The Definitive Guide to Django

Web Development Done Right

Adrian Holovaty and Jacob Kaplan-Moss

Apress®

The Definitive Guide to Django: Web Development Done Right

Copyright © 2008 by Adrian Holovaty and Jacob Kaplan-Moss

ISBN-13 (pbk): 978-1-59059-725-5

ISBN-10 (pbk): 1-59059-725-7

ISBN-13 (electronic): 978-1-4302-0331-5

ISBN-10 (electronic): 1-4302-0331-5

Printed and bound in the United States of America 9 8 7 6 5 4 3 2 1

Lead Editor: Jason Gilmore
Technical Reviewer: Jeremy Dunck
Editorial Board: Steve Anglin, Ewan Buckingham, Tony Campbell, Gary Cornell, Jonathan Gennick, Jason Gilmore, Kevin Goff, Jonathan Hassell, Matthew Moodie, Joseph Ottinger, Jeffrey Pepper, Ben Renow-Clarke, Dominic Shakeshaft, Matt Wade, Tom Welsh
Project Manager | Production Director: Grace Wong
Copy Editor: Nicole Flores
Associate Production Director: Kari Brooks-Copony
Production Editor: Ellie Fountain
Compositor and Artist: Kinetic Publishing Services, LLC
Proofreaders: Lori Bring and Christy Wagner
Indexer: Brenda Miller
Cover Designer: Kurt Krames
Manufacturing Director: Tom Debolski

Distributed to the book trade worldwide by Springer-Verlag New York, Inc., 233 Spring Street, 6th Floor, New York, NY 10013. Phone 1-800-SPRINGER, fax 201-348-4505, e-mail orders-ny@springer-sbm.com, or visit http://www.springeronline.com.

For information on translations, please contact Apress directly at 2855 Telegraph Avenue, Suite 600, Berkeley, CA 94705. Phone 510-549-5930, fax 510-549-5939, e-mail info@apress.com, or visit http://www.apress.com.

The source code for this book is available to readers at http://www.apress.com and at http://www.djangobook.com.

Contents at a Glance

PART 1 ■■■ Getting Started

PART 2 ■■■ Django's Subframeworks

PART 3 ■ ■ ■ Appendixes

v

Contents

PART 1 ■■■ Getting Started

PART 2 ■ ■ ■ Django's Subframeworks

PART 3 ■ ■ ■ Appendixes

█APPENDIX E   Settings 379

About the Authors

ADRIAN HOLOVATY, a Web developer/journalist, is one of the creators and core developers of Django. He is the founder of EveryBlock, a local news Web startup.

When not working on Django improvements, Adrian hacks on side projects for the public good, such as chicagocrime.org, one of the original Google Maps mashups. He lives in Chicago and maintains a weblog at `http://holovaty.com`.

JACOB KAPLAN-MOSS is one of the lead developers of Django. At his day job, he's the lead developer for *Lawrence Journal-World*, a locally-owned newspaper in Lawrence, Kansas, where Django was developed.

At *Journal-World*, Jacob hacks on a number of sites, including lawrence.com, LJworld.com, and KUsports.com, and is continually embarrassed by the multitude of media awards those sites win. In his spare time—what little of it there is—he fancies himself a chef.

About the Technical Reviewer

■**JEREMY DUNCK** is the lead developer of Pegasus News, a personalized local site based in Dallas, Texas. An early contributor to Greasemonkey and Django, he sees technology as a tool for communication and access to knowledge.

Acknowledgments

The most gratifying aspect of working on Django is the community. We've been especially lucky that Django has attracted such a smart, motivated, and friendly bunch. A segment of that community followed us over to the online "beta" release of this book. Their reviews and comments were indispensable; this book wouldn't have been possible without all that wonderful peer review. Almost a thousand people left comments that helped us improve the clarity, quality, and flow of the final book; we'd like to thank each and every one of them.

We're especially grateful to those who took the time to review the book in depth and left dozens (sometimes hundreds) of comments apiece: Marty Alchin, Max Battcher, Oliver Beattie, Rod Begbie, Paul Bissex, Matt Boersma, Robbin Bonthond, Peter Bowyer, Nesta Campbell, Jon Colverson, Jeff Croft, Chris Dary, Alex Dong, Matt Drew, Robert Dzikowski, Nick Efford, Ludvig Ericson, Eric Floehr, Brad Fults, David Grant, Simon Greenhill, Robert Haveman, Kent Johnson, Andrew Kember, Marek Kubica, Eduard Kucera, Anand Kumria, Scott Lamb, Fredrik Lundh, Vadim Macagon, Markus Majer, Orestis Markou, R. Mason, Yasushi Masuda, Kevin Menard, Carlo Miron, James Mulholland, R.D. Nielsen, Michael O'Keefe, Lawrence Oluyede, Andreas Pfrengle, Frankie Robertson, Mike Robinson, Armin Ronacher, Daniel Roseman, Johan Samyn, Ross Shannon, Carolina F. Silva, Paul Smith, Björn Stabell, Bob Stepno, Graeme Stevenson, Justin Stockton, Kevin Teague, Daniel Tietze, Brooks Travis, Peter Tripp, Matthias Urlichs, Peter van Kampen, Alexandre Vassalotti, Jay Wang, Brian Will, and Joshua Works.

Many thanks to our technical editor, Jeremy Dunck. Without Jeremy this book would be littered with errors, inaccuracies, and broken code. We feel very lucky that someone as talented as Jeremy found the time to help us out.

We're grateful for all the hard work the folks at Apress put into this book. They've been amazingly supportive and patient; this book wouldn't have come together without a lot of work on their part. We're especially happy that Apress supported and even encouraged the free release of this book online; it's wonderful seeing a publisher so embracing the spirit of open source.

Finally, of course, thanks to our friends, families, and coworkers who've graciously tolerated our mental absence while we finished this work.

Introduction

In the early days, Web developers wrote every page by hand. Updating a Web site meant editing HTML; a "redesign" involved redoing every single page, one at a time.

As Web sites grew and became more ambitious, it quickly became obvious that that situation was tedious, time-consuming, and ultimately untenable. A group of enterprising hackers at NCSA (the National Center for Supercomputing Applications, where Mosaic, the first graphical Web browser, was developed) solved this problem by letting the Web server spawn external programs that could dynamically generate HTML. They called this protocol the Common Gateway Interface, or CGI, and it changed the Web forever.

It's hard now to imagine what a revelation CGI must have been: instead of treating HTML pages as simple files on disk, CGI allows you to think of your pages as resources generated dynamically on demand. The development of CGI ushered in the first generation of dynamic Web sites.

However, CGI has its problems: CGI scripts need to contain a lot of repetitive "boilerplate" code, they make code reuse difficult, and they can be difficult for first-time developers to write and understand.

PHP fixed many of these problems, and it took the world by storm—it's now by far the most popular tool used to create dynamic Web sites, and dozens of similar languages and environments (ASP, JSP, etc.) followed PHP's design closely. PHP's major innovation is its ease of use: PHP code is simply embedded into plain HTML; the learning curve for someone who already knows HTML is extremely shallow.

But PHP has its own problems; its very ease of use encourages sloppy, repetitive, ill-conceived code. Worse, PHP does little to protect programmers from security vulnerabilities, and thus many PHP developers found themselves learning about security only once it was too late.

These and similar frustrations led directly to the development of the current crop of "third-generation" Web development frameworks. These frameworks—Django and Ruby on Rails appear to be the most popular these days—recognize that the Web's importance has escalated of late. With this new explosion of Web development comes yet another increase in ambition; Web developers are expected to do more and more every day.

Django was invented to meet these new ambitions. Django lets you build deep, dynamic, interesting sites in an extremely short time. Django is designed to let you focus on the fun, interesting parts of your job while easing the pain of the repetitive bits. In doing so, it provides high-level abstractions of common Web development patterns, shortcuts for frequent programming tasks, and clear conventions on how to solve problems. At the same time, Django tries to stay out of your way, letting you work outside the scope of the framework as needed.

We wrote this book because we firmly believe that Django makes Web development better. It's designed to quickly get you moving on your own Django projects, and then ultimately teach you everything you need to know to successfully design, develop, and deploy a site that you'll be proud of.

We're extremely interested in your feedback. The online version of this book—available at http://djangobook.com/—will let you comment on any part of the book, and discuss it with other readers. We'll do our best to read all the comments posted there, and to respond to as many as possible. If you prefer email, please drop us a line at feedback@djangobook.com. Either way, we'd love to hear from you!

We're glad you're here, and we hope you find Django as exciting, fun, and useful as we do.

PART 1

■ ■ ■

Getting Started

CHAPTER 1

■■■

Introduction to Django

This book is about Django, a Web development framework that saves you time and makes Web development a joy. Using Django, you can build and maintain high-quality Web applications with minimal fuss.

At its best, Web development is an exciting, creative act; at its worst, it can be a repetitive, frustrating nuisance. Django lets you focus on the fun stuff—the crux of your Web application—while easing the pain of the repetitive bits. In doing so, it provides high-level abstractions of common Web development patterns, shortcuts for frequent programming tasks, and clear conventions for how to solve problems. At the same time, Django tries to stay out of your way, letting you work outside the scope of the framework as needed.

The goal of this book is to make you a Django expert. The focus is twofold. First, we explain, in depth, what Django does and how to build Web applications with it. Second, we discuss higher-level concepts where appropriate, answering the question "How can I apply these tools effectively in my own projects?" By reading this book, you'll learn the skills needed to develop powerful Web sites quickly, with code that is clean and easy to maintain.

In this chapter, we provide a high-level overview of Django.

What Is a Web Framework?

Django is a prominent member of a new generation of *Web frameworks*. So, what exactly does that term mean?

To answer that question, let's consider the design of a Web application written using the Common Gateway Interface (CGI) standard, a popular way to write Web applications circa 1998. In those days, when you wrote a CGI application, you did everything yourself—the equivalent of baking a cake from scratch. For example, here's a simple CGI script, written in Python, that displays the ten most recently published books from a database:

```
#!/usr/bin/python

import MySQLdb
```

```
print "Content-Type: text/html"
print
print "<html><head><title>Books</title></head>"
print "<body>"
print "<h1>Books</h1>"
print "<ul>"

connection = MySQLdb.connect(user='me', passwd='letmein', db='my_db')
cursor = connection.cursor()
cursor.execute("SELECT name FROM books ORDER BY pub_date DESC LIMIT 10")
for row in cursor.fetchall():
    print "<li>%s</li>" % row[0]

print "</ul>"
print "</body></html>"
connection.close()
```

This code is straightforward. First, it prints a "Content-Type" line, followed by a blank line, as required by CGI. It prints some introductory HTML, connects to a database, and executes a query that retrieves the latest ten books. Looping over those books, it generates an HTML unordered list. Finally, it prints the closing HTML and closes the database connection.

With a one-off dynamic page such as this one, the write-it-from-scratch approach isn't necessarily bad. For one thing, this code is simple to comprehend—even a novice developer can read these 16 lines of Python and understand all it does, from start to finish. There's nothing else to learn; no other code to read. It's also simple to deploy: just save this code in a file called latestbooks.cgi, upload that file to a Web server, and visit that page with a browser.

But as a Web application grows beyond the trivial, this approach breaks down, and you face a number of problems:

- What happens when multiple pages need to connect to the database? Surely that database-connecting code shouldn't be duplicated in each individual CGI script, so the pragmatic thing to do would be to refactor it into a shared function.

- Should a developer *really* have to worry about printing the "Content-Type" line and remembering to close the database connection? This sort of boilerplate reduces programmer productivity and introduces opportunities for mistakes. These setup- and teardown-related tasks would best be handled by some common infrastructure.

- What happens when this code is reused in multiple environments, each with a separate database and password? At this point, some environment-specific configuration becomes essential.

- What happens when a Web designer who has no experience coding Python wishes to redesign the page? Ideally, the logic of the page—the retrieval of books from the database—would be separate from the HTML display of the page, so that a designer could edit the latter without affecting the former.

These problems are precisely what a Web framework intends to solve. A Web framework provides a programming infrastructure for your applications, so that you can focus on writing clean, maintainable code without having to reinvent the wheel. In a nutshell, that's what Django does.

The MVC Design Pattern

Let's dive in with a quick example that demonstrates the difference between the previous approach and that undertaken using a Web framework. Here's how you might write the previous CGI code using Django:

```python
# models.py (the database tables)

from django.db import models

class Book(models.Model):
    name = models.CharField(maxlength=50)
    pub_date = models.DateField()
```

```python
# views.py (the business logic)

from django.shortcuts import render_to_response
from models import Book

def latest_books(request):
    book_list = Book.objects.order_by('-pub_date')[:10]
    return render_to_response('latest_books.html', {'book_list': book_list})
```

```python
# urls.py (the URL configuration)

from django.conf.urls.defaults import *
import views

urlpatterns = patterns('',
    (r'latest/$', views.latest_books),
)
```

```html
# latest_books.html (the template)

<html><head><title>Books</title></head>
<body>
<h1>Books</h1>
<ul>
{% for book in book_list %}
<li>{{ book.name }}</li>
{% endfor %}
</ul>
</body></html>
```

Don't worry about the particulars of *how* this works just yet—we just want you to get a feel for the overall design. The main thing to note here is the *separation of concerns*:

- The models.py file contains a description of the database table, as a Python class. This is called a *model*. Using this class, you can create, retrieve, update, and delete records in your database using simple Python code rather than writing repetitive SQL statements.

- The views.py file contains the business logic for the page, in the latest_books() function. This function is called a *view*.

- The urls.py file specifies which view is called for a given URL pattern. In this case, the URL /latest/ will be handled by the latest_books() function.

- latest_books.html is an HTML template that describes the design of the page.

Taken together, these pieces loosely follow the Model-View-Controller (MVC) design pattern. Simply put, MVC defines a way of developing software so that the code for defining and accessing data (the model) is separate from request routing logic (the controller), which in turn is separate from the user interface (the view).

A key advantage of such an approach is that components are *loosely coupled*. That is, each distinct piece of a Django-powered Web application has a single key purpose and can be changed independently without affecting the other pieces. For example, a developer can change the URL for a given part of the application without affecting the underlying implementation. A designer can change a page's HTML without having to touch the Python code that renders it. A database administrator can rename a database table and specify the change in a single place, rather than having to search and replace through a dozen files.

In this book, each component of this stack gets its own chapter. For example, Chapter 3 covers views, Chapter 4 covers templates, and Chapter 5 covers models. Chapter 5 also discusses Django's MVC philosophies in depth.

Django's History

Before we dive into more code, we should take a moment to explain Django's history. It's helpful to understand why the framework was created, because a knowledge of the history will put into context why Django works the way it does.

If you've been building Web applications for a while, you're probably familiar with the problems in the CGI example we presented earlier. The classic Web developer's path goes something like this:

1. Write a Web application from scratch.

2. Write another Web application from scratch.

3. Realize the application from step 1 shares much in common with the application from step 2.

4. Refactor the code so that application 1 shares code with application 2.

5. Repeat steps 2–4 several times.

6. Realize you've invented a framework.

This is precisely how Django itself was created!

Django grew organically from real-world applications written by a Web development team in Lawrence, Kansas. It was born in the fall of 2003, when the Web programmers at the *Lawrence Journal-World* newspaper, Adrian Holovaty and Simon Willison, began using Python to build applications. The World Online team, responsible for the production and maintenance of several local news sites, thrived in a development environment dictated by journalism deadlines. For the sites—including LJWorld.com, Lawrence.com, and KUsports.com—journalists (and management) demanded that features be added and entire applications be built on an intensely fast schedule, often with only days' or hours' notice. Thus, Adrian and Simon developed a time-saving Web development framework out of necessity—it was the only way they could build maintainable applications under the extreme deadlines.

In summer 2005, after having developed this framework to a point where it was efficiently powering most of World Online's sites, the World Online team, which now included Jacob Kaplan-Moss, decided to release the framework as open source software. They released it in July 2005 and named it Django, after the jazz guitarist Django Reinhardt.

Although Django is now an open source project with contributors across the planet, the original World Online developers still provide central guidance for the framework's growth, and World Online contributes other important aspects such as employee time, marketing materials, and hosting/bandwidth for the framework's Web site (http://www.djangoproject.com/).

This history is relevant because it helps explain two key matters. The first is Django's "sweet spot." Because Django was born in a news environment, it offers several features (particularly its admin interface, covered in Chapter 6) that are particularly well suited for "content" sites—sites like eBay, craigslist.org, and washingtonpost.com that offer dynamic, database-driven information. (Don't let that turn you off, though—although Django is particularly good for developing those sorts of sites, that doesn't preclude it from being an effective tool for building any sort of dynamic Web site. There's a difference between being *particularly effective* at something and being *ineffective* at other things.)

The second matter to note is how Django's origins have shaped the culture of its open source community. Because Django was extracted from real-world code, rather than being an academic exercise or commercial product, it is acutely focused on solving Web development problems that Django's developers themselves have faced—and continue to face. As a result, Django itself is actively improved on an almost daily basis. The framework's developers have a keen interest in making sure Django saves developers time, produces applications that are easy to maintain, and performs well under load. If nothing else, the developers are motivated by their own selfish desires to save themselves time and enjoy their jobs. (To put it bluntly, they eat their own dog food.)

How to Read This Book

In writing this book, we tried to strike a balance between readability and reference, with a bias toward readability. Our goal with this book, as stated earlier, is to make you a Django expert, and we believe the best way to teach is through prose and plenty of examples, rather than a providing an exhaustive but bland catalog of Django features. (As someone once said, you can't expect to teach somebody how to speak merely by teaching them the alphabet.)

With that in mind, we recommend that you read Chapters 1 through 7 in order. They form the foundation of how to use Django; once you've read them, you'll be able to build

Django-powered Web sites. The remaining chapters, which focus on specific Django features, can be read in any order.

The appendixes are for reference. They, along with the free documentation at `http://www.djangoproject.com/`, are probably what you'll flip back to occasionally to recall syntax or find quick synopses of what certain parts of Django do.

Required Programming Knowledge

Readers of this book should understand the basics of procedural and object-oriented programming: control structures (`if`, `while`, and `for`), data structures (lists, hashes/dictionaries), variables, classes, and objects.

Experience in Web development is, as you may expect, very helpful, but it's not required to read this book. Throughout the book, we try to promote best practices in Web development for readers who lack this type of experience.

Required Python Knowledge

At its core, Django is simply a collection of libraries written in the Python programming language. To develop a site using Django, you write Python code that uses these libraries. Learning Django, then, is a matter of learning how to program in Python and understanding how the Django libraries work.

If you have experience programming in Python, you should have no trouble diving in. By and large, the Django code doesn't perform "black magic" (i.e., programming trickery whose implementation is difficult to explain or understand). For you, learning Django will be a matter of learning Django's conventions and APIs.

If you don't have experience programming in Python, you're in for a treat. It's easy to learn and a joy to use! Although this book doesn't include a full Python tutorial, it highlights Python features and functionality where appropriate, particularly when code doesn't immediately make sense. Still, we recommend you read the official Python tutorial, available online at `http://docs.python.org/tut/`. We also recommend Mark Pilgrim's free book *Dive Into Python*, available at `http://www.diveintopython.org/` and published in print by Apress.

New Django Features

As we noted earlier, Django is frequently improved, and it will likely have a number of useful—even *essential*—new features by the time this book is published. Thus, our goal as authors of this book is twofold:

- Make sure this book is as "future-proof" as possible, so that whatever you read here will still be relevant in future Django versions

- Actively update this book on its Web site, `http://www.djangobook.com/`, so you can access the latest and greatest documentation as soon as we write it

If you want to implement something with Django that isn't explained in this book, check the latest version of this book on the aforementioned Web site, and also check the official Django documentation.

Getting Help

One of the greatest benefits of Django is its kind and helpful user community. For help with any aspect of Django—from installation, to application design, to database design, to deployment—feel free to ask questions online.

- The django-users mailing list is where thousands of Django users go to ask and answer questions. Sign up for free at `http://www.djangoproject.com/r/django-users`.

- The Django IRC channel is where Django users hang out to chat and help each other in real time. Join the fun by logging on to `#django` on the Freenode IRC network.

What's Next?

In the next chapter, we'll get started with `Django`, covering installation and initial setup.

CHAPTER 2

■■■

Getting Started

We think it's best to get a running start. The details and extent of the Django framework will be fleshed out in later chapters, but for now, trust us—this chapter will be fun.

Installing Django is easy. Because Django runs anywhere Python does, Django can be configured in many ways. We cover the common scenarios for Django installations in this chapter. Chapter 20 covers deploying Django to production.

Installing Python

Django is written in 100% pure Python code, so you'll need to install Python on your system. Django requires Python 2.3 or higher.

If you're on Linux or Mac OS X, you probably already have Python installed. Type python at a command prompt (or in Terminal, in OS X). If you see something like this, then Python is installed:

```
Python 2.4.1 (#2, Mar 31 2005, 00:05:10)
[GCC 3.3 20030304 (Apple Computer, Inc. build 1666)] on darwin
Type "help", "copyright", "credits" or "license" for more information.
>>>
```

Otherwise, if you see an error such as "command not found", you'll have to download and install Python. See http://www.python.org/download/ to get started. The installation is fast and easy.

Installing Django

In this section, we cover two installation options: installing an official release and installing from Subversion.

Installing an Official Release

Most people will want to install the latest official release from http://www.djangoproject.com/download/. Django uses the standard Python distutils installation method, which in Linux land looks like this:

1. Download the tarball, which will be named something like `Django-0.96.tar.gz`.

2. `tar xzvf Django-*.tar.gz`.

3. `cd Django-*`.

4. `sudo python setup.py install`.

On Windows, we recommend using 7-Zip to handle all manner of compressed files, including `.tar.gz`. You can download 7-Zip from `http://www.djangoproject.com/r/7zip/`.

Change into some other directory and start `python`. If everything worked, you should be able to import the module `django`:

```
>>> import django
>>> django.VERSION
(0, 96, None)
```

■**Note** The Python interactive interpreter is a command-line program that lets you write a Python program interactively. To start it, just run the command `python` at the command line. Throughout this book, we feature example Python code that's printed as if it's being entered in the interactive interpreter. The triple greater-than signs (>>>) signify a Python prompt.

Installing Django from Subversion

If you want to work on the bleeding edge, or if you want to contribute code to Django itself, you should install Django from its Subversion repository.

Subversion is a free, open source revision-control system similar to CVS, and the Django team uses it to manage changes to the Django codebase. You can use a Subversion client to grab the very latest Django source code and, at any given time, you can update your local version of the Django code, known as your *local checkout*, to get the latest changes and improvements made by Django developers.

The latest and greatest Django development code is referred to as the *trunk*. The Django team runs production sites on trunk and strives to keep it stable.

To grab the latest Django trunk, follow these steps:

1. Make sure you have a Subversion client installed. You can get the software free from `http://subversion.tigris.org/`, and you can find excellent documentation at `http://svnbook.red-bean.com/`.

2. Check out the trunk using the command `svn co http://code.djangoproject.com/svn/django/trunk djtrunk`.

3. Create `site-packages/django.pth` and add the `djtrunk` directory to it, or update your `PYTHONPATH` to point to `djtrunk`.

4. Place `djtrunk/django/bin` on your system path. This directory includes management utilities such as `django-admin.py`.

■Tip If you're not familiar with `.pth` files, you can learn more about them at `http://www.djangoproject.com/r/python/site-module/`.

After downloading from Subversion and following the preceding steps, there's no need to `python setup.py install`—you've just done the work by hand!

Because the Django trunk changes often with bug fixes and feature additions, you'll probably want to update it every once in a while—or hourly, if you're really obsessed. To update the code, just run the command `svn update` from within the `djtrunk` directory. When you run that command, Subversion will contact `http://code.djangoproject.com/`, determine if any code has changed, and update your local version of the code with any changes that have been made since you last updated. It's quite slick.

Setting Up a Database

Django's only prerequisite is a working installation of Python. However, this book focuses on one of Django's sweet spots, which is developing *database-backed* Web sites, so you'll need to install a database server of some sort for storing your data.

If you just want to get started playing with Django, skip ahead to the "Starting a Project" section—but trust us, you'll want to install a database eventually. All of the examples in this book assume you have a database set up.

As of the time of this writing, Django supports three database engines:

- PostgreSQL (`http://www.postgresql.org/`)

- SQLite 3 (`http://www.sqlite.org/`)

- MySQL (`http://www.mysql.com/`)

Work is in progress to support Microsoft SQL Server and Oracle. The Django Web site will always have the latest information about supported databases.

We're quite fond of PostgreSQL ourselves, for reasons outside the scope of this book, so we mention it first. However, all the engines listed here will work equally well with Django.

SQLite deserves special notice as a development tool. It's an extremely simple in-process database engine that doesn't require any sort of server setup or configuration. It's by far the easiest to set up if you just want to play around with Django, and it's even included in the standard library of Python 2.5.

On Windows, obtaining database driver binaries is sometimes an involved process. Since you're just getting started with Django, we recommend using Python 2.5 and its built-in support for SQLite. Compiling driver binaries is a downer.

Using Django with PostgreSQL

If you're using PostgreSQL, you'll need the `psycopg` package available from `http://www.djangoproject.com/r/python-pgsql/`. Take note of whether you're using version 1 or 2; you'll need this information later.

If you're using PostgreSQL on Windows, you can find precompiled binaries of `psycopg` at `http://www.djangoproject.com/r/python-pgsql/windows/`.

Using Django with SQLite 3

If you're using a Python version over 2.5, you already have SQLite. If you're working with Python 2.4 or older, you'll need SQLite 3—not version 2—from `http://www.djangoproject.com/r/sqlite/` and the `pysqlite` package from `http://www.djangoproject.com/r/python-sqlite/`. Make sure you have `pysqlite` version 2.0.3 or higher.

On Windows, you can skip installing the separate SQLite binaries, since they're statically linked into the `pysqlite` binaries.

Using Django with MySQL

Django requires MySQL 4.0 or above; the 3.x versions don't support nested subqueries and some other fairly standard SQL statements. You'll also need the `MySQLdb` package from `http://www.djangoproject.com/r/python-mysql/`.

Using Django Without a Database

As mentioned earlier, Django doesn't actually require a database. If you just want to use it to serve dynamic pages that don't hit a database, that's perfectly fine.

With that said, bear in mind that some of the extra tools bundled with Django *do* require a database, so if you choose not to use a database, you'll miss out on those features. (We highlight these features throughout this book.)

Starting a Project

A *project* is a collection of settings for an instance of Django, including database configuration, Django-specific options, and application-specific settings.

If this is your first time using Django, you'll have to take care of some initial setup. Create a new directory to start working in, perhaps something like `/home/username/djcode/`, and change into that directory.

■Note `django-admin.py` should be on your system path if you installed Django via its `setup.py` utility. If you checked out from Subversion, you can find it in `djtrunk/django/bin`. Since you'll be using `django-admin.py` often, consider adding it to your path. On Unix, you can do so by symlinking from `/usr/local/bin` using a command such as `sudo ln -s/path/to/django/bin/django-admin.py /usr/local/bin/django-admin.py`. On Windows, you'll need to update your `PATH` environment variable.

Run the command `django-admin.py startproject mysite` to create a `mysite` directory in your current directory.

Let's look at what startproject created:

```
mysite/
    __init__.py
    manage.py
    settings.py
    urls.py
```

These files are as follows:

- __init__.py: A file required for Python; treat the directory as a package (i.e., a group of modules)

- manage.py: A command-line utility that lets you interact with this Django project in various ways

- settings.py: Settings/configuration for this Django project

- urls.py: The URL declarations for this Django project; a "table of contents" of your Django-powered site

---

WHERE SHOULD THE DIRECTORY LIVE?

If your background is in PHP, you're probably used to putting code under the Web server's document root (in a place such as /var/www). With Django, you don't do that. It's not a good idea to put any of this Python code within your Web server's document root, because in doing so you risk the possibility that people will be able to view your code over the Web. That's not good for security.

Put your code in some directory *outside* of the document root.

The Development Server

Django includes a built-in, lightweight Web server you can use while developing your site. We've included this server so you can develop your site rapidly, without having to deal with configuring your production Web server (e.g., Apache) until you're ready for production. This development server watches your code for changes and automatically reloads, helping you make many rapid changes to your project without needing to restart anything.

Change into the mysite directory, if you haven't done so already, and run the command python manage.py runserver. You'll see something like this:

```
Validating models...
0 errors found.

Django version 0.96, using settings 'mysite.settings'
Development server is running at http://127.0.0.1:8000/
Quit the server with CONTROL-C.
```

Although the development server is extremely nice for, well, development, resist the temptation to use this server in anything resembling a production environment. The development server can handle only a single request at a time reliably, and it has not gone through a security audit of any sort. When the time comes to launch your site, see Chapter 20 for information on how to deploy Django.

CHANGING THE HOST OR THE PORT

By default, the `runserver` command starts the development server on port 8000, listening only for local connections. If you want to change the server's port, pass it as a command-line argument:

```
python manage.py runserver 8080
```

You can also change the IP address that the server listens on. This is especially helpful if you'd like to share a development site with other developers. The following will make Django listen on any network interface, thus allowing other computers to connect to the development server:

```
python manage.py runserver 0.0.0.0:8080
```

Now that the server's running, visit `http://127.0.0.1:8000/` with your Web browser. You'll see a "Welcome to Django" page that's shaded a pleasant pastel blue. It worked!

What's Next?

Now that you have everything installed and the development server running, in the next chapter you'll write some basic code that demonstrates how to serve Web pages using Django.

■ ■ ■

## CHAPTER 3

The Basics of Dynamic Web Pages

In the previous chapter, we explained how to set up a Django project and run the Django development server. Of course, that site doesn't actually do anything useful yet—all it does is display the "It worked!" message. Let's change that. This chapter introduces how to create dynamic Web pages with Django.

Your First View: Dynamic Content

As our first goal, let's create a Web page that displays the current date and time. This is a good example of a *dynamic* Web page, because the contents of the page are not static; rather, the contents change according to the result of a computation (in this case, a calculation of the current time). This simple example doesn't involve a database or any sort of user input—just the output of your server's internal clock.

To create this page, we'll write a *view function*. A view function, or *view* for short, is simply a Python function that takes a Web request and returns a Web response. This response can be the HTML contents of a Web page, or a redirect, or a 404 error, or an XML document, or an image . . . or anything, really. The view itself contains whatever arbitrary logic is necessary to return that response. This code can live anywhere you want, as long as it's on your Python path. There's no other requirement—no "magic," so to speak. For the sake of putting the code *somewhere*, let's create a file called views.py in the mysite directory, which you created in the previous chapter.

Here's a view that returns the current date and time, as an HTML document:

```python
from django.http import HttpResponse
import datetime

def current_datetime(request):
    now = datetime.datetime.now()
    html = "<html><body>It is now %s.</body></html>" % now
    return HttpResponse(html)
```

Let's step through this code one line at a time:

- First, we import the class `HttpResponse`, which lives in the `django.http` module. See Appendix H for further details on the `HttpRequest` and `HttpResponse` objects.

- Then we import the `datetime` module from Python's standard library, the set of useful modules that comes with Python. The `datetime` module contains several functions and classes for dealing with dates and times, including a function that returns the current time.

- Next, we define a function called `current_datetime`. This is the view function. Each view function takes an `HttpRequest` object as its first parameter, which is typically named `request`.

  Note that the name of the view function doesn't matter; it doesn't have to be named in a certain way in order for Django to recognize it. We're calling it `current_datetime` here, because that name clearly indicates what it does, but it could just as well be named `super_duper_awesome_current_time` or something equally revolting. Django doesn't care. The next section explains how Django finds this function.

- The first line of code within the function calculates the current date/time as a `datetime.datetime` object, and stores that as the local variable `now`.

- The second line of code within the function constructs an HTML response using Python's format-string capability. The `%s` within the string is a placeholder, and the percent sign after the string means "Replace the `%s` with the value of the variable `now`." (Yes, the HTML is invalid, but we're trying to keep the example simple and short.)

- Finally, the view returns an `HttpResponse` object that contains the generated response. Each view function is responsible for returning an `HttpResponse` object. (There are exceptions, but we'll get to those later.)

DJANGO'S TIME ZONE

Django includes a `TIME_ZONE` setting that defaults to `America/Chicago`. This probably isn't where you live, so you might want to change it in your `settings.py`. See Appendix E for details.

Mapping URLs to Views

So, to recap, this view function returns an HTML page that includes the current date and time. But how do we tell Django to use this code? That's where *URLconfs* come in.

A *URLconf* is like a table of contents for your Django-powered Web site. Basically, it's a mapping between URL patterns and the view functions that should be called for those URL patterns. It's how you tell Django, "For this URL, call this code, and for that URL, call that code." Remember that the view functions need to be on the Python path.

YOUR PYTHON PATH

Your *Python path* is the list of directories on your system where Python looks when you use the Python `import` statement.

For example, let's say your Python path is set to `['', '/usr/lib/python2.4/site-packages', '/home/username/djcode/']`. If you execute the Python code `from foo import bar`, Python will first check for a module called `foo.py` in the current directory. (The first entry in the Python path, an empty string, means "the current directory.") If that file doesn't exist, Python will look for the file `/usr/lib/python2.4/site-packages/foo.py`. If that file doesn't exist, it will try `/home/username/djcode/foo.py`. Finally, if *that* file doesn't exist, it will raise `ImportError`.

If you're interested in seeing the value of your Python path, start the Python interactive interpreter and type `import sys`, followed by `print sys.path`.

Generally you don't have to worry about setting your Python path—Python and Django will take care of things for you automatically behind the scenes. (If you're curious, setting the Python path is one of the things that the `manage.py` file does.)

When you executed `django-admin.py startproject` in the previous chapter, the script created a URLconf for you automatically: the file `urls.py`. Let's edit that file. By default, it looks something like this:

```
from django.conf.urls.defaults import *

urlpatterns = patterns('',
    # Example:
    # (r'^mysite/', include('mysite.apps.foo.urls.foo')),

    # Uncomment this for admin:
#    (r'^admin/', include('django.contrib.admin.urls')),
)
```

Let's step through this code one line at a time:

- The first line imports all objects from the `django.conf.urls.defaults` module, including a function called `patterns`.

- The second line calls the function `patterns()` and saves the result into a variable called `urlpatterns`. The `patterns()` function gets passed only a single argument—the empty string. The rest of the lines are commented out. (The string can be used to supply a common prefix for view functions, but we'll skip this advanced usage for now.)

The main thing to note here is the variable `urlpatterns`, which Django expects to find in your `ROOT_URLCONF` module. This variable defines the mapping between URLs and the code that handles those URLs.

By default, everything in the URLconf is commented out—your Django application is a blank slate. (As a side note, that's how Django knew to show you the "It worked!" page in the last chapter. If your URLconf is empty, Django assumes you just started a new project and hence displays that message.)

Let's edit this file to expose our current_datetime view:

```
from django.conf.urls.defaults import *
from mysite.views import current_datetime

urlpatterns = patterns('',
    (r'^time/$', current_datetime),
)
```

We made two changes here. First, we imported the current_datetime view from its module (mysite/views.py, which translates into mysite.views in Python import syntax). Next, we added the line (r'^time/$', current_datetime),. This line is referred to as a *URLpattern*—it's a Python tuple in which the first element is a simple regular expression and the second element is the view function to use for that pattern.

In a nutshell, we just told Django that any request to the URL /time/ should be handled by the current_datetime view function.

A few things are worth pointing out:

- Note that, in this example, we passed the current_datetime view function as an object without calling the function. This is a key feature of Python (and other dynamic languages): functions are first-class objects, which means you can pass them around just like any other variables. Cool stuff, eh?

- The r in r'^time/$' means that '^time/$ is a Python raw string. This allows regular expressions to be written without overly verbose escaping.

- You should exclude the expected slash at the beginning of the '^time/$' expression in order to match /time/. Django automatically puts a slash before every expression. At first glance, this may seem odd, but URLconfs can be included in other URLconfs, and leaving off the leading slash simplifies matters. This is further covered in Chapter 8.

- The caret character (^) and dollar sign character ($) are important. The caret means "require that the pattern matches the start of the string," and the dollar sign means "require that the pattern matches the end of the string."

  This concept is best explained by example. If we had instead used the pattern '^time/' (without a dollar sign at the end), then *any* URL that starts with time/ would match, such as /time/foo and /time/bar, not just /time/. Similarly, if we had left off the initial caret character ('time/$'), Django would match *any* URL that ends with time/, such as /foo/bar/time/. Thus, we use both the caret and dollar sign to ensure that only the URL /time/ matches. Nothing more, nothing less.

  You may be wondering what happens if someone requests /time. This is handled as you'd hope (via a redirect) as long as the APPEND_SLASH setting is True. (See Appendix E for some good bedtime reading on this topic.)

To test our changes to the URLconf, start the Django development server, as you did in Chapter 2, by running the command python manage.py runserver. (If you left it running, that's fine, too. The development server automatically detects changes to your Python code and reloads as necessary, so you don't have to restart the server between changes.) The server is running at the address http://127.0.0.1:8000/, so open up a Web browser and go to http://127.0.0.1:8000/time/. You should see the output of your Django view.

Hooray! You've made your first Django-powered Web page.

REGULAR EXPRESSIONS

Regular expressions (or *regexes*) are a compact way of specifying patterns in text. While Django URLconfs allow arbitrary regexes for powerful URL-matching capability, you'll probably use only a few regex patterns in practice. Here's a small selection of common patterns:

Symbol	Matches
. (dot)	Any character
\d	Any digit
[A-Z]	Any character, A–Z (uppercase)
[a-z]	Any character, a–z (lowercase)
[A-Za-z]	Any character, a–z (case insensitive)
+	One or more of the previous character (e.g., \d+ matches one or more digit)
[^/]+	All characters until a forward slash (excluding the slash itself)
?	Zero or more of the previous character (e.g., \d* matches zero or more digits)
{1,3}	Between one and three (inclusive) of the previous expression

How Django Processes a Request

We should point out several things about what just happened. Here's the nitty-gritty of what goes on when you run the Django development server and make requests to Web pages:

- The command python manage.py runserver imports a file called settings.py from the same directory. This file contains all sorts of optional configuration for this particular Django instance, but one of the most important settings is ROOT_URLCONF. The ROOT_URLCONF setting tells Django which Python module should be used as the URLconf for this Web site.

  Remember when django-admin.py startproject created the files settings.py and urls.py? Well, the autogenerated settings.py has a ROOT_URLCONF that points to the autogenerated urls.py. Convenient.

- When a request comes in—say, a request to the URL /time/—Django loads the URLconf pointed to by the ROOT_URLCONF setting. Then it checks each of the URLpatterns in that URLconf in order, comparing the requested URL with the patterns one at a time, until it finds one that matches. When it finds one that matches, it calls the view function associated with that pattern, passing an HttpRequest object as the first parameter to the function. (More on HttpRequest later.)

- The view function is responsible for returning an HttpResponse object.

You now know the basics of how to make Django-powered pages. It's quite simple, really—just write view functions and map them to URLs via URLconfs. You might think it would be slow to map URLs to functions using a series of regular expressions, but you'd be surprised.

How Django Processes a Request: Complete Details

In addition to the straightforward URL-to-view mapping just described, Django provides quite a bit of flexibility in processing requests.

The typical flow—URLconf resolution to a view function that returns an `HttpResponse`—can be short-circuited or augmented via middleware. The deep secrets of middleware are fully covered in Chapter 15, but a quick sketch (see Figure 3-1) should aid you in conceptually fitting the pieces together.

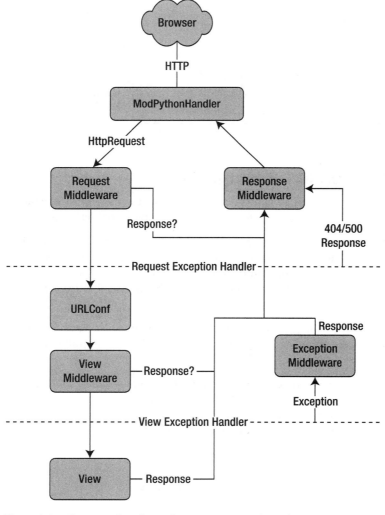

Figure 3-1. *The complete flow of a Django request and response*

When an HTTP request comes in from the browser, a server-specific *handler* constructs the HttpRequest passed to later components and handles the flow of the response processing.

The handler then calls any available Request or View middleware. These types of middleware are useful for augmenting incoming HttpRequest objects as well as providing special handling for specific types of requests. If either returns an HttpResponse, processing bypasses the view.

Bugs slip by even the best programmers, but *exception middleware* can help squash them. If a view function raises an exception, control passes to the exception middleware. If this middleware does not return an HttpResponse, the exception is reraised.

Even then, all is not lost. Django includes default views that create a friendly 404 and 500 response.

Finally, *response middleware* is good for postprocessing an HttpResponse just before it's sent to the browser or doing cleanup of request-specific resources.

URLconfs and Loose Coupling

Now's a good time to highlight a key philosophy behind URLconfs and behind Django in general: the principle of *loose coupling*. Simply put, loose coupling is a software-development approach that values the importance of making pieces interchangeable. If two pieces of code are loosely coupled, then changes made to one of the pieces will have little or no effect on the other.

Django's URLconfs are a good example of this principle in practice. In a Django Web application, the URL definitions and the view functions they call are loosely coupled; that is, the decision of what the URL should be for a given function, and the implementation of the function itself, reside in two separate places. This lets a developer switch out one piece without affecting the other.

In contrast, other Web development platforms couple the URL to the program. In typical PHP (http://www.php.net/) applications, for example, the URL of your application is designated by where you place the code on your filesystem. In early versions of the CherryPy Python Web framework (http://www.cherrypy.org/), the URL of your application corresponded to the name of the method in which your code lived. This may seem like a convenient shortcut in the short term, but it can get unmanageable in the long run.

For example, consider the view function we wrote earlier, which displays the current date and time. If we wanted to change the URL for the application— say, move it from /time/ to /currenttime/—we could make a quick change to the URLconf, without having to worry about the underlying implementation of the function. Similarly, if we wanted to change the view function—altering its logic somehow—we could do that without affecting the URL to which the function is bound. Furthermore, if we wanted to expose the current-date functionality at *several* URLs, we could easily take care of that by editing the URLconf, without having to touch the view code.

That's loose coupling in action. We'll continue to point out examples of this important philosophy throughout this book.

404 Errors

In our URLconf thus far, we've defined only a single URLpattern: the one that handles requests to the URL /time/. What happens when a different URL is requested?

To find out, try running the Django development server and hitting a page such as http://127.0.0.1:8000/hello/ or http://127.0.0.1:8000/does-not-exist/, or even http://127.0.0.1:8000/ (the site "root"). You should see a "Page not found" message (see Figure 3-2). (Pretty, isn't it? We Django people sure do like our pastel colors.) Django displays this message because you requested a URL that's not defined in your URLconf.

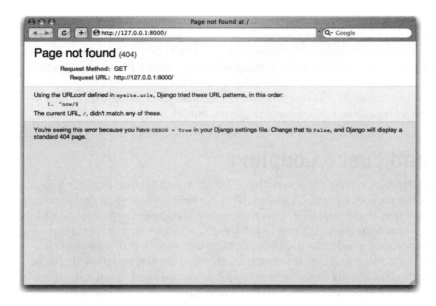

Figure 3-2. *Django's 404 page*

The utility of this page goes beyond the basic 404 error message; it also tells you precisely which URLconf Django used and every pattern in that URLconf. From that information, you should be able to tell why the requested URL threw a 404.

Naturally, this is sensitive information intended only for you, the Web developer. If this were a production site deployed live on the Internet, we wouldn't want to expose that information to the public. For that reason, this "Page not found" page is only displayed if your Django project is in *debug mode*. We'll explain how to deactivate debug mode later. For now, just know that every Django project is in debug mode when you first create it, and if the project is not in debug mode, a different response is given.

Your Second View: Dynamic URLs

In our first view example, the contents of the page—the current date/time—were dynamic, but the URL (/time/) was static. In most dynamic Web applications, though, a URL contains parameters that influence the output of the page.

Let's create a second view that displays the current date and time offset by a certain number of hours. The goal is to craft a site in such a way that the page /time/plus/1/ displays the date/time one hour into the future, the page /time/plus/2/ displays the date/time two hours into the future, the page /time/plus/3/ displays the date/time three hours into the future, and so on.

A novice might think to code a separate view function for each hour offset, which might result in a URLconf like this:

```
urlpatterns = patterns('',
    (r'^time/$', current_datetime),
    (r'^time/plus/1/$', one_hour_ahead),
    (r'^time/plus/2/$', two_hours_ahead),
    (r'^time/plus/3/$', three_hours_ahead),
    (r'^time/plus/4//$', four_hours_ahead),
)
```

Clearly, this line of thought is flawed. Not only would this result in redundant view functions, but also the application is fundamentally limited to supporting only the predefined hour ranges—one, two, three, or four hours. If, all of a sudden, we wanted to create a page that displayed the time *five* hours into the future, we'd have to create a separate view and URLconf line for that, furthering the duplication and insanity. We need to do some abstraction here.

A Word About Pretty URLs

If you're experienced in another Web development platform, such as PHP or Java, you may be thinking, "Hey, let's use a query string parameter!"—something like /time/plus?hours=3, in which the hours would be designated by the hours parameter in the URL's query string (the part after the ?).

You *can* do that with Django (and we'll tell you how later, if you really must know), but one of Django's core philosophies is that URLs should be beautiful. The URL /time/plus/3/ is far cleaner, simpler, more readable, easier to recite to somebody aloud and . . . just plain prettier than its query string counterpart. Pretty URLs are a sign of a quality Web application. Django's URLconf system encourages pretty URLs by making it easier to use pretty URLs than *not* to.

Wildcard URLpatterns

Continuing with our hours_ahead example, let's put a wildcard in the URLpattern. As we mentioned previously, a URLpattern is a regular expression; hence, we can use the regular expression pattern \d+ to match one or more digits:

```
from django.conf.urls.defaults import *
from mysite.views import current_datetime, hours_ahead

urlpatterns = patterns('',
    (r'^time/$', current_datetime),
    (r'^time/plus/\d+/$', hours_ahead),
)
```

This URLpattern will match any URL such as /time/plus/2/, /time/plus/25/, or even /time/plus/100000000000/. Come to think of it, let's limit it so that the maximum allowed offset is 99 hours. That means we want to allow either one- or two-digit numbers—in regular expression syntax, that translates into \d{1,2}:

```
(r'^time/plus/\d{1,2}/$', hours_ahead),
```

■Note When building Web applications, it's always important to consider the most outlandish data input possible, and decide whether or not the application should support that input. We've curtailed the outlandishness here by limiting the offset to 99 hours. And, by the way, The Outlandishness Curtailers would be a fantastic, if verbose, band name.

Now that we've designated a wildcard for the URL, we need a way of passing that data to the view function, so that we can use a single view function for any arbitrary hour offset. We do this by placing parentheses around the data in the URLpattern that we want to save. In the case of our example, we want to save whatever number was entered in the URL, so let's put parentheses around the \d{1,2}:

```
(r'^time/plus/(\d{1,2})/$', hours_ahead),
```

If you're familiar with regular expressions, you'll be right at home here; we're using parentheses to *capture* data from the matched text.

The final URLconf, including our previous current_datetime view, looks like this:

```
from django.conf.urls.defaults import *
from mysite.views import current_datetime, hours_ahead

urlpatterns = patterns('',
    (r'^time/$', current_datetime),
    (r'^time/plus/(\d{1,2})/$', hours_ahead),
)
```

With that taken care of, let's write the hours_ahead view.

CODING ORDER

In this example, we wrote the URLpattern first and the view second, but in the previous example, we wrote the view first, and then the URLpattern. Which technique is better? Well, every developer is different.

If you're a big-picture type of person, it may make the most sense to you to write all of the URLpatterns for your application at the same time, at the start of your project, and then code up the views. This has the advantage of giving you a clear to-do list, and it essentially defines the parameter requirements for the view functions you'll need to write.

If you're more of a bottom-up developer, you might prefer to write the views first, and then anchor them to URLs afterward. That's OK, too.

In the end, it comes down to which technique fits your brain the best. Both approaches are valid.

hours_ahead is very similar to the current_datetime view we wrote earlier, with a key difference: it takes an extra argument, the number of hours of offset. Add this to views.py:

```
def hours_ahead(request, offset):
    offset = int(offset)
    dt = datetime.datetime.now() + datetime.timedelta(hours=offset)
    html = "<html><body>In %s hour(s), it will be %s.</body></html>" % (offset, dt)
    return HttpResponse(html)
```

Let's step through this code one line at a time:

- Just as we did for our current_datetime view, we import the class django.http.
  HttpResponse and the datetime module.

- The view function, hours_ahead, takes *two* parameters: request and offset.

- request is an HttpRequest object, just as in current_datetime. We'll say it again: each
  view *always* takes an HttpRequest object as its first parameter.

- offset is the string captured by the parentheses in the URLpattern. For example, if the
  requested URL were /time/plus/3/, then offset would be the string '3'. If the requested
  URL were /time/plus/21/, then offset would be the string '21'. Note that captured
  strings will always be *strings*, not integers, even if the string is composed of only digits,
  such as '21'.

  We decided to call the variable offset, but you can call it whatever you'd like, as long as
  it's a valid Python identifier. The variable name doesn't matter; all that matters is that it's
  the second argument to the function (after request). It's also possible to use keyword,
  rather than positional, arguments in an URLconf. We cover that in Chapter 8.

- The first thing we do within the function is call int() on offset. This converts the string
  value to an integer.

  Note that Python will raise a ValueError exception if you call int() on a value that cannot
  be converted to an integer, such as the string 'foo'. However, in this example we don't
  have to worry about catching that exception, because we can be certain offset will be
  a string containing only digits. We know that because the regular-expression pattern in
  our URLconf—(\d{1,2})—captures only digits. This illustrates another nicety of URL-
  confs: they provide a fair level of input validation.

- The next line of the function shows why we called int() on offset. On this line, we calculate the current time plus a time offset of offset hours, storing the result in dt. The
  datetime.timedelta function requires the hours parameter to be an integer.

- Next, we construct the HTML output of this view function, just as we did in current_
  datetime. A small difference in this line from the previous line is that it uses Python's
  format-string capability with *two* values, not just one. Hence, there are two %s symbols
  in the string and a tuple of values to insert: (offset, dt).

- Finally, we return an HttpResponse of the HTML—again, just as we did in current_datetime.

With that view function and URLconf written, start the Django development server (if
it's not already running), and visit http://127.0.0.1:8000/time/plus/3/ to verify it works.
Then try http://127.0.0.1:8000/time/plus/5/. Then http://127.0.0.1:8000/time/plus/24/.
Finally, visit http://127.0.0.1:8000/time/plus/100/ to verify that the pattern in your URLconf

only accepts one- or two-digit numbers; Django should display a "Page not found" error in this case, just as we saw in the "404 Errors" section earlier. The URL http://127.0.0.1:8000/time/plus/ (with *no* hour designation) should also throw a 404.

If you're following along while coding at the same time, you'll notice that the views.py file now contains two views. (We omitted the current_datetime view from the last set of examples for clarity.) Put together, views.py should look like this:

```
from django.http import HttpResponse
import datetime

def current_datetime(request):
    now = datetime.datetime.now()
    html = "<html><body>It is now %s.</body></html>" % now
    return HttpResponse(html)

def hours_ahead(request, offset):
    offset = int(offset)
    dt = datetime.datetime.now() + datetime.timedelta(hours=offset)
    html = "<html><body>In %s hour(s), it will be %s.</body></html>" % (offset, dt)
    return HttpResponse(html)
```

Django's Pretty Error Pages

Take a moment to admire the fine Web application we've made so far . . . now let's break it! We'll deliberately introduce a Python error into our views.py file by commenting out the offset = int(offset) line in the hours_ahead view:

```
def hours_ahead(request, offset):
    #offset = int(offset)
    dt = datetime.datetime.now() + datetime.timedelta(hours=offset)
    html = "<html><body>In %s hour(s), it will be %s.</body></html>" % (offset, dt)
    return HttpResponse(html)
```

Load up the development server and navigate to /time/plus/3/. You'll see an error page with a significant amount of information, including a TypeError message displayed at the very top: "unsupported type for timedelta hours component: str".

What happened? Well, the datetime.timedelta function expects the hours parameter to be an integer, and we commented out the bit of code that converted offset to an integer. That caused datetime.timedelta to raise the TypeError. It's the typical kind of small bug that every programmer runs into at some point.

The point of this example was to demonstrate Django's error pages. Take some time to explore the error page and get to know the various bits of information it gives you.

Here are some things to notice:

- At the top of the page, you get the key information about the exception: the type of exception, any parameters to the exception (the `"unsupported type"` message in this case), the file in which the exception was raised, and the offending line number.

- Under the exception information, the page displays the full Python traceback for this exception. This is similar to the standard traceback you get in Python's command-line interpreter, except it's more interactive. For each frame in the stack, Django displays the name of the file, the function/method name, the line number, and the source code of that line.

  Click the line of source code (in dark gray), and you'll see several lines from before and after the erroneous line, to give you context.

  Click "Local vars" under any frame in the stack to view a table of all local variables and their values, in that frame, at the exact point in the code at which the exception was raised. This debugging information is invaluable.

- Note the "Switch to copy-and-paste view" text under the "Traceback" header. Click those words, and the traceback will switch to an alternate version that can be easily copied and pasted. Use this when you want to share your exception traceback with others to get technical support—such as the kind folks in the Django IRC chat room or on the Django users mailing list.

- Next, the "Request information" section includes a wealth of information about the incoming Web request that spawned the error: GET and POST information, cookie values, and metainformation, such as CGI headers. Appendix H has a complete reference of all the information a request object contains.

  Below the "Request information" section, the "Settings" section lists all of the settings for this particular Django installation. All the available settings are covered in detail in Appendix E. For now, take a look at the settings to get an idea of the information available.

The Django error page is capable of displaying more information in certain special cases, such as the case of template syntax errors. We'll get to those later, when we discuss the Django template system. For now, uncomment the `offset = int(offset)` line to get the view function working properly again.

Are you the type of programmer who likes to debug with the help of carefully placed `print` statements? You can use the Django error page to do so—just without the `print` statements. At any point in your view, temporarily insert an `assert False` to trigger the error page. Then, you can view the local variables and state of the program. (There's a more advanced way to debug Django views, which we'll explain later, but this is the quickest and easiest.)

Finally, it's obvious that much of this information is sensitive—it exposes the innards of your Python code and Django configuration—and it would be foolish to show this information on the public Internet. A malicious person could use it to attempt to reverse-engineer your Web application and do nasty things. For that reason, the Django error page is only displayed when your Django project is in debug mode. We'll explain how to deactivate debug mode later.

For now, just know that every Django project is in debug mode automatically when you start it. (Sound familiar? The "Page not found" errors, described in the "404 Errors" section, work the same way.)

What's Next?

We've so far been producing views by hard-coding HTML into the Python code. Unfortunately, this is nearly always a bad idea. Luckily, Django ships with a simple yet powerful template engine that allows you to separate the design of the page from the underlying code. We'll dive into Django's template engine in the next chapter.

CHAPTER 4

■ ■ ■

The Django Template System

In the previous chapter, you may have noticed something peculiar in how we returned the text in our example views. Namely, the HTML was hard-coded directly in our Python code. This arrangement leads to several problems:

- Any change to the design of the page requires a change to the Python code. The design of a site tends to change far more frequently than the underlying Python code, so it would be convenient if the design could change without needing to modify the Python code.

- Writing Python code and designing HTML are two different disciplines, and most professional Web development environments split these responsibilities between separate people (or even separate departments). Designers and HTML/CSS coders shouldn't have to edit Python code to get their job done; they should deal with HTML.

- Similarly, it's most efficient if programmers can work on Python code and designers can work on templates at the same time, rather than one person waiting for the other to finish editing a single file that contains both Python and HTML.

For these reasons, it's much cleaner and more maintainable to separate the design of the page from the Python code itself. We can do this with Django's *template system*, which we discuss in this chapter.

Template System Basics

A Django template is a string of text that is intended to separate the presentation of a document from its data. A template defines placeholders and various bits of basic logic (i.e., template tags) that regulate how the document should be displayed. Usually, templates are used for producing HTML, but Django templates are equally capable of generating any text-based format.

Let's dive in with a simple example template. This template describes an HTML page that thanks a person for placing an order with a company. Think of it as a form letter:

```
<html>
<head><title>Ordering notice</title></head>

<body>

<p>Dear {{ person_name }},</p>
```

```
<p>Thanks for placing an order from {{ company }}. It's scheduled to
ship on {{ ship_date|date:"F j, Y" }}.</p>

<p>Here are the items you've ordered:</p>

<ul>
{% for item in item_list %}
<li>{{ item }}</li>
{% endfor %}
</ul>

{% if ordered_warranty %}
<p>Your warranty information will be included in the packaging.</p>
{% endif %}

<p>Sincerely,<br />{{ company }}</p>

</body>
</html>
```

This template is basic HTML with some variables and template tags thrown in. Let's step through it:

- Any text surrounded by a pair of braces (e.g., {{ person_name }}) is a *variable*. This means "insert the value of the variable with the given name." How do we specify the values of the variables? We'll get to that in a moment.

- Any text that's surrounded by curly braces and percent signs (e.g., {% if ordered_ warranty %}) is a *template tag*. The definition of a tag is quite broad: a tag just tells the template system to "do something."

  This example template contains two tags: the {% for item in item_list %} tag (a for tag) and the {% if ordered_warranty %} tag (an if tag). A for tag acts as a simple loop construct, letting you loop over each item in a sequence. An if tag, as you may expect, acts as a logical "if" statement. In this particular case, the tag checks whether the value of the ordered_warranty variable evaluates to True. If it does, the template system will display everything between the {% if ordered_warranty %} and {% endif %}. If not, the template system won't display it. The template system also supports {% else %} and other various logic statements.

- Finally, the second paragraph of this template has an example of a *filter*, with which you can alter the display of a variable. In this example, {{ ship_date|date:"F j, Y" }}, we're passing the ship_date variable to the date filter, giving the date filter the argument "F j, Y". The date filter formats dates in a given format, as specified by that argument. Filters are attached using a pipe character (|), as a reference to Unix pipes.

Each Django template has access to several built-in tags and filters, many of which are discussed in the sections that follow. Appendix F contains the full list of tags and filters, and it's a good idea to familiarize yourself with that list so you know what's possible. It's also possible to create your own filters and tags, which we cover in Chapter 10.

Using the Template System

To use the template system in Python code, just follow these two steps:

1. Create a `Template` object by providing the raw template code as a string. Django also offers a way to create `Template` objects by designating the path to a template file on the filesystem; we'll examine that in a bit.

2. Call the `render()` method of the `Template` object with a given set of variables (i.e., the context). This returns a fully rendered template as a string, with all of the variables and block tags evaluated according to the context.

The following sections describe each step in more detail.

Creating Template Objects

The easiest way to create a `Template` object is to instantiate it directly. The `Template` class lives in the `django.template` module, and the constructor takes one argument, the raw template code. Let's dip into the Python interactive interpreter to see how this works in code.

INTERACTIVE INTERPRETER EXAMPLES

Throughout this book, we feature example Python interactive interpreter sessions. You can recognize these examples by the triple >> greater-than signs (Python prompt)>>>)>greater-than signs (>>>), which designate the interpreter's prompt. If you're copying examples from this book, don't copy those greater-than signs.

Multiline statements in the interactive interpreter are padded with three dots (. . .), for example:

```
>>> print """This is a
... string that spans
... three lines."""
This is a
string that spans
three lines.
>>> def my_function(value):
...     print value
>>> my_function('hello')
hello
```

Those three dots at the start of the additional lines are inserted by the Python shell—they're not part of our input. We include them here to be faithful to the actual output of the interpreter. If you copy our examples to follow along, don't copy those dots.

From within the project directory created by `django-admin.py startproject` (as covered in Chapter 2), type `python manage.py shell` to start the interactive interpreter. Here's a basic walk-through:

```
>>> from django.template import Template
>>> t = Template("My name is {{ name }}.")
>>> print t
```

If you're following along interactively, you'll see something like this:

```
<django.template.Template object at 0xb7d5f24c>
```

That 0xb7d5f24c part will be different every time, and it doesn't really matter; it's simply the Python "identity" of the Template object.

Note When using Django, you need to tell Django which settings to use. Interactively, this is typically done using python manage.py shell, but you've got a few other options, as described in Appendix E.

When you create a Template object, the template system compiles the raw template code into an internal, optimized form, ready for rendering. But if your template code includes any syntax errors, the call to Template() will cause a TemplateSyntaxError exception:

```
>>> from django.template import Template
>>> t = Template('{% notatag %} ')
Traceback (most recent call last):
  File "<stdin>", line 1, in ?
  ...
  django.template.TemplateSyntaxError: Invalid block tag: 'notatag'
```

The system raises a TemplateSyntaxError exception for any of the following cases:

- Invalid block tags

- Invalid arguments to valid block tags

- Invalid filters

- Invalid arguments to valid filters

- Invalid template syntax

- Unclosed block tags (for block tags that require closing tags)

Rendering a Template

Once you have a Template object, you can pass it data by giving it a *context*. A context is simply a set of variables and their associated values. A template uses this to populate its variable tags and evaluate its block tags.

A context is represented in Django by the Context class, which lives in the django.template module. Its constructor takes one optional argument: a dictionary mapping variable names to variable values. Call the Template object's render() method with the context to "fill" the template:

```
>>> from django.template import Context, Template
>>> t = Template("My name is {{ name }}.")
>>> c = Context({"name": "Stephane"})
>>> t.render(c)
'My name is Stephane.'
```

■Note A Python dictionary is a mapping between known keys and variable values. A `Context` is similar to a dictionary, but a `Context` provides additional functionality, as covered in Chapter 10.

Variable names must begin with a letter (A–Z or a–z) and may contain digits, underscores, and dots. (Dots are a special case we'll get to in a moment.) Variable names are case sensitive.

Here's an example of template compilation and rendering, using the sample template from the beginning of this chapter:

```
>>> from django.template import Template, Context
>>> raw_template = """<p>Dear {{ person_name }},</p>
...
... <p>Thanks for ordering {{ product }} from {{ company }}. It's scheduled
... to ship on {{ ship_date|date:"F j, Y" }}.</p>
...
... {% if ordered_warranty %}
... <p>Your warranty information will be included in the packaging.</p>
... {% endif %}
...
... <p>Sincerely,<br />{{ company }}</p>"""
>>> t = Template(raw_template)
>>> import datetime
>>> c = Context({'person_name': 'John Smith',
...       'product': 'Super Lawn Mower',
...       'company': 'Outdoor Equipment',
...       'ship_date': datetime.date(2009, 4, 2),
...       'ordered_warranty': True})
>>> t.render(c)
"<p>Dear John Smith,</p>\n\n<p>Thanks for ordering Super Lawn Mower from
Outdoor Equipment. It's scheduled \nto ship on April 2, 2009.</p>\n\n\n<p>Your
warranty information will be included in the
packaging.</p>\n\n\n<p>Sincerely,<br />Outdoor Equipment</p>"
```

Let's step through this code one statement at a time:

- First, we import the classes `Template` and `Context`, which both live in the module `django.template`.

- We save the raw text of our template into the variable `raw_template`. Note that we use triple quote marks to designate the string, because it wraps over multiple lines; in Python code, strings designated with single quote marks cannot be wrapped over multiple lines.

- Next, we create a template object, t, by passing `raw_template` to the `Template` class constructor.

- We import the `datetime` module from Python's standard library, because we'll need it in the following statement.

- Then, we create a `Context` object, `c`. The `Context` constructor takes a Python dictionary, which maps variable names to values. Here, for example, we specify that the `person_name` is `'John Smith'`, `product` is `'Super Lawn Mower'`, and so forth.

- Finally, we call the `render()` method on our template object, passing it the context. This returns the rendered template—that is, it replaces template variables with the actual values of the variables, and it executes any block tags.

  Note that the warranty paragraph was displayed because the `ordered_warranty` variable evaluated to `True`. Also note the date, `April 2, 2009`, which is displayed according to the format string `'F j, Y'`. (We explain format strings for the `date` filter shortly.)

  If you're new to Python, you may wonder why this output includes newline characters (`'\n'`) rather than displaying the line breaks. That's happening because of a subtlety in the Python interactive interpreter: the call to `t.render(c)` returns a string, and by default the interactive interpreter displays the *representation* of the string, rather than the printed value of the string. If you want to see the string with line breaks displayed as true line breaks rather than `'\n'` characters, use the `print` statement: `print t.render(c)`.

Those are the fundamentals of using the Django template system: just write a template, create a `Template` object, create a `Context`, and call the `render()` method.

Multiple Contexts, Same Template

Once you have a `Template` object, you can render multiple contexts through it, for example:

```
>>> from django.template import Template, Context
>>> t = Template('Hello, {{ name }}')
>>> print t.render(Context({'name': 'John'}))
Hello, John
>>> print t.render(Context({'name': 'Julie'}))
Hello, Julie
>>> print t.render(Context({'name': 'Pat'}))
Hello, Pat
```

Whenever you're using the same template source to render multiple contexts like this, it's more efficient to create the `Template` object *once*, and then call `render()` on it multiple times:

```
# Bad
for name in ('John', 'Julie', 'Pat'):
    t = Template('Hello, {{ name }}')
    print t.render(Context({'name': name}))

# Good
t = Template('Hello, {{ name }}')
for name in ('John', 'Julie', 'Pat'):
    print t.render(Context({'name': name}))
```

Django's template parsing is quite fast. Behind the scenes, most of the parsing happens via a single call to a short regular expression. This is in stark contrast to XML-based template engines, which incur the overhead of an XML parser and tend to be orders of magnitude slower than Django's template rendering engine.

Context Variable Lookup

In the examples so far, we've passed simple values in the contexts—mostly strings, plus a datetime.date example. However, the template system elegantly handles more complex data structures, such as lists, dictionaries, and custom objects.

The key to traversing complex data structures in Django templates is the dot character (.). Use a dot to access dictionary keys, attributes, indices, or methods of an object.

This is best illustrated with a few examples. For instance, suppose you're passing a Python dictionary to a template. To access the values of that dictionary by dictionary key, use a dot:

```
>>> from django.template import Template, Context
>>> person = {'name': 'Sally', 'age': '43'}
>>> t = Template('{{ person.name }} is {{ person.age }} years old.')
>>> c = Context({'person': person})
>>> t.render(c)
'Sally is 43 years old.'
```

Similarly, dots also allow access of object attributes. For example, a Python datetime.date object has year, month, and day attributes, and you can use a dot to access those attributes in a Django template:

```
>>> from django.template import Template, Context
>>> import datetime
>>> d = datetime.date(1993, 5, 2)
>>> d.year
1993
>>> d.month
5
>>> d.day
2
>>> t = Template('The month is {{ date.month }} and the year is {{ date.year }}.')
>>> c = Context({'date': d})
>>> t.render(c)
'The month is 5 and the year is 1993.'
```

This example uses a custom class:

```
>>> from django.template import Template, Context
>>> class Person(object):
...     def __init__(self, first_name, last_name):
...         self.first_name, self.last_name = first_name, last_name
>>> t = Template('Hello, {{ person.first_name }} {{ person.last_name }}.')
>>> c = Context({'person': Person('John', 'Smith')})
>>> t.render(c)
'Hello, John Smith.'
```

Dots are also used to call methods on objects. For example, each Python string has the methods `upper()` and `isdigit()`, and you can call those in Django templates using the same dot syntax:

```
>>> from django.template import Template, Context
>>> t = Template('{{ var }} -- {{ var.upper }} -- {{ var.isdigit }}')
>>> t.render(Context({'var': 'hello'}))
'hello -- HELLO -- False'
>>> t.render(Context({'var': '123'}))
'123 -- 123 -- True'
```

Note that you don't include parentheses in the method calls. Also, it's not possible to pass arguments to the methods; you can only call methods that have no required arguments. (We explain this philosophy later in this chapter.)

Finally, dots are also used to access list indices, for example:

```
>>> from django.template import Template, Context
>>> t = Template('Item 2 is {{ items.2 }}.')
>>> c = Context({'items': ['apples', 'bananas', 'carrots']})
>>> t.render(c)
'Item 2 is carrots.'
```

Negative list indices are not allowed. For example, the template variable `{{ items.-1 }}` would cause a `TemplateSyntaxError`.

■Note Python lists have 0-based indices so that the first item is at index 0, the second is at index 1, and so on.

The dot lookups can be summarized like this: when the template system encounters a dot in a variable name, it tries the following lookups, in this order:

- Dictionary lookup (e.g., `foo["bar"]`)

- Attribute lookup (e.g., `foo.bar`)

- Method call (e.g., `foo.bar()`)

- List-index lookup (e.g., `foo[bar]`)

The system uses the first lookup type that works. It's short-circuit logic.

Dot lookups can be nested multiple levels deep. For instance, the following example uses `{{ person.name.upper }}`, which translates into a dictionary lookup (`person['name']`) and then a method call (`upper()`):

```
>>> from django.template import Template, Context
>>> person = {'name': 'Sally', 'age': '43'}
>>> t = Template('{{ person.name.upper }} is {{ person.age }} years old.')
>>> c = Context({'person': person})
```

```
>>> t.render(c)
'SALLY is 43 years old.'
```

Method Call Behavior

Method calls are slightly more complex than the other lookup types. Here are some things to keep in mind:

- If, during the method lookup, a method raises an exception, the exception will be propagated, unless the exception has a silent_variable_failure attribute whose value is True. If the exception *does* have a silent_variable_failure attribute, the variable will render as an empty string, for example:

```
>>> t = Template("My name is {{ person.first_name }}.")
>>> class PersonClass3:
...     def first_name(self):
...         raise AssertionError, "foo"
>>> p = PersonClass3()
>>> t.render(Context({"person": p}))
Traceback (most recent call last):
...
AssertionError: foo

>>> class SilentAssertionError(AssertionError):
...     silent_variable_failure = True
>>> class PersonClass4:
...     def first_name(self):
...         raise SilentAssertionError
>>> p = PersonClass4()
>>> t.render(Context({"person": p}))
"My name is ."
```

- A method call will work only if the method has no required arguments. Otherwise, the system will move to the next lookup type (list-index lookup).

- Obviously, some methods have side effects, and it would be foolish at best, and possibly even a security hole, to allow the template system to access them.

  Say, for instance, you have a BankAccount object that has a delete() method. A template shouldn't be allowed to include something like {{ account.delete }}. To prevent this, set the function attribute alters_data on the method:

```
def delete(self):
    # Delete the account
delete.alters_data = True
```

  The template system won't execute any method marked in this way. In other words, if a template includes {{ account.delete }}, that tag will not execute the delete() method. It will fail silently.

How Invalid Variables Are Handled

By default, if a variable doesn't exist, the template system renders it as an empty string, failing silently, for example:

```
>>> from django.template import Template, Context
>>> t = Template('Your name is {{ name }}.')
>>> t.render(Context())
'Your name is .'
>>> t.render(Context({'var': 'hello'}))
'Your name is .'
>>> t.render(Context({'NAME': 'hello'}))
'Your name is .'
>>> t.render(Context({'Name': 'hello'}))
'Your name is .'
```

The system fails silently rather than raising an exception because it's intended to be resilient to human error. In this case, all of the lookups failed because variable names have the wrong case or name. In the real world, it's unacceptable for a Web site to become inaccessible due to a small template syntax error.

Note that it's possible to change Django's default behavior in this regard, by tweaking a setting in your Django configuration. We discuss this further in Chapter 10.

Playing with Context Objects

Most of the time, you'll instantiate Context objects by passing in a fully populated dictionary to Context(). But you can add and delete items from a Context object once it's been instantiated, too, using standard Python dictionary syntax:

```
>>> from django.template import Context
>>> c = Context({"foo": "bar"})
>>> c['foo']
'bar'
>>> del c['foo']
>>> c['foo']
''
>>> c['newvariable']  = 'hello'
>>> c['newvariable']
'hello'
```

Basic Template Tags and Filters

As we've mentioned already, the template system ships with built-in tags and filters. The sections that follow provide a rundown of the most common tags and filters.

Tags

The following sections outline the common Django tags.

if/else

The {% if %} tag evaluates a variable, and if that variable is "true" (i.e., it exists, is not empty, and is not a false Boolean value), the system will display everything between {% if %} and {% endif %}, for example:

```
{% if today_is_weekend %}
    <p>Welcome to the weekend!</p>
{% endif %}
```

An {% else %} tag is optional:

```
{% if today_is_weekend %}
    <p>Welcome to the weekend!</p>
{% else %}
    <p>Get back to work.</p>
{% endif %}
```

PYTHON "TRUTHINESS"

In Python, the empty list ([ ]), tuple (( )), dictionary ({ }), string (' '), zero (0), and the special object None are False in a Boolean context. Everything else is True.

The {% if %} tag accepts and, or, or not for testing multiple variables, or to negate a given variable. Here's an example:

```
{% if athlete_list and coach_list %}
    Both athletes and coaches are available.
{% endif %}

{% if not athlete_list %}
    There are no athletes.
{% endif %}

{% if athlete_list or coach_list %}
    There are some athletes or some coaches.
{% endif %}

{% if not athlete_list or coach_list %}
    There are no athletes or there are some coaches. (OK, so
    writing English translations of Boolean logic sounds
    stupid; it's not our fault.)
{% endif %}

{% if athlete_list and not coach_list %}
    There are some athletes and absolutely no coaches.
{% endif %}
```

{% if %} tags don't allow and and or clauses within the same tag, because the order of logic would be ambiguous. For example, this is invalid:

```
{% if athlete_list and coach_list or cheerleader_list %}
```

The use of parentheses for controlling order of operations is not supported. If you find yourself needing parentheses, consider performing logic in the view code in order to simplify the templates. Even so, if you need to combine and and or to do advanced logic, just use nested {% if %} tags, for example:

```
{% if athlete_list %}
    {% if coach_list or cheerleader_list %}
        We have athletes, and either coaches or cheerleaders!
    {% endif %}
{% endif %}
```

Multiple uses of the same logical operator are fine, but you can't combine different operators. For example, this is valid:

```
{% if athlete_list or coach_list or parent_list or teacher_list %}
```

There is no {% elif %} tag. Use nested {% if %} tags to accomplish the same thing:

```
{% if athlete_list %}
    <p>Here are the athletes: {{ athlete_list }}.</p>
{% else %}
    <p>No athletes are available.</p>
    {% if coach_list %}
        <p>Here are the coaches: {{ coach_list }}.</p>
    {% endif %}
{% endif %}
```

Make sure to close each {% if %} with an {% endif %}. Otherwise, Django will throw a TemplateSyntaxError.

for

The {% for %} tag allows you to loop over each item in a sequence. As in Python's for statement, the syntax is for X in Y, where Y is the sequence to loop over and X is the name of the variable to use for a particular cycle of the loop. Each time through the loop, the template system will render everything between {% for %} and {% endfor %}.

For example, you could use the following to display a list of athletes given a variable athlete_list:

```
<ul>
{% for athlete in athlete_list %}
    <li>{{ athlete.name }}</li>
{% endfor %}
</ul>
```

Add reversed to the tag to loop over the list in reverse:

```
{% for athlete in athlete_list reversed %}
...
{% endfor %}
```

It's possible to nest {% for %} tags:

```
{% for country in countries %}
    <h1>{{ country.name }}</h1>
    <ul>
    {% for city in country.city_list %}
        <li>{{ city }}</li>
    {% endfor %}
    </ul>
{% endfor %}
```

There is no support for "breaking out" of a loop before the loop is finished. If you want to accomplish this, change the variable you're looping over so that it includes only the values you want to loop over. Similarly, there is no support for a "continue" statement that would instruct the loop processor to return immediately to the front of the loop. (See the section "Philosophies and Limitations" later in this chapter for the reasoning behind this design decision.)

The {% for %} tag sets a magic forloop template variable within the loop. This variable has a few attributes that give you information about the progress of the loop:

- forloop.counter is always set to an integer representing the number of times the loop has been entered. This is one-indexed, so the first time through the loop, forloop.counter will be set to 1.

    Here's an example:

    ```
    {% for item in todo_list %}
        <p>{{ forloop.counter }}: {{ item }}</p>
    {% endfor %}
    ```

- forloop.counter0 is like forloop.counter, except it's zero-indexed. Its value will be set to 0 the first time through the loop.

- forloop.revcounter is always set to an integer representing the number of remaining items in the loop. The first time through the loop, forloop.revcounter will be set to the total number of items in the sequence you're traversing. The last time through the loop, forloop.revcounter will be set to 1.

- forloop.revcounter0 is like forloop.revcounter, except it's zero-indexed. The first time through the loop, forloop.revcounter0 will be set to the number of elements in the sequence minus 1. The last time through the loop, it will be set to 0.

- forloop.first is a Boolean value set to True if this is the first time through the loop. This is convenient for special casing:

    ```
    {% for object in objects %}
        {% if forloop.first %}<li class="first">{% else %}<li>{% endif %}
    ```

```
    {{ object }}
    </li>
{% endfor %}
```

- forloop.last is a Boolean value set to True if this is the last time through the loop. A common use for this is to put pipe characters between a list of links:

```
{% for link in links %}{{ link }}{% if not forloop.last %} | {% endif %}➥
{% endfor %}
```

The preceding template code might output something like this:

Link1 | Link2 | Link3 | Link4

- forloop.parentloop is a reference to the forloop object for the *parent* loop, in case of nested loops. Here's an example:

```
{% for country in countries %}
    <table>
    {% for city in country.city_list %}
        <tr>
        <td>Country #{{ forloop.parentloop.counter }}</td>
        <td>City #{{ forloop.counter }}</td>
        <td>{{ city }}</td>
        </tr>
    {% endfor %}
    </table>
{% endfor %}
```

The magic forloop variable is only available within loops. After the template parser has reached {% endfor %}, forloop disappears.

CONTEXT AND THE FORLOOP VARIABLE

Inside the {% for %} block, the existing variables are moved out of the way to avoid overwriting the magic forloop variable. Django exposes this moved context in forloop.parentloop. You generally don't need to worry about this, but if you supply a template variable named forloop (though we advise against it), it will be named forloop.parentloop while inside the {% for %} block.

ifequal/ifnotequal

The Django template system deliberately is not a full-fledged programming language and thus does not allow you to execute arbitrary Python statements (more on this idea in the section "Philosophies and Limitations"). However, it's quite a common template requirement to compare two values and display something if they're equal—and Django provides an {% ifequal %} tag for that purpose.

The {% ifequal %} tag compares two values and displays everything between {% ifequal %} and {% endifequal %} if the values are equal.

This example compares the template variables user and currentuser:

```
{% ifequal user currentuser %}
    <h1>Welcome!</h1>
{% endifequal %}
```

The arguments can be hard-coded strings, with either single or double quotes, so the following is valid:

```
{% ifequal section 'sitenews' %}
    <h1>Site News</h1>
{% endifequal %}
```

```
{% ifequal section "community" %}
    <h1>Community</h1>
{% endifequal %}
```

Just like {% if %}, the {% ifequal %} tag supports an optional {% else %}:

```
{% ifequal section 'sitenews' %}
    <h1>Site News</h1>
{% else %}
    <h1>No News Here</h1>
{% endifequal %}
```

Only template variables, strings, integers, and decimal numbers are allowed as arguments to {% ifequal %}. These are valid examples:

```
{% ifequal variable 1 %}
{% ifequal variable 1.23 %}
{% ifequal variable 'foo' %}
{% ifequal variable "foo" %}
```

Any other types of variables, such as Python dictionaries, lists, or Booleans, can't be hard-coded in {% ifequal %}. These are invalid examples:

```
{% ifequal variable True %}
{% ifequal variable [1, 2, 3] %}
{% ifequal variable {'key': 'value'} %}
```

If you need to test whether something is true or false, use the {% if %} tags instead of {% ifequal %}.

Comments

Just as in HTML or in a programming language such as Python, the Django template language allows for comments. To designate a comment, use {# #}:

```
{# This is a comment #}
```

The comment will not be output when the template is rendered.

A comment cannot span multiple lines. This limitation improves template parsing performance. In the following template, the rendered output will look exactly the same as the template (i.e., the comment tag will not be parsed as a comment):

```
This is a {# this is not
a comment #}
test.
```

Filters

As explained earlier in this chapter, template filters are simple ways of altering the value of variables before they're displayed. Filters look like this:

```
{{ name|lower }}
```

This displays the value of the `{{ name }}` variable after being filtered through the `lower` filter, which converts text to lowercase. Use a pipe (`|`) to apply a filter.

Filters can be *chained*—that is, the output of one filter is applied to the next. Here's a common idiom for escaping text contents and then converting line breaks to <p> tags:

```
{{ my_text|escape|linebreaks }}
```

Some filters take arguments. A filter argument looks like this:

```
{{ bio|truncatewords:"30" }}
```

This displays the first 30 words of the `bio` variable. Filter arguments are always in double quotes.

The following are a few of the most important filters; Appendix F covers the rest.

- `addslashes`: Adds a backslash before any backslash, single quote, or double quote. This is useful if the produced text is included in a JavaScript string.

- `date`: Formats a `date` or `datetime` object according to a format string given in the parameter, for example:

  ```
  {{ pub_date|date:"F j, Y" }}
  ```

  Format strings are defined in Appendix F.

- `escape`: Escapes ampersands, quotes, and angle brackets in the given string. This is useful for sanitizing user-submitted data and for ensuring data is valid XML or XHTML. Specifically, `escape` makes these conversions:

  - Converts & to &

  - Converts < to <

  - Converts > to >

  - Converts " (double quote) to "

  - Converts ' (single quote) to '

- length: Returns the length of the value. You can use this on a list or a string, or any Python object that knows how to determine its length (i.e., any object that has a __len__() method).

Philosophies and Limitations

Now that you've gotten a feel for the Django template language, we should point out some of its intentional limitations, along with some philosophies behind why it works the way it does.

More than any other component of Web applications, programmer opinions on template systems vary wildly. The fact that Python alone has dozens, if not hundreds, of open source template-language implementations supports this point. Each was likely created because its developer deemed all existing template languages inadequate. (In fact, it is said to be a rite of passage for a Python developer to write his or her own template language! If you haven't done this yet, consider it. It's a fun exercise.)

With that in mind, you might be interested to know that Django doesn't require that you use its template language. Because Django is intended to be a full-stack Web framework that provides all the pieces necessary for Web developers to be productive, many times it's *more convenient* to use Django's template system than other Python template libraries, but it's not a strict requirement in any sense. As you'll see in the upcoming section "Using Templates in Views," it's very easy to use another template language with Django.

Still, it's clear we have a strong preference for the way Django's template language works. The template system has roots in how Web development is done at World Online and the combined experience of Django's creators. Here are a few of those philosophies:

- *Business logic should be separated from presentation logic*. We see a template system as a tool that controls presentation and presentation-related logic—and that's it. The template system shouldn't support functionality that goes beyond this basic goal.

  For that reason, it's impossible to call Python code directly within Django templates. All "programming" is fundamentally limited to the scope of what template tags can do. It *is* possible to write custom template tags that do arbitrary things, but the out-of-the-box Django template tags intentionally do not allow for arbitrary Python code execution.

- *Syntax should be decoupled from HTML/XML*. Although Django's template system is used primarily to produce HTML, it's intended to be just as usable for non-HTML formats, such as plain text. Some other template languages are XML based, placing all template logic within XML tags or attributes, but Django deliberately avoids this limitation. Requiring valid XML to write templates introduces a world of human mistakes and hard-to-understand error messages, and using an XML engine to parse templates incurs an unacceptable level of overhead in template processing.

- *Designers are assumed to be comfortable with HTML code*. The template system isn't designed so that templates necessarily are displayed nicely in WYSIWYG editors such as Dreamweaver. That is too severe a limitation and wouldn't allow the syntax to be as nice as it is. Django expects template authors to be comfortable editing HTML directly.

- *Designers are assumed not to be Python programmers*. The template system authors recognize that Web page templates are most often written by *designers*, not *programmers*, and therefore should not assume Python knowledge.

However, the system also intends to accommodate small teams in which the templates *are* created by Python programmers. It offers a way to extend the system's syntax by writing raw Python code (more on this in Chapter 10).

- *The goal is not to invent a programming language.* The goal is to offer just enough programming-esque functionality, such as branching and looping, that is essential for making presentation-related decisions.

As a result of these design philosophies, the Django template language has the following limitations:

- *A template cannot set a variable or change the value of a variable.* It's possible to write custom template tags that accomplish these goals (see Chapter 10), but the stock Django template tags do not allow it.

- *A template cannot call raw Python code.* There's no way to "drop into Python mode" or use raw Python constructs. Again, it's possible to write custom template tags to do this, but the stock Django template tags don't allow it.

Using Templates in Views

You've learned the basics of using the template system; now let's use this knowledge to create a view. Recall the `current_datetime` view in `mysite.views`, which we started in the previous chapter. Here's what it looks like:

```
from django.http import HttpResponse
import datetime

def current_datetime(request):
    now = datetime.datetime.now()
    html = "<html><body>It is now %s.</body></html>" % now
    return HttpResponse(html)
```

Let's change this view to use Django's template system. At first, you might think to do something like this:

```
from django.template import Template, Context
from django.http import HttpResponse
import datetime

def current_datetime(request):
    now = datetime.datetime.now()
    t = Template("<html><body>It is now {{ current_date }}.</body></html>")
    html = t.render(Context({'current_date': now}))
    return HttpResponse(html)
```

Sure, that uses the template system, but it doesn't solve the problems we pointed out in the introduction of this chapter. Namely, the template is still embedded in the Python code. Let's fix that by putting the template in a *separate file*, which this view will load.

You might first consider saving your template somewhere on your filesystem and using Python's built-in file-opening functionality to read the contents of the template. Here's what that might look like, assuming the template was saved as the file /home/djangouser/templates/ mytemplate.html:

```
from django.template import Template, Context
from django.http import HttpResponse
import datetime

def current_datetime(request):
    now = datetime.datetime.now()
    # Simple way of using templates from the filesystem.
    # This doesn't account for missing files!
    fp = open('/home/djangouser/templates/mytemplate.html')
    t = Template(fp.read())
    fp.close()
    html = t.render(Context({'current_date': now}))
    return HttpResponse(html)
```

This approach, however, is inelegant for these reasons:

- It doesn't handle the case of a missing file. If the file mytemplate.html doesn't exist or isn't readable, the open() call will raise an IOError exception.

- It hard-codes your template location. If you were to use this technique for every view function, you'd be duplicating the template locations. Not to mention it involves a lot of typing!

- It includes a lot of boring boilerplate code. You've got better things to do than write calls to open(), fp.read(), and fp.close() each time you load a template.

To solve these issues, we'll use *template loading* and *template directories*, both of which are described in the sections that follow.

Template Loading

Django provides a convenient and powerful API for loading templates from disk, with the goal of removing redundancy both in your template-loading calls and in your templates themselves.

In order to use this template-loading API, first you'll need to tell the framework where you store your templates. The place to do this is in your *settings file*.

A Django settings file is the place to put configuration for your Django instance (aka your Django project). It's a simple Python module with module-level variables, one for each setting.

When you ran django-admin.py startproject mysite in Chapter 2, the script created a default settings file for you, aptly named settings.py. Have a look at the file's contents. It contains variables that look like this (though not necessarily in this order):

```
DEBUG = True
TIME_ZONE = 'America/Chicago'
USE_I18N = True
ROOT_URLCONF = 'mysite.urls'
```

This is pretty self-explanatory; the settings and their respective values are simple Python variables. And because the settings file is just a plain Python module, you can do dynamic things such as checking the value of one variable before setting another. (This also means that you should avoid Python syntax errors in your settings file.)

We'll cover settings files in depth in Appendix E, but for now, have a look at the TEMPLATE_DIRS setting. This setting tells Django's template-loading mechanism where to look for templates. By default, it's an empty tuple. Pick a directory where you'd like to store your templates and add it to TEMPLATE_DIRS, like so:

```
TEMPLATE_DIRS = (
    '/home/django/mysite/templates',
)
```

There are a few things to note:

- You can specify any directory you want, as long as the directory and templates within that directory are readable by the user account under which your Web server runs. If you can't think of an appropriate place to put your templates, we recommend creating a templates directory within your Django project (i.e., within the mysite directory you created in Chapter 2, if you've been following along with this book's examples).

- Don't forget the comma at the end of the template directory string! Python requires commas within single-element tuples to disambiguate the tuple from a parenthetical expression. This is a common newbie gotcha.

  If you want to avoid this error, you can make TEMPLATE_DIRS a list instead of a tuple, because single-element lists don't require a trailing comma:

```
TEMPLATE_DIRS = [
    '/home/django/mysite/templates'
]
```

  A tuple is slightly more semantically correct than a list (tuples cannot be changed after being created, and nothing should be changing settings once they've been read), so we recommend using a tuple for your TEMPLATE_DIRS setting.

- If you're on Windows, include your drive letter and use Unix-style forward slashes rather than backslashes, as follows:

- It's simplest to use absolute paths (i.e., directory paths that start at the root of the filesystem). If you want to be a bit more flexible and decoupled, though, you can take advantage of the fact that Django settings files are just Python code by constructing the contents of TEMPLATE_DIRS dynamically, for example:

```
import os.path

TEMPLATE_DIRS = (
    os.path.join(os.path.dirname(__file__), 'templates').replace('\\', '/'),
)
```

  This example uses the "magic" Python variable __file__, which is automatically set to the file name of the Python module in which the code lives.

```
TEMPLATE_DIRS = (
    'C:/www/django/templates',
)
```

With TEMPLATE_DIRS set, the next step is to change the view code to use Django's template-loading functionality rather than hard-coding the template paths. Returning to our current_datetime view, let's change it like so:

```
from django.template.loader import get_template
from django.template import Context
from django.http import HttpResponse
import datetime

def current_datetime(request):
    now = datetime.datetime.now()
    t = get_template('current_datetime.html')
    html = t.render(Context({'current_date': now}))
    return HttpResponse(html)
```

In this example, we're using the function django.template.loader.get_template() rather than loading the template from the filesystem manually. The get_template() function takes a template name as its argument, figures out where the template lives on the filesystem, opens that file, and returns a compiled Template object.

If get_template() cannot find the template with the given name, it raises a TemplateDoesNotExist exception. To see what that looks like, fire up the Django development server again, as in Chapter 3, by running python manage.py runserver within your Django project's directory. Then, point your browser at the page that activates the current_datetime view (e.g., http://127.0.0.1:8000/time/). Assuming your DEBUG setting is set to True and you haven't yet created a current_datetime.html template, you should see a Django error page highlighting the TemplateDoesNotExist error, as shown in Figure 4-1.

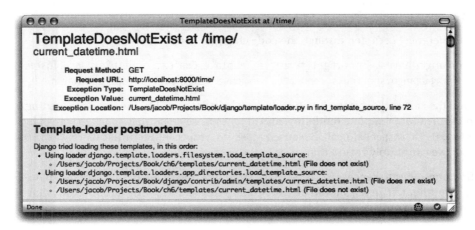

Figure 4-1. *The error page shown when a template cannot be found*

This error page is similar to the one we explained in Chapter 3, with one additional piece of debugging information: a "Template-loader postmortem" section. This section tells you which templates Django tried to load, along with the reason each attempt failed (e.g., "File does not exist"). This information is invaluable when you're trying to debug template-loading errors.

As you can probably tell from the error messages found in the Figure 4-1, Django attempted to find the template by combining the directory in the TEMPLATE_DIRS setting with the template name passed to get_template(). So if your TEMPLATE_DIRS contains '/home/django/templates', Django looks for the file '/home/django/templates/current_datetime.html'. If TEMPLATE_DIRS contains more than one directory, each is checked until the template is found or they've all been checked.

Moving along, create the current_datetime.html file within your template directory using the following template code:

```
<html><body>It is now {{ current_date }}.</body></html>
```

Refresh the page in your Web browser, and you should see the fully rendered page.

render_to_response()

Because it's such a common idiom to load a template, fill a Context, and return an HttpResponse object with the result of the rendered template, Django provides a shortcut that lets you do those things in one line of code. This shortcut is a function called render_to_response(), which lives in the module django.shortcuts. Most of the time, you'll be using render_to_response() rather than loading templates and creating Context and HttpResponse objects manually.

Here's the ongoing current_datetime example rewritten to use render_to_response():

```
from django.shortcuts import render_to_response
import datetime

def current_datetime(request):
    now = datetime.datetime.now()
    return render_to_response('current_datetime.html', {'current_date': now})
```

What a difference! Let's step through the code changes:

- We no longer have to import get_template, Template, Context, or HttpResponse. Instead, we import django.shortcuts.render_to_response. The import datetime remains.

- Within the current_datetime function, we still calculate now, but the template loading, context creation, template rendering, and HttpResponse creation is all taken care of by the render_to_response() call. Because render_to_response() returns an HttpResponse object, we can simply return that value in the view.

The first argument to render_to_response() should be the name of the template to use. The second argument, if given, should be a dictionary to use in creating a Context for that template. If you don't provide a second argument, render_to_response() will use an empty dictionary.

The locals() Trick

Consider our latest incarnation of current_datetime:

```
def current_datetime(request):
    now = datetime.datetime.now()
    return render_to_response('current_datetime.html', {'current_date': now})
```

Many times, as in this example, you'll find yourself calculating some values, storing them in variables (e.g., now in the preceding code), and sending those variables to the template. Particularly lazy programmers should note that it's slightly redundant to have to give names for temporary variables *and* give names for the template variables. Not only is it redundant, but also it's extra typing.

So if you're one of those lazy programmers and you like keeping code particularly concise, you can take advantage of a built-in Python function called locals(). It returns a dictionary mapping all local variable names to their values. Thus, the preceding view could be rewritten like so:

```
def current_datetime(request):
    current_date = datetime.datetime.now()
    return render_to_response('current_datetime.html', locals())
```

Here, instead of manually specifying the context dictionary as before, we pass the value of locals(), which will include all variables defined at that point in the function's execution. As a consequence, we've renamed the now variable to current_date, because that's the variable name that the template expects. In this example, locals() doesn't offer a *huge* improvement, but this technique can save you some typing if you have several template variables to define— or if you're lazy.

One thing to watch out for when using locals() is that it includes *every* local variable, which may comprise more variables than you actually want your template to have access to. In the previous example, locals() will also include request. Whether this matters to you depends on your application.

A final thing to consider is that locals() incurs a small bit of overhead, because when you call it, Python has to create the dictionary dynamically. If you specify the context dictionary manually, you avoid this overhead.

Subdirectories in get_template()

It can get unwieldy to store all of your templates in a single directory. You might like to store templates in subdirectories of your template directory, and that's fine. In fact, we recommend doing so; some more advanced Django features (such as the generic views system, which we cover in Chapter 9) expect this template layout as a default convention.

Storing templates in subdirectories of your template directory is easy. In your calls to get_template(), just include the subdirectory name and a slash before the template name, like so:

```
t = get_template('dateapp/current_datetime.html')
```

Because `render_to_response()` is a small wrapper around `get_template()`, you can do the same thing with the first argument to `render_to_response()`.

There's no limit to the depth of your subdirectory tree. Feel free to use as many as you like.

■**Note** Windows users, be sure to use forward slashes rather than backslashes. `get_template()` assumes a Unix-style file name designation.

The include Template Tag

Now that we've covered the template-loading mechanism, we can introduce a built-in template tag that takes advantage of it: `{% include %}`. This tag allows you to include the contents of another template. The argument to the tag should be the name of the template to include, and the template name can be either a variable or a hard-coded (quoted) string, in either single or double quotes. Anytime you have the same code in multiple templates, consider using an `{% include %}` to remove the duplication.

These two examples include the contents of the template `nav.html`. The examples are equivalent and illustrate that either single or double quotes are allowed:

```
{% include 'nav.html' %}
{% include "nav.html" %}
```

This example includes the contents of the template `includes/nav.html`:

```
{% include 'includes/nav.html' %}
```

This example includes the contents of the template whose name is contained in the variable `template_name`:

```
{% include template_name %}
```

As in `get_template()`, the file name of the template is determined by adding the template directory from `TEMPLATE_DIRS` to the requested template name.

Included templates are evaluated with the context of the template that's including them. If a template with the given name isn't found, Django will do one of two things:

- If `DEBUG` is set to `True`, you'll see the `TemplateDoesNotExist` exception on a Django error page.

- If `DEBUG` is set to `False`, the tag will fail silently, displaying nothing in the place of the tag.

Template Inheritance

Our template examples so far have been tiny HTML snippets, but in the real world, you'll be using Django's template system to create entire HTML pages. This leads to a common Web development problem: across a Web site, how do you reduce the duplication and redundancy of common page areas, such as sitewide navigation?

A classic way of solving this problem is to use *server-side includes*, directives you can embed within your HTML pages to "include" one Web page inside another. Indeed, Django supports that approach, with the {% include %} template tag just described. But the preferred way of solving this problem with Django is to use a more elegant strategy called *template inheritance*.

In essence, template inheritance lets you build a base "skeleton" template that contains all the common parts of your site and defines "blocks" that child templates can override.

Let's see an example of this by creating a more complete template for our current_datetime view, by editing the current_datetime.html file:

```
<!DOCTYPE HTML PUBLIC "-//W3C//DTD HTML 4.01//EN">
<html lang="en">
<head>
    <title>The current time</title>
</head>
<body>
    <h1>My helpful timestamp site</h1>
    <p>It is now {{ current_date }}.</p>

    <hr>
    <p>Thanks for visiting my site.</p>
</body>
</html>
```

That looks just fine, but what happens when we want to create a template for another view—say, the hours_ahead view from Chapter 3? If we want to again make a nice, valid, full HTML template, we'd create something like this:

```
<!DOCTYPE HTML PUBLIC "-//W3C//DTD HTML 4.01//EN">
<html lang="en">
<head>
    <title>Future time</title>
</head>
<body>
    <h1>My helpful timestamp site</h1>
    <p>In {{ hour_offset }} hour(s), it will be {{ next_time }}.</p>

    <hr>
    <p>Thanks for visiting my site.</p>
</body>
</html>
```

Clearly, we've just duplicated a lot of HTML. Imagine if we had a more typical site, including a navigation bar, a few style sheets, perhaps some JavaScript—we'd end up putting all sorts of redundant HTML into each template.

The server-side include solution to this problem is to factor out the common bits in both templates and save them in separate template snippets, which are then included in each template. Perhaps you'd store the top bit of the template in a file called header.html:

```
<!DOCTYPE HTML PUBLIC "-//W3C//DTD HTML 4.01//EN">
<html lang="en">
<head>
```

And perhaps you'd store the bottom bit in a file called footer.html:

```
<hr>
<p>Thanks for visiting my site.</p>
</body>
</html>
```

With an include-based strategy, headers and footers are easy. It's the middle ground that's messy. In this example, both pages feature a title—<h1>My helpful timestamp site</h1>—but that title can't fit into header.html because the <title> on both pages is different. If we included the <h1> in the header, we'd have to include the <title>, which wouldn't allow us to customize it per page. See where this is going?

Django's template inheritance system solves these problems. You can think of it as an "inside-out" version of server-side includes. Instead of defining the snippets that are *common*, you define the snippets that are *different*.

The first step is to define a *base template*—a skeleton of your page that *child templates* will later fill in. Here's a base template for our ongoing example:

```
<!DOCTYPE HTML PUBLIC "-//W3C//DTD HTML 4.01//EN">
<html lang="en">
<head>
    <title>{% block title %}{% endblock %}</title>
</head>
<body>
    <h1>My helpful timestamp site</h1>
    {% block content %}{% endblock %}
    {% block footer %}
    <hr>
    <p>Thanks for visiting my site.</p>
    {% endblock %}
</body>
</html>
```

This template, which we'll call base.html, defines a simple HTML skeleton document that we'll use for all the pages on the site. It's the job of child templates to override, or add to, or leave alone the contents of the blocks. (If you're following along at home, save this file to your template directory.)

We're using a template tag here that you haven't seen before: the {% block %} tag. All the {% block %} tags do is tell the template engine that a child template may override those portions of the template.

Now that we have this base template, we can modify our existing current_datetime.html template to use it:

```
{% extends "base.html" %}

{% block title %}The current time{% endblock %}

{% block content %}
<p>It is now {{ current_date }}.</p>
{% endblock %}
```

While we're at it, let's create a template for the hours_ahead view from Chapter 3. (If you're following along with code, we'll leave it up to you to change hours_ahead to use the template system.) Here's what that would look like:

```
{% extends "base.html" %}

{% block title %}Future time{% endblock %}

{% block content %}
<p>In {{ hour_offset }} hour(s), it will be {{ next_time }}.</p>
{% endblock %}
```

Isn't this beautiful? Each template contains only the code that's *unique* to that template. No redundancy needed. If you need to make a sitewide design change, just make the change to base.html, and all of the other templates will immediately reflect the change.

Here's how it works. When you load the template current_datetime.html, the template engine sees the {% extends %} tag, noting that this template is a child template. The engine immediately loads the parent template—in this case, base.html.

At that point, the template engine notices the three {% block %} tags in base.html and replaces those blocks with the contents of the child template. So, the title we've defined in {% block title %} will be used, as will the {% block content %}.

Note that since the child template doesn't define the footer block, the template system uses the value from the parent template instead. Content within a {% block %} tag in a parent template is always used as a fallback.

Inheritance doesn't affect the way the context works, and you can use as many levels of inheritance as needed. One common way of using inheritance is the following three-level approach:

1. Create a base.html template that holds the main look and feel of your site. This is the stuff that rarely, if ever, changes.

2. Create a base_SECTION.html template for each "section" of your site (e.g., base_photos.html and base_forum.html). These templates extend base.html and include section-specific styles/design.

3. Create individual templates for each type of page, such as a forum page or a photo gallery. These templates extend the appropriate section template.

This approach maximizes code reuse and makes it easy to add items to shared areas, such as sectionwide navigation.

Here are some tips for working with template inheritance:

- If you use {% extends %} in a template, it must be the first template tag in that template. Otherwise, template inheritance won't work.

- Generally, the more {% block %} tags in your base templates, the better. Remember, child templates don't have to define all parent blocks, so you can fill in reasonable defaults in a number of blocks, and then define only the ones you need in the child templates. It's better to have more hooks than fewer hooks.

- If you find yourself duplicating code in a number of templates, it probably means you should move that code to a {% block %} in a parent template.

- If you need to get the content of the block from the parent template, the {{ block.super }} variable will do the trick. This is useful if you want to add to the contents of a parent block instead of completely overriding it.

- You may not define multiple {% block %} tags with the same name in the same template. This limitation exists because a block tag works in "both" directions. That is, a block tag doesn't just provide a hole to fill, it also defines the content that fills the hole in the *parent*. If there were two similarly named {% block %} tags in a template, that template's parent wouldn't know which one of the blocks' content to use.

- The template name you pass to {% extends %} is loaded using the same method that get_template() uses. That is, the template name is appended to your TEMPLATE_DIRS setting.

- In most cases, the argument to {% extends %} will be a string, but it can also be a variable, if you don't know the name of the parent template until runtime. This lets you do some cool, dynamic stuff.

What's Next?

Most modern Web sites are *database driven*, meaning the site content is stored in a relational database. This allows a clean separation of data and logic (in the same way views and templates allow the separation of logic and display). The next chapter covers the tools Django provides to interact with a database.

CHAPTER 5

■■■

Interacting with a Database: Models

In Chapter 3, we covered the fundamentals of building dynamic Web sites with Django: setting up views and URLconfs. As we explained, a view is responsible for doing *some arbitrary logic* and then returning a response. In the example, our arbitrary logic was to calculate the current date and time.

In modern Web applications, the arbitrary logic often involves interacting with a database. Behind the scenes, a *database-driven Web site* connects to a database server, retrieves some data out of it, and displays that data, nicely formatted, on a Web page. Or, similarly, the site could provide functionality that lets site visitors populate the database on their own.

Many complex Web sites provide some combination of the two. Amazon.com, for instance, is a great example of a database-driven site. Each product page is essentially a query into Amazon's product database formatted as HTML, and when you post a customer review, it gets inserted into the database of reviews.

Django is well suited for making database-driven Web sites, as it comes with easy yet powerful ways of performing database queries using Python. This chapter explains that functionality: Django's database layer.

Note While it's not strictly necessary to know basic database theory and SQL in order to use Django's database layer, it's highly recommended. An introduction to those concepts is beyond the scope of this book, but keep reading even if you're a database newbie. You'll probably be able to follow along and grasp concepts based on the context.

The "Dumb" Way to Do Database Queries in Views

Just as Chapter 3 detailed a "dumb" way to produce output within a view (by hard-coding the text directly within the view), there's a "dumb" way to retrieve data from a database in a view. It's simple: just use any existing Python library to execute an SQL query and do something with the results.

In this example view, we use the MySQLdb library (available at http://www.djangoproject.com/r/python-mysql/) to connect to a MySQL database, retrieve some records, and feed them to a template for display as a Web page:

```
from django.shortcuts import render_to_response
import MySQLdb

def book_list(request):
    db = MySQLdb.connect(user='me', db='mydb', passwd='secret', host='localhost')
    cursor = db.cursor()
    cursor.execute('SELECT name FROM books ORDER BY name')
    names = [row[0] for row in cursor.fetchall()]
    db.close()
    return render_to_response('book_list.html', {'names': names})
```

This approach works, but some problems should jump out at you immediately:

- We're hard-coding the database connection parameters. Ideally, these parameters would be stored in the Django configuration.

- We're having to write a fair bit of boilerplate code: creating a connection, creating a cursor, executing a statement, and closing the connection. Ideally, all we'd have to do is specify which results we wanted.

- It ties us to MySQL. If, down the road, we switch from MySQL to PostgreSQL, we'll have to use a different database adapter (e.g., psycopg rather than MySQLdb), alter the connection parameters, and—depending on the nature of the SQL statement—possibly rewrite the SQL. Ideally, the database server we're using would be abstracted, so that a database server change could be made in a single place.

As you might expect, Django's database layer aims to solve these problems. Here's a sneak preview of how the previous view can be rewritten using Django's database API:

```
from django.shortcuts import render_to_response
from mysite.books.models import Book

def book_list(request):
    books = Book.objects.order_by('name')
    return render_to_response('book_list.html', {'books': books})
```

We'll explain this code a little later in the chapter. For now, just get a feel for how it looks.

The MTV Development Pattern

Before we delve into any more code, let's take a moment to consider the overall design of a database-driven Django Web application.

As we mentioned in previous chapters, Django is designed to encourage loose coupling and strict separation between pieces of an application. If you follow this philosophy, it's easy to make changes to a particular piece of the application without affecting the other pieces. In view functions, for instance, we discussed the importance of separating the business logic from the presentation logic by using a template system. With the database layer, we're applying that same philosophy to data access logic.

Those three pieces together—data access logic, business logic, and presentation logic—comprise a concept that's sometimes called the *Model-View-Controller* (MVC) pattern of software architecture. In this pattern, "Model" refers to the data access layer, "View" refers to the part of the system that selects what to display and how to display it, and "Controller" refers to the part of the system that decides which view to use, depending on user input, accessing the model as needed.

WHY THE ACRONYM?

The goal of explicitly defining patterns such as MVC is mostly to streamline communication among developers. Instead of having to tell your coworkers, "Let's make an abstraction of the data access, then let's have a separate layer that handles data display, and let's put a layer in the middle that regulates this," you can take advantage of a shared vocabulary and say, "Let's use the MVC pattern here."

Django follows this MVC pattern closely enough that it can be called an MVC framework. Here's roughly how the M, V, and C break down in Django:

- *M*, the data-access portion, is handled by Django's database layer, which is described in this chapter.

- *V*, the portion that selects which data to display and how to display it, is handled by views and templates.

- *C*, the portion that delegates to a view depending on user input, is handled by the framework itself by following your URLconf and calling the appropriate Python function for the given URL.

Because the "C" is handled by the framework itself and most of the excitement in Django happens in models, templates, and views, Django has been referred to as an *MTV framework*. In the MTV development pattern,

- *M* stands for "Model," the data access layer. This layer contains anything and everything about the data: how to access it, how to validate it, which behaviors it has, and the relationships between the data.

- *T* stands for "Template," the presentation layer. This layer contains presentation-related decisions: how something should be displayed on a Web page or other type of document.

- *V* stands for "View," the business logic layer. This layer contains the logic that accesses the model and defers to the appropriate template(s). You can think of it as the bridge between models and templates.

If you're familiar with other MVC Web-development frameworks, such as Ruby on Rails, you may consider Django views to be the "controllers" and Django templates to be the "views." This is an unfortunate confusion brought about by differing interpretations of MVC. In Django's interpretation of MVC, the "view" describes the data that gets presented to the user; it's not necessarily just *how* the data looks, but *which* data is presented. In contrast, Ruby on Rails and similar frameworks suggest that the controller's job includes deciding which data gets presented to the user, whereas the view is strictly *how* the data looks, not *which* data is presented.

Neither interpretation is more "correct" than the other. The important thing is to understand the underlying concepts.

Configuring the Database

With all of that philosophy in mind, let's start exploring Django's database layer. First, we need to take care of some initial configuration: we need to tell Django which database server to use and how to connect to it.

We'll assume you've set up a database server, activated it, and created a database within it (e.g., using a `CREATE DATABASE` statement). SQLite is a special case; in that case, there's no database to create, because SQLite uses standalone files on the filesystem to store its data.

As with `TEMPLATE_DIRS` in the previous chapter, database configuration lives in the Django settings file, called `settings.py` by default. Edit that file and look for the database settings:

```
DATABASE_ENGINE = ''
DATABASE_NAME = ''
DATABASE_USER = ''
DATABASE_PASSWORD = ''
DATABASE_HOST = ''
DATABASE_PORT = ''
```

Here's a rundown of each setting.

- `DATABASE_ENGINE` tells Django which database engine to use. If you're using a database with Django, `DATABASE_ENGINE` must be set to one of the strings shown in Table 5-1.

Table 5-1. *Database Engine Settings*

Setting	Database	Required Adapter
postgresql	PostgreSQL	psycopg version 1.x, http://www.djangoproject.com/r/python-pgsql/1/.
postgresql_psycopg2	PostgreSQL	psycopg version 2.x, http://www.djangoproject.com/r/python-pgsql/.
mysql	MySQL	MySQLdb, http://www.djangoproject.com/r/python-mysql/.
sqlite3	SQLite	No adapter needed if using Python 2.5+. Otherwise, pysqlite, http://www.djangoproject.com/r/python-sqlite/.
oracle	Oracle	cx_Oracle, http://www.djangoproject.com/r/python-oracle/.

Note that for whichever database back-end you use, you'll need to download and install the appropriate database adapter. Each one is available for free on the Web; just follow the links in the "Required Adapter" column in Table 5-1.

- DATABASE_NAME tells Django the name of your database. If you're using SQLite, specify the full filesystem path to the database file on your filesystem (e.g., '/home/django/mydata.db').

- DATABASE_USER tells Django which username to use when connecting to your database. If you're using SQLite, leave this blank.

- DATABASE_PASSWORD tells Django which password to use when connecting to your database. If you're using SQLite or have an empty password, leave this blank.

- DATABASE_HOST tells Django which host to use when connecting to your database. If your database is on the same computer as your Django installation (i.e., localhost), leave this blank. If you're using SQLite, leave this blank.

  MySQL is a special case here. If this value starts with a forward slash (/) and you're using MySQL, MySQL will connect via a Unix socket to the specified socket, for example:

  ```
  DATABASE_HOST = '/var/run/mysql'
  ```

  If you're using MySQL and this value *doesn't* start with a forward slash, then this value is assumed to be the host.

- DATABASE_PORT tells Django which port to use when connecting to your database. If you're using SQLite, leave this blank. Otherwise, if you leave this blank, the underlying database adapter will use whichever port is default for your given database server. In most cases, the default port is fine, so you can leave this blank.

Once you've entered those settings, test your configuration. First, from within the mysite project directory you created in Chapter 2, run the command python manage.py shell.

You'll notice this starts a Python interactive interpreter. Looks can be deceiving, though! There's an important difference between running the command python manage.py shell within your Django project directory and the more generic python. The latter is the basic Python shell, but the former tells Django which settings file to use before it starts the shell. This is a key requirement for doing database queries: Django needs to know which settings file to use in order to get your database connection information.

Behind the scenes, python manage.py shell simply assumes that your settings file is in the same directory as manage.py. There are other ways to tell Django which settings module to use; we'll cover those options later. For now, use python manage.py shell whenever you need to drop into the Python interpreter to do Django-specific tinkering.

Once you've entered the shell, type these commands to test your database configuration:

```
>>> from django.db import connection
>>> cursor = connection.cursor()
```

If nothing happens, then your database is configured properly. Otherwise, check the error message for clues about what's wrong. Table 5-2 shows some common errors.

Table 5-2. *Database Configuration Error Messages*

Error Message	Solution
You haven't set the DATABASE_ENGINE setting yet.	Set the DATABASE_ENGINE setting to something other than an empty string.
Environment variable DJANGO_SETTINGS_MODULE is undefined.	Run the command python manage.py shell rather than python.
Error loading _____ module: No module named _____.	You haven't installed the appropriate database-specific adapter (e.g., psycopg or MySQLdb).
_____ isn't an available database backend.	Set your DATABASE_ENGINE setting to one of the valid engine settings described previously. Perhaps you made a typo?
database _____ does not exist	Change the DATABASE_NAME setting to point to a database that exists, or execute the appropriate CREATE DATABASE statement in order to create it.
role _____ does not exist	Change the DATABASE_USER setting to point to a user that exists, or create the user in your database.
could not connect to server	Make sure DATABASE_HOST and DATABASE_PORT are set correctly, and make sure the server is running.

Your First App

Now that you've verified the connection is working, it's time to create a *Django app*—a bundle of Django code, including models and views, that lives together in a single Python package and represents a full Django application.

It's worth explaining the terminology here, because this tends to trip up beginners. We already created a *project*, in Chapter 2, so what's the difference between a *project* and an *app*? The difference is that of configuration vs. code:

- A project is an instance of a certain set of Django apps, plus the configuration for those apps. Technically, the only requirement of a project is that it supplies a settings file, which defines the database connection information, the list of installed apps, the TEMPLATE_DIRS, and so forth.

- An app is a portable set of Django functionality, usually including models and views, that lives together in a single Python package. For example, Django comes with a number of apps, such as a commenting system and an automatic admin interface. A key thing to note about these apps is that they're portable and reusable across multiple projects.

There are very few hard-and-fast rules about how you fit your Django code into this scheme; it's flexible. If you're building a simple Web site, you may use only a single app. If you're building a complex Web site with several unrelated pieces such as an e-commerce system and a message board, you'll probably want to split those into separate apps so that you'll be able to reuse them individually in the future.

Indeed, you don't necessarily need to create apps at all, as evidenced by the example view functions we've created so far in this book. In those cases, we simply created a file called `views.py`, filled it with view functions, and pointed our URLconf at those functions. No "apps" were needed.

However, there's one requirement regarding the app convention: if you're using Django's database layer (models), you must create a Django app. Models must live within apps. Thus, in order to start writing our models, we'll need to create a new app.

Within the `mysite` project directory you created in Chapter 2, type this command to create a new app named `books`:

```
python manage.py startapp books
```

This command does not produce any output, but it does create a `books` directory within the `mysite` directory. Let's look at the contents of that directory:

```
books/
    __init__.py
    models.py
    views.py
```

These files will contain the models and views for this app.

Have a look at `models.py` and `views.py` in your favorite text editor. Both files are empty, except for an import in `models.py`. This is the blank slate for your Django app.

Defining Models in Python

As we discussed earlier in this chapter, the "M" in "MTV" stands for "Model." A Django model is a description of the data in your database, represented as Python code. It's your data layout—the equivalent of your SQL `CREATE TABLE` statements—except it's in Python instead of SQL, and it includes more than just database column definitions. Django uses a model to execute SQL code behind the scenes and return convenient Python data structures representing the rows in your database tables. Django also uses models to represent higher-level concepts that SQL can't necessarily handle.

If you're familiar with databases, your immediate thought might be, "Isn't it redundant to define data models in Python *and* in SQL?" Django works the way it does for several reasons:

- Introspection requires overhead and is imperfect. In order to provide convenient data-access APIs, Django needs to know the database layout *somehow*, and there are two ways of accomplishing this. The first way is to explicitly describe the data in Python, and the second way is to introspect the database at runtime to determine the data models.

    This second way seems cleaner, because the metadata about your tables lives in only one place, but it introduces a few problems. First, introspecting a database at runtime obviously requires overhead. If the framework had to introspect the database each time it processed a request, or even when the Web server was initialized, this would incur an unacceptable level of overhead. (While some believe that level of overhead is acceptable, Django's developers aim to trim as much framework overhead as possible, and this approach has succeeded in making Django faster than its high-level framework competitors in benchmarks.) Second, some databases, notably older versions of MySQL, do not store sufficient metadata for accurate and complete introspection.

- Writing Python is fun, and keeping everything in Python limits the number of times your brain has to do a "context switch." It helps productivity if you keep yourself in a single programming environment/mentality for as long as possible. Having to write SQL, then Python, and then SQL again is disruptive.

- Having data models stored as code rather than in your database makes it easier to keep your models under version control. This way, you can easily keep track of changes to your data layouts.

- SQL allows for only a certain level of metadata about a data layout. Most database systems, for example, do not provide a specialized data type for representing email addresses or URLs. Django models do. The advantage of higher-level data types is higher productivity and more reusable code.

- SQL is inconsistent across database platforms. If you're distributing a Web application, for example, it's much more pragmatic to distribute a Python module that describes your data layout than separate sets of CREATE TABLE statements for MySQL, PostgreSQL, and SQLite.

A drawback of this approach, however, is that it's possible for the Python code to get out of sync with what's actually in the database. If you make changes to a Django model, you'll need to make the same changes inside your database to keep your database consistent with the model. We'll detail some strategies for handling this problem later in this chapter.

Finally, we should note that Django includes a utility that can generate models by introspecting an existing database. This is useful for quickly getting up and running with legacy data.

Your First Model

As an ongoing example in this chapter and the next chapter, we'll focus on a basic book/author/publisher data layout. We use this as our example because the conceptual relationships between books, authors, and publishers are well known, and this is a common data layout used in introductory SQL textbooks. You're also reading a book that was written by authors and produced by a publisher!

We'll suppose the following concepts, fields, and relationships:

- An author has a salutation (e.g., Mr. or Mrs.), a first name, a last name, an email address, and a headshot photo.

- A publisher has a name, a street address, a city, a state/province, a country, and a Web site.

- A book has a title and a publication date. It also has one or more authors (a many-to-many relationship with authors) and a single publisher (a one-to-many relationship—aka foreign key—to publishers).

The first step in using this database layout with Django is to express it as Python code. In the models.py file that was created by the startapp command, enter the following:

```
from django.db import models

class Publisher(models.Model):
    name = models.CharField(maxlength=30)
    address = models.CharField(maxlength=50)
    city = models.CharField(maxlength=60)
    state_province = models.CharField(maxlength=30)
    country = models.CharField(maxlength=50)
    website = models.URLField()

class Author(models.Model):
    salutation = models.CharField(maxlength=10)
    first_name = models.CharField(maxlength=30)
    last_name = models.CharField(maxlength=40)
    email = models.EmailField()
    headshot = models.ImageField(upload_to='/tmp')

class Book(models.Model):
    title = models.CharField(maxlength=100)
    authors = models.ManyToManyField(Author)
    publisher = models.ForeignKey(Publisher)
    publication_date = models.DateField()
```

Let's quickly examine this code to cover the basics. The first thing to notice is that each model is represented by a Python class that is a subclass of django.db.models.Model. The parent class, Model, contains all the machinery necessary to make these objects capable of interacting with a database—and that leaves our models responsible solely for defining their fields, in a nice and compact syntax. Believe it or not, this is all the code we need to write to have basic data access with Django.

Each model generally corresponds to a single database table, and each attribute on a model generally corresponds to a column in that database table. The attribute name corresponds to the column's name, and the type of field (e.g., CharField) corresponds to the database column type (e.g., varchar). For example, the Publisher model is equivalent to the following table (assuming PostgreSQL CREATE TABLE syntax):

```
CREATE TABLE "books_publisher" (
    "id" serial NOT NULL PRIMARY KEY,
    "name" varchar(30) NOT NULL,
    "address" varchar(50) NOT NULL,
    "city" varchar(60) NOT NULL,
    "state_province" varchar(30) NOT NULL,
    "country" varchar(50) NOT NULL,
    "website" varchar(200) NOT NULL
);
```

Indeed, Django can generate that CREATE TABLE statement automatically, as we'll show in a moment.

The exception to the one-class-per-database-table rule is the case of many-to-many relationships. In our example models, Book has a ManyToManyField called authors. This designates that a book has one or many authors, but the Book database table doesn't get an authors column. Rather, Django creates an additional table—a many-to-many "join table"—that handles the mapping of books to authors.

■**Note** For a full list of field types and model syntax options, see Appendix B.

Finally, note we haven't explicitly defined a primary key in any of these models. Unless you instruct it otherwise, Django automatically gives every model an integer primary key field called id. Each Django model is required to have a single-column primary key.

Installing the Model

We've written the code; now let's create the tables in our database. In order to do that, the first step is to *activate* these models in our Django project. We do that by adding the books app to the list of installed apps in the settings file.

Edit the settings.py file again, and look for the INSTALLED_APPS setting. INSTALLED_APPS tells Django which apps are activated for a given project. By default, it looks something like this:

```
INSTALLED_APPS = (
    'django.contrib.auth',
    'django.contrib.contenttypes',
    'django.contrib.sessions',
    'django.contrib.sites',
)
```

Temporarily comment out all four of those strings by putting a hash character (#) in front of them. (They're included by default as a common-case convenience, but we'll activate and discuss them later.) While you're at it, modify the default MIDDLEWARE_CLASSES and TEMPLATE_CONTEXT_PROCESSORS settings. These depend on some of the apps we just commented out. Then, add 'mysite.books' to the INSTALLED_APPS list, so the setting ends up looking like this:

```
MIDDLEWARE_CLASSES = []
TEMPLATE_CONTEXT_PROCESSORS = []
INSTALLED_APPS = (
    #'django.contrib.auth',
    #'django.contrib.contenttypes',
    #'django.contrib.sessions',
    #'django.contrib.sites',
    'mysite.books',
)
```

> ▓**Note** As we're dealing with a single-element tuple here, don't forget the trailing comma. By the way, this book's authors prefer to put a comma after *every* element of a tuple, regardless of whether the tuple has only a single element. This avoids the issue of forgetting commas, and there's no penalty for using that extra comma.

'mysite.books' refers to the books app we're working on. Each app in INSTALLED_APPS is represented by its full Python path—that is, the path of packages, separated by dots, leading to the app package.

Now that the Django app has been activated in the settings file, we can create the database tables in our database. First, let's validate the models by running this command:

```
python manage.py validate
```

The validate command checks whether your models' syntax and logic are correct. If all is well, you'll see the message 0 errors found. If you don't, make sure you typed in the model code correctly. The error output should give you helpful information about what was wrong with the code.

Anytime you think you have problems with your models, run python manage.py validate. It tends to catch all the common model problems.

If your models are valid, run the following command for Django to generate CREATE TABLE statements for your models in the books app (with colorful syntax highlighting available if you're using Unix):

```
python manage.py sqlall books
```

In this command, books is the name of the app. It's what you specified when you ran the command manage.py startapp. When you run the command, you should see something like this:

```
BEGIN;
CREATE TABLE "books_publisher" (
    "id" serial NOT NULL PRIMARY KEY,
    "name" varchar(30) NOT NULL,
    "address" varchar(50) NOT NULL,
    "city" varchar(60) NOT NULL,
    "state_province" varchar(30) NOT NULL,
    "country" varchar(50) NOT NULL,
    "website" varchar(200) NOT NULL
);
CREATE TABLE "books_book" (
    "id" serial NOT NULL PRIMARY KEY,
    "title" varchar(100) NOT NULL,
    "publisher_id" integer NOT NULL REFERENCES "books_publisher" ("id"),
    "publication_date" date NOT NULL
);
```

```
CREATE TABLE "books_author" (
    "id" serial NOT NULL PRIMARY KEY,
    "salutation" varchar(10) NOT NULL,
    "first_name" varchar(30) NOT NULL,
    "last_name" varchar(40) NOT NULL,
    "email" varchar(75) NOT NULL,
    "headshot" varchar(100) NOT NULL
);
CREATE TABLE "books_book_authors" (
    "id" serial NOT NULL PRIMARY KEY,
    "book_id" integer NOT NULL REFERENCES "books_book" ("id"),
    "author_id" integer NOT NULL REFERENCES "books_author" ("id"),
    UNIQUE ("book_id", "author_id")
);
CREATE INDEX books_book_publisher_id ON "books_book" ("publisher_id");
COMMIT;
```

Note the following:

- Table names are automatically generated by combining the name of the app (books) and the lowercased name of the model (publisher, book, and author). You can override this behavior, as detailed in Appendix B.

- As we mentioned earlier, Django adds a primary key for each table automatically—the id fields. You can override this, too.

- By convention, Django appends "_id" to the foreign key field name. As you might have guessed, you can override this behavior as well.

- The foreign key relationship is made explicit by a REFERENCES statement.

- These CREATE TABLE statements are tailored to the database you're using, so database-specific field types such as auto_increment (MySQL), serial (PostgreSQL), or integer primary key (SQLite) are handled for you automatically. The same goes for quoting of column names (e.g., using double quotes or single quotes). This example output is in PostgreSQL syntax.

The sqlall command doesn't actually create the tables or otherwise touch your database—it just prints output to the screen so you can see what SQL Django would execute if you asked it. If you wanted to, you could copy and paste this SQL into your database client, or use Unix pipes to pass it directly. However, Django provides an easier way of committing the SQL to the database. Run the syncdb command, like so:

```
python manage.py syncdb
```

You'll see something like this:

```
Creating table books_publisher
Creating table books_book
Creating table books_author
Installing index for books.Book model
```

The syncdb command is a simple "sync" of your models to your database. It looks at all of the models in each app in your INSTALLED_APPS setting, checks the database to see whether the appropriate tables exist yet, and creates the tables if they don't yet exist. Note that syncdb does *not* sync changes in models or deletions of models; if you make a change to a model or delete a model, and you want to update the database, syncdb will not handle that. (More on this later.)

If you run python manage.py syncdb again, nothing happens, because you haven't added any models to the books app or added any apps to INSTALLED_APPS. Ergo, it's always safe to run python manage.py syncdb—it won't clobber things.

If you're interested, take a moment to dive into your database server's command-line client and see the database tables Django created. You can manually run the command-line client (e.g., psql for PostgreSQL) or you can run the command python manage.py dbshell, which will figure out which command-line client to run, depending on your DATABASE_SERVER setting. The latter is almost always more convenient.

Basic Data Access

Once you've created a model, Django automatically provides a high-level Python API for working with those models. Try it out by running python manage.py shell and typing the following:

```
>>> from books.models import Publisher
>>> p1 = Publisher(name='Addison-Wesley',
        address='75 Arlington St.',
...     city='Boston', state_province='MA', country='U.S.A.',
...     website='http://www.addison-wesley.com/')
>>> p.save()
>>> p2 = Publisher(name="O'Reilly", address='10 Fawcett St.',
...     city='Cambridge', state_province='MA', country='U.S.A.',
...     website='http://www.oreilly.com/')
>>> p2.save()
>>> publisher_list = Publisher.objects.all()
>>> publisher_list
[<Publisher: Publisher object>, <Publisher: Publisher object>]
```

These few lines of code accomplish quite a bit. Here are the highlights:

- To create an object, just import the appropriate model class and instantiate it by passing in values for each field.

- To save the object to the database, call the save() method on the object. Behind the scenes, Django executes an SQL INSERT statement here.

- To retrieve objects from the database, use the attribute Publisher.objects. Fetch a list of all Publisher objects in the database with the statement Publisher.objects.all(). Behind the scenes, Django executes an SQL SELECT statement here.

Naturally, you can do quite a lot with the Django database API—but first, let's take care of a small annoyance.

Adding Model String Representations

When we printed out the list of publishers, all we got was this unhelpful display, which makes it difficult to tell the Publisher objects apart:

```
[<Publisher: Publisher object>, <Publisher: Publisher object>]
```

We can fix this easily by adding a method called __str__() to our Publisher object. A __str__() method tells Python how to display the "string" representation of an object. You can see this in action by adding a __str__() method to the three models:

```
from django.db import models
class Publisher(models.Model):
    name = models.CharField(maxlength=30)
    address = models.CharField(maxlength=50)
    city = models.CharField(maxlength=60)
    state_province = models.CharField(maxlength=30)
    country = models.CharField(maxlength=50)
    website = models.URLField()

    def __str__(self):
        return self.name

class Author(models.Model):
    salutation = models.CharField(maxlength=10)
    first_name = models.CharField(maxlength=30)
    last_name = models.CharField(maxlength=40)
    email = models.EmailField()
    headshot = models.ImageField(upload_to='/tmp')

    def __str__(self):
        return '%s %s' % (self.first_name, self.last_name)

class Book(models.Model):
    title = models.CharField(maxlength=100)
    authors = models.ManyToManyField(Author)
    publisher = models.ForeignKey(Publisher)
    publication_date = models.DateField()

    def __str__(self):
        return self.title
```

As you can see, a __str__() method can do whatever it needs to do in order to return a string representation. Here, the __str__() methods for Publisher and Book simply return the object's name and title, respectively, but the __str__() for Author is slightly more complex: it pieces together the first_name and last_name fields. The only requirement for __str__() is that it return a string. If __str__() doesn't return a string—if it returns, say, an integer—then Python will raise a TypeError with a message like "__str__ returned non-string".

For the changes to take effect, exit out of the Python shell and enter it again with python manage.py shell. (This is the simplest way to make code changes take effect.) Now the list of Publisher objects is much easier to understand:

```
>>> from books.models import Publisher
>>> publisher_list = Publisher.objects.all()
>>> publisher_list
[<Publisher: Addison-Wesley>, <Publisher: O'Reilly>]
```

Make sure any model you define has a __str__() method—not only for your own convenience when using the interactive interpreter, but also because Django uses the output of __str__() in several places when it needs to display objects.

Finally, note that __str__() is a good example of adding *behavior* to models. A Django model describes more than the database table layout for an object; it also describes any functionality that object knows how to do. __str__() is one example of such functionality—a model knows how to display itself.

Inserting and Updating Data

You've already seen this done—to insert a row into your database, first create an instance of your model using keyword arguments, like so:

```
>>> p = Publisher(name='Apress',
...           address='2855 Telegraph Ave.',
...           city='Berkeley',
...           state_province='CA',
...           country='U.S.A.',
...           website='http://www.apress.com/')
```

This act of instantiating a model class does *not* touch the database.

To save the record into the database (i.e., to perform the SQL INSERT statement), call the object's save() method:

```
>>> p.save()
```

In SQL, this can roughly be translated into the following:

```
INSERT INTO book_publisher
    (name, address, city, state_province, country, website)
VALUES
    ('Apress', '2855 Telegraph Ave.', 'Berkeley', 'CA',
     'U.S.A.', 'http://www.apress.com/');
```

Because the Publisher model uses an autoincrementing primary key id, the initial call to save() does one more thing: it calculates the primary key value for the record and sets it to the id attribute on the instance:

```
>>> p.id
52    # this will differ based on your own data
```

Subsequent calls to save() will save the record in place, without creating a new record (i.e., performing an SQL UPDATE statement instead of an INSERT):

```
>>> p.name = 'Apress Publishing'
>>> p.save()
```

The preceding save() statement will result in roughly the following SQL:

```
UPDATE book_publisher SET
    name = 'Apress Publishing',
    address = '2855 Telegraph Ave.',
    city = 'Berkeley',
    state_province = 'CA',
    country = 'U.S.A.',
    website = 'http://www.apress.com'
WHERE id = 52;
```

Selecting Objects

Creating and updating data sure is fun, but it is also useless without a way to sift through that data. We've already seen a way to look up all the data for a certain model:

```
>>> Publisher.objects.all()
[<Publisher: Addison-Wesley>, <Publisher: O'Reilly>, <Publisher: Apress Publishing>
```

This roughly translates to the following SQL:

```
SELECT
    id, name, address, city, state_province, country, website
FROM book_publisher;
```

Notice that Django doesn't use SELECT * when looking up data and instead lists all fields explicitly. This is by design, as in certain circumstances SELECT * can be slower, and (more important) listing fields more closely follows one tenet of the Zen of Python: "Explicit is better than implicit." For more on the Zen of Python, try typing import this at a Python prompt.

Let's take a close look at each part of this Publisher.objects.all() line:

- First, we have the model we defined, Publisher. No surprise here: when you want to look up data, you use the model for that data.

- Next, we have this objects business. Technically, this is a *manager*. Managers are discussed in detail in Appendix B. For now, all you need to know is that managers take care of all "table-level" operations on data including, most important, data lookup. All objects automatically get an objects manager; you'll use it any time you want to look up model instances.

- Finally, we have all(). This is a method on the objects manager that returns all the rows in the database. Though this object *looks* like a list, it's actually a QuerySet—an object that represents some set of rows from the database. Appendix C deals with QuerySets in detail. For the rest of this chapter, we'll just treat them like the lists they emulate.

Any database lookup is going to follow this general pattern—we'll call methods on the manager attached to the model we want to query against.

Filtering Data

While fetching all objects certainly has its uses, most of the time we're going to want to deal with a subset of the data. We do this with the `filter()` method:

```
>>> Publisher.objects.filter(name="Apress Publishing")
[<Publisher: Apress Publishing>]
```

`filter()` takes keyword arguments that get translated into the appropriate SQL `WHERE` clauses. The preceding example would get translated into something like this:

```
SELECT
    id, name, address, city, state_province, country, website
FROM book_publisher
WHERE name = 'Apress Publishing';
```

You can pass multiple arguments into `filter()` to narrow down things further:

```
>>> Publisher.objects.filter(country="U.S.A.", state_province="CA")
[<Publisher: Apress Publishing>]
```

Those multiple arguments get translated into SQL `AND` clauses. Thus, the example in the code snippet translates into the following:

```
SELECT
    id, name, address, city, state_province, country, website
FROM book_publisher
WHERE country = 'U.S.A.' AND state_province = 'CA';
```

Notice that by default the lookups use the SQL = operator to do exact match lookups. Other lookup types are available:

```
>>> Publisher.objects.filter(name__contains="press")
[<Publisher: Apress Publishing>]
```

That's a double underscore there between `name` and `contains`. Like Python itself, Django uses the double underscore to signal that something "magic" is happening—here, the `__contains` part gets translated by Django into an SQL `LIKE` statement:

```
SELECT
    id, name, address, city, state_province, country, website
FROM book_publisher
WHERE name LIKE '%press%';
```

Many other types of lookups are available, including `icontains` (case-insensitive `LIKE`), `startswith` and `endswith`, and `range` (SQL `BETWEEN` queries). Appendix C describes all of these lookup types in detail.

Retrieving Single Objects

Sometimes you want to fetch only a single object. That's what the get() method is for:

```
>>> Publisher.objects.get(name="Apress Publishing")
<Publisher: Apress Publishing>
```

Instead of a list (rather, QuerySet), only a single object is returned. Because of that, a query resulting in multiple objects will cause an exception:

```
>>> Publisher.objects.get(country="U.S.A.")
Traceback (most recent call last):
    ...
AssertionError: get() returned more than one Publisher—it returned 2!
```

A query that returns no objects also causes an exception:

```
>>> Publisher.objects.get(name="Penguin")
Traceback (most recent call last):
    ...
DoesNotExist: Publisher matching query does not exist.
```

Ordering Data

As you play around with the previous examples, you might discover that the objects are being returned in a seemingly random order. You aren't imagining things—so far we haven't told the database how to order its results, so we're simply getting back data in some arbitrary order chosen by the database.

That's obviously a bit silly; we wouldn't want a Web page listing publishers to be ordered randomly. So, in practice, we'll probably want to use order_by() to reorder our data into a useful list:

```
>>> Publisher.objects.order_by("name")
[<Publisher: Apress Publishing>, <Publisher: Addison-Wesley>, <Publisher: O'Reilly>]
```

This doesn't look much different from the earlier all() example, but the SQL now includes a specific ordering:

```
SELECT
    id, name, address, city, state_province, country, website
FROM book_publisher
ORDER BY name;
```

We can order by any field we like:

```
>>> Publisher.objects.order_by("address")
[<Publisher: O'Reilly>, <Publisher: Apress Publishing>, <Publisher: Addison-Wesley>]

>>> Publisher.objects.order_by("state_province")
[<Publisher: Apress Publishing>, <Publisher: Addison-Wesley>, <Publisher: O'Reilly>]
```

and by multiple fields:

```
>>> Publisher.objects.order_by("country", "address")
[<Publisher: Apress Publishing>, <Publisher: O'Reilly>, <Publisher: Addison-Wesley>]
```

We can also specify reverse ordering by prefixing the field name with a – (a minus sign character):

```
>>> Publisher.objects.order_by("-name")
[<Publisher: O'Reilly>, <Publisher: Apress Publishing>, <Publisher: Addison-Wesley>]
```

While this flexibility is useful, using order_by() all the time can be quite repetitive. Most of the time you'll have a particular field you usually want to order by. In these cases, Django lets you attach a default ordering to the model:

```
class Publisher(models.Model):
    name = models.CharField(maxlength=30)
    address = models.CharField(maxlength=50)
    city = models.CharField(maxlength=60)
    state_province = models.CharField(maxlength=30)
    country = models.CharField(maxlength=50)
    website = models.URLField()

    def __str__(self):
        return self.name

    class Meta:
        ordering = ["name"]
```

This ordering = ["name"] bit tells Django that unless an ordering is given explicitly with order_by(), all publishers should be ordered by name.

Note Django uses the internal class Meta as a place to specify additional metadata about a model. It's completely optional, but it can do some very useful things. See Appendix B for the options you can put under Meta.

Chaining Lookups

You've seen how you can filter data, and you've seen how you can order it. At times, of course, you're going to want to do both. In these cases, you simply "chain" the lookups together:

```
>>> Publisher.objects.filter(country="U.S.A.").order_by("-name")
[<Publisher: O'Reilly>, <Publisher: Apress Publishing>, <Publisher: Addison-Wesley>]
```

As you might expect, this translates to an SQL query with both a WHERE and an ORDER BY:

```
SELECT
    id, name, address, city, state_province, country, website
FROM book_publisher
WHERE country = 'U.S.A'
ORDER BY name DESC;
```

You can keep chaining queries as long as you like. There's no limit.

Slicing Data

Another common need is to look up only a fixed number of rows. Imagine you have thousands of publishers in your database, but you want to display only the first one. You can do this using Python's standard list slicing syntax:

```
>>> Publisher.objects.all()[0]
<Publisher: Addison-Wesley>
```

This translates roughly to the following:

```
SELECT
    id, name, address, city, state_province, country, website
FROM book_publisher
ORDER BY name
LIMIT 1;
```

■**Note** We've just scratched the surface of dealing with models, but you should now know enough to understand all the examples in the rest of this book. When you're ready to learn the complete details behind object lookups, turn to Appendix C.

Deleting Objects

To delete objects, simply call the delete() method on your object:

```
>>> apress = Publisher.objects.get(name="Addison-Wesley")
>>> apress.delete()
>>> Publisher.objects.all()
[<Publisher: Apress Publishing>, <Publisher: O'Reilly>]
```

You can also delete objects in bulk by calling delete() on the result of some lookup:

```
>>> publishers = Publisher.objects.all()
>>> publishers.delete()
>>> Publisher.objects.all()
[]
```

Deletions are *permanent*, so be careful! In fact, it's usually a good idea to avoid deleting objects unless you absolutely have to—relational databases don't do "undo" so well, and restoring from backups is painful.

It's often a good idea to add "active" flags to your data models. You can look up only "active" objects, and simply set the active field to `False` instead of deleting the object. Then, if you realize you've made a mistake, you can simply flip the flag back.

Making Changes to a Database Schema

When we introduced the `syncdb` command earlier in this chapter, we noted that `syncdb` merely creates tables that don't yet exist in your database—it does *not* sync changes in models or perform deletions of models. If you add or change a model's field, or if you delete a model, you'll need to make the change in your database manually. This section explains how to do that.

When dealing with schema changes, it's important to keep a few things in mind about how Django's database layer works:

- Django will complain loudly if a model contains a field that has not yet been created in the database table. This will cause an error the first time you use the Django database API to query the given table (i.e., it will happen at code execution time, not at compilation time).

- Django does *not* care if a database table contains columns that are not defined in the model.

- Django does *not* care if a database contains a table that is not represented by a model.

Making schema changes is a matter of changing the various pieces—the Python code and the database itself—in the right order.

Adding Fields

When adding a field to a table/model in a production setting, the trick is to take advantage of the fact that Django doesn't care if a table contains columns that aren't defined in the model. The strategy is to add the column in the database and then update the Django model to include the new field.

However, there's a bit of a chicken-and-egg problem here, because in order to know how the new database column should be expressed in SQL, you need to look at the output of Django's `manage.py sqlall` command, which requires that the field exist in the model. (Note that you're not *required* to create your column with exactly the same SQL that Django would, but it's a good idea to do so, just to be sure everything's in sync.)

The solution to the chicken-and-egg problem is to use a development environment instead of making the changes on a production server. (You *are* using a testing/development environment, right?) Here are the detailed steps to take.

First, take these steps in the development environment (i.e., not on the production server):

1. Add the field to your model.

2. Run `manage.py sqlall [yourapp]` to see the new `CREATE TABLE` statement for the model. Note the column definition for the new field.

3. Start your database's interactive shell (e.g., `psql` or `mysql`, or you can use `manage.py dbshell`). Execute an `ALTER TABLE` statement that adds your new column.

4. (Optional.) Launch the Python interactive shell with `manage.py shell` and verify that the new field was added properly by importing the model and selecting from the table (e.g., `MyModel.objects.all()[:5]`).

Then on the production server perform these steps:

1. Start your database's interactive shell.

2. Execute the `ALTER TABLE` statement you used in step 3 of the development environment steps.

3. Add the field to your model. If you're using source-code revision control and you checked in your change in development environment step 1, now is the time to update the code (e.g., `svn update`, with Subversion) on the production server.

4. Restart the Web server for the code changes to take effect.

For example, let's walk through what we'd do if we added a `num_pages` field to the `Book` model described earlier in this chapter. First, we'd alter the model in our development environment to look like this:

```
class Book(models.Model):
    title = models.CharField(maxlength=100)
    authors = models.ManyToManyField(Author)
    publisher = models.ForeignKey(Publisher)
    publication_date = models.DateField()
    num_pages = models.IntegerField(blank=True, null=True)

    def __str__(self):
        return self.title
```

■**Note** Read the "Adding NOT NULL Columns" sidebar for important details on why we included `blank=True` and `null=True`.

Then we'd run the command `manage.py sqlall books` to see the `CREATE TABLE` statement. It would look something like this:

```
CREATE TABLE "books_book" (
    "id" serial NOT NULL PRIMARY KEY,
    "title" varchar(100) NOT NULL,
    "publisher_id" integer NOT NULL REFERENCES "books_publisher" ("id"),
    "publication_date" date NOT NULL,
    "num_pages" integer NULL
);
```

The new column is represented like this:

```
"num_pages" integer NULL
```

Next, we'd start the database's interactive shell for our development database by typing psql (for PostgreSQL), and we'd execute the following statements:

```
ALTER TABLE books_book ADD COLUMN num_pages integer;
```

ADDING NOT NULL COLUMNS

There's a subtlety here that deserves mention. When we added the num_pages field to our model, we included the blank=True and null=True options. We did this because a database column will contain NULL values when you first create it.

However, it's also possible to add columns that cannot contain NULL values. To do this, you have to create the column as NULL, then populate the column's values using some default(s), and then alter the column to set the NOT NULL modifier. For example:

```
BEGIN;
ALTER TABLE books_book ADD COLUMN num_pages integer;
UPDATE books_book SET num_pages=0;
ALTER TABLE books_book ALTER COLUMN num_pages SET NOT NULL;
COMMIT;
```

If you go down this path, remember that you should leave off blank=True and null=True in your model.

After the ALTER TABLE statement, we'd verify that the change worked properly by starting the Python shell and running this code:

```
>>> from mysite.books.models import Book
>>> Book.objects.all()[:5]
```

If that code didn't cause errors, we'd switch to our production server and execute the ALTER TABLE statement on the production database. Then, we'd update the model in the production environment and restart the Web server.

Removing Fields

Removing a field from a model is a lot easier than adding one. To remove a field, just follow these steps:

1. Remove the field from your model and restart the Web server.

2. Remove the column from your database, using a command like this:

   ```
   ALTER TABLE books_book DROP COLUMN num_pages;
   ```

Removing Many-to-Many Fields

Because many-to-many fields are different from normal fields, the removal process is different:

1. Remove the `ManyToManyField` from your model and restart the Web server.

2. Remove the many-to-many table from your database, using a command like this:

   ```
   DROP TABLE books_books_publishers;
   ```

Removing Models

Removing a model entirely is as easy as removing a field. To remove a model, just follow these steps:

1. Remove the model from your `models.py` file and restart the Web server.

2. Remove the table from your database, using a command like this:

   ```
   DROP TABLE books_book;
   ```

What's Next?

Once you've defined your models, the next step is to populate your database with data. You might have legacy data, in which case Chapter 16 will give you advice about integrating with legacy databases. You might rely on site users to supply your data, in which case Chapter 7 will teach you how to process user-submitted form data.

But in some cases, you or your team might need to enter data manually, in which case it would be helpful to have a Web-based interface for entering and managing data. The next chapter covers Django's admin interface, which exists precisely for that reason.

■ ■ ■

## CHAPTER 6

The Django Administration Site

For a certain class of Web sites, an *admin interface* is an essential part of the infrastructure. This is a Web-based interface, limited to trusted site administrators, that enables the addition, editing, and deletion of site content. The interface you use to post to your blog, the back-end site managers use to moderate reader-generated comments, the tool your clients use to update the press releases on the Web site you built for them—these are all examples of admin interfaces.

There's a problem with admin interfaces, though: it's boring to build them. Web development is fun when you're developing public-facing functionality, but building admin interfaces is always the same. You have to authenticate users, display and handle forms, validate input, and so on. It's boring, and it's repetitive.

So what's Django's approach to these boring, repetitive tasks? It does it all for you—in just a couple of lines of code, no less. With Django, building an admin interface is a solved problem.

This chapter is about Django's automatic admin interface. This feature works by reading metadata in your model to provide a powerful and production-ready interface that site administrators can start using immediately. Here, we discuss how to activate, use, and customize this feature.

Activating the Admin Interface

We think the admin interface is the coolest part of Django—and most Djangonauts agree—but since not everyone actually needs it, it's an optional piece. That means there are three steps you'll need to follow to activate it:

1. Add admin metadata to your models. Not all models can (or should) be editable by admin users, so you need to "mark" models that should have an admin interface. You do that by adding an inner Admin class to your model (alongside the Meta class, if you have one). So, to add an admin interface to our Book model from the previous chapter, we use this:

```
class Book(models.Model):
    title = models.CharField(maxlength=100)
    authors = models.ManyToManyField(Author)
    publisher = models.ForeignKey(Publisher)
    publication_date = models.DateField()
    num_pages = models.IntegerField(blank=True, null=True)

    class Admin: pass
```

The Admin declaration flags the class as having an admin interface. There are a number of options that you can put beneath Admin, but for now we're sticking with all the defaults, so we put pass in there to signify to Python that the Admin class is empty.

If you're following this example with your own code, it's probably a good idea to add Admin declarations to the Publisher and Author classes at this point.

2. Install the admin application. Do this by adding django.contrib.admin to your INSTALLED_APPS setting and running python manage.py syncdb. This second step will install the extra database tables the admin interface uses.

■**Note** When you first ran syncdb, you were probably asked about creating a superuser. If you didn't do so at that time, you'll need to run django/contrib/auth/bin/create_superuser.py to create an admin user. Otherwise, you won't be able to log in to the admin interface.

---

3. Add the URL pattern to your urls.py. If you're still using the one created by startproject, the admin URL pattern should be already there, but commented out. Either way, your URL patterns should look like the following:

```
from django.conf.urls.defaults import *

urlpatterns = patterns('',
    (r'^admin/', include('django.contrib.admin.urls')),
)
```

That's it. Now run python manage.py runserver to start the development server. You'll see something like this:

```
Validating models...
0 errors found.

Django version 0.96, using settings 'mysite.settings'
Development server is running at http://127.0.0.1:8000/
Quit the server with CONTROL-C.
```

Now you can visit the URL given to you by Django (http://127.0.0.1:8000/admin/ in the preceding example), log in, and play around.

Using the Admin Interface

The admin interface is designed to be used by nontechnical users, and as such it should be pretty self-explanatory. Nevertheless, a few notes about the features of the admin interface are in order.

The first thing you'll see is a login screen, as shown in Figure 6-1.

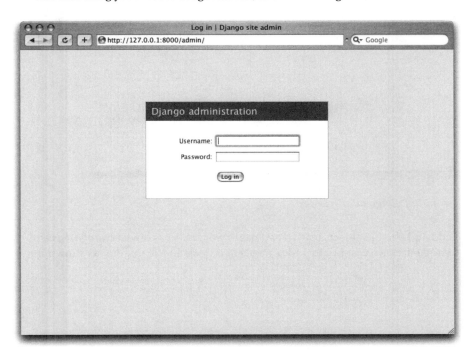

Figure 6-1. *Django's login screen*

You'll use the username and password you set up when you first added your superuser account. Once you're logged in, you'll see that you can manage users, groups, and permissions (more on that shortly).

Each object given an Admin declaration shows up on the main index page, as shown in Figure 6-2.

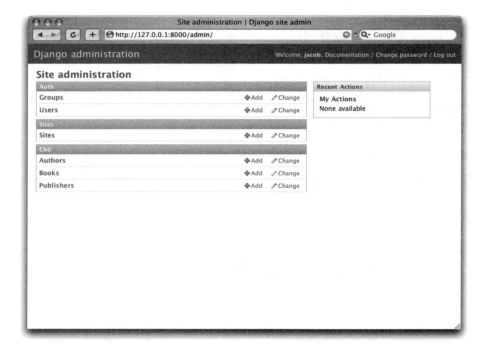

Figure 6-2. *The main Django admin index*

Links to add and change objects lead to two pages we refer to as object *change lists* and *edit forms*. Change lists are essentially index pages of objects in the system, as shown in Figure 6-3.

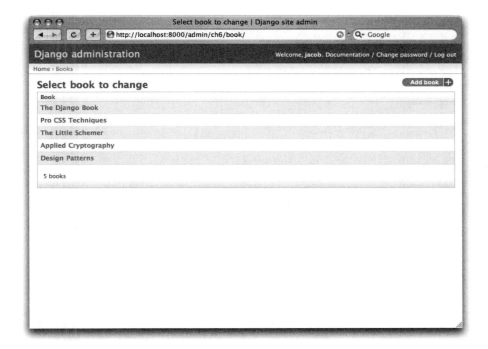

Figure 6-3. *A typical change list view*

A number of options control which fields appear on these lists and the appearance of extra features like date drill-downs, search fields, and filter interfaces. We discuss these features in more detail shortly.

Edit forms are used to modify existing objects and create new ones (see Figure 6-4). Each field defined in your model appears here, and you'll notice that fields of different types get different widgets (e.g., date/time fields have calendar controls, foreign keys use a select box, etc.).

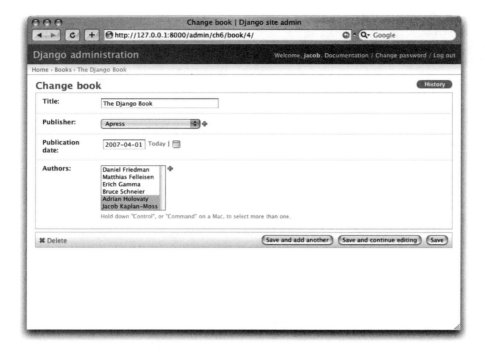

Figure 6-4. *A typical edit form*

You'll notice that the admin interface also handles input validation for you. Try leaving a required field blank or putting an invalid time into a time field, and you'll see those errors when you try to save, as shown in Figure 6-5.

When you edit an existing object, you'll notice a History button in the upper-right corner of the window. Every change made through the admin interface is logged, and you can examine this log by clicking the History button (see Figure 6-6).

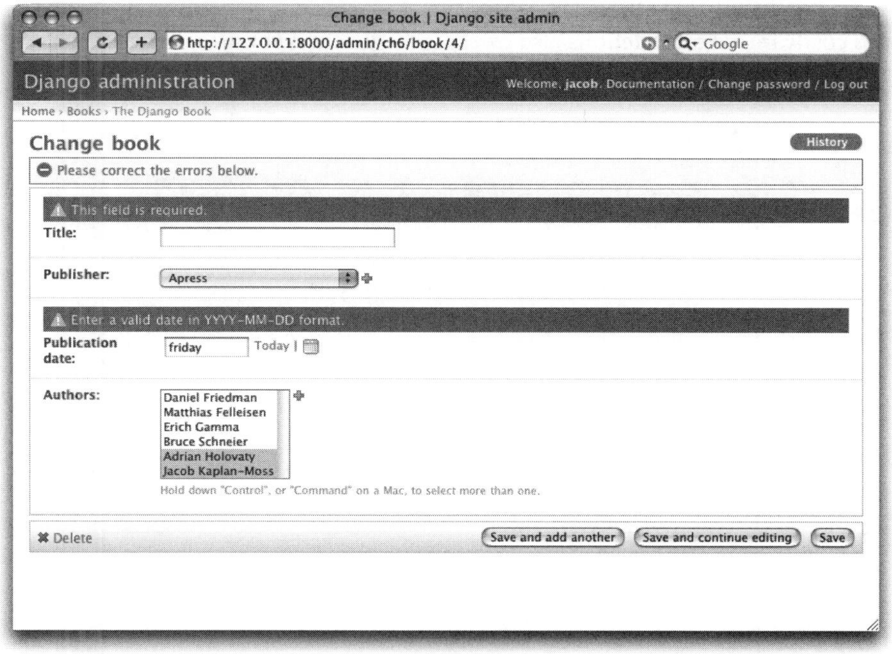

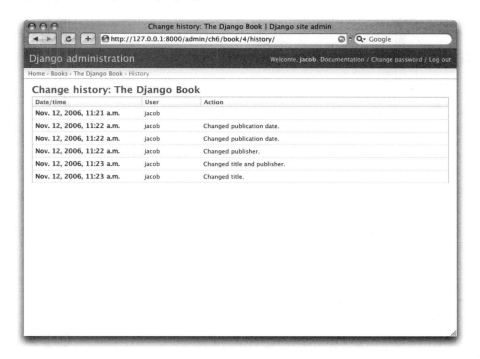

Figure 6-5. *An edit form displaying errors*

Figure 6-6. *Django's object history page*

When you delete an existing object, the admin interface asks you to confirm the delete action to avoid costly mistakes. Deletions also *cascade*; the deletion confirmation page shows you all the related objects that will be deleted as well (see Figure 6-7).

Figure 6-7. *Django's delete confirmation page*

Users, Groups, and Permissions

Since you're logged in as a superuser, you have access to create, edit, and delete any object. However, the admin interface has a user permissions system that you can use to give other users access only to the portions of the interface that they need.

You edit these users and permissions through the admin interface just like any other object. The link to the User and Group models is there on the admin index along with all the objects you've defined yourself.

User objects have the standard username, password, e-mail, and real name fields you might expect, along with a set of fields that define what the user is allowed to do in the admin interface. First, there's a set of three flags:

- The "is active" flag controls whether the user is active at all. If this flag is off, the user has no access to any URLs that require login.

- The "is staff" flag controls whether the user is allowed to log in to the admin interface (i.e., whether that user is considered a "staff member" in your organization). Since this same user system can be used to control access to public (i.e., nonadmin) sites (see Chapter 12), this flag differentiates between public users and administrators.

- The "is superuser" flag gives the user full, unfettered access to every item in the admin interface; regular permissions are ignored.

"Normal" admin users—that is, active, nonsuperuser staff members—are granted access that depends on a set of assigned permissions. Each object editable through the admin interface has three permissions: a *create* permission, an *edit* permission, and a *delete* permission. Assigning permissions to a user grants the user access to do what is described by those permissions.

■Note Access to edit users and permissions is also controlled by this permission system. If you give someone permission to edit users, she will be able to edit her own permissions, which might not be what you want!

You can also assign users to groups. A *group* is simply a set of permissions to apply to all members of that group. Groups are useful for granting identical permissions to a large number of users.

Customizing the Admin Interface

You can customize the way the admin interface looks and behaves in a number of ways. We cover just a few of them in this section as they relate to our Book model; Chapter 17 covers customizing the admin interface in detail.

As it stands now, the change list for our books shows only the string representation of the model we added to its __str__. This works fine for just a few books, but if we had hundreds or thousands of books, it would be very hard to locate a single needle in the haystack. However, we can easily add some display, searching, and filtering functions to this interface. Change the Admin declaration as follows:

```
class Book(models.Model):
    title = models.CharField(maxlength=100)
    authors = models.ManyToManyField(Author)
    publisher = models.ForeignKey(Publisher)
    publication_date = models.DateField()

    class Admin:
        list_display = ('title', 'publisher', 'publication_date')
        list_filter = ('publisher', 'publication_date')
        ordering = ('-publication_date',)
        search_fields = ('title',)
```

These four lines of code dramatically change our list interface, as shown in Figure 6-8.

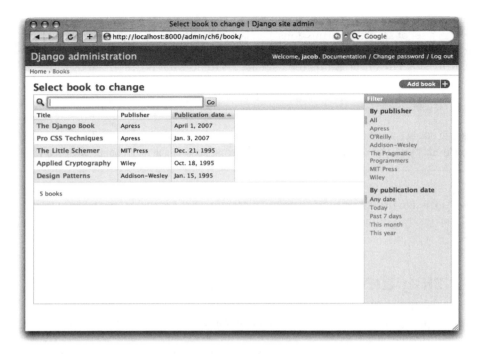

Figure 6-8. *Modified change list page*

Each of those lines instructed the admin interface to construct a different piece of this interface:

- The list_display option controls which columns appear in the change list table. By default, the change list displays only a single column that contains the object's string representation. Here, we've changed that to show the title, publisher, and publication date.

- The list_filter option creates the filtering bar on the right side of the list. We've allowed filtering by date (which allows you to see only books published in the last week, month, etc.) and by publisher. The filters show up as long as there are at least two values to choose from.

  You can instruct the admin interface to filter by any field, but foreign keys, dates, Booleans, and fields with a choices attribute work best.

- The ordering option controls the order in which the objects are presented in the admin interface. It's simply a list of fields by which to order the results; prefixing a field with a minus sign reverses the given order. In this example, we're ordering by publication date, with the most recent first.

- Finally, the search_fields option creates a field that allows text searches. It allows searches by the title field (so you could type **Django** to show all books with "Django" in the title).

Using these options (and the others described in Chapter 12) you can, with only a few lines of code, make a very powerful, production-ready interface for data editing.

Customizing the Admin Interface's Look and Feel

Clearly, having the phrase "Django administration" at the top of each admin page is ridiculous. It's just placeholder text.

It's easy to change, though, using Django's template system. The Django admin site is powered by Django itself, and its interfaces use Django's own template system. (Django's template system was covered in Chapter 4.)

As we explained in Chapter 4, the TEMPLATE_DIRS setting specifies a list of directories to check when loading Django templates. To customize Django's admin templates, simply copy the relevant stock admin template from the Django distribution into one of the directories pointed to by TEMPLATE_DIRS.

The admin site finds the "Django administration" header by looking for the template admin/base_site.html. By default, this template lives in the Django admin template directory, django/contrib/admin/templates, which you can find by looking in your Python site-packages directory, or wherever Django was installed. To customize this base_site.html template, copy that template into an admin subdirectory of whichever directory you're using in TEMPLATE_DIRS. For example, if your TEMPLATE_DIRS includes "/home/mytemplates", then copy django/contrib/admin/templates/admin/base_site.html to /home/mytemplates/admin/base_site.html. Don't forget that admin subdirectory.

Then, just edit the new admin/base_site.html file to replace the generic Django text with your own site's name as you see fit.

Note that any of Django's default admin templates can be overridden. To override a template, just do the same thing you did with base_site.html: copy it from the default directory into your custom directory and make changes to the copy.

You might wonder how, if TEMPLATE_DIRS was empty by default, Django found the default admin templates. The answer is that, by default, Django automatically looks for templates within a templates/ subdirectory in each application package as a fallback. See the "Writing Custom Template Loaders" section in Chapter 10 for more information about how this works.

Customizing the Admin Index Page

On a similar note, you might want to customize the look and feel of the Django admin index page. By default, it displays all available applications, according to your INSTALLED_APPS setting, sorted by the name of the application. You might, however, want to change this order to make it easier to find the applications you're looking for. After all, the index is probably the most important page of the admin interface, so it should be easy to use.

The template to customize is admin/index.html. (Remember to copy admin/index.html to your custom template directory as in the previous example.) Edit the file, and you'll see it uses a template tag called {% get_admin_app_list as app_list %}. This tag retrieves every installed Django application. Instead of using the tag, you can hard-code links to object-specific admin pages in whatever way you think is best. If hard-coding links doesn't appeal to you, see Chapter 10 for details on implementing your own template tags.

Django offers another shortcut in this department. Run the command python manage.py adminindex <app> to get a chunk of template code for inclusion in the admin index template. It's a useful starting point.

For full details on customizing the look and feel of the Django admin site in general, see Chapter 17.

When and Why to Use the Admin Interface

We think Django's admin interface is pretty spectacular. In fact, we'd call it one of Django's "killer features." However, we often get asked about "use cases" for the admin interface—when do *we* use it, and why? Over the years, we've discovered a number of patterns for using the admin interface that we think are helpful.

Obviously, the admin interface is extremely useful for editing data (fancy that). If you have any sort of data entry tasks, the admin interface simply can't be beat. We suspect that the vast majority of readers of this book will have a whole host of data entry tasks.

Django's admin interface especially shines when nontechnical users need to be able to enter data; that's the purpose behind the feature, after all. At the newspaper where Django was first developed, development of a typical online feature—a special report on water quality in the municipal supply, say—goes something like this:

- The reporter responsible for the story meets with one of the developers and goes over the available data.

- The developer designs a model around this data and then opens up the admin interface to the reporter.

- While the reporter enters data into Django, the programmer can focus on developing the publicly accessible interface (the fun part!).

In other words, the raison d'être of Django's admin interface is facilitating the simultaneous work of content producers and programmers.

However, beyond the obvious data entry tasks, we find the admin interface useful in a few other cases:

- *Inspecting data models*: The first thing we do when we've defined a new model is to call it up in the admin interface and enter some dummy data. This is usually when we find any data modeling mistakes; having a graphical interface to a model quickly reveals problems.

- *Managing acquired data*: There's little actual data entry associated with a site like `http://chicagocrime.org`, since most of the data comes from an automated source. However, when problems with the automatically acquired data crop up, it's useful to be able to go in and edit that data easily.

What's Next?

So far we've created a few models and configured a top-notch interface for editing data. In the next chapter, we'll move on to the real "meat and potatoes" of Web development: form creation and processing.

■ ■ ■

## CHAPTER 7

Form Processing

Guest author: Simon Willison

After following along with the last chapter, you should now have a fully functioning if some-what simple site. In this chapter, we'll deal with the next piece of the puzzle: building views that take input from readers.

We'll start by making a simple search form "by hand" and looking at how to handle data submitted from the browser. From there, we'll move on to using Django's forms framework.

Search

The Web is all about search. Two of the Net's biggest success stories, Google and Yahoo, built their multibillion-dollar businesses around search. Nearly every site sees a large percentage of traffic coming to and from its search pages. Often the difference between a site's success or failure is the quality of its search. So it looks like we'd better add some searching to our fledgling books site, no?

We'll start by adding the search view to our URLconf (mysite.urls). Recall that this means adding something like (r'^search/$', 'mysite.books.views.search') to the set of URL patterns.

Next, we'll write this search view into our view module (mysite.books.views):

```
from django.db.models import Q
from django.shortcuts import render_to_response
from mysite.books.models import Book

def search(request):
    query = request.GET.get('q', '')
    if query:
        qset = (
            Q(title__icontains=query) |
            Q(authors__first_name__icontains=query) |
            Q(authors__last_name__icontains=query)
        )
        results = Book.objects.filter(qset).distinct()
```

```
else:
    results = []
return render_to_response("books/search.html", {
    "results": results,
    "query": query
})
```

There are a couple of things going on here that you haven't yet seen. First, there's `request.GET`. This is how you access GET data from Django; POST data is accessed through a similar `request.POST` object. These objects behave exactly like standard Python dictionaries with some extra features covered in Appendix H.

So the line

```
query = request.GET.get('q', '')
```

looks for a GET parameter named q and returns an empty string if that parameter wasn't submitted.

Note that we're using the `get()` method on `request.GET`, which is potentially confusing. The `get()` method here is the one that every Python dictionary has. We're using it here to be careful: it is *not* safe to assume that `request.GET` contains a `'q'` key, so we use `get('q', '')` to provide a default fallback value of `''` (the empty string). If we merely accessed the variable using `request.GET['q']`, that code would raise a `KeyError` if q wasn't available in the GET data.

Second, what about this Q business? Q objects are used to build up complex queries—in this case, we're searching for any books where either the title or the name of one of the authors matches the search query. Technically, these Q objects comprise a `QuerySet`, and you can read more about them in Appendix C.

In these queries, `icontains` is a case-insensitive search that uses the SQL `LIKE` operator in the underlying database.

Since we're searching against a many-to-many field, it's possible for the same book to be returned more than once by the query (e.g., a book with two authors who both match the search query). Adding `.distinct()` to the filter lookup eliminates any duplicate results.

There's still no template for this search view, however. This should do the trick:

```
<!DOCTYPE HTML PUBLIC "-//W3C/DTD HTML 4.01//EN">
<html lang="en">
<head>
  <title>Search {% if query %}Results{% endif %}</title>
</head>
<body>
  <h1>Search</h1>
  <form action="." method="GET">
    <label for="q">Search: </label>
    <input type="text" name="q" value="{{ query|escape }}">
    <input type="submit" value="Search">
  </form>

  {% if query %}
    <h2>Results for "{{ query|escape }}":</h2>

    {% if results %}
      <ul>
      {% for book in results %}
        <li>{{ book }}</l1>
      {% endfor %}
      </ul>
    {% else %}
      <p>No books found</p>
    {% endif %}
  {% endif %}
</body>
</html>
```

Hopefully by now what this does is fairly obvious. However, there are a few subtleties worth pointing out:

- The form's action is ., which means "the current URL." This is a standard best practice: don't use separate views for the form page and the results page—use a single one that serves the form and search results.

- We reinsert the value of the query back into the <input>. This lets readers easily refine their searches without having to retype what they searched for.

- Everywhere query is used, we pass it through the escape filter to make sure that any potentially malicious search text is filtered out before being inserted into the page.

  It's *vital* that you do this with any user-submitted content! Otherwise you open your site up to cross-site scripting (XSS) attacks. Chapter 19 discusses XSS and security in more detail.

- However, we don't need to worry about harmful content in your database lookups—we can simply pass the query into the lookup as is. This is because Django's database layer handles this aspect of security for you.

Now we have a working search. A further improvement would be putting a search form on every page (i.e., in the base template); we'll let you handle that one yourself.

Next, we'll look at a more complex example. But before we do, let's discuss a more abstract topic: the "perfect form."

The "Perfect Form"

Forms can often be a major cause of frustration for the users of your site. Let's consider the behavior of a hypothetical perfect form:

- It should ask the user for some information, obviously. Accessibility and usability matter here, so smart use of the HTML <label> element and useful contextual help are important.

- The submitted data should be subjected to extensive validation. The golden rule of Web application security is "never trust incoming data," so validation is essential.

- If the user has made any mistakes, the form should be redisplayed with detailed, informative error messages. The original data should be prefilled, to save the user from having to reenter everything.

- The form should continue to redisplay until all of the fields have been correctly filled.

Constructing the perfect form seems like a lot of work! Thankfully, Django's forms framework is designed to do most of the work for you. You provide a description of the form's fields, the validation rules, and a simple template, and Django does the rest. The result is a "perfect form" with very little effort.

Creating a Feedback Form

The best way to build a site that people love is to listen to their feedback. Many sites appear to have forgotten this; they hide their contact details behind layers of FAQs, and they seem to make it as difficult as possible to get in touch with an actual human being.

When your site has millions of users, this may be a reasonable strategy. When you're trying to build up an audience, though, you should actively encourage feedback at every opportunity. Let's build a simple feedback form and use it to illustrate Django's forms framework in action.

We'll start by defining our form. Forms in Django are created in a similar way to models: declaratively, using a Python class. Here's the class for our simple form. By convention, we'll insert it into a new forms.py file within our application directory.

```
from django import newforms as forms

TOPIC_CHOICES = (
    ('general', 'General enquiry'),
    ('bug', 'Bug report'),
    ('suggestion', 'Suggestion'),
)
```

```
class ContactForm(forms.Form):
    topic = forms.ChoiceField(choices=TOPIC_CHOICES)
    message = forms.CharField()
    sender = forms.EmailField(required=False)
```

"NEW" FORMS? WHAT?

When Django was first released to the public, it had a complicated, confusing forms system. It made producing forms far too difficult, so it was completely rewritten and is now called "newforms." However, there's still a fair amount of code that depends on the "old" form system, so for the time being Django ships with two form packages.

As we write this book, Django's old form system is still available as django.forms and the new form package as django.newforms. At some point that will change and django.forms will point to the new form package. However, to make sure the examples in this book work as widely as possible, all the examples will refer to django.newforms.

A Django form is a subclass of django.newforms.Form, just as a Django model is a subclass of django.db.models.Model. The django.newforms module also contains a number of Field classes; a full list is available in Django's documentation at http://www.djangoproject.com/documentation/0.96/newforms/.

Our ContactForm consists of three fields: a topic, which is a choice among three options; a message, which is a character field; and a sender, which is an email field and is optional (because even anonymous feedback can be useful). There are a number of other field types available, and you can write your own if they don't cover your needs.

The form object itself knows how to do a number of useful things. It can validate a collection of data, it can generate its own HTML "widgets," it can construct a set of useful error messages and, if we're feeling lazy, it can even draw the entire form for us. Let's hook it into a view and see it in action. In views.py:

```
from django.shortcuts import render_to_response
from mysite.books.forms import ContactForm

def contact(request):
    form = ContactForm()
    return render_to_response('contact.html', {'form': form})
```

and in contact.html:

```
<!DOCTYPE HTML PUBLIC "-//W3C//DTD HTML 4.01//EN">
<html lang="en">
<head>
    <title>Contact us</title>
</head>
<body>
    <h1>Contact us</h1>
    <form action="." method="POST">
```

```
        <table>
            {{ form.as_table }}
        </table>
        <p><input type="submit" value="Submit"></p>
    </form>
</body>
</html>
```

The most interesting line here is {{ form.as_table }}. form is our ContactForm instance, as passed to render_to_response. as_table is a method on that object that renders the form as a sequence of table rows (as_ul and as_p can also be used). The generated HTML looks like this:

```
<tr>
    <th><label for="id_topic">Topic:</label></th>
    <td>
        <select name="topic" id="id_topic">
            <option value="general">General enquiry</option>
            <option value="bug">Bug report</option>
            <option value="suggestion">Suggestion</option>
        </select>
    </td>
</tr>
<tr>
    <th><label for="id_message">Message:</label></th>
    <td><input type="text" name="message" id="id_message" /></td>
</tr>
<tr>
    <th><label for="id_sender">Sender:</label></th>
    <td><input type="text" name="sender" id="id_sender" /></td>
</tr>
```

Note that the <table> and <form> tags are not included; you need to define those yourself in the template, which gives you control over how the form behaves when it is submitted. Label elements *are* included, making forms accessible out of the box.

Our form is currently using a <input type="text"> widget for the message field. We don't want to restrict our users to a single line of text, so we'll swap in a <textarea> widget instead:

```
class ContactForm(forms.Form):
    topic = forms.ChoiceField(choices=TOPIC_CHOICES)
    message = forms.CharField(widget=forms.Textarea())
    sender = forms.EmailField(required=False)
```

The forms framework separates out the presentation logic for each field into a set of widgets. Each field type has a default widget, but you can easily override the default, or provide a custom widget of your own.

At the moment, submitting the form doesn't actually do anything. Let's hook in our validation rules:

```
def contact(request):
    if request.method == 'POST':
        form = ContactForm(request.POST)
    else:
        form = ContactForm()
    return render_to_response('contact.html', {'form': form})
```

A form instance can be in one of two states: bound or unbound. A *bound* instance is attached to a dictionary (or dictionary-like object) and knows how to validate and redisplay the data from it. An *unbound* form has no data associated with it and simply knows how to display itself.

Try clicking Submit on the blank form. The page should redisplay, showing a validation error that informs us that our message field is required.

Try entering an invalid email address as well. The EmailField knows how to validate email addresses, at least to a reasonable level of doubt.

SETTING INITIAL DATA

Passing data directly to the form constructor binds that data and indicates that validation should be performed. Often, though, we need to display an initial form with some of the fields prefilled—for example, an "edit" form. We can do this with the initial keyword argument:

```
form = CommentForm(initial={'sender': 'user@example.com'})
```

If our form will *always* use the same default values, we can configure them in the form definition itself:

```
message = forms.CharField(initial="Replace with your feedback"
```

Processing the Submission

Once the user has filled the form to the point that it passes our validation rules, we need to do something useful with the data. In this case, we want to construct and send an email containing the user's feedback. We'll use Django's email package to do this.

First, though, we need to tell if the data is indeed valid, and if it is, we need access to the validated data. The forms framework does more than just validate the data; it also converts it into Python types. Our contact form only deals with strings, but if we were to use an IntegerField or DateTimeField, the forms framework would ensure that we got back a Python integer or datetime object, respectively.

To tell whether a form is bound to valid data, call the is_valid() method:

```
form = ContactForm(request.POST)
if form.is_valid():
    # Process form data
```

Now we need access to the data. We could pull it straight out of request.POST, but if we did, we'd miss out on the type conversions performed by the forms framework. Instead, we use form.clean_data:

```
if form.is_valid():
    topic = form.clean_data['topic']
    message = form.clean_data['message']
    sender = form.clean_data['sender']
    # ...
```

Finally, we need to record the user's feedback. The easiest way to do this is to email it to a site administrator. We can do that using the send_mail function:

```
from django.core.mail import send_mail

# ...

send_mail(
    'Feedback from your site, topic: %s' % topic,
    message, sender,
    ['administrator@example.com']
)
```

The send_mail function has four required arguments: the email subject, the email body, the "from" address, and a list of recipient addresses. send_mail is a convenient wrapper around Django's EmailMessage class, which provides advanced features such as attachments, multipart emails, and full control over email headers.

Having sent the feedback email, we'll redirect our user to a static confirmation page. The finished view function looks like this:

```
from django.http import HttpResponseRedirect
from django.shortcuts import render_to_response
from django.core.mail import send_mail
from forms import ContactForm

def contact(request):
    if request.method == 'POST':
        form = ContactForm(request.POST)
        if form.is_valid():
            topic = form.cleaned_data['topic']
            message = form.cleaned_data['message']
            sender = form.cleaned_data.get('sender', 'noreply@example.com')
            send_mail(
                'Feedback from your site, topic: %s' % topic,
                message, sender,
                ['administrator@example.com']
            )
            return HttpResponseRedirect('/contact/thanks/')
    else:
        form = ContactForm()
    return render_to_response('contact.html', {'form': form})
```

■Note If a user selects Refresh on a page that was displayed by a POST request, that request will be repeated. This can often lead to undesired behavior, such as a duplicate record being added to the database. Redirect after POST is a useful pattern that can help avoid this scenario: after a successful POST has been processed, redirect the user to another page rather than returning HTML directly.

Custom Validation Rules

Imagine we've launched our feedback form, and the emails have started tumbling in. There's just one problem: some of the emails contain just one or two words, hardly enough for a detailed missive. We decide to adopt a new validation policy: four words or more, please.

There are a number of ways to hook custom validation into a Django form. If our rule is something we will reuse again and again, we can create a custom field type. Most custom validations are one-off affairs, though, and can be tied directly to the form class.

We want additional validation on the message field, so we need to add a clean_message method to our form:

```
class ContactForm(forms.Form):
    topic = forms.ChoiceField(choices=TOPIC_CHOICES)
    message = forms.CharField(widget=forms.Textarea())
    sender = forms.EmailField(required=False)

    def clean_message(self):
        message = self.clean_data.get('message', '')
        num_words = len(message.split())
        if num_words < 4:
            raise forms.ValidationError("Not enough words!")
        return message
```

This new method will be called after the default field validator (in this case, the validator for a required CharField). Because the field data has already been partially processed, we need to pull it out of the form's clean_data dictionary.

We naively use a combination of len() and split() to count the number of words. If the user has entered too few words, we raise a ValidationError. The string attached to this exception will be displayed to the user as an item in the error list.

It is important that we explicitly return the value for the field at the end of the method. This allows us to modify the value (or convert it to a different Python type) within our custom validation method. If we forget, the return statement and then None will be returned, and the original value will be lost.

A Custom Look and Feel

The quickest way to customize the form's presentation is with CSS. The list of errors in particular could do with some visual enhancement, and the <ul> has a class attribute of errorlist for that exact purpose. The following CSS really makes our errors stand out:

```
<style type="text/css">
    ul.errorlist {
        margin: 0;
        padding: 0;
    }
    .errorlist li {
        background-color: red;
        color: white;
        display: block;
        font-size: 10px;
        margin: 0 0 3px;
        padding: 4px 5px;
    }
</style>
```

While it's convenient to have our form's HTML generated for us, in many cases the default rendering won't be right for our application. {{ form.as_table }} and friends are useful shortcuts while we develop our application, but everything about the way a form is displayed can be overridden, mostly within the template itself.

Each field widget (<input type="text">, <select>, <textarea>, or similar) can be rendered individually by accessing {{ form.fieldname }}. Any errors associated with a field are available as {{ form.fieldname.errors }}. We can use these form variables to construct a custom template for our contact form:

```
<form action="." method="POST">
    <div class="fieldWrapper">
        {{ form.topic.errors }}
        <label for="id_topic">Kind of feedback:</label>
        {{ form.topic }}
    </div>
    <div class="fieldWrapper">
        {{ form.message.errors }}
        <label for="id_message">Your message:</label>
        {{ form.message }}
    </div>
    <div class="fieldWrapper">
        {{ form.sender.errors }}
        <label for="id_sender">Your email (optional):</label>
        {{ form.sender }}
    </div>
    <p><input type="submit" value="Submit"></p>
</form>
```

{{ form.message.errors }} will display as a <ul class="errorlist"> if errors are present and a blank string if the field is valid (or the form is unbound). We can also treat form.message.errors as a Boolean or even iterate over it as a list, for example:

```
<div class="fieldWrapper{% if form.message.errors %} errors{% endif %}">
    {% if form.message.errors %}
        <ol>
        {% for error in form.message.errors %}
            <li><strong>{{ error|escape }}</strong></li>
        {% endfor %}
        </ol>
    {% endif %}
    {{ form.message }}
</div>
```

In the case of validation errors, this will add an "errors" class to the containing <div> and display the list of errors in an ordered list.

Creating Forms from Models

Let's build something a little more interesting: a form that submits a new publisher to our book application from Chapter 5.

An important principle in software development that Django tries to adhere to is Don't Repeat Yourself (DRY). Andy Hunt and Dave Thomas in *The Pragmatic Programmer* (Addison-Wesley, 1999) define this as follows:

> *Every piece of knowledge must have a single, unambiguous, authoritative representation within a system.*

Our Publisher model class says that a publisher has a name, address, city, state_province, country, and website. Duplicating this information in a form definition would break the DRY rule. Instead, we can use a useful shortcut: form_for_model():

```
from models import Publisher
from django.newforms import form_for_model

PublisherForm = form_for_model(Publisher)
```

PublisherForm is a Form subclass, just like the ContactForm class we created manually earlier on. We can use it in much the same way:

```
def add_publisher(request):
    if request.method == 'POST':
        form = PublisherForm(request.POST)
        if form.is_valid():
            form.save()
            return HttpResponseRedirect('/add_publisher/thanks/')
    else:
        form = PublisherForm()
    return render_to_response('add_publisher.html', {'form': form})
```

The add_publisher.html file is almost identical to our original contact.html template, so it has been omitted.

There's one more shortcut being demonstrated here. Since forms derived from models are often used to save new instances of the model to the database, the form class created by form_for_model includes a convenient save() method. This deals with the common case; you're welcome to ignore it if you want to do something a bit more involved with the submitted data.

form_for_instance() is a related method that can create a preinitialized form from an instance of a model class. This is useful for creating "edit" forms.

What's Next?

This chapter concludes the introductory material in this book. The next 13 chapters deal with various advanced topics, including generating content other than HTML (Chapter 11), security (Chapter 19), and deployment (Chapter 20).

After these first seven chapters, you should know enough to start writing your own Django projects. The rest of the material in this book will help fill in the missing pieces as you need them.

We'll start in Chapter 8 by doubling back and taking a closer look at views and URLconfs (introduced first in Chapter 3).

CHAPTER 8

■ ■ ■ ■

Advanced Views and URLconfs

In Chapter 3, we explained the basics of Django view functions and URLconfs. This chapter goes into more detail about advanced functionality in those two pieces of the framework.

URLconf Tricks

There's nothing "special" about URLconfs—like anything else in Django, they're just Python code. You can take advantage of this in several ways, as described in the sections that follow.

Streamlining Function Imports

Consider this URLconf, which builds on the example in Chapter 3:

```
from django.conf.urls.defaults import *
from mysite.views import current_datetime, hours_ahead, hours_behind,
now_in_chicago, now_in_london

urlpatterns = patterns('',
    (r'^now/$', current_datetime),
    (r'^now/plus(\d{1,2})hours/$', hours_ahead),
    (r'^now/minus(\d{1,2})hours/$', hours_behind),
    (r'^now/in_chicago/$', now_in_chicago),
    (r'^now/in_london/$', now_in_london),
)
```

As explained in Chapter 3, each entry in the URLconf includes its associated view function, passed directly as a function object. This means it's necessary to import the view functions at the top of the module.

But as a Django application grows in complexity, its URLconf grows, too, and keeping those imports can be tedious to manage. (For each new view function, you have to remember to import it, and the import statement tends to get overly long if you use this approach.) It's possible to avoid that tedium by importing the views module itself. This example URLconf is equivalent to the previous one:

```
from django.conf.urls.defaults import *
from mysite import views
```

```
urlpatterns = patterns('',
    (r'^now/$', views.current_datetime),
    (r'^now/plus(\d{1,2})hours/$', views.hours_ahead),
    (r'^now/minus(\d{1,2})hours/$', views.hours_behind),
    (r'^now/in_chicago/$', views.now_in_chicago),
    (r'^now/in_london/$', views.now_in_london),
)
```

Django offers another way of specifying the view function for a particular pattern in the URLconf: you can pass a string containing the module name and function name rather than the function object itself. Continuing the ongoing example:

```
from django.conf.urls.defaults import *

urlpatterns = patterns('',
    (r'^now/$', 'mysite.views.current_datetime'),
    (r'^now/plus(\d{1,2})hours/$', 'mysite.views.hours_ahead'),
    (r'^now/minus(\d{1,2})hours/$', 'mysite.views.hours_behind'),
    (r'^now/in_chicago/$', 'mysite.views.now_in_chicago'),
    (r'^now/in_london/$', 'mysite.views.now_in_london'),
)
```

(Note the quotes around the view names. We're using 'mysite.views.current_datetime'—with quotes—instead of mysite.views.current_datetime.)

Using this technique, it's no longer necessary to import the view functions. Django automatically imports the appropriate view function the first time it's needed, according to the string describing the name and path of the view function.

A further shortcut you can take when using the string technique is to factor out a common "view prefix." In our URLconf example, each of the view strings starts with 'mysite.views', which is redundant to type. We can factor out that common prefix and pass it as the first argument to patterns(), like this:

```
from django.conf.urls.defaults import *

urlpatterns = patterns('mysite.views',
    (r'^now/$', 'current_datetime'),
    (r'^now/plus(\d{1,2})hours/$', 'hours_ahead'),
    (r'^now/minus(\d{1,2})hours/$', 'hours_behind'),
    (r'^now/in_chicago/$', 'now_in_chicago'),
    (r'^now/in_london/$', 'now_in_london'),
)
```

Note that you don't put a trailing dot (".") in the prefix, nor do you put a leading dot in the view strings. Django puts those in automatically.

With these two approaches in mind, which is better? It really depends on your personal coding style and needs.

Advantages of the string approach are as follows:

- It's more compact, because it doesn't require you to import the view functions.

- It results in more readable and manageable URLconfs if your view functions are spread across several different Python modules.

Advantages of the function object approach are as follows:

- It allows for easy "wrapping" of view functions.

- It's more "Pythonic"—that is, it's more in line with Python traditions, such as passing functions as objects.

Both approaches are valid, and you can even mix them within the same URLconf. The choice is yours.

Using Multiple View Prefixes

In practice, if you use the string technique, you'll probably end up mixing views to the point where the views in your URLconf won't have a common prefix. However, you can still take advantage of the view prefix shortcut to remove duplication. Just add multiple patterns() objects together, like this:

Old:

```
from django.conf.urls.defaults import *

urlpatterns = patterns('',
    (r'^/?$', 'mysite.views.archive_index'),
    (r'^(\d{4})/([a-z]{3})/$', 'mysite.views.archive_month'),
    (r'^tag/(\w+)/$', 'weblog.views.tag'),
)
```

New:

```
from django.conf.urls.defaults import *

urlpatterns = patterns('mysite.views',
    (r'^/?$', 'archive_index'),
    (r'^(\d{4})/([a-z]{3})/$', 'archive_month'),
)

urlpatterns += patterns('weblog.views',
    (r'^tag/(\w+)/$', 'tag'),
)
```

All the framework cares about is that there's a module-level variable called urlpatterns. This variable can be constructed dynamically, as we do in this example.

Special-Casing URLs in Debug Mode

Speaking of constructing urlpatterns dynamically, you might want to take advantage of this technique to alter your URLconf's behavior while in Django's debug mode. To do this, just check the value of the DEBUG setting at runtime, like so:

```
from django.conf.urls.defaults import*
from django.conf import settings
```

```
urlpatterns = patterns('',
    (r'^$', 'mysite.views.homepage'),
    (r'^(\d{4})/([a-z]{3})/$', 'mysite.views.archive_month'),
)

if settings.DEBUG:
    urlpatterns += patterns('',
        (r'^debuginfo$', 'mysite.views.debug'),
    )
```

In this example, the URL /debuginfo/ will be available only if your DEBUG setting is set to True.

Using Named Groups

In all of our URLconf examples so far, we've used simple, *non-named* regular expression groups—that is, we put parentheses around parts of the URL we wanted to capture, and Django passes that captured text to the view function as a positional argument. In more advanced usage, it's possible to use *named* regular expression groups to capture URL bits and pass them as *keyword* arguments to a view.

KEYWORD ARGUMENTS VS. POSITIONAL ARGUMENTS

A Python function can be called using keyword arguments or positional arguments—and, in some cases, both at the same time. In a keyword argument call, you specify the names of the arguments along with the values you're passing. In a positional argument call, you simply pass the arguments without explicitly specifying which argument matches which value; the association is implicit in the arguments' order.

For example, consider this simple function:

```
def sell(item, price, quantity):
    print "Selling %s unit(s) of %s at %s" % (quantity, item, price)
```

To call it with positional arguments, you specify the arguments in the order in which they're listed in the function definition:

```
sell('Socks', '$2.50', 6)
```

To call it with keyword arguments, you specify the names of the arguments along with the values. The following statements are equivalent:

```
sell(item='Socks', price='$2.50', quantity=6)
sell(item='Socks', quantity=6, price='$2.50')
sell(price='$2.50', item='Socks', quantity=6)
sell(price='$2.50', quantity=6, item='Socks')
sell(quantity=6, item='Socks', price='$2.50')
sell(quantity=6, price='$2.50', item='Socks')
```

Finally, you can mix keyword and positional arguments, as long as all positional arguments are listed before keyword arguments. The following statements are equivalent to the previous examples:

```
sell('Socks', '$2.50', quantity=6)
sell('Socks', price='$2.50', quantity=6)
sell('Socks', quantity=6, price='$2.50')
```

In Python regular expressions, the syntax for named regular expression groups is (?P<name>pattern), where name is the name of the group and pattern is some pattern to match.

Here's an example URLconf that uses non-named groups:

```
from django.conf.urls.defaults import *
from mysite import views

urlpatterns = patterns('',
    (r'^articles/(\d{4})/$', views.year_archive),
    (r'^articles/(\d{4})/(\d{2})/$', views.month_archive),
)
```

Here's the same URLconf rewritten to use named groups:

```
from django.conf.urls.defaults import *
from mysite import views

urlpatterns = patterns('',
    (r'^articles/(?P<year>\d{4})/$', views.year_archive),
    (r'^articles/(?P<year>\d{4})/(?P<month>\d{2})/$', views.month_archive),
)
```

This accomplishes exactly the same thing as the previous example, with one subtle difference: the captured values are passed to view functions as keyword arguments rather than positional arguments.

For example, with non-named groups, a request to /articles/2006/03/ would result in a function call equivalent to this:

```
month_archive(request, '2006', '03')
```

With named groups, though, the same request would result in this function call:

```
month_archive(request, year='2006', month='03')
```

In practice, using named groups makes your URLconfs slightly more explicit and less prone to argument-order bugs—and you can reorder the arguments in your views' function definitions. Following the preceding example, if we wanted to change the URLs to include the month *before* the year, and we were using non-named groups, we'd have to remember to change the order of arguments in the month_archive view. If we were using named groups, changing the order of the captured parameters in the URL would have no effect on the view.

Of course, the benefits of named groups come at the cost of brevity; some developers find the named-group syntax ugly and too verbose. Still, another advantage of named groups is readability, especially for those who aren't intimately familiar with regular expressions or your particular Django application. It's easier to see what's happening, at a glance, in a URLconf that uses named groups.

Understanding the Matching/Grouping Algorithm

A caveat with using named groups in a URLconf is that a single URLconf pattern cannot contain both named and non-named groups. If you do this, Django won't throw any errors, but you'll probably find that your URLs aren't matching as you expect. Specifically, here's the algorithm the URLconf parser follows with respect to named groups vs. non-named groups in a regular expression:

- If there are any named arguments, it will use those, ignoring non-named arguments.

- Otherwise, it will pass all non-named arguments as positional arguments.

- In both cases, it will pass any extra options as keyword arguments. See the next section for more information.

Passing Extra Options to View Functions

Sometimes you'll find yourself writing view functions that are quite similar, with only a few small differences. For example, say you have two views whose contents are identical except for the template they use:

```
# urls.py

from django.conf.urls.defaults import *
from mysite import views

urlpatterns = patterns('',
    (r'^foo/$', views.foo_view),
    (r'^bar/$', views.bar_view),
)
```

```
# views.py

from django.shortcuts import render_to_response
from mysite.models import MyModel

def foo_view(request):
    m_list = MyModel.objects.filter(is_new=True)
    return render_to_response('template1.html', {'m_list': m_list})

def bar_view(request):
    m_list = MyModel.objects.filter(is_new=True)
    return render_to_response('template2.html', {'m_list': m_list})
```

We're repeating ourselves in this code, and that's inelegant. At first, you may think to remove the redundancy by using the same view for both URLs, putting parentheses around the URL to capture it, and checking the URL within the view to determine the template, like so:

```
# urls.py

from django.conf.urls.defaults import *
from mysite import views

urlpatterns = patterns('',
    (r'^(foo)/$', views.foobar_view),
    (r'^(bar)/$', views.foobar_view),
)
```

```
# views.py

from django.shortcuts import render_to_response
from mysite.models import MyModel

def foobar_view(request, url):
    m_list = MyModel.objects.filter(is_new=True)
    if url == 'foo':
        template_name = 'template1.html'
    elif url == 'bar':
        template_name = 'template2.html'
    return render_to_response(template_name, {'m_list': m_list})
```

The problem with that solution, though, is that it couples your URLs to your code. If you decide to rename /foo/ to /fooey/, you'll have to remember to change the view code.

The elegant solution involves an optional URLconf parameter. Each pattern in a URLconf may include a third item: a dictionary of keyword arguments to pass to the view function.

With this in mind, we can rewrite our ongoing example like this:

```
# urls.py

from django.conf.urls.defaults import *
from mysite import views

urlpatterns = patterns('',
    (r'^foo/$', views.foobar_view, {'template_name': 'template1.html'}),
    (r'^bar/$', views.foobar_view, {'template_name': 'template2.html'}),
)
```

```
# views.py

from django.shortcuts import render_to_response
from mysite.models import MyModel
```

```
def foobar_view(request, template_name):
    m_list = MyModel.objects.filter(is_new=True)
    return render_to_response(template_name, {'m_list': m_list})
```

As you can see, the URLconf in this example specifies `template_name` in the URLconf. The view function treats it as just another parameter.

This extra URLconf options technique is a nice way of sending additional information to your view functions with minimal fuss. As such, it's used by a couple of Django's bundled applications, most notably its generic views system, which we cover in Chapter 9.

The following sections contain a couple of ideas about how you can use the extra URLconf options technique in your own projects.

Faking Captured URLconf Values

Say you have a set of views that match a pattern, along with another URL that doesn't fit the pattern but whose view logic is the same. In this case, you can "fake" the capturing of URL values by using extra URLconf options to handle that extra URL with the same view.

For example, you might have an application that displays some data for a particular day, with URLs such as these:

```
/mydata/jan/01/
/mydata/jan/02/
/mydata/jan/03/
# ...
/mydata/dec/30/
/mydata/dec/31/
```

This is simple enough to deal with—you can capture those in a URLconf like this (using named group syntax):

```
urlpatterns = patterns('',
    (r'^mydata/(?P<month>\w{3})/(?P<day>\d\d)/$', views.my_view),
)
```

and the view function signature will look like this:

```
def my_view(request, month, day):
    # ....
```

This approach is straightforward—it's nothing you haven't seen before. The trick comes in when you want to add another URL that uses `my_view` but whose URL doesn't include a `month` and/or `day`.

For example, you might want to add another URL, `/mydata/birthday/`, which would be equivalent to `/mydata/jan/06/`. You can take advantage of extra URLconf options like so:

```
urlpatterns = patterns('',
    (r'^mydata/birthday/$', views.my_view, {'month': 'jan', 'day': '06'}),
    (r'^mydata/(?P<month>\w{3})/(?P<day>\d\d)/$', views.my_view),
)
```

The cool thing here is that you don't have to change your view function at all. The view function only cares that it *gets* month and day parameters—it doesn't matter whether they come from the URL capturing itself or extra parameters.

Making a View Generic

It's good programming practice to "factor out" commonalities in code. For example, with these two Python functions:

```python
def say_hello(person_name):
    print 'Hello, %s' % person_name

def say_goodbye(person_name):
    print 'Goodbye, %s' % person_name
```

we can factor out the greeting to make it a parameter:

```python
def greet(person_name, greeting):
    print '%s, %s' % (greeting, person_name)
```

You can apply this same philosophy to your Django views by using extra URLconf parameters. With this in mind, you can start making higher-level abstractions of your views. Instead of thinking to yourself, "This view displays a list of Event objects," and "That view displays a list of BlogEntry objects," realize they're both specific cases of "A view that displays a list of objects, where the type of object is variable."

Take this code, for example:

```python
# urls.py

from django.conf.urls.defaults import *
from mysite import views

urlpatterns = patterns('',
    (r'^events/$', views.event_list),
    (r'^blog/entries/$', views.entry_list),
)
```

```python
# views.py

from django.shortcuts import render_to_response
from mysite.models import Event, BlogEntry

def event_list(request):
    obj_list = Event.objects.all()
    return render_to_response('mysite/event_list.html', {'event_list': obj_list})

def entry_list(request):
    obj_list = BlogEntry.objects.all()
    return render_to_response('mysite/blogentry_list.html',
                              {'entry_list': obj_list})
```

The two views do essentially the same thing: they display a list of objects. So let's factor out the type of object they're displaying:

```
# urls.py

from django.conf.urls.defaults import *
from mysite import models, views

urlpatterns = patterns('',
    (r'^events/$', views.object_list, {'model': models.Event}),
    (r'^blog/entries/$', views.object_list, {'model': models.BlogEntry}),
)

# views.py

from django.shortcuts import render_to_response

def object_list(request, model):
    obj_list = model.objects.all()
    template_name = 'mysite/%s_list.html' % model.__name__.lower()
    return render_to_response(template_name, {'object_list': obj_list})
```

With those small changes, we suddenly have a reusable, model-agnostic view! From now on, anytime we need a view that lists a set of objects, we can simply reuse this object_list view rather than writing view code. Here are a couple of notes about what we did:

- We passed the model classes directly, as the model parameter. The dictionary of extra URLconf options can pass any type of Python object—not just strings.

- The model.objects.all() line is an example of *duck typing*: "If it walks like a duck and talks like a duck, we can treat it like a duck." Note the code doesn't know what type of object model is; the only requirement is that model have an objects attribute, which in turn has an all() method.

- We used model.__name__.lower() in determining the template name. Every Python class has a __name__ attribute that returns the class name. This feature is useful at times like this, when we don't know the type of class until runtime. For example, the BlogEntry class's __name__ is the string 'BlogEntry'.

- In a slight difference between this example and the previous example, we passed the generic variable name object_list to the template. We could easily change this variable name to be blogentry_list or event_list, but we've left that as an exercise for the reader.

Because database-driven Web sites have several common patterns, Django comes with a set of "generic views" that use this exact technique to save you time. We cover Django's built-in generic views in the next chapter.

Giving a View Configuration Options

If you're distributing a Django application, chances are that your users will want some degree of configuration. In this case, it's a good idea to add hooks to your views for any configuration options you think people may want to change. You can use extra URLconf parameters for this purpose.

A common bit of an application to make configurable is the template name:

```
def my_view(request, template_name):
    var = do_something()
    return render_to_response(template_name, {'var': var})
```

Understanding Precedence of Captured Values vs. Extra Options

When there's a conflict, extra URLconf parameters get precedence over captured parameters. In other words, if your URLconf captures a named-group variable and an extra URLconf parameter includes a variable with the same name, the extra URLconf parameter value will be used.

For example, consider this URLconf:

```
from django.conf.urls.defaults import *

urlpatterns = patterns('',
    (r'^mydata/(?P<id>\d+)/$', views.my_view, {'id': 3}),
)
```

Here, both the regular expression and the extra dictionary include an id. The hard-coded id gets precedence. That means any request (e.g., /mydata/2/ or /mydata/432432/) will be treated as if id is set to 3, regardless of the value captured in the URL.

Astute readers will note that in this case, it's a waste of time and typing to capture the id in the regular expression, because its value will always be overridden by the dictionary's value. That's correct—we bring this up only to help you avoid making the mistake.

Using Default View Arguments

Another convenient trick is to specify default parameters for a view's arguments. This tells the view which value to use for a parameter by default if none is specified.

Here's an example:

```
# urls.py

from django.conf.urls.defaults import *

urlpatterns = patterns('',
    (r'^blog/$', views.page),
    (r'^blog/page(?P<num>\d+)/$', views.page),
)

# views.py

def page(request, num="1"):
    # Output the appropriate page of blog entries, according to num.
    # ...
```

Here, both URL patterns point to the same view—`views.page`—but the first pattern doesn't capture anything from the URL. If the first pattern matches, the `page()` function will use its default argument for `num`, `"1"`. If the second pattern matches, `page()` will use whatever `num` value was captured by the regular expression.

It's common to use this technique in conjunction with configuration options, as explained earlier. This example makes a slight improvement to the example in the "Giving a View Configuration Options" section by providing a default value for `template_name`:

```
def my_view(request, template_name='mysite/my_view.html'):
    var = do_something()
    return render_to_response(template_name, {'var': var})
```

Special-Casing Views

Sometimes you'll have a pattern in your URLconf that handles a large set of URLs, but you'll need to special-case one of them. In this case, take advantage of the linear way a URLconf is processed and put the special case first.

For example, the "add an object" pages in Django's admin site are represented by this URLconf line:

```
urlpatterns = patterns('',
    # ...
    ('^([^/]+)/([^/]+)/add/$', 'django.contrib.admin.views.main.add_stage'),
    # ...
)
```

This matches URLs such as `/myblog/entries/add/` and `/auth/groups/add/`. However, the "add" page for a user object (`/auth/user/add/`) is a special case—it doesn't display all of the form fields, it displays two password fields, and so forth. We *could* solve this problem by special-casing in the view, like so:

```
def add_stage(request, app_label, model_name):
    if app_label == 'auth' and model_name == 'user':
        # do special-case code
    else:
        # do normal code
```

but that's inelegant for a reason we've touched on multiple times in this chapter: it puts URL logic in the view. As a more elegant solution, we can take advantage of the fact that URLconfs are processed in order from top to bottom:

```
urlpatterns = patterns('',
    # ...
    ('^auth/user/add/$', 'django.contrib.admin.views.auth.user_add_stage'),
    ('^([^/]+)/([^/]+)/add/$', 'django.contrib.admin.views.main.add_stage'),
    # ...
)
```

With this in place, a request to `/auth/user/add/` will be handled by the `user_add_stage` view. Although that URL matches the second pattern, it matches the top one first. (This is short-circuit logic.)

Capturing Text in URLs

Each captured argument is sent to the view as a plain Python string, regardless of what sort of match the regular expression makes. For example, in the following URLconf line:

```
(r'^articles/(?P<year>\d{4})/$', views.year_archive),
```

the year argument to views.year_archive() will be a string, not an integer, even though \d{4} will only match integer strings.

This is important to keep in mind when you're writing view code. Many built-in Python functions are fussy (and rightfully so) about accepting only objects of a certain type. A common error is to attempt to create a datetime.date object with string values instead of integer values:

```
>>> import datetime
>>> datetime.date('1993', '7', '9')
Traceback (most recent call last):
    ...
TypeError: an integer is required
>>> datetime.date(1993, 7, 9)
datetime.date(1993, 7, 9)
```

Translated to a URLconf and view, the error looks like this:

```
# urls.py

from django.conf.urls.defaults import *

urlpatterns = patterns('',
    (r'^articles/(\d{4})/(\d{2})/(\d{2})/$', views.day_archive),
)
```

```
# views.py

import datetime

def day_archive(request, year, month, day)
    # The following statement raises a TypeError!
    date = datetime.date(year, month, day)
```

Instead, day_archive() can be written correctly like this:

```
def day_archive(request, year, month, day)
    date = datetime.date(int(year), int(month), int(day))
```

Note that int() itself raises a ValueError when you pass it a string that is not composed solely of digits, but we're avoiding that error in this case because the regular expression in our URLconf has ensured that only strings containing digits are passed to the view function.

Determining What the URLconf Searches Against

When a request comes in, Django tries to match the URLconf patterns against the requested URL, as a normal Python string (not as a Unicode string). This does not include GET or POST parameters, or the domain name. It also does not include the leading slash, because every URL has a leading slash.

For example, in a request to http://www.example.com/myapp/, Django will try to match myapp/. In a request to http://www.example.com/myapp/?page=3, Django will try to match myapp/.

The request method (e.g., POST, GET, HEAD) is *not* taken into account when traversing the URLconf. In other words, all request methods will be routed to the same function for the same URL. It's the responsibility of a view function to perform branching based on request method.

Including Other URLconfs

If you intend your code to be used on multiple Django-based sites, you should consider arranging your URLconfs in such a way that allows for "including."

At any point, your URLconf can "include" other URLconf modules. This essentially "roots" a set of URLs below other ones. For example, this URLconf includes other URLconfs:

```
from django.conf.urls.defaults import *

urlpatterns = patterns('',
    (r'^weblog/', include('mysite.blog.urls')),
    (r'^photos/', include('mysite.photos.urls')),
    (r'^about/$', 'mysite.views.about'),
)
```

There's an important gotcha here: the regular expressions in this example that point to an include() do *not* have a $ (end-of-string match character) but *do* include a trailing slash. Whenever Django encounters include(), it chops off whatever part of the URL matched up to that point and sends the remaining string to the included URLconf for further processing.

Continuing this example, here's the URLconf mysite.blog.urls:

```
from django.conf.urls.defaults import *

urlpatterns = patterns('',
    (r'^(\d\d\d\d)/$', 'mysite.blog.views.year_detail'),
    (r'^(\d\d\d\d)/(\d\d)/$', 'mysite.blog.views.month_detail'),
)
```

With these two URLconfs, here's how a few sample requests would be handled:

- /weblog/2007/: In the first URLconf, the pattern r'^weblog/' matches. Because it is an include(), Django strips all the matching text, which is 'weblog/' in this case. The remaining part of the URL is 2007/, which matches the first line in the mysite.blog.urls URLconf.

- /weblog//2007/: In the first URLconf, the pattern r'^weblog/' matches. Because it is an include(), Django strips all the matching text, which is 'weblog/' in this case. The remaining part of the URL is /2007/ (with a leading slash), which does not match any of the lines in the mysite.blog.urls URLconf.

- /about/: This matches the view mysite.views.about in the first URLconf, demonstrating that you can mix include() patterns with non-include() patterns.

How Captured Parameters Work with include()

An included URLconf receives any captured parameters from parent URLconfs, for example:

```
# root urls.py

from django.conf.urls.defaults import *

urlpatterns = patterns('',
    (r'^(?P<username>\w+)/blog/', include('foo.urls.blog')),
)

# foo/urls/blog.py

from django.conf.urls.defaults import *

urlpatterns = patterns('',
    (r'^$', 'foo.views.blog_index'),
    (r'^archive/$', 'foo.views.blog_archive'),
)
```

In this example, the captured `username` variable is passed to the included URLconf and, hence, to *every* view function within that URLconf.

Note that the captured parameters will *always* be passed to *every* line in the included URLconf, regardless of whether the line's view actually accepts those parameters as valid. For this reason, this technique is useful only if you're certain that every view in the included URLconf accepts the parameters you're passing.

How Extra URLconf Options Work with include()

Similarly, you can pass extra URLconf options to `include()`, just as you can pass extra URLconf options to a normal view—as a dictionary. When you do this, *each* line in the included URLconf will be passed the extra options.

For example, the following two URLconf sets are functionally identical.

Set 1:

```
# urls.py

from django.conf.urls.defaults import *

urlpatterns = patterns('',
    (r'^blog/', include('inner'), {'blogid': 3}),
)

# inner.py

from django.conf.urls.defaults import *
```

```
urlpatterns = patterns('',
    (r'^archive/$', 'mysite.views.archive'),
    (r'^about/$', 'mysite.views.about'),
    (r'^rss/$', 'mysite.views.rss'),
)
```

Set 2:

```
# urls.py

from django.conf.urls.defaults import *

urlpatterns = patterns('',
    (r'^blog/', include('inner')),
)

# inner.py

from django.conf.urls.defaults import *

urlpatterns = patterns('',
    (r'^archive/$', 'mysite.views.archive', {'blogid': 3}),
    (r'^about/$', 'mysite.views.about', {'blogid': 3}),
    (r'^rss/$', 'mysite.views.rss', {'blogid': 3}),
)
```

As is the case with captured parameters (explained in the previous section), extra options will *always* be passed to *every* line in the included URLconf, regardless of whether the line's view actually accepts those options as valid. For this reason, this technique is useful only if you're certain that every view in the included URLconf accepts the extra options you're passing.

What's Next?

One of Django's main goals is to reduce the amount of code developers need to write, and in this chapter we suggested how to cut down the code of your views and URLconfs.

The next logical step in code elimination is removing the need to write views entirely. That's the topic of the next chapter.

PART 2

■ ■ ■

Django's Subframeworks

CHAPTER 9

■■■

Generic Views

Here again is a recurring theme of this book: at its worst, Web development is boring and monotonous. So far, we've covered how Django tries to take away some of that monotony at the model and template layers, but Web developers also experience this boredom at the view level.

Django's *generic views* were developed to ease that pain. They take certain common idioms and patterns found in view development and abstract them so that you can quickly write common views of data without having to write too much code. In fact, nearly every view example in the preceding chapters could be rewritten with the help of generic views.

Chapter 8 touched briefly on how you'd go about making a view "generic." To review, we can recognize certain common tasks, like displaying a list of objects, and write code that displays a list of *any* object. Then the model in question can be passed as an extra argument to the URLconf.

Django ships with generic views to do the following:

- Perform common "simple" tasks: redirect to a different page and render a given template.

- Display list and detail pages for a single object. The event_list and entry_list views from Chapter 8 are examples of list views. A single event page is an example of what we call a "detail" view.

- Present date-based objects in year/month/day archive pages, associated detail, and "latest" pages. The Django Weblog's (http://www.djangoproject.com/weblog/) year, month, and day archives are built with these, as would be a typical newspaper's archives.

- Allow users to create, update, and delete objects—with or without authorization.

Taken together, these views provide easy interfaces to perform the most common tasks developers encounter.

Using Generic Views

All of these views are used by creating configuration dictionaries in your URLconf files and passing those dictionaries as the third member of the URLconf tuple for a given pattern.

For example, here's a simple URLconf you could use to present a static "about" page:

```
from django.conf.urls.defaults import *
from django.views.generic.simple import direct_to_template

urlpatterns = patterns('',
    ('^about/$', direct_to_template, {
        'template': 'about.html'
    })
)
```

Though this might seem a bit "magical" at first glance—look, a view with no code!— it's actually exactly the same as the examples in Chapter 8. The direct_to_template view simply grabs information from the extra-parameters dictionary and uses that information when rendering the view.

Because this generic view—and all the others—is a regular view function like any other, we can reuse it inside our own views. As an example, let's extend our "about" example to map URLs of the form /about/<whatever>/ to statically rendered about/<whatever>.html. We'll do this by first modifying the URLconf to point to a view function:

```
from django.conf.urls.defaults import *
from django.views.generic.simple import direct_to_template
from mysite.books.views import about_pages

urlpatterns = patterns('',
    ('^about/$', direct_to_template, {
        'template': 'about.html'
    }),
    ('^about/(w+)/$', about_pages),
)
```

Next, we'll write the about_pages view:

```
from django.http import Http404
from django.template import TemplateDoesNotExist
from django.views.generic.simple import direct_to_template

def about_pages(request, page):
    try:
        return direct_to_template(request, template="about/%s.html" % page)
    except TemplateDoesNotExist:
        raise Http404()
```

Here we're treating direct_to_template like any other function. Since it returns an HttpResponse, we can simply return it as is. The only slightly tricky business here is dealing with missing templates. We don't want a nonexistent template to cause a server error, so we catch TemplateDoesNotExist exceptions and return 404 errors instead.

> **IS THERE A SECURITY VULNERABILITY HERE?**
>
> Sharp-eyed readers may have noticed a possible security hole: we're constructing the template name using interpolated content from the browser (`template="about/%s.html" % page`). At first glance, this looks like a classic *directory traversal* vulnerability (discussed in detail in Chapter 19). But is it really?
>
> Not exactly. Yes, a maliciously crafted value of `page` could cause directory traversal, but although `page` *is* taken from the request URL, not every value will be accepted. They key is in the URLconf: we're using the regular expression `\w+` to match the `page` part of the URL, and `\w` accepts only letters and numbers. Thus, any malicious characters (dots and slashes, here) will be rejected by the URL resolver before they reach the view itself.

Generic Views of Objects

The `direct_to_template` view certainly is useful, but Django's generic views really shine when it comes to presenting views on your database content. Because it's such a common task, Django comes with a handful of built-in generic views that make generating list and detail views of objects incredibly easy.

Let's take a look at one of these generic views: the "object list" view. We'll be using this `Publisher` object from Chapter 5:

```
class Publisher(models.Model):
    name = models.CharField(maxlength=30)
    address = models.CharField(maxlength=50)
    city = models.CharField(maxlength=60)
    state_province = models.CharField(maxlength=30)
    country = models.CharField(maxlength=50)
    website = models.URLField()

    def __str__(self):
        return self.name

    class Meta:
        ordering = ["-name"]
```

To build a list page of all books, we'd use a URLconf along these lines:

```
from django.conf.urls.defaults import *
from django.views.generic import list_detail
from mysite.books.models import Publisher

publisher_info = {
    "queryset" : Publisher.objects.all(),
}

urlpatterns = patterns('',
    (r'^publishers/$', list_detail.object_list, publisher_info)
)
```

That's all the Python code we need to write. We still need to write a template, however. We could explicitly tell the object_list view which template to use by including a template_name key in the extra arguments dictionary, but in the absence of an explicit template Django will infer one from the object's name. In this case, the inferred template will be "books/publisher_list.html"—the "books" part comes from the name of the app that defines the model, while the "publisher" bit is just the lowercased version of the model's name.

This template will be rendered against a context containing a variable called object_list that contains all the book objects. A very simple template might look like the following:

```
{% extends "base.html" %}

{% block content %}
    <h2>Publishers</h2>
    <ul>
        {% for publisher in object_list %}
            <li>{{ publisher.name }}</li>
        {% endfor %}
    </ul>
{% endblock %}
```

That's really all there is to it. All the cool features of generic views come from changing the "info" dictionary passed to the generic view. Appendix D documents all the generic views and their options in detail. In the rest of this chapter, we'll consider some of the common ways you might customize and extend generic views.

Extending Generic Views

There's no question that using generic views can speed up development substantially. In most projects, however, there comes a moment when the generic views no longer suffice. Indeed, the most common question asked by new Django developers is how to make generic views handle a wider array of situations.

Luckily, in nearly every one of these cases, there are ways to simply extend generic views to handle a larger array of use cases. These situations usually fall into a handful of patterns dealt with in the sections that follow.

Making "Friendly" Template Contexts

You might have noticed that the sample publisher list template stores all the books in a variable named object_list. While this works just fine, it isn't all that "friendly" to template authors: they have to "just know" that they're dealing with books here. A better name for that variable would be publisher_list; that variable's content is pretty obvious.

We can change the name of that variable easily with the template_object_name argument:

```
publisher_info = {
    "queryset" : Publisher.objects.all(),
    "template_object_name" : "publisher",
}
```

```
urlpatterns = patterns('',
    (r'^publishers/$', list_detail.object_list, publisher_info)
)
```

Providing a useful `template_object_name` is always a good idea. Your co-workers who design templates will thank you.

Adding Extra Context

Often you simply need to present some extra information beyond that provided by the generic view. For example, think of showing a list of all the other publishers on each publisher detail page. The `object_detail` generic view provides the publisher to the context, but it seems there's no way to get a list of *all* publishers in that template.

But there is: all generic views take an extra optional parameter, `extra_context`. This is a dictionary of extra objects that will be added to the template's context. So, to provide the list of all publishers on the detail view, we'd use an info dict like this:

```
publisher_info = {
    "queryset" : Publisher.objects.all(),
    "extra_context" : {"publisher_list" : Publisher.objects.all()}
}
```

This would populate a `{{ publisher_list }}` variable in the template context. This pattern can be used to pass any information down into the template for the generic view. It's very handy.

However, there's actually a subtle bug here—can you spot it? The problem has to do with when the queries in `extra_context` are evaluated. Because this example puts `Publisher.objects.all()` in the URLconf, it will be evaluated only once (when the URLconf is first loaded). Once you add or remove publishers, you'll notice that the generic view doesn't reflect those changes until you reload the Web server (see "Caching and QuerySets" in Appendix C for more information about when QuerySets are cached and evaluated).

Note This problem doesn't apply to the `queryset` generic view argument. Since Django knows that particular `QuerySet` should *never* be cached, the generic view takes care of clearing the cache when each view is rendered.

The solution is to use a callback in `extra_context` instead of a value. Any callable (i.e., a function) that's passed to `extra_context` will be evaluated when the view is rendered (instead of only once). You could do this with an explicitly defined function:

```
def get_publishers():
    return Publisher.objects.all()

book_info = {
    "queryset" : Publisher.objects.all(),
    "extra_context" : {"publisher_list" : get_publishers}
}
```

or you could use a less obvious but shorter version that relies on the fact that `Publisher.objects.all` is itself a callable:

```
book_info = {
    "queryset" : Book.objects.all(),
    "extra_context" : {"publisher_list" : Publisher.objects.all}
}
```

Notice the lack of parentheses after `Publisher.objects.all`; this references the function without actually calling it (which the generic view will do later).

Viewing Subsets of Objects

Now let's take a closer look at this `queryset` key we've been using all along. Most generic views take one of these `queryset` arguments—it's how the view knows which set of objects to display (see "Selecting Objects" in Chapter 5 for an introduction to `QuerySets`, and see Appendix C for the complete details).

To pick a basic example, we might want to order a list of books by publication date, with the most recent first:

```
book_info = {
    "queryset" : Book.objects.all().order_by("-publication_date"),
}
```

That's a pretty simple example, but it illustrates the idea nicely. Of course, you'll usually want to do more than just reorder objects. If you want to present a list of books by a particular publisher, you can use the same technique:

```
apress_books = {
    "queryset": Book.objects.filter(publisher__name="Apress Publishing"),
    "template_name" : "books/apress_list.html"
}

urlpatterns = patterns('',
    (r'^publishers/$', list_detail.object_list, publisher_info),
    (r'^books/apress/$', list_detail.object_list, apress_books),
)
```

Notice that along with a filtered `queryset`, we're also using a custom template name. If we didn't, the generic view would use the same template as the "vanilla" object list, which might not be what we want.

Also notice that this isn't a very elegant way of doing publisher-specific books. If we want to add another publisher page, we need another handful of lines in the URLconf, and more than a few publishers would get unreasonable. We'll deal with this problem in the next section.

■**Note** If you get a 404 when requesting /books/apress/, check to ensure that you actually have a publisher with the name "Apress Publishing." If you don't have that publisher, you'll get a 404. Generic views have an `allow_empty` parameter that changes this behavior; see Appendix D for details.

Complex Filtering with Wrapper Functions

Another common need is to filter down the objects given in a list page by some key in the URL. Earlier we hard-coded the publisher's name in the URLconf, but what if we wanted to write a view that displayed all the books by some arbitrary publisher? We can "wrap" the object_list generic view to avoid writing a lot of code by hand. As usual, we'll start by writing a URLconf:

```
urlpatterns = patterns('',
    (r'publishers/$', list_detail.object_list, publisher_info),
    (r'books/(w+)/$', books_by_publisher),
)
```

Next, we'll write the books_by_publisher view itself:

```
from django.http import Http404
from django.views.generic import list_detail
from mysite.books.models import Book, Publisher

def books_by_publisher(request, name):

    # Look up the publisher (and raise a 404 if it can't be found).
    try:
        publisher = Publisher.objects.get(name__iexact=name)
    except Publisher.DoesNotExist:
        raise Http404

    # Use the object_list view for the heavy lifting.
    return list_detail.object_list(
        request,
        queryset = Book.objects.filter(publisher=publisher),
        template_name = "books/books_by_publisher.html",
        template_object_name = "books",
        extra_context = {"publisher" : publisher}
    )
```

This works because there's really nothing special about generic views—they're just Python functions. Like any view function, generic views expect a certain set of arguments and return HttpResponse objects. Thus, it's incredibly easy to wrap a small function around a generic view that does additional work before (or after; see the next section) handing things off to the generic view.

Notice that in the preceding example we passed the current publisher being displayed in the extra_context. This is usually a good idea in wrappers of this nature; it lets the template know which "parent" object is currently being browsed.

Performing Extra Work

The last common pattern we'll look at involves doing some extra work before or after calling the generic view.

Imagine we had a last_accessed field on our Author object that we were using to keep track of the last time anybody looked at that author. The generic object_detail view, of course, wouldn't know anything about this field, but once again we could easily write a custom view to keep that field updated.

First, we'd need to add an author detail bit in the URLconf to point to a custom view:

```
from mysite.books.views import author_detail

urlpatterns = patterns('',
    #...
    (r'^authors/(?P<author_id>d+)/$', author_detail),
)
```

Then we'd write our wrapper function:

```
import datetime
from mysite.books.models import Author
from django.views.generic import list_detail
from django.shortcuts import get_object_or_404

def author_detail(request, author_id):
    # Look up the Author (and raise a 404 if she's not found)
    author = get_object_or_404(Author, pk=author_id)

    # Record the last accessed date
    author.last_accessed = datetime.datetime.now()
    author.save()

    # Show the detail page
    return list_detail.object_detail(
        request,
        queryset = Author.objects.all(),
        object_id = author_id,
    )
```

This code won't actually work unless you add a last_accessed field to your Author model and create a books/author_detail.html template.

We can use a similar idiom to alter the response returned by the generic view. If we wanted to provide a downloadable plain-text version of the list of authors, we could use a view like this:

```
def author_list_plaintext(request):
    response = list_detail.object_list(
        request,
        queryset = Author.objects.all(),
        mimetype = "text/plain",
        template_name = "books/author_list.txt"
    )
    response["Content-Disposition"] = "attachment; filename=authors.txt"
    return response
```

This works because the generic views return simple HttpResponse objects that can be treated like dictionaries to set HTTP headers. This Content-Disposition business, by the way, instructs the browser to download and save the page instead of displaying it in the browser.

What's Next?

In this chapter we looked at only a couple of the generic views Django ships with, but the general ideas presented here should apply pretty closely to any generic view. Appendix D covers all the available views in detail, and it's recommended reading if you want to get the most out of this powerful feature.

In the next chapter we delve deep into the inner workings of Django's templates, showing all the cool ways they can be extended. Until now, we've treated the template engine as a mostly static tool you can use to render your content.

CHAPTER 10

■ ■ ■

Extending the Template Engine

Although most of your interactions with Django's template language will be in the role of template author, you may want to customize and extend the template engine—either to make it do something it doesn't already do, or to make your job easier in some other way.

This chapter delves deep into the guts of Django's template system. It covers what you need to know if you plan to extend the system or if you're just curious about how it works.

If you're looking to use the Django template system as part of another application (i.e., without the rest of the framework), make sure to read the "Configuring the Template System in Standalone Mode" section later in the chapter.

Template Language Review

First, let's quickly review a number of terms introduced in Chapter 4:

- A *template* is a text document, or a normal Python string, that is marked up using the Django template language. A template can contain block tags and variables.

- A *block tag* is a symbol within a template that does something. This definition is deliberately vague. For example, a block tag can produce content, serve as a control structure (an if statement or for loop), grab content from a database, or enable access to other template tags.

  Block tags are surrounded by {% and %}:

  ```
  {% if is_logged_in %}
    Thanks for logging in!
  {% else %}
    Please log in.
  {% endif %}
  ```

- A *variable* is a symbol within a template that outputs a value. Variable tags are surrounded by {{ and }}:

  ```
  My first name is {{ first_name }}. My last name is {{ last_name }}.
  ```

- A *context* is a name-value mapping (similar to a Python dictionary) that is passed to a template.

- A template *renders* a context by replacing the variable "holes" with values from the context and executing all block tags.

For more details about the basics of these terms, refer back to Chapter 4.

The rest of this chapter discusses ways of extending the template engine. First, though, let's take a quick look at a few internals left out of Chapter 4 for simplicity.

RequestContext and Context Processors

When rendering a template, you need a context. Usually this is an instance of django.template. Context, but Django also comes with a special subclass, django.template.RequestContext, that acts slightly differently. RequestContext adds a bunch of variables to your template context by default—things like the HttpRequest object or information about the currently logged-in user.

Use RequestContext when you don't want to have to specify the same set of variables in a series of templates. For example, consider these four views:

```
from django.template import loader, Context

def view_1(request):
    # ...
    t = loader.get_template('template1.html')
    c = Context({
        'app': 'My app',
        'user': request.user,
        'ip_address': request.META['REMOTE_ADDR'],
        'message': 'I am view 1.'
    })
    return t.render(c)

def view_2(request):
    # ...
    t = loader.get_template('template2.html')
    c = Context({
        'app': 'My app',
        'user': request.user,
        'ip_address': request.META['REMOTE_ADDR'],
        'message': 'I am the second view.'
    })
    return t.render(c)

def view_3(request):
# ...
    t = loader.get_template('template3.html')
    c = Context({
        'app': 'My app',
```

```
        'user': request.user,
        'ip_address': request.META['REMOTE_ADDR'],
        'message': 'I am the third view.'
    })
    return t.render(c)

def view_4(request):
    # ...
    t = loader.get_template('template4.html')
    c = Context({
        'app': 'My app',
        'user': request.user,
        'ip_address': request.META['REMOTE_ADDR'],
        'message': 'I am the fourth view.'
    })
    return t.render(c)
```

(Note that we're deliberately *not* using the render_to_response() shortcut in these examples—
we're manually loading the templates, constructing the context objects, and rendering the
templates. We're "spelling out" all of the steps for the purpose of clarity.)

Each view passes the same three variables—app, user, and ip_address—to its template.
Wouldn't it be nice if we could remove that redundancy?

RequestContext and *context processors* were created to solve this problem. Context
processors let you specify a number of variables that get set in each context automatically—
without you having to specify the variables in each render_to_response() call. The catch is
that you have to use RequestContext instead of Context when you render a template.

The most low-level way of using context processors is to create some processors and pass
them to RequestContext. Here's how the preceding example could be written with context
processors:

```
from django.template import loader, RequestContext

def custom_proc(request):
    "A context processor that provides 'app', 'user' and 'ip_address'."
    return {
        'app': 'My app',
        'user': request.user,
        'ip_address': request.META['REMOTE_ADDR']
    }

def view_1(request):
    # ...
    t = loader.get_template('template1.html')
    c = RequestContext(request, {'message': 'I am view 1.'},
            processors=[custom_proc])
    return t.render(c)
```

```
def view_2(request):
    # ...
    t = loader.get_template('template2.html')
    c = RequestContext(request, {'message': 'I am the second view.'},
            processors=[custom_proc])
    return t.render(c)

def view_3(request):
    # ...
    t = loader.get_template('template3.html')
    c = RequestContext(request, {'message': 'I am the third view.'},
            processors=[custom_proc])
    return t.render(c)

def view_4(request):
    # ...
    t = loader.get_template('template4.html')
    c = RequestContext(request, {'message': 'I am the fourth view.'},
            processors=[custom_proc])
    return t.render(c)
```

Let's step through this code:

- First, we define a function custom_proc. This is a context processor—it takes an HttpRequest object and returns a dictionary of variables to use in the template context. That's all it does.

- We've changed the four view functions to use RequestContext instead of Context. There are two differences in how the context is constructed. First, RequestContext requires the first argument to be an HttpRequest object—the one that was passed into the view function in the first place (request). Second, RequestContext takes an optional processors argument, which is a list or tuple of context processor functions to use. Here, we pass in custom_proc, the custom processor we defined earlier.

- Each view no longer has to include app, user, or ip_address in its context construction, because those are provided by custom_proc.

- Each view *still* has the flexibility to introduce any custom template variables it might need. In this example, the message template variable is set differently in each view.

In Chapter 4, we introduced the render_to_response() shortcut, which saves you from having to call loader.get_template(), then create a Context, and then call the render() method on the template. In order to demonstrate the lower-level workings of context processors, the previous examples didn't use render_to_response(). But it's possible—and preferable—to use context processors with render_to_response(). Do this with the context_instance argument, like so:

```
from django.shortcuts import render_to_response
from django.template import RequestContext
```

```
def custom_proc(request):
    "A context processor that provides 'app', 'user' and 'ip_address'."
    return {
        'app': 'My app',
        'user': request.user,
        'ip_address': request.META['REMOTE_ADDR']
    }

def view_1(request):
    # ...
    return render_to_response('template1.html',
        {'message': 'I am view 1.'},
        context_instance=RequestContext(request, processors=[custom_proc]))

def view_2(request):
    # ...
    return render_to_response('template2.html',
        {'message': 'I am the second view.'},
        context_instance=RequestContext(request, processors=[custom_proc]))

def view_3(request):
    # ...
    return render_to_response('template3.html',
        {'message': 'I am the third view.'},
        context_instance=RequestContext(request, processors=[custom_proc]))

def view_4(request):
    # ...
    return render_to_response('template4.html',
        {'message': 'I am the fourth view.'},
        context_instance=RequestContext(request, processors=[custom_proc]))
```

Here, we've trimmed down each view's template rendering code to a single (wrapped) line.

This is an improvement, but, evaluating the conciseness of this code, we have to admit we're now almost overdosing on the *other* end of the spectrum. We've removed redundancy in data (our template variables) at the cost of adding redundancy in code (in the processors call). Using context processors doesn't save you much typing if you have to type processors all the time.

For that reason, Django provides support for *global* context processors. The TEMPLATE_CONTEXT_PROCESSORS setting designates which context processors should *always* be applied to RequestContext. This removes the need to specify processors each time you use RequestContext.

By default, TEMPLATE_CONTEXT_PROCESSORS is set to the following:

```
TEMPLATE_CONTEXT_PROCESSORS = (
    'django.core.context_processors.auth',
    'django.core.context_processors.debug',
    'django.core.context_processors.i18n',
)
```

This setting is a tuple of callables that use the same interface as the preceding custom_ proc function—functions that take a request object as their argument and return a dictionary of items to be merged into the context. Note that the values in TEMPLATE_CONTEXT_PROCESSORS are specified as *strings*, which means the processors are required to be somewhere on your Python path (so you can refer to them from the setting).

Each processor is applied in order. That is, if one processor adds a variable to the context and a second processor adds a variable with the same name, the second will override the first.

Django provides a number of simple context processors, including the ones that are enabled by default. We describe these in the sections that follow.

django.core.context_processors.auth

If TEMPLATE_CONTEXT_PROCESSORS contains this processor, every RequestContext will contain these variables:

- user: A django.contrib.auth.models.User instance representing the currently logged-in user (or an AnonymousUser instance, if the client isn't logged in).

- messages: A list of messages (as strings) for the currently logged-in user. Behind the scenes, this variable calls request.user.get_and_delete_messages() for every request. That method collects the user's messages and deletes them from the database.

- perms: An instance of django.core.context_processors.PermWrapper, which represents the permissions the currently logged-in user has.

See Chapter 12 for more information on users, permissions, and messages.

django.core.context_processors.debug

This processor pushes debugging information down to the template layer. If TEMPLATE_CONTEXT_ PROCESSORS contains this processor, every RequestContext will contain these variables:

- debug: The value of your DEBUG setting (either True or False). You can use this variable in templates to test whether you're in debug mode.

- sql_queries: A list of {'sql': ..., 'time': ...} dictionaries representing every SQL query that has happened so far during the request and how long it took. The list is in the order in which the queries were issued.

Because debugging information is sensitive, this context processor will add variables to the context only if both of the following conditions are true:

- The DEBUG setting is True.

- The request came from an IP address in the INTERNAL_IPS setting.

django.core.context_processors.i18n

If this processor is enabled, every RequestContext will contain these variables:

- LANGUAGES: The value of the LANGUAGES setting

- LANGUAGE_CODE: request.LANGUAGE_CODE if it exists; otherwise, the value of the LANGUAGE_CODE setting

Appendix E provides more information about these two settings.

django.core.context_processors.request

If this processor is enabled, every RequestContext will contain a variable request, which is the current HttpRequest object. Note that this processor is not enabled by default; you have to activate it.

Guidelines for Writing Your Own Context Processors

Here are a few tips for rolling your own:

- Make each context processor responsible for the smallest subset of functionality possible. It's easy to use multiple processors, so you might as well split functionality into logical pieces for future reuse.

- Keep in mind that any context processor in TEMPLATE_CONTEXT_PROCESSORS will be available in *every* template powered by that settings file, so try to pick variable names that are unlikely to conflict with variable names your templates might be using independently. Because variable names are case sensitive, it's not a bad idea to use all uppercase letters for variables a processor provides.

- It doesn't matter where on the filesystem the processors live, as long as they're on your Python path so you can point to them from the TEMPLATE_CONTEXT_PROCESSORS setting. With that said, the convention is to save them in a file called context_processors.py within your application or project.

Inside Template Loading

Generally, you'll store templates in files on your filesystem, but you can use custom *template loaders* to load templates from other sources.

Django has two ways to load templates:

- django.template.loader.get_template(template_name): get_template returns the compiled template (a Template object) for the template with the given name. If the template doesn't exist, a TemplateDoesNotExist exception will be raised.

- django.template.loader.select_template(template_name_list): select_template is just like get_template, except it takes a list of template names. Of the list, it returns the first template that exists. If none of the templates exist, a TemplateDoesNotExist exception will be raised.

As covered in Chapter 4, each of these functions by default uses your `TEMPLATE_DIRS` setting to load templates. Internally, however, these functions actually delegate to a template loader for the heavy lifting.

Some of loaders are disabled by default, but you can activate them by editing the `TEMPLATE_LOADERS` setting. `TEMPLATE_LOADERS` should be a tuple of strings, where each string represents a template loader. These template loaders ship with Django:

- `django.template.loaders.filesystem.load_template_source`: This loader loads templates from the filesystem, according to `TEMPLATE_DIRS`. It is enabled by default.

- `django.template.loaders.app_directories.load_template_source`: This loader loads templates from Django applications on the filesystem. For each application in `INSTALLED_APPS`, the loader looks for a `templates` subdirectory. If the directory exists, Django looks for templates there.

  This means you can store templates with your individual applications, making it easy to distribute Django applications with default templates. For example, if `INSTALLED_APPS` contains (`'myproject.polls'`, `'myproject.music'`), then `get_template('foo.html')` will look for templates in this order:

  - `/path/to/myproject/polls/templates/foo.html`

  - `/path/to/myproject/music/templates/foo.html`

  Note that the loader performs an optimization when it is first imported: it caches a list of the `INSTALLED_APPS` packages that have a `templates` subdirectory. This loader is enabled by default.

- `django.template.loaders.eggs.load_template_source`: This loader is just like `app_directories`, except it loads templates from Python eggs rather than from the filesystem. This loader is disabled by default; you'll need to enable it if you're using eggs to distribute your application.

Django uses the template loaders in order according to the `TEMPLATE_LOADERS` setting. It uses each loader until a loader finds a match.

Extending the Template System

Now that you understand a bit more about the internals of the template system, let's look at how to extend the system with custom code.

Most template customization comes in the form of custom template tags and/or filters. Although the Django template language comes with many built-in tags and filters, you'll probably assemble your own libraries of tags and filters that fit your own needs. Fortunately, it's quite easy to define your own functionality.

Creating a Template Library

Whether you're writing custom tags or filters, the first thing to do is to create a *template library*—a small bit of infrastructure Django can hook into.

Creating a template library is a two-step process:

1. Decide which Django application should house the template library. If you've created an application via manage.py startapp, you can put it in there, or you can create another application solely for the template library.

   Whichever route you take, make sure to add the application to your INSTALLED_APPS setting. We'll explain this shortly.

2. Create a templatetags directory in the appropriate Django application's package. It should be on the same level as models.py, views.py, and so forth. Here's an example:

   ```
   books/
       __init__.py
       models.py
       templatetags/
       views.py
   ```

   Create two empty files in the templatetags directory: an __init__.py file (to indicate to Python that this is a package containing Python code) and a file that will contain your custom tag/filter definitions. The name of the latter file is what you'll use to load the tags later. For example, if your custom tags/filters are in a file called poll_extras.py, you'd write the following in a template:

   ```
   {% load poll_extras %}
   ```

   The {% load %} tag looks at your INSTALLED_APPS setting and only allows the loading of template libraries within installed Django applications. This is a security feature; it allows you to host Python code for many template libraries on a single computer without enabling access to all of them for every Django installation.

If you write a template library that isn't tied to any particular models/views, it's valid and quite normal to have a Django application package that contains only a templatetags package. There's no limit on how many modules you put in the templatetags package. Just keep in mind that a {% load %} statement will load tags/filters for the given Python module name, not the name of the application.

Once you've created that Python module, you'll just have to write a bit of Python code, depending on whether you're writing filters or tags.

To be a valid tag library, the module must contain a module-level variable named register that is a template.Library instance. This template.Library instance is the data structure in which all the tags and filters are registered. So, near the top of your module, insert the following:

```
from django import template

register = template.Library()
```

Note For a good number of examples, read the source code for Django's default filters and tags. They're in django/template/defaultfilters.py and django/template/defaulttags.py, respectively. Some applications in django.contrib also contain template libraries.

Once you've created this register variable, you'll use it to create template filters and tags.

Writing Custom Template Filters

Custom filters are just Python functions that take one or two arguments:

- The value of the variable (input)

- The value of the argument, which can have a default value or be left out altogether

For example, in the filter {{ var|foo:"bar" }}, the filter foo would be passed the contents of the variable var and the argument "bar".

Filter functions should always return something. They shouldn't raise exceptions, and they should fail silently. If there's an error, they should return either the original input or an empty string, whichever makes more sense.

Here's an example filter definition:

```
def cut(value, arg):
    "Removes all values of arg from the given string"
    return value.replace(arg, '')
```

And here's an example of how that filter would be used:

```
{{ somevariable|cut:"0" }}
```

Most filters don't take arguments. In this case, just leave the argument out of your function:

```
def lower(value): # Only one argument.
    "Converts a string into all lowercase"
    return value.lower()
```

When you've written your filter definition, you need to register it with your Library instance, to make it available to Django's template language:

```
register.filter('cut', cut)
register.filter('lower', lower)
```

The Library.filter() method takes two arguments:

- The name of the filter (a string)

- The filter function itself

If you're using Python 2.4 or above, you can use register.filter() as a decorator instead:

```
@register.filter(name='cut')
def cut(value, arg):
    return value.replace(arg, '')

@register.filter
def lower(value):
    return value.lower()
```

If you leave off the name argument, as in the second example, Django will use the function's name as the filter name.

Here, then, is a complete template library example, using the cut filter:

```
from django import template

register = template.Library()

@register.filter(name='cut')
def cut(value, arg):
    return value.replace(arg, '')
```

Writing Custom Template Tags

Tags are more complex than filters, because tags can do nearly anything.

Chapter 4 describes how the template system works in a two-step process: compiling and rendering. To define a custom template tag, you need to tell Django how to manage both steps when it gets to your tag.

When Django compiles a template, it splits the raw template text into *nodes*. Each node is an instance of django.template.Node and has a render() method. Thus, a compiled template is simply a list of Node objects.

When you call render() on a compiled template, the template calls render() on each Node in its node list, with the given context. The results are all concatenated to form the output of the template. Thus, to define a custom template tag, you specify how the raw template tag is converted into a Node (the compilation function) and what the node's render() method does.

In the sections that follow, we cover all the steps in writing a custom tag.

Writing the Compilation Function

For each template tag it encounters, the template parser calls a Python function with the tag contents and the parser object itself. This function is responsible for returning a Node instance based on the contents of the tag.

For example, let's write a template tag, {% current_time %}, that displays the current date/time, formatted according to a parameter given in the tag, in strftime syntax (see http://www.djangoproject.com/r/python/strftime/). It's a good idea to decide the tag syntax before anything else. In our case, let's say the tag should be used like this:

```
<p>The time is {% current_time "%Y-%m-%d %I:%M %p" %}.</p>
```

■Note Yes, this template tag is redundant—Django's default {% now %} tag does the same task with simpler syntax. This template tag is presented here just for example purposes.

The parser for this function should grab the parameter and create a `Ode` object:

```
from django import template

def do_current_time(parser, token):
    try:
        # split_contents() knows not to split quoted strings.
        tag_name, format_string = token.split_contents()
    except ValueError:
        msg = '%r tag requires a single argument' % token.contents[0]
        raise template.TemplateSyntaxError(msg)
    return CurrentTimeNode(format_string[1:-1])
```

There's actually a lot going on here:

- `parser` is the template parser object. We don't need it in this example.

- `token.contents` is a string of the raw contents of the tag. In our example, it's `'current_time "%Y-%m-%d %I:%M %p"'`.

- The `token.split_contents()` method separates the arguments on spaces while keeping quoted strings together. Avoid using `token.contents.split()` (which just uses Python's standard string-splitting semantics). It's not as robust, as it naively splits on *all* spaces, including those within quoted strings.

- This function is responsible for raising `django.template.TemplateSyntaxError`, with helpful messages, for any syntax error.

- Don't hard-code the tag's name in your error messages, because that couples the tag's name to your function. `token.split_contents()[0]` will *always* be the name of your tag—even when the tag has no arguments.

- The function returns a `CurrentTimeNode` (which we'll create shortly) containing everything the node needs to know about this tag. In this case, it just passes the argument `"%Y-%m-%d %I:%M %p"`. The leading and trailing quotes from the template tag are removed with `format_string[1:-1]`.

- Template tag compilation functions *must* return a `Node` subclass; any other return value is an error.

Writing the Template Node

The second step in writing custom tags is to define a `Node` subclass that has a `render()` method. Continuing the preceding example, we need to define `CurrentTimeNode`:

```
import datetime

class CurrentTimeNode(template.Node):

    def __init__(self, format_string):
        self.format_string = format_string
```

```
def render(self, context):
    now = datetime.datetime.now()
    return now.strftime(self.format_string)
```

These two functions (__init__ and render) map directly to the two steps in template processing (compilation and rendering). Thus, the initialization function only needs to store the format string for later use, and the render() function does the real work.

Like template filters, these rendering functions should fail silently instead of raising errors. The only time that template tags are allowed to raise errors is at compilation time.

Registering the Tag

Finally, you need to register the tag with your module's Library instance. Registering custom tags is very similar to registering custom filters (as explained previously). Just instantiate a template.Library instance and call its tag() method, for example:

```
register.tag('current_time', do_current_time)
```

The tag() method takes two arguments:

- The name of the template tag (string). If this is left out, the name of the compilation function will be used.

- The compilation function.

As with filter registration, it is also possible to use register.tag as a decorator in Python 2.4 and above:

```
@register.tag(name="current_time")
def do_current_time(parser, token):
    # ...


@register.tag
def shout(parser, token):
    # ...
```

If you leave off the name argument, as in the second example, Django will use the function's name as the tag name.

Setting a Variable in the Context

The previous section's example simply returned a value. Often it's useful to set template variables instead of returning values. That way, template authors can just use the variables that your template tags set.

To set a variable in the context, use dictionary assignment on the context object in the render() method. Here's an updated version of CurrentTimeNode that sets a template variable, current_time, instead of returning it:

```
class CurrentTimeNode2(template.Node):

    def __init__(self, format_string):
        self.format_string = format_string
```

```
def render(self, context):
    now = datetime.datetime.now()
    context['current_time'] = now.strftime(self.format_string)
    return ''
```

Note that render() returns an empty string. render() should always return a string, so if all the template tag does is set a variable, render() should return an empty string.

Here's how you'd use this new version of the tag:

```
{% current_time2 "%Y-%M-%d %I:%M %p" %}
<p>The time is {{ current_time }}.</p>
```

But there's a problem with CurrentTimeNode2: the variable name current_time is hard-coded. This means you'll need to make sure your template doesn't use {{ current_time }} anywhere else, because {% current_time2 %} will blindly overwrite that variable's value.

A cleaner solution is to make the template tag specify the name of the variable to be set, like so:

```
{% get_current_time "%Y-%M-%d %I:%M %p" as my_current_time %}
<p>The current time is {{ my_current_time }}.</p>
```

To do so, you'll need to refactor both the compilation function and the Node class, as follows:

```
import re

class CurrentTimeNode3(template.Node):

    def __init__(self, format_string, var_name):
        self.format_string = format_string
        self.var_name = var_name

    def render(self, context):
        now = datetime.datetime.now()
        context[self.var_name] = now.strftime(self.format_string)
        return ''

def do_current_time(parser, token):
    # This version uses a regular expression to parse tag contents.
    try:
        # Splitting by None == splitting by spaces.
        tag_name, arg = token.contents.split(None, 1)
    except ValueError:
        msg = '%r tag requires arguments' % token.contents[0]
        raise template.TemplateSyntaxError(msg)

    m = re.search(r'(.*?) as (\w+)', arg)
    if m:
        fmt, var_name = m.groups()
```

```
    else:
        msg = '%r tag had invalid arguments' % tag_name
        raise template.TemplateSyntaxError(msg)

    if not (fmt[0] == fmt[-1] and fmt[0] in ('"', "'")):
        msg = "%r tag's argument should be in quotes" % tag_name
        raise template.TemplateSyntaxError(msg)

    return CurrentTimeNode3(fmt[1:-1], var_name)
```

Now do_current_time() passes the format string and the variable name to CurrentTimeNode3.

Parsing Until Another Block Tag

Template tags can work as blocks containing other tags (think {% if %}, {% for %}, etc.). To create a template tag like this, use parser.parse() in your compilation function.

Here's how the standard {% comment %} tag is implemented:

```
def do_comment(parser, token):
    nodelist = parser.parse(('endcomment',))
    parser.delete_first_token()
    return CommentNode()

class CommentNode(template.Node):
    def render(self, context):
        return ''
```

parser.parse() takes a tuple of names of block tags to parse until. It returns an instance of django.template.NodeList, which is a list of all Node objects that the parser encountered *before* it encountered any of the tags named in the tuple. So in the preceding example, nodelist is a list of all nodes between {% comment %} and {% endcomment %}, not counting {% comment %} and {% endcomment %} themselves.

After parser.parse() is called, the parser hasn't yet "consumed" the {% endcomment %} tag, so the code needs to explicitly call parser.delete_first_token() to prevent that tag from being processed twice.

Then CommentNode.render() simply returns an empty string. Anything between {% comment %} and {% endcomment %} is ignored.

Parsing Until Another Block Tag and Saving Contents

In the previous example, do_comment() discarded everything between {% comment %} and {% endcomment %}. It's also possible to do something with the code between block tags instead.

For example, here's a custom template tag, {% upper %}, that capitalizes everything between itself and {% endupper %}:

```
{% upper %}
    This will appear in uppercase, {{ your_name }}.
{% endupper %}
```

As in the previous example, we'll use parser.parse(). This time, we pass the resulting nodelist to Node:

```
@register.tag
def do_upper(parser, token):
    nodelist = parser.parse(('endupper',))
    parser.delete_first_token()
    return UpperNode(nodelist)

class UpperNode(template.Node):

    def __init__(self, nodelist):
        self.nodelist = nodelist

    def render(self, context):
        output = self.nodelist.render(context)
        return output.upper()
```

The only new concept here is self.nodelist.render(context) in UpperNode.render(). This simply calls render() on each Node in the node list.

For more examples of complex rendering, see the source code for {% if %}, {% for %}, {% ifequal %}, and {% ifchanged %}. They live in django/template/defaulttags.py.

Shortcut for Simple Tags

Many template tags take a single argument—a string or a template variable reference—and return a string after doing some processing based solely on the input argument and some external information. For example, the current_time tag we wrote earlier is of this variety. We give it a format string, and it returns the time as a string.

To ease the creation of these types of tags, Django provides a helper function, simple_tag. This function, which is a method of django.template.Library, takes a function that accepts one argument, wraps it in a render function and the other necessary bits mentioned previously, and registers it with the template system.

Our earlier current_time function could thus be written like this:

```
def current_time(format_string):
    return datetime.datetime.now().strftime(format_string)

register.simple_tag(current_time)
```

In Python 2.4, the decorator syntax also works:

```
@register.simple_tag
def current_time(token):
    ...
```

A couple of things to notice about the `simple_tag` helper function are as follows:

- Only the (single) argument is passed into our function.

- Checking for the required number of arguments has already been done by the time our function is called, so we don't need to do that.

- The quotes around the argument (if any) have already been stripped away, so we receive a plain string.

Inclusion Tags

Another common template tag is the type that displays some data by rendering *another* template. For example, Django's admin interface uses custom template tags to display the buttons along the bottom of the "add/change" form pages. Those buttons always look the same, but the link targets change depending on the object being edited. They're a perfect case for using a small template that is filled with details from the current object.

These sorts of tags are called *inclusion tags*. Writing inclusion tags is probably best demonstrated by example. Let's write a tag that produces a list of choices for a simple multiple-choice Poll object. We'll use the tag like this:

```
{% show_results poll %}
```

The result will be something like this:

```
<ul>
  <li>First choice</li>
  <li>Second choice</li>
  <li>Third choice</li>
</ul>
```

First, we define the function that takes the argument and produces a dictionary of data for the result. Notice that we need to return only a dictionary, not anything more complex. This will be used as the context for the template fragment:

```
def show_results(poll):
    choices = poll.choice_set.all()
    return {'choices': choices}
```

Next, we create the template used to render the tag's output. Following our example, the template is very simple:

```
<ul>
{% for choice in choices %}
    <li> {{ choice }} </li>
{% endfor %}
</ul>
```

Finally, we create and register the inclusion tag by calling the `inclusion_tag()` method on a `Library` object.

Following our example, if the preceding template is in a file called `polls/result_snippet.html`, we register the tag like this:

```
register.inclusion_tag('polls/result_snippet.html')(show_results)
```

As always, Python 2.4 decorator syntax works as well, so we could have instead written this:

```
@register.inclusion_tag('results.html')
def show_results(poll):
    ...
```

Sometimes, your inclusion tags need access to values from the parent template's context. To solve this, Django provides a `takes_context` option for inclusion tags. If you specify `takes_context` in creating a template tag, the tag will have no required arguments, and the underlying Python function will have one argument: the template context as of when the tag was called.

For example, say you're writing an inclusion tag that will always be used in a context that contains `home_link` and `home_title` variables that point back to the main page. Here's what the Python function would look like:

```
@register.inclusion_tag('link.html', takes_context=True)
def jump_link(context):
    return {
        'link': context['home_link'],
        'title': context['home_title'],
    }
```

■**Note** The first parameter to the function *must* be called `context`.

The template `link.html` might contain the following:

```
Jump directly to <a href="{{ link }}">{{ title }}</a>.
```

Then, anytime you want to use that custom tag, load its library and call it without any arguments, like so:

```
{% jump_link %}
```

Writing Custom Template Loaders

Django's built-in template loaders (described in the "Inside Template Loading" section) will usually cover all your template-loading needs, but it's pretty easy to write your own if you need special loading logic. For example, you could load templates from a database, or directly from a Subversion repository using Subversion's Python bindings, or (as shown shortly) from a ZIP archive.

A template loader—that is, each entry in the `TEMPLATE_LOADERS` setting—is expected to be a callable with this interface:

```
load_template_source(template_name, template_dirs=None)
```

The template_name argument is the name of the template to load (as passed to loader.get_template() or loader.select_template()), and template_dirs is an optional list of directories to search instead of TEMPLATE_DIRS.

If a loader is able to successfully load a template, it should return a tuple: (template_source, template_path). Here, template_source is the template string that will be compiled by the template engine, and template_path is the path the template was loaded from. That path might be shown to the user for debugging purposes, so it should quickly identify where the template was loaded from.

If the loader is unable to load a template, it should raise django.template. TemplateDoesNotExist.

Each loader function should also have an is_usable function attribute. This is a Boolean that informs the template engine whether this loader is available in the current Python installation. For example, the eggs loader (which is capable of loading templates from Python eggs) sets is_usable to False if the pkg_resources module isn't installed, because pkg_resources is necessary to read data from eggs.

An example should help clarify all of this. Here's a template loader function that can load templates from a ZIP file. It uses a custom setting, TEMPLATE_ZIP_FILES, as a search path instead of TEMPLATE_DIRS, and it expects each item on that path to be a ZIP file containing templates:

```python
import zipfile
from django.conf import settings
from django.template import TemplateDoesNotExist

def load_template_source(template_name, template_dirs=None):
    """Template loader that loads templates from a ZIP file."""

    # Look up ZIP file list from settings if it's not already given.
    template_zipfiles = getattr(settings, "TEMPLATE_ZIP_FILES", [])
    # Try each ZIP file in TEMPLATE_ZIP_FILES.
    for fname in template_zipfiles:
        try:
            z = zipfile.ZipFile(fname)
            source = z.read(template_name)
        except (IOError, KeyError):
            continue

        # We found a template, so return the source.
        template_path = "%s:%s" % (fname, template_name)
        return (source, template_path)

    # If we reach here, the template couldn't be loaded
    raise TemplateDoesNotExist(template_name)

# This loader is always usable (since zipfile is included with Python)
load_template_source.is_usable = True
```

The only step left if we want to use this loader is to add it to the TEMPLATE_LOADERS setting. If we put this code in a module called mysite.zip_loader, then we add mysite.zip_loader.load_template_source to TEMPLATE_LOADERS.

Using the Built-in Template Reference

Django's admin interface includes a complete reference of all template tags and filters available for a given site. It's designed to be a tool that Django programmers give to template developers. To see it, go to the admin interface and click the Documentation link at the upper right of the page.

The reference is divided into four sections: tags, filters, models, and views. The *tags* and *filters* sections describe all the built-in tags (in fact, the tag and filter references in Chapter 4 come directly from those pages) as well as any custom tag or filter libraries available.

The *views* page is the most valuable. Each URL in your site has a separate entry here, and clicking a URL will show you the following:

- The name of the view function that generates that view

- A short description of what the view does

- The context, or a list of variables available in the view's template

- The name of the template or templates that are used for that view

Because Django-powered sites usually use database objects, the *models* pages describe each type of object in the system along with all the fields available on that object.

Taken together, the documentation pages should tell you every tag, filter, variable, and object available to you in a given template.

Configuring the Template System in Standalone Mode

■**Note** This section is only of interest to people trying to use the template system as an output component in another application. If you are using the template system as part of a Django application, the information presented here doesn't apply to you.

Normally, Django will load all the configuration information it needs from its own default configuration file, combined with the settings in the module given in the DJANGO_SETTINGS_MODULE environment variable. But if you're using the template system independently of the rest of Django, the environment variable approach isn't very convenient, because you probably want to configure the template system in line with the rest of your application rather than dealing with settings files and pointing to them via environment variables.

To solve this problem, you need to use the manual configuration option described fully in Appendix E. In a nutshell, you need to import the appropriate pieces of the template system and then, *before* you call any of the template functions, call `django.conf.settings.configure()` with any settings you wish to specify.

You might want to consider setting at least `TEMPLATE_DIRS` (if you are going to use template loaders), `DEFAULT_CHARSET` (although the default of `utf-8` is probably fine), and `TEMPLATE_DEBUG`. All available settings are described in Appendix E, and any setting starting with `TEMPLATE_` is of obvious interest.

What's Next?

So far this book has assumed that the content you're displaying is HTML. This isn't a bad assumption for a book about Web development, but at times you'll want to use Django to output other data formats. The next chapter describes how you can use Django to produce images, PDFs, and any other data format you can imagine.

CHAPTER 11

■ ■ ■

Generating Non-HTML Content

Usually when we talk about developing Web sites, we're talking about producing HTML. Of course, there's a lot more to the Web than HTML; we use the Web to distribute data in all sorts of formats: RSS, PDFs, images, and so forth.

So far we've focused on the common case of HTML production, but in this chapter we'll take a detour and look at using Django to produce other types of content.

Django has convenient built-in tools that you can use to produce some common non-HTML content:

- RSS/Atom syndication feeds

- Sitemaps (an XML format originally developed by Google that gives hints to search engines)

We'll examine each of those tools a little later on, but first we'll cover the basic principles.

The Basics: Views and MIME Types

Remember this from Chapter 3?

> *A view function, or view for short, is simply a Python function that takes a Web request and returns a Web response. This response can be the HTML contents of a Web page, or a redirect, or a 404 error, or an XML document, or an image . . . or anything, really.*

More formally, a Django view function must

- Accept an `HttpRequest` instance as its first argument

- Return an `HttpResponse` instance

The key to returning non-HTML content from a view lies in the `HttpResponse` class, specifically the `mimetype` constructor argument. By tweaking the MIME type, we can indicate to the browser that we've returned a response of a different format.

For example, let's look at a view that returns a PNG image. To keep things simple, we'll just read the file off the disk:

```
from django.http import HttpResponse

def my_image(request):
    image_data = open("/path/to/my/image.png", "rb").read()
    return HttpResponse(image_data, mimetype="image/png")
```

That's it! If you replace the image path in the open() call with a path to a real image, you can use this very simple view to serve an image, and the browser will display it correctly.

The other important thing to keep in mind is that HttpResponse objects implement Python's standard file API. This means that you can use an HttpResponse instance in any place Python (or a third-party library) expects a file.

For an example of how that works, let's take a look at producing CSV with Django.

Producing CSV

CSV is a simple data format usually used by spreadsheet software. It's basically a series of table rows, with each cell in the row separated by a comma (CSV stands for comma-separated values). For example, here's some data on "unruly" airline passengers in CSV format:

```
Year,Unruly Airline Passengers
1995,146
1996,184
1997,235
1998,200
1999,226
2000,251
2001,299
2002,273
2003,281
2004,304
2005,203
```

The preceding listing contains real numbers; they come courtesy of the US Federal Aviation Administration. See http://www.faa.gov/data_statistics/passengers_cargo/unruly_passengers/.

Though CSV looks simple, it's not a format that's ever been formally defined. Different pieces of software produce and consume different variants of CSV, making it a bit tricky to use. Luckily, Python comes with a standard CSV library, csv, that is pretty much bulletproof.

Because the csv module operates on filelike objects, it's a snap to use an HttpResponse instead:

```
import csv
from django.http import HttpResponse
```

```
# Number of unruly passengers each year 1995 - 2005. In a real application
# this would likely come from a database or some other back-end data store.
UNRULY_PASSENGERS = [146,184,235,200,226,251,299,273,281,304,203]

def unruly_passengers_csv(request):
    # Create the HttpResponse object with the appropriate CSV header.
    response = HttpResponse(mimetype='text/csv')
    response['Content-Disposition'] = 'attachment; filename=unruly.csv'

    # Create the CSV writer using the HttpResponse as the "file"
    writer = csv.writer(response)
    writer.writerow(['Year', 'Unruly Airline Passengers'])
    for (year, num) in zip(range(1995, 2006), UNRULY_PASSENGERS):
        writer.writerow([year, num])

    return response
```

The code and comments should be pretty clear, but a few things deserve special mention:

- The response is given the text/csv MIME type (instead of the default text/html). This tells browsers that the document is a CSV file.

- The response gets an additional Content-Disposition header, which contains the name of the CSV file. This header (well, the "attachment" part) will instruct the browser to prompt for a location to save the file (instead of just displaying it). This file name is arbitrary; call it whatever you want. It will be used by browsers in the Save As dialog.

- Hooking into the CSV-generation API is easy: just pass response as the first argument to csv.writer. The csv.writer function expects a filelike object, and HttpResponse objects fit the bill.

- For each row in your CSV file, call writer.writerow, passing it an iterable object such as a list or tuple.

- The CSV module takes care of quoting for you, so you don't have to worry about escaping strings with quotes or commas in them. Just pass information to writerow(), and it will do the right thing.

This is the general pattern you'll use any time you need to return non-HTML content: create an HttpResponse response object (with a special MIME type), pass it to something expecting a file, and then return the response.

Let's look at a few more examples.

Generating PDFs

Portable Document Format (PDF) is a format developed by Adobe that's used to represent printable documents, complete with pixel-perfect formatting, embedded fonts, and 2D vector graphics. You can think of a PDF document as the digital equivalent of a printed document; indeed, PDFs are usually used when someone needs to give a document to someone else to print.

You can easily generate PDFs with Python and Django thanks to the excellent open source ReportLab library (`http://www.reportlab.org/rl_toolkit.html`). The advantage of generating PDF files dynamically is that you can create customized PDFs for different purposes—say, for different users or different pieces of content.

For example, we used Django and ReportLab at KUSports.com to generate customized, printer-ready NCAA tournament brackets.

Installing ReportLab

Before you do any PDF generation, however, you'll need to install ReportLab. It's usually pretty simple: just download and install the library from `http://www.reportlab.org/downloads.html`. The user guide (naturally available only as a PDF file) at `http://www.reportlab.org/rsrc/userguide.pdf` has additional installation instructions.

If you're using a modern Linux distribution, you might want to check your package management utility before installing ReportLab. Most package repositories have added ReportLab. For example, if you're using the (excellent) Ubuntu distribution, a simple `apt-get install python-reportlab` will do the trick nicely.

Test your installation by importing it in the Python interactive interpreter:

```
>>> import reportlab
```

If that command doesn't raise any errors, the installation worked.

Writing Your View

Like CSV, generating PDFs dynamically with Django is easy because the ReportLab API acts on filelike objects. Here's a "Hello World" example:

```
from reportlab.pdfgen import canvas
from django.http import HttpResponse

def hello_pdf(request):
    # Create the HttpResponse object with the appropriate PDF headers.
    response = HttpResponse(mimetype='application/pdf')
    response['Content-Disposition'] = 'attachment; filename=hello.pdf'

    # Create the PDF object, using the response object as its "file."
    p = canvas.Canvas(response)

    # Draw things on the PDF. Here's where the PDF generation happens.
    # See the ReportLab documentation for the full list of functionality.
    p.drawString(100, 100, "Hello world.")

    # Close the PDF object cleanly, and we're done.
    p.showPage()
    p.save()
    return response
```

A few notes are in order:

- Here we use the application/pdf MIME type. This tells browsers that the document is a PDF file, rather than an HTML file. If you leave off this information, browsers will probably interpret the response as HTML, which will result in scary gobbledygook in the browser window.

- Hooking into the ReportLab API is easy: just pass response as the first argument to canvas.Canvas. The Canvas class expects a filelike object, and HttpResponse objects fit the bill.

- All subsequent PDF-generation methods are called on the PDF object (in this case, p), not on response.

- Finally, it's important to call showPage() and save() on the PDF file (or you'll end up with a corrupted PDF file).

Complex PDFs

If you're creating a complex PDF document (or any large data blob), consider using the cStringIO library as a temporary holding place for your PDF file. The cStringIO library provides a filelike object interface that is written in C for maximum efficiency.

Here's the previous "Hello World" example rewritten to use cStringIO:

```
from cStringIO import StringIO
from reportlab.pdfgen import canvas
from django.http import HttpResponse

def hello_pdf(request):
    # Create the HttpResponse object with the appropriate PDF headers.
    response = HttpResponse(mimetype='application/pdf')
    response['Content-Disposition'] = 'attachment; filename=hello.pdf'

    pdfbuffer = StringIO()

    # Create the PDF object, using the StringIO object as its "file."
    p = canvas.Canvas(pdfbuffer)

    # Draw things on the PDF. Here's where the PDF generation happens.
    # See the ReportLab documentation for the full list of functionality.
    p.drawString(100, 100, "Hello world.")

    # Close the PDF object cleanly.
    p.showPage()
    p.save()

    # Get the value of the StringIO buffer and write it to the response.
    response.write(pdfbuffer.getvalue())
    return response
```

Other Possibilities

There's a whole host of other types of content you can generate in Python. Here are a few more ideas and some pointers to libraries you could use to implement them:

- *ZIP files*: Python's standard library ships with the `zipfile` module, which can both read and write compressed ZIP files. You could use it to provide on-demand archives of a bunch of files, or perhaps compress large documents when requested. You could similarly produce TAR files using the standard library `tarfile` module.

- *Dynamic images*: The Python Imaging Library (PIL; `http://www.pythonware.com/products/pil/`) is a fantastic toolkit for producing images (PNG, JPEG, GIF, and a whole lot more). You could use it to automatically scale down images into thumbnails, composite multiple images into a single frame, or even do Web-based image processing.

- *Plots and charts*: There are a number of incredibly powerful Python plotting and charting libraries you could use to produce on-demand maps, charts, plots, and graphs. We can't possibly list them all, so here are a couple of the highlights:

  - `matplotlib` (`http://matplotlib.sourceforge.net/`) can be used to produce the type of high-quality plots usually generated with MatLab or Mathematica.

  - `pygraphviz` (`https://networkx.lanl.gov/wiki/pygraphviz`), an interface to the Graphviz graph layout toolkit (`http://graphviz.org/`), can be used for generating structured diagrams of graphs and networks.

In general, any Python library capable of writing to a file can be hooked into Django. The possibilities really are endless.

Now that we've looked at the basics of generating non-HTML content, let's step up a level of abstraction. Django ships with some pretty nifty built-in tools for generating some common types of non-HTML content.

The Syndication Feed Framework

Django comes with a high-level syndication feed–generating framework that makes creating RSS and Atom feeds easy.

■**Note** RSS and Atom are both XML-based formats you can use to provide automatically updating "feeds" of your site's content. Read more about RSS at `http://www.whatisrss.com/`, and get information on Atom at `http://www.atomenabled.org/`.

To create any syndication feed, all you have to do is write a short Python class. You can create as many feeds as you want.

The high-level feed-generating framework is a view that's hooked to `/feeds/` by convention. Django uses the remainder of the URL (everything after `/feeds/`) to determine which feed to return.

To create a feed, you'll write a `Feed` class and point to it in your URLconf (see Chapters 3 and 8 for more about URLconfs).

Initialization

To activate syndication feeds on your Django site, add this URLconf:

```
(r'^feeds/(?P<url>.*)/$',
 'django.contrib.syndication.views.feed',
 {'feed_dict': feeds}
),
```

This line tells Django to use the RSS framework to handle all URLs starting with `"feeds/"`. (You can change that `"feeds/"` prefix to fit your own needs.)

This URLconf line has an extra argument: `{'feed_dict': feeds}`. Use this extra argument to pass the syndication framework the feeds that should be published under that URL.

Specifically, `feed_dict` should be a dictionary that maps a feed's slug (a short URL label) to its `Feed` class. You can define the `feed_dict` in the URLconf itself. Here's a full example URLconf:

```
from django.conf.urls.defaults import *
from myproject.feeds import LatestEntries, LatestEntriesByCategory

feeds = {
    'latest': LatestEntries,
    'categories': LatestEntriesByCategory,
}

urlpatterns = patterns('',
    # ...
    (r'^feeds/(?P<url>.*)/$', 'django.contrib.syndication.views.feed',
        {'feed_dict': feeds}),
    # ...
)
```

The preceding example registers two feeds:

- The feed represented by `LatestEntries` will live at `feeds/latest/`.

- The feed represented by `LatestEntriesByCategory` will live at `feeds/categories/`.

Once that's set up, you'll need to define the `Feed` classes themselves.

A `Feed` class is a simple Python class that represents a syndication feed. A feed can be simple (e.g., a "site news" feed, or a basic feed displaying the latest entries of a blog) or more complex (e.g., a feed displaying all the blog entries in a particular category, where the category is variable).

`Feed` classes must subclass `django.contrib.syndication.feeds.Feed`. They can live anywhere in your code tree.

A Simple Feed

This simple example, taken from chicagocrime.org, describes a feed of the latest five news items:

```
from django.contrib.syndication.feeds import Feed
from chicagocrime.models import NewsItem

class LatestEntries(Feed):
    title = "Chicagocrime.org site news"
    link = "/sitenews/"
    description = "Updates on changes and additions to chicagocrime.org."

    def items(self):
        return NewsItem.objects.order_by('-pub_date')[:5]
```

The important things to notice here are as follows:

- The class subclasses `django.contrib.syndication.feeds.Feed`.

- `title`, `link`, and `description` correspond to the standard RSS `<title>`, `<link>`, and `<description>` elements, respectively.

- `items()` is simply a method that returns a list of objects that should be included in the feed as `<item>` elements. Although this example returns `NewsItem` objects using Django's database API, `items()` doesn't have to return model instances.

- You do get a few bits of functionality "for free" by using Django models, but `items()` can return any type of object you want.

There's just one more step. In an RSS feed, each `<item>` has a `<title>`, `<link>`, and `<description>`. We need to tell the framework what data to put into those elements.

- To specify the contents of `<title>` and `<description>`, create Django templates (see Chapter 4) called `feeds/latest_title.html` and `feeds/latest_description.html`, where `latest` is the `slug` specified in the URLconf for the given feed. Note that the `.html` extension is required. The RSS system renders that template for each item, passing it two template context variables:

  - `obj`: The current object (one of whichever objects you returned in `items()`).

  - `site`: A `django.models.core.sites.Site` object representing the current site. This is useful for `{{ site.domain }}` or `{{ site.name }}`.

  If you don't create a template for either the title or description, the framework will use the template `"{{ obj }}"` by default—that is, the normal string representation of the object.

  You can also change the names of these two templates by specifying `title_template` and `description_template` as attributes of your `Feed` class.

- To specify the contents of `<link>`, you have two options. For each item in `items()`, Django first tries executing a `get_absolute_url()` method on that object. If that method doesn't exist, it tries calling a method `item_link()` in the `Feed` class, passing it a single parameter, `item`, which is the object itself. Both `get_absolute_url()` and `item_link()` should return the item's URL as a normal Python string.

- For the previous `LatestEntries` example, we could have very simple feed templates. `latest_title.html` contains

  `{{ obj.title }}`

  and `latest_description.html` contains

  `{{ obj.description }}`

  It's almost too easy . . .

A More Complex Feed

The framework also supports more complex feeds, via parameters.

For example, chicagocrime.org offers an RSS feed of recent crimes for every police beat in Chicago. It would be silly to create a separate `Feed` class for each police beat; that would violate the Don't Repeat Yourself (DRY) principle and would couple data to programming logic. Instead, the syndication framework lets you make generic feeds that return items based on information in the feed's URL.

On chicagocrime.org, the police-beat feeds are accessible via URLs like this:

- `http://www.chicagocrime.org/rss/beats/0613/`: Returns recent crimes for beat 0613

- `http://www.chicagocrime.org/rss/beats/1424/`: Returns recent crimes for beat 1424

The slug here is "beats". The syndication framework sees the extra URL bits after the slug—0613 and 1424—and gives you a hook to tell it what those URL bits mean and how they should influence which items get published in the feed.

An example makes this clear. Here's the code for these beat-specific feeds:

```
from django.core.exceptions import ObjectDoesNotExist

class BeatFeed(Feed):
    def get_object(self, bits):
        # In case of "/rss/beats/0613/foo/bar/baz/", or other such
        # clutter, check that bits has only one member.
        if len(bits) != 1:
            raise ObjectDoesNotExist
        return Beat.objects.get(beat__exact=bits[0])

    def title(self, obj):
        return "Chicagocrime.org: Crimes for beat %s" % obj.beat
```

```
def link(self, obj):
    return obj.get_absolute_url()

def description(self, obj):
    return "Crimes recently reported in police beat %s" % obj.beat

def items(self, obj):
    crimes = Crime.objects.filter(beat__id__exact=obj.id)
    return crimes.order_by('-crime_date')[:30]
```

Here's the basic algorithm the RSS framework, given this class and a request to the URL /rss/beats/0613/:

1. The framework gets the URL /rss/beats/0613/ and notices there's an extra bit of URL after the slug. It splits that remaining string by the slash character ("/") and calls the Feed class's get_object() method, passing it the bits.

   In this case, bits is ['0613']. For a request to /rss/beats/0613/foo/bar/, bits would be ['0613', 'foo', 'bar'].

2. get_object() is responsible for retrieving the given beat, from the given bits.

   In this case, it uses the Django database API to retrieve the beat. Note that get_object() should raise django.core.exceptions.ObjectDoesNotExist if given invalid parameters. There's no try/except around the Beat.objects.get() call, because it's not necessary. That function raises Beat.DoesNotExist on failure, and Beat.DoesNotExist is a subclass of ObjectDoesNotExist. Raising ObjectDoesNotExist in get_object() tells Django to produce a 404 error for that request.

3. To generate the feed's <title>, <link>, and <description>, Django uses the title(), link(), and description() methods. In the previous example, they were simple string class attributes, but this example illustrates that they can be either strings or methods. For each of title, link, and description, Django follows this algorithm:

   a. It tries to call a method, passing the obj argument, where obj is the object returned by get_object().

   b. Failing that, it tries to call a method with no arguments.

   c. Failing that, it uses the class attribute.

4. Finally, note that items() in this example also takes the obj argument. The algorithm for items is the same as described in the previous step—first, it tries items(obj), then items(), and then finally an items class attribute (which should be a list).

Full documentation of all the methods and attributes of the Feed classes is always available from the official Django documentation (http://www.djangoproject.com/documentation/syndication/).

Specifying the Type of Feed

By default, the syndication framework produces RSS 2.0. To change that, add a feed_type attribute to your Feed class:

```
from django.utils.feedgenerator import Atom1Feed

class MyFeed(Feed):
    feed_type = Atom1Feed
```

Note that you set feed_type to a class object, not an instance. Currently available feed types are shown in Table 11-1.

Table 11-1. *Feed Types*

Feed Class	Format
django.utils.feedgenerator.Rss201rev2Feed	RSS 2.01 (default)
django.utils.feedgenerator.RssUserland091Feed	RSS 0.91
django.utils.feedgenerator.Atom1Feed	Atom 1.0

Enclosures

To specify enclosures (i.e., media resources associated with feed items such as MP3 podcast feeds), use the item_enclosure_url, item_enclosure_length, and item_enclosure_mime_type hooks:

```
from myproject.models import Song

class MyFeedWithEnclosures(Feed):
    title = "Example feed with enclosures"
    link = "/feeds/example-with-enclosures/"

    def items(self):
        return Song.objects.all()[:30]

    def item_enclosure_url(self, item):
        return item.song_url

    def item_enclosure_length(self, item):
        return item.song_length

    item_enclosure_mime_type = "audio/mpeg"
```

This assumes, of course, that you've created a Song object with song_url and song_length (i.e., the size in bytes) fields.

Language

Feeds created by the syndication framework automatically include the appropriate `<language>` tag (RSS 2.0) or `xml:lang` attribute (Atom). This comes directly from your `LANGUAGE_CODE` setting.

URLs

The `link` method/attribute can return either an absolute URL (e.g., `"/blog/"`) or a URL with the fully qualified domain and protocol (e.g., `"http://www.example.com/blog/"`). If `link` doesn't return the domain, the syndication framework will insert the domain of the current site, according to your `SITE_ID` setting.

Atom feeds require a `<link rel="self">` that defines the feed's current location. The syndication framework populates this automatically, using the domain of the current site according to the `SITE_ID` setting.

Publishing Atom and RSS Feeds in Tandem

Some developers like to make available both Atom and RSS versions of their feeds. That's easy to do with Django: just create a subclass of your `feed` class and set the `feed_type` to something different. Then update your URLconf to add the extra versions. Here's a full example:

```
from django.contrib.syndication.feeds import Feed
from chicagocrime.models import NewsItem
from django.utils.feedgenerator import Atom1Feed

class RssSiteNewsFeed(Feed):
    title = "Chicagocrime.org site news"
    link = "/sitenews/"
    description = "Updates on changes and additions to chicagocrime.org."

    def items(self):
        return NewsItem.objects.order_by('-pub_date')[:5]

class AtomSiteNewsFeed(RssSiteNewsFeed):
    feed_type = Atom1Feed
```

And here's the accompanying URLconf:

```
from django.conf.urls.defaults import *
from myproject.feeds import RssSiteNewsFeed, AtomSiteNewsFeed

feeds = {
    'rss': RssSiteNewsFeed,
    'atom': AtomSiteNewsFeed,
}

urlpatterns = patterns('',
    # ...
    (r'^feeds/(?P<url>.*)/$', 'django.contrib.syndication. views.feed',
```

```
        {'feed_dict': feeds}),
    # ...
)
```

The Sitemap Framework

A *sitemap* is an XML file on your Web site that tells search engine indexers how frequently your pages change and how "important" certain pages are in relation to other pages on your site. This information helps search engines index your site.

For example, here's a piece of the sitemap for Django's Web site (`http://www.djangoproject.com/sitemap.xml`):

```
<?xml version="1.0" encoding="UTF-8"?>
<urlset xmlns="http://www.sitemaps.org/schemas/sitemap/0.9">
  <url>
    <loc>http://www.djangoproject.com/documentation/</loc>
    <changefreq>weekly</changefreq>
    <priority>0.5</priority>
  </url>
  <url>
    <loc>http://www.djangoproject.com/documentation/0_90/</loc>
    <changefreq>never</changefreq>
    <priority>0.1</priority>
  </url>
  ...
</urlset>
```

For more on sitemaps, see `http://www.sitemaps.org/`.

The Django sitemap framework automates the creation of this XML file by letting you express this information in Python code. To create a sitemap, you just need to write a `Sitemap` class and point to it in your URLconf.

Installation

To install the sitemap application, follow these steps:

1. Add `'django.contrib.sitemaps'` to your `INSTALLED_APPS` setting.

2. Make sure `'django.template.loaders.app_directories.load_template_source'` is in your `TEMPLATE_LOADERS` setting. It's in there by default, so you'll need to change this only if you've changed that setting.

3. Make sure you've installed the sites framework (see Chapter 14).

The sitemap application doesn't install any database tables. The only reason it needs to go into `INSTALLED_APPS` is so the `load_template_source` template loader can find the default templates.

Initialization

To activate sitemap generation on your Django site, add this line to your URLconf:

```
(r'^sitemap.xml$', 'django.contrib.sitemaps.views.sitemap', {'sitemaps': sitemaps})
```

This line tells Django to build a sitemap when a client accesses /sitemap.xml.

The name of the sitemap file is not important, but the location is. Search engines will only index links in your sitemap for the current URL level and below. For instance, if sitemap.xml lives in your root directory, it may reference any URL in your site. However, if your sitemap lives at /content/sitemap.xml, it may only reference URLs that begin with /content/.

The sitemap view takes an extra, required argument: {'sitemaps': sitemaps}. sitemaps should be a dictionary that maps a short section label (e.g., blog or news) to its Sitemap class (e.g., BlogSitemap or NewsSitemap). It may also map to an instance of a Sitemap class (e.g., BlogSitemap(some_var)).

Sitemap Classes

A Sitemap class is a simple Python class that represents a "section" of entries in your sitemap. For example, one Sitemap class could represent all the entries of your Weblog, while another could represent all of the events in your events calendar.

In the simplest case, all these sections get lumped together into one sitemap.xml, but it's also possible to use the framework to generate a sitemap index that references individual sitemap files, one per section (as described shortly).

Sitemap classes must subclass django.contrib.sitemaps.Sitemap. They can live anywhere in your code tree.

For example, assume you have a blog system, with an Entry model, and you want your sitemap to include all the links to your individual blog entries. Here's how your Sitemap class might look:

```
from django.contrib.sitemaps import Sitemap
from mysite.blog.models import Entry

class BlogSitemap(Sitemap):
    changefreq = "never"
    priority = 0.5

    def items(self):
        return Entry.objects.filter(is_draft=False)

    def lastmod(self, obj):
        return obj.pub_date
```

Declaring a Sitemap should look very similar to declaring a Feed; that's by design. Like Feed classes, Sitemap members can be either methods or attributes. See the steps in the earlier "A Complex Example" section for more about how this works.

A `Sitemap` class can define the following methods/attributes:

- `items` *(required)*: Provides list of objects. The framework doesn't care what type of objects they are; all that matters is that these objects get passed to the `location()`, `lastmod()`, `changefreq()`, and `priority()` methods.

- `location` *(optional)*: Gives the absolute URL for a given object. Here, "absolute URL" means a URL that doesn't include the protocol or domain. Here are some examples:

  - Good: `'/foo/bar/'`

  - Bad: `'example.com/foo/bar/'`

  - Bad: `'http://example.com/foo/bar/'`

  If `location` isn't provided, the framework will call the `get_absolute_url()` method on each object as returned by `items()`.

- `lastmod` *(optional)*: The object's "last modification" date, as a Python `datetime` object.

- `changefreq` *(optional)*: How often the object changes. Possible values (as given by the Sitemaps specification) are as follows:

  - `'always'`

  - `'hourly'`

  - `'daily'`

  - `'weekly'`

  - `'monthly'`

  - `'yearly'`

  - `'never'`

- `priority` *(optional)*: A suggested indexing priority between `0.0` and `1.0`. The default priority of a page is `0.5`. See the `http://sitemaps.org` documentation for more about how `priority` works.

Shortcuts

The sitemap framework provides a couple convenience classes for common cases. These are described in the sections that follow.

FlatPageSitemap

The `django.contrib.sitemaps.FlatPageSitemap` class looks at all flat pages defined for the current site and creates an entry in the sitemap. These entries include only the `location` attribute—not `lastmod`, `changefreq`, or `priority`.

See Chapter 14 for more about flat pages.

GenericSitemap

The GenericSitemap class works with any generic views (see Chapter 9) you already have.

To use it, create an instance, passing in the same info_dict you pass to the generic views. The only requirement is that the dictionary have a queryset entry. It may also have a date_field entry that specifies a date field for objects retrieved from the queryset. This will be used for the lastmod attribute in the generated sitemap. You may also pass priority and changefreq keyword arguments to the GenericSitemap constructor to specify these attributes for all URLs.

Here's an example of a URLconf using both FlatPageSitemap and GenericSiteMap (with the hypothetical Entry object from earlier):

```
from django.conf.urls.defaults import *
from django.contrib.sitemaps import FlatPageSitemap, GenericSitemap
from mysite.blog.models import Entry

info_dict = {
    'queryset': Entry.objects.all(),
    'date_field': 'pub_date',
}

sitemaps = {
    'flatpages': FlatPageSitemap,
    'blog': GenericSitemap(info_dict, priority=0.6),
}

urlpatterns = patterns('',
    # some generic view using info_dict
    # ...

    # the sitemap
    (r'^sitemap.xml$',
     'django.contrib.sitemaps.views.sitemap',
     {'sitemaps': sitemaps})
)
```

Creating a Sitemap Index

The sitemap framework also has the ability to create a sitemap index that references individual sitemap files, one per each section defined in your sitemaps dictionary. The only differences in usage are as follows:

- You use two views in your URLconf: django.contrib.sitemaps.views.index and django.contrib.sitemaps.views.sitemap.

- The django.contrib.sitemaps.views.sitemap view should take a section keyword argument.

Here is what the relevant URLconf lines would look like for the previous example:

```
(r'^sitemap.xml$',
 'django.contrib.sitemaps.views.index',
 {'sitemaps': sitemaps}),

(r'^sitemap-(?P<section>.+).xml$',
 'django.contrib.sitemaps.views.sitemap',
 {'sitemaps': sitemaps})
```

This will automatically generate a `sitemap.xml` file that references both `sitemap-flatpages.xml` and `sitemap-blog.xml`. The `Sitemap` classes and the `sitemaps` dictionary don't change at all.

Pinging Google

You may want to "ping" Google when your sitemap changes, to let it know to reindex your site. The framework provides a function to do just that: `django.contrib.sitemaps.ping_google()`.

■**Note** At the time of this writing, only Google responds to sitemap pings. However, it's quite likely that Yahoo and/or MSN will soon support these pings as well. At that time, we'll likely change the name of `ping_google()` to something like `ping_search_engines()`, so make sure to check the latest sitemap documentation at `http://www.djangoproject.com/documentation/sitemaps/`.

`ping_google()` takes an optional argument, `sitemap_url`, which should be the absolute URL of your site's sitemap (e.g., `'/sitemap.xml'`). If this argument isn't provided, `ping_google()` will attempt to figure out your sitemap by performing a reverse lookup on your URLconf. `ping_google()` raises the exception `django.contrib.sitemaps.SitemapNotFound` if it cannot determine your sitemap URL.

One useful way to call `ping_google()` is from a model's `save()` method:

```
from django.contrib.sitemaps import ping_google

class Entry(models.Model):
    # ...
    def save(self):
        super(Entry, self).save()
        try:
            ping_google()
        except Exception:
            # Bare 'except' because we could get a variety
            # of HTTP-related exceptions.
            pass
```

A more efficient solution, however, would be to call ping_google() from a cron script or some other scheduled task. The function makes an HTTP request to Google's servers, so you may not want to introduce that network overhead each time you call save().

What's Next?

Next, we'll continue to dig deeper into all the nifty built-in tools Django gives you. Chapter 12 looks at all the tools you need to provide user-customized sites: sessions, users, and authentication.

Onward!

CHAPTER 12

■■■

Sessions, Users, and Registration

It's time for a confession: we've been deliberately ignoring an incredibly important aspect of Web development prior to this point. So far, we've thought of the traffic visiting our sites as some faceless, anonymous mass hurtling itself against our carefully designed pages.

This isn't true, of course. The browsers hitting our sites have real humans behind them (some of the time, at least). That's a big thing to ignore: the Internet is at its best when it serves to connect *people*, not machines. If we're going to develop truly compelling sites, eventually we're going to have to deal with the bodies behind the browsers.

Unfortunately, it's not all that easy. HTTP is designed to be *stateless*—that is, each and every request happens in a vacuum. There's no persistence between one request and the next, and we can't count on any aspects of a request (IP address, user agent, etc.) to consistently indicate successive requests from the same person.

In this chapter you'll learn how to handle this lack of state. We'll start at the lowest level (cookies), and work up to the high-level tools for handling sessions, users, and registration.

Cookies

Browser developers long ago recognized that HTTP's statelessness poses a huge problem for Web developers, and thus *cookies* were born. A cookie is a small piece of information that browsers store on behalf of Web servers. Every time a browser requests a page from a certain server, it gives back the cookie that it initially received.

Let's take a look how this might work. When you open your browser and type in **google.com**, your browser sends an HTTP request to Google that starts something like this:

```
GET / HTTP/1.1
Host: google.com
...
```

When Google replies, the HTTP response looks something like the following:

```
HTTP/1.1 200 OK
Content-Type: text/html
Set-Cookie: PREF=ID=5b14f22bdaf1e81c:TM=1167000671:LM=1167000671;
            expires=Sun, 17-Jan-2038 19:14:07 GMT;
            path=/; domain=.google.com
Server: GWS/2.1
...
```

Notice the `Set-Cookie` header. Your browser will store that cookie value (`PREF=ID=5b14f22bdaf1e81c:TM=1167000671:LM=1167000671`) and serve it back to Google every time you access the site. So the next time you access Google, your browser is going to send a request like this:

```
GET / HTTP/1.1
Host: google.com
Cookie: PREF=ID=5b14f22bdaf1e81c:TM=1167000671:LM=1167000671
...
```

Google then can use that `Cookie` value to know that you're the same person who accessed the site earlier. This value might, for example, be a key into a database that stores user information. Google could (and does) use it to display your name on the page.

Getting and Setting Cookies

When dealing with persistence in Django, most of the time you'll want to use the higher-level session and/or user frameworks discussed a little later in this chapter. However, we'll pause and look at how to read and write cookies at a low level. This should help you understand how the rest of the tools discussed in the chapter actually work, and it will come in handy if you ever need to play with cookies directly.

Reading cookies that are already set is incredibly simple. Every request object has a `COOKIES` object that acts like a dictionary; you can use it to read any cookies that the browser has sent to the view:

```
def show_color(request):
    if "favorite_color" in request.COOKIES:
        return HttpResponse("Your favorite color is %s" % \
            request.COOKIES["favorite_color"])
    else:
        return HttpResponse("You don't have a favorite color.")
```

Writing cookies is slightly more complicated. You need to use the `set_cookie()` method on an `HttpResponse` object. Here's an example that sets the `favorite_color` cookie based on a `GET` parameter:

```
def set_color(request):
    if "favorite_color" in request.GET:

        # Create an HttpResponse object...
```

```
    response = HttpResponse("Your favorite color is now %s" % \
        request.GET["favorite_color"])

    # ... and set a cookie on the response
    response.set_cookie("favorite_color",
                            request.GET["favorite_color"])

    return response

else:
    return HttpResponse("You didn't give a favorite color.")
```

You can also pass a number of optional arguments to response.set_cookie() that control aspects of the cookie, as shown in Table 12-1.

Table 12-1. *Cookie Options*

Parameter	Default	Description
max_age	None	Age (in seconds) that the cookie should last. If this parameter is None, the cookie will last only until the browser is closed.
expires	None	The date/time when the cookie should expire. It needs to be in the format "Wdy, DD-Mth-YY HH:MM:SS GMT". If given, this parameter overrides the max_age parameter.
path	"/"	The path prefix that this cookie is valid for. Browsers will only pass the cookie back to pages below this path prefix, so you can use this to prevent cookies from being sent to other sections of your site. This parameter is especially useful when you don't control the top level of your site's domain.
domain	None	The domain that this cookie is valid for. You can use this parameter to set a cross-domain cookie. For example, domain=".example.com" will set a cookie that is readable by the domains www.example.com, www2.example.com, and an.other.sub.domain.example.com. If this parameter is set to None, a cookie will only be readable by the domain that set it.
secure	False	If set to True, this parameter instructs the browser to return this cookie only to pages accessed over HTTPS.

The Mixed Blessing of Cookies

You might notice a number of potential problems with the way cookies work. Let's look at some of the more important ones:

- Storage of cookies is essentially voluntary; browsers don't guarantee anything. In fact, all browsers enable users to control the policy for accepting cookies. If you want to see just how vital cookies are to the Web, try turning on your browser's "prompt to accept every cookie" option.

  Despite their nearly universal use, cookies are still the definition of unreliability. This means that developers should check that a user actually accepts cookies before relying on them.

More important, you should *never* store important data in cookies. The Web is filled with horror stories of developers who have stored unrecoverable information in browser cookies, only to have that data purged by the browser for one reason or another.

- Cookies (especially those not sent over HTTPS) are not secure. Because HTTP data is sent in cleartext, cookies are extremely vulnerable to *snooping* attacks. That is, an attacker snooping on the wire can intercept a cookie and read it. This means you should never store sensitive information in a cookie.

    There's an even more insidious attack, known as a *man-in-the-middle* attack, wherein an attacker intercepts a cookie and uses it to pose as another user. Chapter 19 discusses attacks of this nature in depth, as well as ways to prevent them.

- Cookies aren't even secure from their intended recipients. Most browsers provide easy ways to edit the content of individual cookies, and resourceful users can always use tools like mechanize (`http://wwwsearch.sourceforge.net/mechanize/`) to construct HTTP requests by hand.

    So you can't store data in cookies that might be sensitive to tampering. The canonical mistake in this scenario is storing something like `IsLoggedIn=1` in a cookie when a user logs in. You'd be amazed at the number of sites that make mistakes of this nature; it takes only a second to fool these sites' "security" systems.

Django's Session Framework

With all of these limitations and potential security holes, it's obvious that cookies and persistent sessions are examples of those "pain points" in Web development. Of course, Django's goal is to be an effective painkiller, so it comes with a session framework designed to smooth over these difficulties for you.

This session framework lets you store and retrieve arbitrary data on a per-site-visitor basis. It stores data on the server side and abstracts the sending and receiving of cookies. Cookies use only a hashed session ID—not the data itself—thus protecting you from most of the common cookie problems.

Let's look at how to enable sessions and use them in views.

Enabling Sessions

Sessions are implemented via a piece of middleware (see Chapter 15) and a Django model. To enable sessions, you'll need to follow these steps:

1. Edit your `MIDDLEWARE_CLASS` setting and make sure `MIDDLEWARE_CLASSES` contains `'django.contrib.sessions.middleware.SessionMiddleware'`.

2. Make sure `'django.contrib.sessions'` is in your `INSTALLED_APPS` setting (and run `manage.py syncdb` if you have to add it).

The default skeleton settings created by `startproject` have both of these bits already installed, so unless you've removed them, you probably don't have to change anything to get sessions to work.

If you don't want to use sessions, you might want to remove the `SessionMiddleware` line from `MIDDLEWARE_CLASSES` and `'django.contrib.sessions'` from your `INSTALLED_APPS`. Doing so will save you only a small amount of overhead, but every little bit counts.

Using Sessions in Views

When `SessionMiddleware` is activated, each `HttpRequest` object—the first argument to any Django view function—will have a `session` attribute, which is a dictionary-like object. You can read it and write to it in the same way you'd use a normal dictionary. For example, in a view you could do stuff like this:

```
# Set a session value:
request.session["fav_color"] = "blue"

# Get a session value -- this could be called in a different view,
# or many requests later (or both):
fav_color = request.session["fav_color"]

# Clear an item from the session:
del request.session["fav_color"]

# Check if the session has a given key:
if "fav_color" in request.session:
    ...
```

You can also use other mapping methods like `keys()` and `items()` on `request.session`. There are a couple of simple rules for using Django's sessions effectively:

- Use normal Python strings as dictionary keys on `request.session` (as opposed to integers, objects, etc.). This is more of a convention than a hard-and-fast rule, but it's worth following.

- Session dictionary keys that begin with an underscore are reserved for internal use by Django. In practice, the framework uses only a small number of underscore-prefixed session variables, but unless you know what they all are (and you are willing to keep up with any changes in Django itself), staying away from underscore prefixes will keep Django from interfering with your application.

- Don't replace `request.session` with a new object, and don't access or set its attributes. Use it like a Python dictionary.

Let's take a look at a few quick examples. This simplistic view sets a `has_commented` variable to `True` after a user posts a comment. It's a simple (but not particularly secure) way of preventing a user from posting more than one comment:

```
def post_comment(request, new_comment):
    if request.session.get('has_commented', False):
        return HttpResponse("You've already commented.")
    c = comments.Comment(comment=new_comment)
    c.save()
```

```
    request.session['has_commented'] = True
    return HttpResponse('Thanks for your comment!')
```

This simplistic view logs in a "member" of the site:

```
def login(request):
try:

    m = Member.objects.get(username__exact=request.POST['username'])
    if m.password == request.POST['password']:
        request.session['member_id'] = m.id
        return HttpResponse("You're logged in.")
except Member.DoesNotExist:
    pass
return HttpResponse("Your username and password didn't match.")
```

And this one logs out a member, according to login():

```
def logout(request):
    try:
        del request.session['member_id']
    except KeyError:
        pass
    return HttpResponse("You're logged out.")
```

■**Note** In practice, this is a lousy way of logging users in. The authentication framework discussed shortly handles this task for you in a much more robust and useful manner. These examples are deliberately simplistic so that you can easily see what's going on.

Setting Test Cookies

As mentioned earlier, you can't rely on every browser accepting cookies. So, as a convenience, Django provides an easy way to test whether a user's browser accepts cookies. You just need to call request.session.set_test_cookie() in a view and check request.session.test_cookie_worked() in a subsequent view—not in the same view call.

This awkward split between set_test_cookie() and test_cookie_worked() is necessary due to the way cookies work. When you set a cookie, you can't actually tell whether a browser accepted it until the browser's next request.

It's good practice to use delete_test_cookie() to clean up after yourself. Do this after you've verified that the test cookie worked.

Here's a typical usage example:

```
def login(request):

    # If we submitted the form...
    if request.method == 'POST':
```

```
    # Check that the test cookie worked (we set it below):
    if request.session.test_cookie_worked():

        # The test cookie worked, so delete it.
        request.session.delete_test_cookie()

        # In practice, we'd need some logic to check username/password
        # here, but since this is an example...
        return HttpResponse("You're logged in.")

    # The test cookie failed, so display an error message. If this
    # was a real site we'd want to display a friendlier message.
    else:
        return HttpResponse("Please enable cookies and try again.")

# If we didn't post, send the test cookie along with the login form.
request.session.set_test_cookie()
return render_to_response('foo/login_form.html')
```

■**Note** Again, the built-in authentication functions handle this check for you.

Using Sessions Outside of Views

Internally, each session is just a normal Django model defined in `django.contrib.sessions.models`. Each session is identified by a more-or-less random 32-character hash stored in a cookie. Because it's a normal model, you can access sessions using the normal Django database API:

```
>>> from django.contrib.sessions.models import Session
>>> s = Session.objects.get(pk='2b1189a188b44ad18c35e113ac6ceead')
>>> s.expire_date
datetime.datetime(2005, 8, 20, 13, 35, 12)
```

You'll need to call `get_decoded()` to get the actual session data. This is necessary because the dictionary is stored in an encoded format:

```
>>> s.session_data
'KGRwMQpTJ19hdXRoX3VzZXJfaWQnCnAyCkkxCnMuMTExY2ZjODI2Yj...'
>>> s.get_decoded()
{'user_id': 42}
```

When Sessions Are Saved

By default, Django only saves to the database if the session has been modified—that is, if any of its dictionary values have been assigned or deleted:

```
# Session is modified.
request.session['foo'] = 'bar'
```

```
# Session is modified.
del request.session['foo']

# Session is modified.
request.session['foo'] = {}

# Gotcha: Session is NOT modified, because this alters
# request.session['foo'] instead of request.session.
request.session['foo']['bar'] = 'baz'
```

To change this default behavior, set SESSION_SAVE_EVERY_REQUEST to True. If SESSION_SAVE_EVERY_REQUEST is True, Django will save the session to the database on every single request, even if it wasn't changed.

Note that the session cookie is sent only when a session has been created or modified. If SESSION_SAVE_EVERY_REQUEST is True, the session cookie will be sent on every request. Similarly, the expires part of a session cookie is updated each time the session cookie is sent.

Browser-Length Sessions vs. Persistent Sessions

You might have noticed that the cookie Google sent us contained expires=Sun, 17-Jan-2038 19:14:07 GMT;. Cookies can optionally contain an expiration date that advises the browser on when to remove the cookie. If a cookie doesn't contain an expiration value, the browser will expire it when the user closes his or her browser window. You can control the session framework's behavior in this regard with the SESSION_EXPIRE_AT_BROWSER_CLOSE setting.

By default, SESSION_EXPIRE_AT_BROWSER_CLOSE is set to False, which means session cookies will be stored in users' browsers for SESSION_COOKIE_AGE seconds (which defaults to two weeks, or 1,209,600 seconds). Use this if you don't want people to have to log in every time they open a browser.

If SESSION_EXPIRE_AT_BROWSER_CLOSE is set to True, Django will use browser-length cookies.

Other Session Settings

Besides the settings already mentioned, a few other settings influence how Django's session framework uses cookies, as shown in Table 12-2.

Table 12-2. *Settings That Influence Cookie Behavior*

Setting	Default	Description
SESSION_COOKIE_DOMAIN	None	The domain to use for session cookies. Set this to a string such as ".lawrence.com" for cross-domain cookies, or use None for a standard cookie.
SESSION_COOKIE_NAME	"sessionid"	The name of the cookie to use for sessions. This can be any string.
SESSION_COOKIE_SECURE	False	Indication of whether to use a "secure" cookie for the session cookie. If this is set to True, the cookie will be marked as "secure," which means that browsers will ensure that the cookie is only sent via HTTPS.

TECHNICAL DETAILS

For the curious, here are a few technical notes about the inner workings of the session framework:

- The session dictionary accepts any Python object capable of being "pickled." See the documentation for Python's built-in `pickle` module for information about how this works.

- Session data is stored in a database table named `django_session`.

- Session data is fetched upon demand. If you never access `request.session`, Django won't hit that database table.

- Django sends a cookie only if it needs to. If you don't set any session data, it won't send a session cookie (unless `SESSION_SAVE_EVERY_REQUEST` is set to `True`).

- The Django sessions framework is entirely, and solely, cookie based. It does not fall back to putting session IDs in URLs as a last resort, as some other tools (e.g., PHP, JSP) do. This is an intentional design decision. Putting sessions in URLs doesn't just make URLs ugly, but it also makes your site vulnerable to a certain form of session ID theft via the `Referer` header.

If you're still curious, the source is pretty straightforward. Look in `django.contrib.sessions` for more details.

Users and Authentication

We're now halfway to linking browsers directly to real people. Sessions give us a way of persisting data through multiple browser requests; the second part of the equation is using those sessions for user login. Of course, we can't just trust that users are who they say they are, so we need to authenticate them along the way.

Naturally, Django provides tools to handle this common task (and many others). Django's user authentication system handles user accounts, groups, permissions, and cookie-based user sessions. This system is often referred to as an *auth/auth* (authentication and authorization) system. That name recognizes that dealing with users is often a two-step process. We need to

1. Verify (*authenticate*) that a user is who he or she claims to be (usually by checking a username and password against a database of users).

2. Verify that the user is *authorized* to perform some given operation (usually by checking against a table of permissions).

Following these needs, Django's auth/auth system consists of a number of parts:

- *Users*: People registered with your site

- *Permissions*: Binary (yes/no) flags designating whether a user may perform a certain task

- *Groups*: A generic way of applying labels and permissions to more than one user

- *Messages*: A simple way to queue and display system messages to users

- *Profiles*: A mechanism to extend the user object with custom fields

If you've used the admin tool (detailed in Chapter 6), you've already seen many of these tools, and if you've edited users or groups in the admin tool, you've actually been editing data in the auth system's database tables.

Enabling Authentication Support

Like the session tools, authentication support is bundled as a Django application in django. contrib, which needs to be installed. Like the session system, it's also installed by default, but if you've removed it, you'll need to follow these steps to install it:

1. Make sure the session framework is installed as described earlier in this chapter. Keeping track of users obviously requires cookies, and thus builds on the session framework.

2. Put 'django.contrib.auth' in your INSTALLED_APPS setting and run manage.py syncdb.

3. Make sure that 'django.contrib.auth.middleware.AuthenticationMiddleware' is in your MIDDLEWARE_CLASSES setting—*after* SessionMiddleware.

With that installation out of the way, we're ready to deal with users in view functions. The main interface you'll use to access users within a view is request.user; this is an object that represents the currently logged-in user. If the user isn't logged in, this will instead be an AnonymousUser object (see the following section for more details).

You can easily tell if a user is logged in with the is_authenticated() method:

```
if request.user.is_authenticated():
    # Do something for authenticated users.
else:
    # Do something for anonymous users.
```

Using Users

Once you have a User—often from request.user, but possibly through one of the other methods discussed shortly—you have a number of fields and methods available on that object. AnonymousUser objects emulate *some* of this interface, but not all of it, so you should always check user.is_authenticated() before assuming you're dealing with a bona fide user object. Tables 12-3 and 12-4 list the fields and methods, respectively, on User objects.

Table 12-3. *Fields on User Objects*

Field	Description
username	Required; 30 characters or fewer. Alphanumeric characters only (letters, digits, and underscores).
first_name	Optional; 30 characters or fewer.
last_name	Optional; 30 characters or fewer.
email	Optional. Email address.
password	Required. A hash of, and metadata about, the password (Django doesn't store the raw password). See the "Passwords" section for more about this value.
is_staff	Boolean. Designates whether this user can access the admin site.

Field	Description
`is_active`	Boolean. Designates whether this account can be used to log in. Set this flag to `False` instead of deleting accounts.
`is_superuser`	Boolean. Designates that this user has all permissions without explicitly assigning them.
`last_login`	A datetime of the user's last login. This is set to the current date/time by default.
`date_joined`	A datetime designating when the account was created. This is set to the current date/time by default when the account is created.

Table 12-4. *Methods on User Objects*

Method	Description
`is_authenticated()`	Always returns `True` for "real" User objects. This is a way to tell if the user has been authenticated. This does not imply any permissions, and it doesn't check if the user is active. It only indicates that the user has successfully authenticated.
`is_anonymous()`	Returns `True` only for `AnonymousUser` objects (and `False` for "real" User objects). Generally, you should prefer using `is_authenticated()` to this method.
`get_full_name()`	Returns the `first_name` plus the `last_name`, with a space in between.
`set_password(passwd)`	Sets the user's password to the given raw string, taking care of the password hashing. This doesn't actually save the `User` object.
`check_password(passwd)`	Returns `True` if the given raw string is the correct password for the user. This takes care of the password hashing in making the comparison.
`get_group_permissions()`	Returns a list of permission strings that the user has through the groups he or she belongs to.
`get_all_permissions()`	Returns a list of permission strings that the user has, both through group and user permissions.
`has_perm(perm)`	Returns `True` if the user has the specified permission, where `perm` is in the format `"package.codename"`. If the user is inactive, this method will always return `False`.
`has_perms(perm_list)`	Returns `True` if the user has *all* of the specified permissions. If the user is inactive, this method will always return `False`.
`has_module_perms(app_label)`	Returns `True` if the user has any permissions in the given `appname`. If the user is inactive, this method will always return `False`.
`get_and_delete_messages()`	Returns a list of `Message` objects in the user's queue and deletes the messages from the queue.
`email_user(subj, msg)`	Sends an email to the user. This email is sent from the `DEFAULT_FROM_EMAIL` setting. You can also pass a third argument, `from_email`, to override the From address on the email.
`get_profile()`	Returns a site-specific profile for this user. See the "Profiles" section for more on this method.

Finally, User objects have two many-to-many fields: groups and permissions. User objects can access their related objects in the same way as any other many-to-many field:

```
# Set a user's groups:
myuser.groups = group_list

# Add a user to some groups:
myuser.groups.add(group1, group2,...)

# Remove a user from some groups:
myuser.groups.remove(group1, group2,...)

# Remove a user from all groups:
myuser.groups.clear()

# Permissions work the same way
myuser.permissions = permission_list
myuser.permissions.add(permission1, permission2, ...)
myuser.permissions.remove(permission1, permission2, ...)
myuser.permissions.clear()
```

Logging In and Out

Django provides built-in view functions for handling logging in and out (and a few other nifty tricks), but before we get to those, let's take a look at how to log users in and out "by hand." Django provides two functions to perform these actions in django.contrib.auth: authenticate() and login().

To authenticate a given username and password, use authenticate(). It takes two keyword arguments, username and password, and it returns a User object if the password is valid for the given username. If the password is invalid, authenticate() returns None:

```
>>> from django.contrib import auth
>>> user = auth.authenticate(username='john', password='secret')
>>> if user is not None:
...     print "Correct!"
... else:
...     print "Oops, that's wrong!"
```

authenticate() only verifies a user's credentials. To log in a user, use login(). It takes an HttpRequest object and a User object and saves the user's ID in the session, using Django's session framework.

This example shows how you might use both authenticate() and login() within a view function:

```
from django.contrib import auth

def login(request):
    username = request.POST['username']
    password = request.POST['password']
```

```
user = auth.authenticate(username=username, password=password)
if user is not None and user.is_active:
    # Correct password, and the user is marked "active"
    auth.login(request, user)
    # Redirect to a success page.
    return HttpResponseRedirect("/account/loggedin/")
else:
    # Show an error page
    return HttpResponseRedirect("/account/invalid/")
```

To log out a user, use `django.contrib.auth.logout()` within your view. It takes an `HttpRequest` object and has no return value:

```
from django.contrib import auth

def logout(request):
    auth.logout(request)
    # Redirect to a success page.
    return HttpResponseRedirect("/account/loggedout/")
```

Note that `logout()` doesn't throw any errors if the user wasn't logged in.

In practice, you usually will not need to write your own login/logout functions; the authentication system comes with a set of views for generically handling logging in and out.

The first step in using the authentication views is to wire them up in your URLconf. You'll need to add this snippet:

```
from django.contrib.auth.views import login, logout

urlpatterns = patterns('',
    # existing patterns here...
    (r'^accounts/login/$',  login),
    (r'^accounts/logout/$', logout),
)
```

`/accounts/login/` and `/accounts/logout/` are the default URLs that Django uses for these views.

By default, the `login` view renders a template at `registration/login.html` (you can change this template name by passing an extra view argument, `template_name`). This form needs to contain a username and a password field. A simple template might look like this:

```
{% extends "base.html" %}

{% block content %}

  {% if form.errors %}
    <p class="error">Sorry, that's not a valid username or password</p>
  {% endif %}

  <form action='.' method='post'>
    <label for="username">User name:</label>
```

```
    <input type="text" name="username" value="" id="username">
    <label for="password">Password:</label>
    <input type="password" name="password" value="" id="password">

    <input type="submit" value="login" />
    <input type="hidden" name="next" value="{{ next|escape }}" />
  <form action='.' method='post'>
```

{% endblock %}

If the user successfully logs in, he or she will be redirected to /accounts/profile/ by default. You can override this by providing a hidden field called next with the URL to redirect to after logging in. You can also pass this value as a GET parameter to the login view and it will be automatically added to the context as a variable called next that you can insert into that hidden field.

The logout view works a little differently. By default it renders a template at registration/ logged_out.html (which usually contains a "You've successfully logged out" message). However, you can call the view with an extra argument, next_page, which will instruct the view to redirect after a logout.

Limiting Access to Logged-in Users

Of course, the reason we're going through all this trouble is so we can limit access to parts of our site.

The simple, raw way to limit access to pages is to check request.user.is_authenticated() and redirect to a login page:

```
from django.http import HttpResponseRedirect

def my_view(request):
    if not request.user.is_authenticated():
        return HttpResponseRedirect('/login/?next=%s' % request.path)
    # ...
```

or perhaps display an error message:

```
def my_view(request):
    if not request.user.is_authenticated():
        return render_to_response('myapp/login_error.html')
    # ...
```

As a shortcut, you can use the convenient login_required decorator:

```
from django.contrib.auth.decorators import login_required

@login_required
def my_view(request):
    # ...
```

login_required does the following:

- If the user isn't logged in, redirect to /accounts/login/, passing the current absolute URL in the query string as next, for example: /accounts/login/?next=/polls/3/.

- If the user is logged in, execute the view normally. The view code can then assume that the user is logged in.

Limiting Access to Users Who Pass a Test

Limiting access based on certain permissions or some other test, or providing a different location for the login view works essentially the same way.

The raw way is to run your test on request.user in the view directly. For example, this view checks to make sure the user is logged in and has the permission polls.can_vote (more about how permissions works follows):

```
def vote(request):
    if request.user.is_authenticated() and request.user.has_perm('polls.can_vote')):
        # vote here
    else:
        return HttpResponse("You can't vote in this poll.")
```

Again, Django provides a shortcut called user_passes_test. It takes arguments and generates a specialized decorator for your particular situation:

```
def user_can_vote(user):
    return user.is_authenticated() and user.has_perm("polls.can_vote")

@user_passes_text(user_can_vote, login_url="/login/")
def vote(request):
    # Code here can assume a logged-in user with the correct permission.
    ...
```

user_passes_test takes one required argument: a callable that takes a User object and returns True if the user is allowed to view the page. Note that user_passes_test does not automatically check that the User is authenticated; you should do that yourself.

In this example we're also showing the second optional argument, login_url, which lets you specify the URL for your login page (/accounts/login/ by default).

Since it's a relatively common task to check whether a user has a particular permission, Django provides a shortcut for that case: the permission_required() decorator. Using this decorator, the earlier example can be written as follows:

```
from django.contrib.auth.decorators import permission_required

@permission_required('polls.can_vote', login_url="/login/")
def vote(request):
    # ...
```

Note that permission_required() also takes an optional login_url parameter, which also defaults to '/accounts/login/'.

LIMITING ACCESS TO GENERIC VIEWS

One of the most frequently asked questions on the Django users list deals with limiting access to a generic view. To pull this off, you'll need to write a thin wrapper around the view and point your URLconf to your wrapper instead of the generic view itself:

```
from dango.contrib.auth.decorators import login_required
from django.views.generic.date_based import object_detail


@login_required
def limited_object_detail(*args, **kwargs):
    return object_detail(*args, **kwargs)
```

You can, of course, replace login_required with any of the other limiting decorators.

Managing Users, Permissions, and Groups

The easiest way by far to manage the auth system is through the admin interface. Chapter 6 discusses how to use Django's admin interface to edit users and control their permissions and access, and most of the time you'll just use that interface.

However, there are low-level APIs you can delve into when you need absolute control, and we discuss these in the sections that follow.

Creating Users

Create users with the create_user helper function:

```
>>> from django.contrib.auth.models import User
>>> user = User.objects.create_user(username='john',
...                                 email='jlennon@beatles.com',
...                                 password='glass onion')
```

At this point, user is a User instance ready to be saved to the database (create_user() doesn't actually call save() itself). You can continue to change its attributes before saving, too:

```
>>> user.is_staff = True
>>> user.save()
```

Changing Passwords

You can change a password with set_password():

```
>>> user = User.objects.get(username='john')
>>> user.set_password('goo goo goo joob')
>>> user.save()
```

Don't set the password attribute directly unless you know what you're doing. The password is actually stored as a *salted hash* and thus can't be edited directly.

More formally, the password attribute of a User object is a string in this format:

hashtype$salt$hash

That's a hash type, the salt, and the hash itself, separated by the dollar sign ($) character. hashtype is either sha1 (default) or md5, the algorithm used to perform a one-way hash of the password. salt is a random string used to salt the raw password to create the hash, for example:

sha1$a1976$a36cc8cbf81742a8fb52e221aaeab48ed7f58ab4

The User.set_password() and User.check_password() functions handle the setting and checking of these values behind the scenes.

IS A "SALTED HASH" SOME KIND OF DRUG?

No, a *salted hash* has nothing to do with marijuana; it's actually a common way to securely store passwords. A *hash* is a one-way cryptographic function—that is, you can easily compute the hash of a given value, but it's nearly impossible to take a hash and reconstruct the original value.

If we stored passwords as plain text, anyone who got their hands on the password database would instantly know everyone's password. Storing passwords as hashes reduces the value of a compromised database.

However, an attacker with the password database could still run a *brute-force* attack, hashing millions of passwords and comparing those hashes against the stored values. This takes some time, but less than you might think—computers are incredibly fast.

Worse, there are publicly available *rainbow tables*, or databases of precomputed hashes of millions of passwords. With a rainbow table, an attacker can break most passwords in seconds.

Adding a *salt*—basically an initial random value—to the stored hash adds another layer of difficulty to breaking passwords. Since salts differ from password to password, they also prevent the use of a rainbow table, thus forcing attackers to fall back on a brute-force attack, itself made more difficult by the extra entropy added to the hash by the salt.

While salted hashes aren't absolutely the most secure way of storing passwords, they're a good middle ground between security and convenience.

Handling Registration

We can use these low-level tools to create views that allow users to sign up. Nearly every developer wants to implement registration differently, so Django leaves writing a registration view up to you. Luckily, it's pretty easy.

At its simplest, we could provide a small view that prompts for the required user information and creates those users. Django provides a built-in form you can use for this purpose, which we'll use in this example:

```
from django import oldforms as forms
from django.http import HttpResponseRedirect
from django.shortcuts import render_to_response
from django.contrib.auth.forms import UserCreationForm
```

```
def register(request):
    form = UserCreationForm()

    if request.method == 'POST':
        data = request.POST.copy()
        errors = form.get_validation_errors(data)
        if not errors:
            new_user = form.save(data)
            return HttpResponseRedirect("/books/")
    else:
        data, errors = {}, {}

    return render_to_response("registration/register.html", {
        'form' : forms.FormWrapper(form, data, errors)
    })
```

This form assumes a template named `registration/register.html`. Here's an example of what that template might look like:

```
{% extends "base.html" %}

{% block title %}Create an account{% endblock %}

{% block content %}
  <h1>Create an account</h1>
  <form action="." method="post">
    {% if form.error_dict %}
      <p class="error">Please correct the errors below.</p>
    {% endif %}

    {% if form.username.errors %}
      {{ form.username.html_error_list }}
    {% endif %}
    <label for="id_username">Username:</label> {{ form.username }}

    {% if form.password1.errors %}
      {{ form.password1.html_error_list }}
    {% endif %}
    <label for="id_password1">Password: {{ form.password1 }}

    {% if form.password2.errors %}
      {{ form.password2.html_error_list }}
    {% endif %}
    <label for="id_password2">Password (again): {{ form.password2 }}

    <input type="submit" value="Create the account" />
  </label>
{% endblock %}
```

Using Authentication Data in Templates

The currently logged-in user and his or her permissions are made available in the template context when you use RequestContext (see Chapter 10).

■**Note** Technically, these variables are only made available in the template context if you use RequestContext *and* your TEMPLATE_CONTEXT_PROCESSORS setting contains "django.core.context_processors.auth", which is the default. Again, see Chapter 10 for more information.

When using RequestContext, the current user (either a User instance or an AnonymousUser instance) is stored in the template variable {{ user }}:

```
{% if user.is_authenticated %}
  <p>Welcome, {{ user.username }}. Thanks for logging in.</p>
{% else %}
  <p>Welcome, new user. Please log in.</p>
{% endif %}
```

This user's permissions are stored in the template variable {{ perms }}. This is a template-friendly proxy to a couple of permission methods described shortly.

There are two ways you can use this perms object. You can use something like {{ perms.polls }} to check if the user has *any* permissions for some given application, or you can use something like {{ perms.polls.can_vote }} to check if the user has a specific permission.

Thus, you can check permissions in template {% if %} statements:

```
{% if perms.polls %}
  <p>You have permission to do something in the polls app.</p>
  {% if perms.polls.can_vote %}
    <p>You can vote!</p>
  {% endif %}
{% else %}
  <p>You don't have permission to do anything in the polls app.</p>
{% endif %}
```

The Other Bits: Permissions, Groups, Messages, and Profiles

There are a few other bits of the authentication framework that we've only dealt with in passing. We'll take a closer look at them in the following sections.

Permissions

Permissions are a simple way to "mark" users and groups as being able to perform some action. They are usually used by the Django admin site, but you can easily use them in your own code.

The Django admin site uses permissions as follows:

- Access to view the "add" form and add an object is limited to users with the *add* permission for that type of object.

- Access to view the change list, view the "change" form, and change an object is limited to users with the *change* permission for that type of object.

- Access to delete an object is limited to users with the *delete* permission for that type of object.

Permissions are set globally per type of object, not per specific object instance. For example, it's possible to say "Mary may change news stories," but it's not currently possible to say "Mary may change news stories, but only the ones she created herself" or "Mary may only change news stories that have a certain status, publication date, or ID."

These three basic permissions—add, change, and delete—are automatically created for each Django model that has a `class Admin`. Behind the scenes, these permissions are added to the `auth_permission` database table when you run `manage.py syncdb`.

These permissions will be of the form `"<app>.<action>_<object_name>"`. That is, if you have a `polls` application with a `Choice` model, you'll get permissions named `"polls.add_choice"`, `"polls.change_choice"`, and `"polls.delete_choice"`.

Note that if your model doesn't have `class Admin` set when you run `syncdb`, the permissions won't be created. If you initialize your database and add `class Admin` to models after the fact, you'll need to run `syncdb` again to create any missing permissions for your installed applications.

You can also create custom permissions for a given model object using the `permissions` attribute on `Meta`. This example model creates three custom permissions:

```
class USCitizen(models.Model):
    # ...
    class Meta:
        permissions = (
            # Permission identifier    human-readable permission name
            ("can_drive",              "Can drive"),
            ("can_vote",               "Can vote in elections"),
            ("can_drink",              "Can drink alcohol"),
        )
```

This only creates those extra permissions when you run `syncdb`; it's up to you to check for these permissions in your views.

Just like users, permissions are implemented in a Django model that lives in `django.contrib.auth.models`. This means that you can use Django's database API to interact directly with permissions if you like.

Groups

Groups are a generic way of categorizing users so you can apply permissions, or some other label, to those users. A user can belong to any number of groups.

A user in a group automatically has the permissions granted to that group. For example, if the group `Site editors` has the permission `can_edit_home_page`, any user in that group will have that permission.

Groups are also a convenient way to categorize users to give them some label, or extended functionality. For example, you could create a group 'Special users', and you could write code that could, say, give those users access to a members-only portion of your site, or send them members-only email messages.

Like users, the easiest way to manage groups is through the admin interface. However, groups are also just Django models that live in django.contrib.auth.models, so once again you can always use Django's database APIs to deal with groups at a low level.

Messages

The message system is a lightweight way to queue messages for given users. A message is associated with a User. There's no concept of expiration or timestamps.

Messages are used by the Django admin interface after successful actions. For example, when you create an object, you'll notice a "The object was created successfully" message at the top of the admin page.

You can use the same API to queue and display messages in your own application. The API is simple:

- To create a new message, use user.message_set.create(message='message_text').

- To retrieve/delete messages, use user.get_and_delete_messages(), which returns a list of Message objects in the user's queue (if any) and deletes the messages from the queue.

In this example view, the system saves a message for the user after creating a playlist:

```
def create_playlist(request, songs):
    # Create the playlist with the given songs.
    # ...
    request.user.message_set.create(
        message="Your playlist was added successfully."
    )
    return render_to_response("playlists/create.html",
        context_instance=RequestContext(request))
```

When you use RequestContext, the currently logged-in user and his or her messages are made available in the template context as the template variable {{ messages }}. Here's an example of template code that displays messages:

```
{% if messages %}
<ul>
    {% for message in messages %}
    <li>{{ message }}</li>
    {% endfor %}
</ul>
{% endif %}
```

Note that RequestContext calls get_and_delete_messages behind the scenes, so any messages will be deleted even if you don't display them.

Finally, note that this messages framework only works with users in the user database. To send messages to anonymous users, use the session framework directly.

Profiles

The final piece of the puzzle is the profile system. To understand what profiles are all about, let's first look at the problem.

In a nutshell, many sites need to store more user information than is available on the standard User object. To compound the problem, most sites will have different "extra" fields. Thus, Django provides a lightweight way of defining a "profile" object that's linked to a given user. This profile object can differ from project to project, and it can even handle different profiles for different sites served from the same database.

The first step in creating a profile is to define a model that holds the profile information. The only requirement Django places on this model is that it have a unique ForeignKey to the User model; this field must be named user. Other that that, you can use any other fields you like. Here's a strictly arbitrary profile model:

```
from django.db import models
from django.contrib.auth.models import User

class MySiteProfile(models.Model):
    # This is the only required field
    user = models.ForeignKey(User, unique=True)

    # The rest is completely up to you...
    favorite_band = models.CharField(maxlength=100, blank=True)
    favorite_cheese = models.CharField(maxlength=100, blank=True)
    lucky_number = models.IntegerField()
```

Next, you'll need to tell Django where to look for this profile object. You do that by setting the AUTH_PROFILE_MODULE setting to the identifier for your model. So, if your model lives in an application called myapp, you'd put this in your settings file:

```
AUTH_PROFILE_MODULE = "myapp.mysiteprofile"
```

Once that's done, you can access a user's profile by calling user.get_profile(). This function could raise a SiteProfileNotAvailable exception if AUTH_PROFILE_MODULE isn't defined, or it could raise a DoesNotExist exception if the user doesn't have a profile already (you'll usually catch that exception and create a new profile at that time).

What's Next?

Yes, the session and authorization system is a lot to absorb. Most of the time you won't need all the features described in this chapter, but when you need to allow complex interactions between users, it's good to have all that power available.

In the next chapter, we'll take a look at a piece of Django that builds on top of this session/user system: the comments application. It allows you to easily attach comments—from anonymous or authenticated users—to arbitrary objects.

Onward and upward!

CHAPTER 13

■■■

Caching

Static Web sites, in which simple files are served directly to the Web, scale like crazy. But a fundamental tradeoff in dynamic Web sites is, well, they're dynamic. Each time a user requests a page, the Web server makes all sorts of calculations—from database queries, to template rendering, to business logic—to create the page that your site's visitor sees. From a processing-overhead perspective, this is quite expensive.

For most Web applications, this overhead isn't a big deal. Most Web applications aren't washingtonpost.com or Slashdot; they're small- to medium-sized sites with so-so traffic. But for medium- to high-traffic sites, it's essential to cut as much overhead as possible. That's where caching comes in.

To *cache* something is to save the result of an expensive calculation so that you don't have to perform the calculation next time. Here's some pseudocode explaining how this would work for a dynamically generated Web page:

```
given a URL, try finding that page in the cache
if the page is in the cache:
    return the cached page
else:
    generate the page
    save the generated page in the cache (for next time)
    return the generated page
```

Django comes with a robust cache system that lets you save dynamic pages so they don't have to be calculated for each request. For convenience, Django offers different levels of cache granularity. You can cache the response of specific views, you can cache only the pieces that are difficult to produce, or you can cache your entire site.

Django also works well with "upstream" caches, such as Squid (http://www.squid-cache.org/) and browser-based caches. These are the types of caches that you don't directly control but to which you can provide hints (via HTTP headers) about which parts of your site should be cached, and how.

Read on to discover how to use Django's caching system. When your site gets Slashdotted you'll be happy you understand this material.

Setting Up the Cache

The cache system requires a small amount of setup. Namely, you have to tell it where your cached data should live, whether in a database, on the filesystem, or directly in memory. This is an important decision that affects your cache's performance (yes, some cache types are faster than others). In-memory caching will generally be much faster than filesystem or database caching, because it lacks the overhead of hitting the filesystem or database.

Your cache preference goes in the CACHE_BACKEND setting in your settings file. If you use caching and do not specify CACHE_BACKEND, Django will use simple:/// by default. The following sections explain all available values for CACHE_BACKEND.

Memcached

By far the fastest, most efficient type of cache available to Django, Memcached is an entirely memory-based cache framework originally developed to handle high loads at LiveJournal (http://www.livejournal.com/) and subsequently open-sourced by Danga Interactive (http://danga.com/). It's used by sites such as Slashdot and Wikipedia to reduce database access and dramatically increase site performance.

Memcached is available for free at http://danga.com/memcached/. It runs as a daemon and is allotted a specified amount of RAM. Its primary feature is to provide an interface—a *super-lightning-fast* interface—for adding, retrieving, and deleting arbitrary data in the cache. All data is stored directly in memory, so there's no overhead of database or filesystem usage.

After installing Memcached itself, you'll need to install the Memcached Python bindings, which are not bundled with Django directly. These bindings are in a single Python module, memcache.py, which is available at http://www.tummy.com/Community/software/python-memcached/.

To use Memcached with Django, set CACHE_BACKEND to memcached://ip:port/, where ip is the IP address of the Memcached daemon and port is the port on which Memcached is running.

In this example, Memcached is running on localhost (127.0.0.1) port 11211:

```
CACHE_BACKEND = 'memcached://127.0.0.1:11211/'
```

One excellent feature of Memcached is its ability to share cache over multiple servers. This means you can run Memcached daemons on multiple machines, and the program will treat the group of machines as a *single* cache, without the need to duplicate cache values on each machine. To take advantage of this feature with Django, include all server addresses in CACHE_BACKEND, separated by semicolons.

In this example, the cache is shared over Memcached instances running on the IP addresses 172.19.26.240 and 172.19.26.242, both of which are on port 11211:

```
CACHE_BACKEND = 'memcached://172.19.26.240:11211;172.19.26.242:11211/'
```

In the following example, the cache is shared over Memcached instances running on the IP addresses 172.19.26.240 (port 11211), 172.19.26.242 (port 11212), and 172.19.26.244 (port 11213):

```
CACHE_BACKEND =
'memcached://172.19.26.240:11211;172.19.26.242:11212;172.19.26.244:11213/'
```

A final point about Memcached is that memory-based caching has one important disadvantage. Because the cached data is stored only in memory, the data will be lost if your server crashes. Clearly, memory isn't intended for permanent data storage, so don't rely on memory-based caching as your only data storage. Without a doubt, *none* of the Django caching back-ends should be used for permanent storage—they're all intended to be solutions for caching, not storage—but we point this out here because memory-based caching is particularly temporary.

Database Caching

To use a database table as your cache back-end, create a cache table in your database and point Django's cache system at that table.

First, create a cache table by running this command:

```
python manage.py createcachetable [cache_table_name]
```

where [cache_table_name] is the name of the database table to create. This name can be whatever you want, as long as it's a valid table name that's not already being used in your database. This command creates a single table in your database that is in the proper format Django's database-cache system expects.

Once you've created that database table, set your CACHE_BACKEND setting to "db://tablename", where tablename is the name of the database table. In this example, the cache table's name is my_cache_table:

```
CACHE_BACKEND = 'db://my_cache_table'
```

The database caching back-end uses the same database as specified in your settings file. You can't use a different database back-end for your cache table.

Filesystem Caching

To store cached items on a filesystem, use the "file://" cache type for CACHE_BACKEND, specifying the directory on your filesystem that should store the cached data.

For example, to store cached data in /var/tmp/django_cache, use this setting:

```
CACHE_BACKEND = 'file:///var/tmp/django_cache'
```

Note that there are three forward slashes toward the beginning of the preceding example. The first two are for file://, and the third is the first character of the directory path, /var/tmp/django_cache. If you're on Windows, put the drive letter after the file://, like so: file://c:/foo/bar.

The directory path should be *absolute*—that is, it should start at the root of your filesystem. It doesn't matter whether you put a slash at the end of the setting.

Make sure the directory pointed to by this setting exists and is readable and writable by the system user under which your Web server runs. Continuing the preceding example, if your server runs as the user apache, make sure the directory /var/tmp/django_cache exists and is readable and writable by the user apache.

Each cache value will be stored as a separate file whose contents are the cache data saved in a serialized ("pickled") format, using Python's pickle module. Each file's name is the cache key, escaped for safe filesystem use.

Local-Memory Caching

If you want the speed advantages of in-memory caching but don't have the capability of running Memcached, consider the local-memory cache back-end. This cache is thread-safe, but not multi-process. It isn't nearly as efficient as Memcached, which has much more advanced memory allocation strategies.

To use it, set CACHE_BACKEND to 'locmem:///', for example:

```
CACHE_BACKEND = 'locmem:///'
```

Simple Caching (for Development)

A simple, single-process memory cache is available as 'simple:///', for example:

```
CACHE_BACKEND = 'simple:///'
```

This cache merely saves cached data in process, which means it should be used only in development or testing environments.

Dummy Caching (for Development)

Finally, Django comes with a "dummy" cache that doesn't actually cache; it just implements the cache interface without doing anything.

This is useful if you have a production site that uses heavy-duty caching in various places and a development/test environment on which you don't want to cache. In that case, set CACHE_BACKEND to 'dummy:///' in the settings file for your development environment, for example:

```
CACHE_BACKEND = 'dummy:///'
```

As a result, your development environment won't use caching, but your production environment still will.

CACHE_BACKEND Arguments

Each cache back-end may take arguments. They're given in query-string style on the CACHE_BACKEND setting. Valid arguments are as follows:

- timeout: The default timeout, in seconds, to use for the cache. This argument defaults to 300 seconds (5 minutes).

- max_entries: For the simple, local-memory, and database back-ends, the maximum number of entries allowed in the cache before old values are deleted. This argument defaults to 300.

- cull_frequency: The ratio of entries that are culled when max_entries is reached. The actual ratio is 1/cull_frequency, so set cull_frequency=2 to cull half of the entries when max_entries is reached.

  A value of 0 for cull_frequency means that the entire cache will be dumped when max_entries is reached. This makes culling *much* faster at the expense of more cache misses. This argument defaults to 3.

In this example, `timeout` is set to 60:

```
CACHE_BACKEND = "locmem:///?timeout=60"
```

In this example, `timeout` is 30 and `max_entries` is 400:

```
CACHE_BACKEND = "locmem:///?timeout=30&max_entries=400"
```

Invalid arguments are silently ignored, as are invalid values of known arguments.

The Per-Site Cache

Once you've specified `CACHE_BACKEND`, the simplest way to use caching is to cache your entire site. This means each page that doesn't have GET or POST parameters will be cached for a specified amount of time the first time it's requested.

To activate the per-site cache, just add `'django.middleware.cache.CacheMiddleware'` to your `MIDDLEWARE_CLASSES` setting, as in this example:

```
MIDDLEWARE_CLASSES = (
    'django.middleware.cache.CacheMiddleware',
    'django.middleware.common.CommonMiddleware',
)
```

■**Note** The order of `MIDDLEWARE_CLASSES` matters. See the section "Order of MIDDLEWARE_CLASSES" later in this chapter.

Then, add the following required settings to your Django settings file:

- `CACHE_MIDDLEWARE_SECONDS`: The number of seconds each page should be cached.

- `CACHE_MIDDLEWARE_KEY_PREFIX`: If the cache is shared across multiple sites using the same Django installation, set this to the name of the site, or some other string that is unique to this Django instance, to prevent key collisions. Use an empty string if you don't care.

The cache middleware caches every page that doesn't have GET or POST parameters. That is, if a user requests a page and passes GET parameters in a query string, or passes POST parameters, the middleware will *not* attempt to retrieve a cached version of the page. If you intend to use the per-site cache, keep this in mind as you design your application; don't use URLs with query strings, for example, unless it is acceptable for your application not to cache those pages.

The cache middleware supports another setting, `CACHE_MIDDLEWARE_ANONYMOUS_ONLY`. If you've defined this setting, and it's set to `True`, then the cache middleware will only cache anonymous requests (i.e., those requests made by a non-logged-in user). This is a simple and effective way of disabling caching for any user-specific pages, such as Django's admin interface. Note that if you use `CACHE_MIDDLEWARE_ANONYMOUS_ONLY`, you should make sure you've activated `AuthenticationMiddleware` and that `AuthenticationMiddleware` appears before `CacheMiddleware` in your `MIDDLEWARE_CLASSES`.

Finally, note that CacheMiddleware automatically sets a few headers in each HttpResponse:

- It sets the Last-Modified header to the current date/time when a fresh (uncached) version of the page is requested.

- It sets the Expires header to the current date/time plus the defined CACHE_MIDDLEWARE_SECONDS.

- It sets the Cache-Control header to give a maximum age for the page, again from the CACHE_MIDDLEWARE_SECONDS setting.

The Per-View Cache

A more granular way to use the caching framework is by caching the output of individual views. This has the same effects as the per-site cache (including the omission of caching on requests with GET and POST parameters). It applies to whichever views you specify, rather than the whole site.

Do this by using a *decorator*, which is a wrapper around your view function that alters its behavior to use caching. The per-view cache decorator is called cache_page and is located in the django.views.decorators.cache module, for example:

```
from django.views.decorators.cache import cache_page

def my_view(request, param):
    # ...
my_view = cache_page(my_view, 60 * 15)
```

Alternatively, if you're using Python 2.4 or greater, you can use decorator syntax. This example is equivalent to the preceding one:

```
from django.views.decorators.cache import cache_page

@cache_page(60 * 15)
def my_view(request, param):
    # ...
```

cache_page takes a single argument: the cache timeout, in seconds. In the preceding example, the result of the my_view() view will be cached for 15 minutes. (Note that we've written it as 60 * 15 for the purpose of readability. 60 * 15 will be evaluated to 900—that is, 15 minutes multiplied by 60 seconds per minute.)

The per-view cache, like the per-site cache, is keyed off of the URL. If multiple URLs point at the same view, each URL will be cached separately. Continuing the my_view example, if your URLconf looks like this:

```
urlpatterns = ('',
    (r'^foo/(\d{1,2})/$', my_view),
)
```

then requests to /foo/1/ and /foo/23/ will be cached separately, as you may expect. But once a particular URL (e.g., /foo/23/) has been requested, subsequent requests to that URL will use the cache.

Specifying Per-View Cache in the URLconf

The examples in the previous section have hard-coded the fact that the view is cached, because cache_page alters the my_view function in place. This approach couples your view to the cache system, which is not ideal for several reasons. For instance, you might want to reuse the view functions on another, cacheless site, or you might want to distribute the views to people who might want to use them without being cached. The solution to these problems is to specify the per-view cache in the URLconf rather than next to the view functions themselves.

Doing so is easy: simply wrap the view function with cache_page when you refer to it in the URLconf. Here's the old URLconf from earlier:

```
urlpatterns = ('',
    (r'^foo/(\d{1,2})/$', my_view),
)
```

Here's the same thing, with my_view wrapped in cache_page:

```
from django.views.decorators.cache import cache_page

urlpatterns = ('',
    (r'^foo/(\d{1,2})/$', cache_page(my_view, 60 * 15)),
)
```

If you take this approach, don't forget to import cache_page within your URLconf.

The Low-Level Cache API

Sometimes, caching an entire rendered page doesn't gain you very much and is, in fact, inconvenient overkill.

Perhaps, for instance, your site includes a view whose results depend on several expensive queries, the results of which change at different intervals. In this case, it would not be ideal to use the full-page caching that the per-site or per-view cache strategies offer, because you wouldn't want to cache the entire result (since some of the data changes often), but you'd still want to cache the results that rarely change.

For cases like this, Django exposes a simple, low-level cache API, which lives in the module django.core.cache. You can use the low-level cache API to store objects in the cache with any level of granularity you like. You can cache any Python object that can be pickled safely: strings, dictionaries, lists of model objects, and so forth. (Most common Python objects can be pickled; refer to the Python documentation for more information about pickling.)

Here's how to import the API:

```
>>> from django.core.cache import cache
```

The basic interface is set(key, value, timeout_seconds) and get(key):

```
>>> cache.set('my_key', 'hello, world!', 30)
>>> cache.get('my_key')
'hello, world!'
```

The timeout_seconds argument is optional and defaults to the timeout argument in the CACHE_BACKEND setting explained earlier.

If the object doesn't exist in the cache, or the cache back-end is unreachable, cache.get() returns None:

```
# Wait 30 seconds for 'my_key' to expire...

>>> cache.get('my_key')
None

>>> cache.get('some_unset_key')
None
```

We advise against storing the literal value None in the cache, because you won't be able to distinguish between your stored None value and a cache miss signified by a return value of None.

cache.get() can take a default argument. This specifies which value to return if the object doesn't exist in the cache:

```
>>> cache.get('my_key', 'has expired')
'has expired'
```

To retrieve multiple cache values in a single shot, use cache.get_many(). If possible for the given cache back-end, get_many() will hit the cache only once, as opposed to hitting it once per cache key. get_many() returns a dictionary with all of the keys you asked for that exist in the cache and haven't expired:

```
>>> cache.set('a', 1)
>>> cache.set('b', 2)
>>> cache.set('c', 3)
>>> cache.get_many(['a', 'b', 'c'])
{'a': 1, 'b': 2, 'c': 3}
```

If a cache key doesn't exist or is expired, it won't be included in the dictionary. The following is a continuation of the example:

```
>>> cache.get_many(['a', 'b', 'c', 'd'])
{'a': 1, 'b': 2, 'c': 3}
```

Finally, you can delete keys explicitly with cache.delete(). This is an easy way of clearing the cache for a particular object:

```
>>> cache.delete('a')
```

cache.delete() has no return value, and it works the same way whether or not a value with the given cache key exists.

Upstream Caches

So far, this chapter has focused on caching your *own* data. But another type of caching is relevant to Web development, too: caching performed by *upstream* caches. These are systems that cache pages for users even before the request reaches your Web site.

Here are a few examples of upstream caches:

- Your ISP may cache certain pages, so if you requested a page from `http://example.com/`, your ISP would send you the page without having to access example.com directly. The maintainers of example.com have no knowledge of this caching; the ISP sits between example.com and your Web browser, handling all of the caching transparently.

- Your Web site may sit behind a *proxy cache*, such as Squid Web Proxy Cache (`http://www.squid-cache.org/`), that caches pages for performance. In this case, each request first would be handled by the proxy, and it would be passed to your application only if needed.

- Your Web browser caches pages, too. If a Web page sends out the appropriate headers, your browser will use the local cached copy for subsequent requests to that page, without even contacting the Web page again to see whether it has changed.

Upstream caching is a nice efficiency boost, but there's a danger to it. The content of many Web pages differs based on authentication and a host of other variables, and cache systems that blindly save pages based purely on URLs could expose incorrect or sensitive data to subsequent visitors to those pages.

For example, say you operate a Web-based e-mail system, and the contents of the "inbox" page obviously depend on which user is logged in. If an ISP blindly cached your site, then the first user who logged in through that ISP would have his or her user-specific inbox page cached for subsequent visitors to the site. That's not cool.

Fortunately, HTTP provides a solution to this problem. A number of HTTP headers exist to instruct upstream caches to differ their cache contents depending on designated variables, and to tell caching mechanisms not to cache particular pages. We'll look at some of these headers in the sections that follow.

Using Vary Headers

The Vary header defines which request headers a cache mechanism should take into account when building its cache key. For example, if the contents of a Web page depend on a user's language preference, the page is said to "vary on language."

By default, Django's cache system creates its cache keys using the requested path (e.g., `"/stories/2005/jun/23/bank_robbed/"`). This means every request to that URL will use the same cached version, regardless of user-agent differences such as cookies or language preferences. However, if this page produces different content based on some difference in request headers—such as a cookie, or a language, or a user-agent—you'll need to use the Vary header to tell caching mechanisms that the page output depends on those things.

To do this in Django, use the convenient vary_on_headers view decorator, like so:

```
from django.views.decorators.vary import vary_on_headers

# Python 2.3 syntax.
def my_view(request):
    # ...
my_view = vary_on_headers(my_view, 'User-Agent')
```

```
# Python 2.4+ decorator syntax.
@vary_on_headers('User-Agent')
def my_view(request):
    # ...
```

In this case, a caching mechanism (such as Django's own cache middleware) will cache a separate version of the page for each unique user-agent.

The advantage to using the vary_on_headers decorator rather than manually setting the Vary header (using something like response['Vary'] = 'user-agent') is that the decorator *adds* to the Vary header (which may already exist), rather than setting it from scratch and potentially overriding anything that was already in there.

You can pass multiple headers to vary_on_headers():

```
@vary_on_headers('User-Agent', 'Cookie')
def my_view(request):
    # ...
```

This tells upstream caches to vary on *both*, which means each combination of user-agent and cookie will get its own cache value. For example, a request with the user-agent Mozilla and the cookie value foo=bar will be considered different from a request with the user-agent Mozilla and the cookie value foo=ham.

Because varying on cookie is so common, there's a vary_on_cookie decorator. These two views are equivalent:

```
@vary_on_cookie
def my_view(request):
    # ...

@vary_on_headers('Cookie')
def my_view(request):
    # ...
```

The headers you pass to vary_on_headers are not case sensitive; "User-Agent" is the same thing as "user-agent".

You can also use a helper function, django.utils.cache.patch_vary_headers, directly. This function sets, or adds to, the Vary header, for example:

```
from django.utils.cache import patch_vary_headers

def my_view(request):
    # ...
    response = render_to_response('template_name', context)
    patch_vary_headers(response, ['Cookie'])
    return response
```

patch_vary_headers takes an HttpResponse instance as its first argument and a list/tuple of case-insensitive header names as its second argument.

Other Cache Headers

Other problems with caching are the privacy of data and the question of where data should be stored in a cascade of caches.

A user usually faces two kinds of caches: his or her own browser cache (a private cache) and his or her provider's cache (a public cache). A public cache is used by multiple users and controlled by someone else. This poses problems with sensitive data—you don't want, say, your bank account number stored in a public cache. So Web applications need a way to tell caches which data is private and which is public.

The solution is to indicate a page's cache should be "private." To do this in Django, use the cache_control view decorator:

```
from django.views.decorators.cache import cache_control

@cache_control(private=True)
def my_view(request):
    # ...
```

This decorator takes care of sending out the appropriate HTTP header behind the scenes.

There are a few other ways to control cache parameters. For example, HTTP allows applications to do the following:

- Define the maximum time a page should be cached.

- Specify whether a cache should always check for newer versions, only delivering the cached content when there are no changes. (Some caches might deliver cached content even if the server page changed, simply because the cache copy isn't yet expired.)

In Django, use the cache_control view decorator to specify these cache parameters. In this example, cache_control tells caches to revalidate the cache on every access and to store cached versions for, at most, 3,600 seconds:

```
from django.views.decorators.cache import cache_control
@cache_control(must_revalidate=True, max_age=3600)
def my_view(request):
    ...
```

Any valid Cache-Control HTTP directive is valid in cache_control(). Here's a full list:

- public=True

- private=True

- no_cache=True

- no_transform=True

- must_revalidate=True

- proxy_revalidate=True

- max_age=num_seconds

- s_maxage=num_seconds

■Tip For explanation of Cache-Control HTTP directives, see the specification at http://www.w3.org/ Protocols/rfc2616/rfc2616-sec14.html#sec14.9.

■Note The caching middleware already sets the cache header's max-age with the value of the CACHE_ MIDDLEWARE_SETTINGS setting. If you use a custom max_age in a cache_control decorator, the decorator will take precedence, and the header values will be merged correctly.

Other Optimizations

Django comes with a few other pieces of middleware that can help optimize your applications' performance:

- django.middleware.http.ConditionalGetMiddleware adds support for modern browsers to conditionally GET responses based on the ETag and Last-Modified headers.

- django.middleware.gzip.GZipMiddleware compresses responses for all modern browsers, saving bandwidth and transfer time.

Order of MIDDLEWARE_CLASSES

If you use CacheMiddleware, it's important to put it in the right place within the MIDDLEWARE_ CLASSES setting, because the cache middleware needs to know the headers by which to vary the cache storage.

Put the CacheMiddleware after any middlewares that might add something to the Vary header, including the following:

- SessionMiddleware, which adds Cookie

- GZipMiddleware, which adds Accept-Encoding

What's Next?

Django ships with a number of "contrib" packages—cool, optional features. We've already covered a few of them: the admin system (Chapter 6) and the session/user framework (Chapter 11).

The next chapter covers the rest of the "contributed" subframeworks. There are a lot of cool tools available—you won't want to miss any of them.

■ ■ ■ ■

Other Contributed Subframeworks

One of the many strengths of Python is its "batteries included" philosophy: when you install Python, it comes with a large standard library of modules that you can start using immediately, without having to download anything else. Django aims to follow this philosophy, and it includes its own standard library of add-ons useful for common Web development tasks. This chapter covers that collection of add-ons.

The Django Standard Library

Django's standard library lives in the package `django.contrib`. Within each subpackage is a separate piece of add-on functionality. These pieces are not necessarily related, but some `django.contrib` subpackages may require other ones.

There's no hard requirement for the types of functionality in `django.contrib`. Some of the packages include models (and hence require you to install their database tables into your database), but others consist solely of middleware or template tags.

The single characteristic the `django.contrib` packages have in common is this: if you were to remove the `django.contrib` package entirely, you could still use Django's fundamental features with no problems. When the Django developers add new functionality to the framework, they use this rule of thumb in deciding whether the new functionality should live in `django.contrib` or elsewhere.

`django.contrib` consists of these packages:

- `admin`: The automatic admin site. See Chapters 6 and 18.

- `auth`: Django's authentication framework. See Chapter 12.

- `comments`: A comments application. This application is currently under heavy development and thus couldn't be covered fully in time for this book's publication. Check the Django Web site for the latest information about the comments application.

- contenttypes: A framework for hooking into "types" of content, where each installed Django model is a separate content type. This framework is used internally by other "contrib" applications and is mostly intended for very advanced Django developers. Those developers should find out more about this application by reading the source code in django/contrib/contenttypes/.

- csrf: Protection against cross-site request forgery (CSRF). See the later section titled "CSRF Protection."

- databrowse: An application for browsing your data. Databrowse was released too recently to be covered in this book, but you can read the latest documentation online at http://www.djangoproject.com/documentation/databrowse/.

- flatpages: A framework for managing simple "flat" HTML content in a database. See the later section titled "Flatpages."

- formtools: A set of high-level abstractions for Django forms. See the later section titled "Form Tools."

- humanize: A set of Django template filters useful for adding a "human touch" to data. See the later section titled "Humanizing Data."

- markup: A set of Django template filters that implement a number of common markup languages. See the later section titled "Markup Filters."

- redirects: A framework for managing redirects. See the later section titled "Redirects."

- sessions: Django's session framework. See Chapter 12.

- sitemaps: A framework for generating sitemap XML files. This feature is not covered in this book, but you can read the latest documentation online at http://www.djangoproject.com/documentation/sitemaps/.

- sites: A framework that lets you operate multiple Web sites from the same database and Django installation. See the next section, "Sites."

- syndication: A framework for generating syndication feeds in RSS and Atom. See Chapter 11.

The rest of this chapter goes into detail about each django.contrib package that we haven't yet covered in this book.

Sites

Django's sites system is a generic framework that lets you operate multiple Web sites from the same database and Django project. This is an abstract concept, and it can be tricky to understand, so we'll start with a couple of scenarios where it would be useful.

Scenario 1: Reusing Data on Multiple Sites

As we explained in Chapter 1, the Django-powered sites LJWorld.com and Lawrence.com are operated by the same news organization: the *Lawrence Journal-World* newspaper in Lawrence,

Kansas. LJWorld.com focuses on news, while Lawrence.com focuses on local entertainment. But sometimes editors want to publish an article on *both* sites.

The brain-dead way of solving the problem would be to use a separate database for each site and to require site producers to publish the same story twice: once for LJWorld.com and again for Lawrence.com. But that's inefficient for site producers, and it's redundant to store multiple copies of the same story in the database.

The better solution? Both sites use the same article database, and an article is associated with one or more sites via a many-to-many relationship. The Django sites framework provides the database table to which articles can be related. It's a hook for associating data with one or more "sites."

Scenario 2: Storing Your Site Name/Domain in One Place

LJWorld.com and Lawrence.com both have e-mail alert functionality, which lets readers sign up to get notifications when news happens. It's pretty basic: a reader signs up on a Web form, and he immediately gets an e-mail saying, "Thank you for your subscription."

It would be inefficient and redundant to implement this signup-processing code twice, so the sites use the same code behind the scenes. But the "Thank you for your subscription" notice needs to be different for each site. By using Site objects, we can abstract the thank-you notice to use the values of the current site's name (e.g., 'LJWorld.com') and domain (e.g., 'www.ljworld.com').

The Django sites framework provides a place for you to store the name and domain for each site in your Django project, which means you can reuse those values in a generic way.

How to Use the Sites Framework

The sites framework is more a series of conventions than a framework. The whole thing is based on two simple concepts:

- The Site model, found in django.contrib.sites, has domain and name fields.

- The SITE_ID setting specifies the database ID of the Site object associated with that particular settings file.

How you use these two concepts is up to you, but Django uses them in a couple of ways automatically via simple conventions.

To install the sites application, follow these steps:

1. Add 'django.contrib.sites' to your INSTALLED_APPS.

2. Run the command manage.py syncdb to install the django_site table into your database.

3. Add one or more Site objects, either through the Django admin site or via the Python API. Create a Site object for each site/domain that this Django project powers.

4. Define the SITE_ID setting in each of your settings files. This value should be the database ID of the Site object for the site powered by that settings file.

The Sites Framework's Capabilities

The sections that follow describe the various things you can do with the sites framework.

Reusing Data on Multiple Sites

To reuse data on multiple sites, as explained in the first scenario, just create a ManyToManyField to Site in your models, for example:

```
from django.db import models
from django.contrib.sites.models import Site

class Article(models.Model):
    headline = models.CharField(maxlength=200)
    # ...
    sites = models.ManyToManyField(Site)
```

That's the infrastructure you need to associate articles with multiple sites in your database. With that in place, you can reuse the same Django view code for multiple sites. Continuing the Article model example, here's what an article_detail view might look like:

```
from django.conf import settings

def article_detail(request, article_id):
    try:
        a = Article.objects.get(id=article_id, sites__id=settings.SITE_ID)
    except Article.DoesNotExist:
        raise Http404
    # ...
```

This view function is reusable because it checks the article's site dynamically, according to the value of the SITE_ID setting.

For example, say LJWorld.com's settings file has a SITE_ID set to 1, and Lawrence.com's settings file has a SITE_ID set to 2. If this view is called when LJWorld.com's settings file is active, then it will limit the article lookup to articles in which the list of sites includes LJWorld.com.

Associating Content with a Single Site

Similarly, you can associate a model to the Site model in a many-to-one relationship using ForeignKey.

For example, if an article is allowed on only a single site, you could use a model like this:

```
from django.db import models
from django.contrib.sites.models import Site

class Article(models.Model):
    headline = models.CharField(maxlength=200)
    # ...
    site = models.ForeignKey(Site)
```

This has the same benefits as described in the last section.

Hooking Into the Current Site from Views

On a lower level, you can use the sites framework in your Django views to do particular things based on the site in which the view is being called, for example:

```
from django.conf import settings

def my_view(request):
    if settings.SITE_ID == 3:
        # Do something.
    else:
        # Do something else.
```

Of course, it's ugly to hard-code the site IDs like that. A slightly cleaner way of accomplishing the same thing is to check the current site's domain:

```
from django.conf import settings
from django.contrib.sites.models import Site

def my_view(request):
    current_site = Site.objects.get(id=settings.SITE_ID)
    if current_site.domain == 'foo.com':
        # Do something
    else:
        # Do something else.
```

The idiom of retrieving the Site object for the value of settings.SITE_ID is quite common, so the Site model's manager (Site.objects) has a get_current() method. This example is equivalent to the previous one:

```
from django.contrib.sites.models import Site

def my_view(request):
    current_site = Site.objects.get_current()
    if current_site.domain == 'foo.com':
        # Do something
    else:
        # Do something else.
```

■**Note** In this final example, you don't have to import django.conf.settings.

Getting the Current Domain for Display

For a DRY (Don't Repeat Yourself) approach to storing your site's name and domain name, as explained in "Scenario 2: Storing Your Site Name/Domain in One Place," just reference the name and domain of the current Site object, for example:

```
from django.contrib.sites.models import Site
from django.core.mail import send_mail

def register_for_newsletter(request):
    # Check form values, etc., and subscribe the user.
    # ...
    site = Site.objects.get_current()
    subject = 'Thanks for subscribing to %s alerts' % site.name
    message = ('Thanks for your subscription.\n\n'
               'We appreciate it. The %s team') % site.name
    from_address = 'editor@%s' % current_site.domain
    send_mail(subject, message, from_address, [user_email])
    # ...
```

Continuing our ongoing example of LJWorld.com and Lawrence.com, on Lawrence.com this e-mail has the subject line "Thanks for subscribing to lawrence.com alerts." On LJWorld.com, the e-mail has the subject line "Thanks for subscribing to LJWorld.com alerts." This same site-specific behavior is applied to the e-mails' message body.

An even more flexible (but more heavyweight) way of doing this would be to use Django's template system. Assuming Lawrence.com and LJWorld.com have different template directories (TEMPLATE_DIRS), you could simply delegate to the template system like so:

```
from django.core.mail import send_mail
from django.template import loader, Context

def register_for_newsletter(request):
    # Check form values, etc., and subscribe the user.
    # ...
    subject = loader.get_template('alerts/subject.txt').render(Context({}))
    message = loader.get_template('alerts/message.txt').render(Context({}))
    send_mail(subject, message, 'do-not-reply@example.com', [user_email])
    # ...
```

In this case, you have to create subject.txt and message.txt templates in both the LJWorld.com and Lawrence.com template directories. As mentioned previously, that gives you more flexibility, but it's also more complex.

It's a good idea to exploit the Site objects as much as possible to remove unneeded complexity and redundancy.

Getting the Current Domain for Full URLs

Django's get_absolute_url() convention is nice for getting your objects' URLs without the domain name, but in some cases you might want to display the full URL—with http:// and the domain and everything—for an object. To do this, you can use the sites framework. Here's a simple example:

```
>>> from django.contrib.sites.models import Site
>>> obj = MyModel.objects.get(id=3)
>>> obj.get_absolute_url()
```

```
'/mymodel/objects/3/'
>>> Site.objects.get_current().domain
'example.com'
>>> 'http://%s%s' % (Site.objects.get_current().domain, obj.get_absolute_url())
'http://example.com/mymodel/objects/3/'
```

CurrentSiteManager

If Sites play a key role in your application, consider using the helpful CurrentSiteManager in your model(s). It's a model manager (see Appendix B) that automatically filters its queries to include only objects associated with the current Site.

Use CurrentSiteManager by adding it to your model explicitly, for example:

```
from django.db import models
from django.contrib.sites.models import Site
from django.contrib.sites.managers import CurrentSiteManager

class Photo(models.Model):
    photo = models.FileField(upload_to='/home/photos')
    photographer_name = models.CharField(maxlength=100)
    pub_date = models.DateField()
    site = models.ForeignKey(Site)
    objects = models.Manager()
    on_site = CurrentSiteManager()
```

With this model, Photo.objects.all() will return all Photo objects in the database, but Photo.on_site.all() will return only the Photo objects associated with the current site, according to the SITE_ID setting.

In other words, these two statements are equivalent:

```
Photo.objects.filter(site=settings.SITE_ID)
Photo.on_site.all()
```

How did CurrentSiteManager know which field of Photo was the Site? It defaults to looking for a field called site. If your model has a ForeignKey or ManyToManyField called something *other* than site, you need to explicitly pass that as the parameter to CurrentSiteManager. The following model, which has a field called publish_on, demonstrates this:

```
from django.db import models
from django.contrib.sites.models import Site
from django.contrib.sites.managers import CurrentSiteManager

class Photo(models.Model):
    photo = models.FileField(upload_to='/home/photos')
    photographer_name = models.CharField(maxlength=100)
    pub_date = models.DateField()
    publish_on = models.ForeignKey(Site)
    objects = models.Manager()
    on_site = CurrentSiteManager('publish_on')
```

If you attempt to use `CurrentSiteManager` and pass a field name that doesn't exist, Django will raise a `ValueError`.

■Note You'll probably want to keep a normal (non-site-specific) `Manager` on your model, even if you use `CurrentSiteManager`. As explained in Appendix B, if you define a manager manually, then Django won't create the automatic `objects = models.Manager()` manager for you.

Also, certain parts of Django—namely, the Django admin site and generic views—use whichever manager is defined *first* in the model, so if you want your admin site to have access to all objects (not just site-specific ones), put `objects = models.Manager()` in your model, before you define `CurrentSiteManager`.

How Django Uses the Sites Framework

Although it's not required that you use the sites framework, it's strongly encouraged, because Django takes advantage of it in a few places. Even if your Django installation is powering only a single site, you should take a few seconds to create the site object with your `domain` and `name`, and point to its ID in your `SITE_ID` setting.

Here's how Django uses the sites framework:

- In the redirects framework (see the later section "Redirects"), each redirect object is associated with a particular site. When Django searches for a redirect, it takes into account the current `SITE_ID`.

- In the comments framework, each comment is associated with a particular site. When a comment is posted, its `site` is set to the current `SITE_ID`, and when comments are listed via the appropriate template tag, only the comments for the current site are displayed.

- In the flatpages framework (see the later section "Flatpages"), each flatpage is associated with a particular site. When a flatpage is created, you specify its `site`, and the flatpage middleware checks the current `SITE_ID` in retrieving flatpages to display.

- In the syndication framework (see Chapter 11), the templates for `title` and `description` automatically have access to a variable `{{ site }}`, which is the `Site` object representing the current site. Also, the hook for providing item URLs will use the `domain` from the current `Site` object if you don't specify a fully qualified domain.

- In the authentication framework (see Chapter 12), the `django.contrib.auth.views.login` view passes the current `Site` name to the template as `{{ site_name }}`.

Flatpages

Often you'll have a database-driven Web application up and running, but you'll need to add a couple of one-off static pages, such as an About page or a Privacy Policy page. It would be possible to use a standard Web server such as Apache to serve these files as flat HTML files, but that introduces an extra level of complexity into your application, because then you have to worry about configuring Apache, you have to set up access for your team to edit those files, and you can't take advantage of Django's template system to style the pages.

The solution to this problem is Django's flatpages application, which lives in the package `django.contrib.flatpages`. This application lets you manage such one-off pages via Django's admin site, and it lets you specify templates for them using Django's template system. It uses Django models behind the scenes, which means it stores the pages in a database, just like the rest of your data, and you can access flatpages with the standard Django database API.

Flatpages are keyed by their URL and site. When you create a flatpage, you specify which URL it's associated with, along with which site(s) it's on. (For more on sites, see the "Sites" section.)

Using Flatpages

To install the flatpages application, follow these steps:

1. Add `'django.contrib.flatpages'` to your `INSTALLED_APPS`. `django.contrib.flatpages` depends on `django.contrib.sites`, so make sure both packages are in `INSTALLED_APPS`.

2. Add `'django.contrib.flatpages.middleware.FlatpageFallbackMiddleware'` to your `MIDDLEWARE_CLASSES` setting.

3. Run the command `manage.py syncdb` to install the two required tables into your database.

The flatpages application creates two tables in your database: `django_flatpage` and `django_flatpage_sites`. `django_flatpage` simply maps a URL to a title and bunch of text content. `django_flatpage_sites` is a many-to-many table that associates a flatpage with one or more sites.

The application comes with a single `FlatPage` model, defined in `django/contrib/flatpages/models.py`. It looks like this:

```
from django.db import models
from django.contrib.sites.models import Site

class FlatPage(models.Model):
    url = models.CharField(maxlength=100)
    title = models.CharField(maxlength=200)
    content = models.TextField()
    enable_comments = models.BooleanField()
    template_name = models.CharField(maxlength=70, blank=True)
    registration_required = models.BooleanField()
    sites = models.ManyToManyField(Site)
```

Let's examine these fields one at a time:

- `url`: The URL at which this flatpage lives, excluding the domain name but including the leading slash (e.g., /about/contact/).

- `title`: The title of the flatpage. The framework doesn't do anything special with this. It's your responsibility to display it in your template.

- `content`: The content of the flatpage (i.e., the HTML of the page). The framework doesn't do anything special with this. It's your responsibility to display it in the template.

- enable_comments: Whether to enable comments on this flatpage. The framework doesn't do anything special with this. You can check this value in your template and display a comment form if needed.

- template_name: The name of the template to use for rendering this flatpage. This is optional; if it's not given or if this template doesn't exist, the framework will fall back to the template flatpages/default.html.

- registration_required: Whether registration is required for viewing this flatpage. This integrates with Django's authentication/user framework, which is explained further in Chapter 12.

- sites: The sites that this flatpage lives on. This integrates with Django's sites framework, which is explained in the "Sites" section of this chapter.

You can create flatpages through either the Django admin interface or the Django database API. For more information on this, see the section "Adding, Changing, and Deleting Flatpages."

Once you've created flatpages, FlatpageFallbackMiddleware does all of the work. Each time any Django application raises a 404 error, this middleware checks the flatpages database for the requested URL as a last resort. Specifically, it checks for a flatpage with the given URL with a site ID that corresponds to the SITE_ID setting.

If it finds a match, it loads the flatpage's template or flatpages/default.html if the flatpage has not specified a custom template. It passes that template a single context variable, flatpage, which is the flatpage object. It uses RequestContext in rendering the template.

If FlatpageFallbackMiddleware doesn't find a match, the request continues to be processed as usual.

■Note This middleware only gets activated for 404 (page not found) errors—not for 500 (server error) or other error responses. Also note that the order of MIDDLEWARE_CLASSES matters. Generally, you can put FlatpageFallbackMiddleware at or near the end of the list, because it's a last resort.

Adding, Changing, and Deleting Flatpages

You can add, change, and delete flatpages in two ways: via the admin interface and via the Python API.

Via the Admin Interface

If you've activated the automatic Django admin interface, you should see a "Flatpages" section on the admin index page. Edit flatpages as you would edit any other object in the system.

Via the Python API

As described previously, flatpages are represented by a standard Django model that lives in django/contrib/flatpages/models.py. Hence, you can access flatpage objects via the Django database API, for example:

```
>>> from django.contrib.flatpages.models import FlatPage
>>> from django.contrib.sites.models import Site
>>> fp = FlatPage(
...     url='/about/',
...     title='About',
...     content='<p>About this site...</p>',
...     enable_comments=False,
...     template_name='',
...     registration_required=False,
... )
>>> fp.save()
>>> fp.sites.add(Site.objects.get(id=1))
>>> FlatPage.objects.get(url='/about/')
<FlatPage: /about/ -- About>
```

Using Flatpage Templates

By default, flatpages are rendered via the template flatpages/default.html, but you can override that for a particular flatpage with the template_name field on the FlatPage object.

Creating the flatpages/default.html template is your responsibility. In your template directory, just create a flatpages directory containing a default.html file.

Flatpage templates are passed a single context variable, flatpage, which is the flatpage object.

Here's a sample flatpages/default.html template:

```
<!DOCTYPE HTML PUBLIC "-//W3C//DTD HTML 4.0 Transitional//EN"
    "http://www.w3.org/TR/REC-html40/loose.dtd">
<html>
<head>
<title>{{ flatpage.title }}</title>
</head>
<body>
{{ flatpage.content }}
</body>
</html>
```

Redirects

Django's redirects framework lets you manage redirects easily by storing them in a database and treating them as any other Django model object. For example, you can use the redirects framework to tell Django, "Redirect any request to /music/ to /sections/arts/music/." This comes in handy when you need to move things around on your site; Web developers should do whatever is necessary to avoid broken links.

Using the Redirects Framework

To install the redirects application, follow these steps:

1. Add `'django.contrib.redirects'` to your `INSTALLED_APPS`.

2. Add `'django.contrib.redirects.middleware.RedirectFallbackMiddleware'` to your `MIDDLEWARE_CLASSES` setting.

3. Run the command `manage.py syncdb` to install the single required table into your database.

`manage.py syncdb` creates a `django_redirect` table in your database. This is a simple lookup table with `site_id`, `old_path`, and `new_path` fields.

You can create redirects through either the Django admin interface or the Django database API. For more, see the section "Adding, Changing, and Deleting Redirects."

Once you've created redirects, the `RedirectFallbackMiddleware` class does all of the work. Each time any Django application raises a 404 error, this middleware checks the redirects database for the requested URL as a last resort. Specifically, it checks for a redirect with the given `old_path` with a site ID that corresponds to the `SITE_ID` setting. (See the earlier section "Sites" for more information on `SITE_ID` and the sites framework.) Then it follows these steps:

- If it finds a match, and `new_path` is not empty, it redirects to `new_path`.

- If it finds a match, and `new_path` is empty, it sends a 410 ("Gone") HTTP header and an empty (contentless) response.

- If it doesn't find a match, the request continues to be processed as usual.

The middleware only gets activated for 404 errors—not for 500 errors or responses of any other status code.

Note that the order of `MIDDLEWARE_CLASSES` matters. Generally, you can put `RedirectFallbackMiddleware` toward the end of the list, because it's a last resort.

■Note If you're using both the redirect and flatpage fallback middleware, consider which one (redirect or flatpage) you'd like checked first. We suggest flatpages before redirects (thus putting the flatpage middleware before the redirect middleware), but you might feel differently.

Adding, Changing, and Deleting Redirects

You can add, change, and delete redirects in two ways: via the admin interface and via the Python API.

Via the Admin Interface

If you've activated the automatic Django admin interface, you should see a "Redirects" section on the admin index page. Edit redirects as you would edit any other object in the system.

Via the Python API

Redirects are represented by a standard Django model that lives in `django/contrib/redirects/models.py`. Hence, you can access redirect objects via the Django database API, for example:

```
>>> from django.contrib.redirects.models import Redirect
>>> from django.contrib.sites.models import Site
>>> red = Redirect(
...     site=Site.objects.get(id=1),
...     old_path='/music/',
...     new_path='/sections/arts/music/',
... )
>>> red.save()
>>> Redirect.objects.get(old_path='/music/')
<Redirect: /music/ ---> /sections/arts/music/>
```

CSRF Protection

The `django.contrib.csrf` package protects against cross-site request forgery (CSRF).

CSRF, also known as "session riding," is a Web site security exploit. It happens when a malicious Web site tricks a user into unknowingly loading a URL from a site at which that user is already authenticated, hence taking advantage of the user's authenticated status. This can be a bit tricky to understand at first, so we walk through two examples in this section.

A Simple CSRF Example

Suppose you're logged in to a Webmail account at `example.com`. This Webmail site has a Log Out button that points to the URL `example.com/logout`—that is, the only action you need to take in order to log out is to visit the page `example.com/logout`.

A malicious site can coerce you to visit the URL `example.com/logout` by including that URL as a hidden `<iframe>` on its own (malicious) page. Thus, if you're logged in to the `example.com` Webmail account and visit the malicious page that has an `<iframe>` to `example.com/logout`, the act of visiting the malicious page will log you out from `example.com`.

Clearly, being logged out of a Webmail site against your will is not a terrifying breach of security, but this same type of exploit can happen to *any* site that "trusts" users, such as an online banking site or an e-commerce site.

A More Complex CSRF Example

In the previous example, `example.com` was partially at fault because it allowed a state change (i.e., logging the user out) to be requested via the HTTP `GET` method. It's much better practice to require an HTTP `POST` for any request that changes state on the server. But even Web sites that require `POST` for state-changing actions are vulnerable to CSRF.

Suppose `example.com` has upgraded its Log Out functionality so that it's a `<form>` button that is requested via `POST` to the URL `example.com/logout`. Furthermore, the logout `<form>` includes this hidden field:

```
<input type="hidden" name="confirm" value="true" />
```

This ensures that a simple POST to the URL example.com/logout won't log a user out; in order for a user to log out, the user must request example.com/logout via POST *and* send the confirm POST variable with a value of 'true'.

Well, despite the extra security, this arrangement can still be exploited by CSRF—the malicious page just needs to do a little more work. Attackers can create an entire form targeting your site, hide it in an invisible <iframe>, and then use JavaScript to submit that form automatically.

Preventing CSRF

How, then, can your site protect itself from this exploit? The first step is to make sure all GET requests are free of side effects. That way, if a malicious site includes one of your pages as an <iframe>, it won't have a negative effect.

That leaves POST requests. The second step is to give each POST <form> a hidden field whose value is secret and is generated from the user's session ID. Then, when processing the form on the server side, check for that secret field and raise an error if it doesn't validate.

This is exactly what Django's CSRF prevention layer does, as explained in the sections that follow.

Using the CSRF Middleware

The django.csrf package contains only one module: middleware.py. This module contains a Django middleware class, CsrfMiddleware, which implements the CSRF protection.

To activate this CSRF protection, add 'django.contrib.csrf.middleware.CsrfMiddleware' to the MIDDLEWARE_CLASSES setting in your settings file. This middleware needs to process the response *after* SessionMiddleware, so CsrfMiddleware must appear *before* SessionMiddleware in the list (because the response middleware is processed last-to-first). Also, it must process the response before the response gets compressed or otherwise mangled, so CsrfMiddleware must come after GZipMiddleware. Once you've added that to your MIDDLEWARE_CLASSES setting, you're done.

In case you're interested, here's how CsrfMiddleware works. It does these two things:

1. It modifies outgoing requests by adding a hidden form field to all POST forms, with the name csrfmiddlewaretoken and a value that is a hash of the session ID plus a secret key. The middleware does *not* modify the response if there's no session ID set, so the performance penalty is negligible for requests that don't use sessions.

2. On all incoming POST requests that have the session cookie set, it checks that csrfmiddlewaretoken is present and correct. If it isn't, the user will get a 403 HTTP error. The content of the 403 error page is the message "Cross Site Request Forgery detected. Request aborted."

This ensures that only forms originating from your Web site can be used to POST data back.

This middleware deliberately targets only HTTP POST requests (and the corresponding POST forms). As we explained, GET requests ought never to have side effects; it's your own responsibility to ensure this.

POST requests not accompanied by a session cookie are not protected, but they don't *need* to be protected, because a malicious Web site could make these kinds of requests anyway.

To avoid altering non-HTML requests, the middleware checks the response's Content-Type header before modifying it. Only pages that are served as text/html or application/xml+xhtml are modified.

Limitations of the CSRF Middleware

CsrfMiddleware requires Django's session framework to work. (See Chapter 12 for more on sessions.) If you're using a custom session or authentication framework that manually manages session cookies, this middleware will not help you.

If your application creates HTML pages and forms in some unusual way (e.g., if it sends fragments of HTML in JavaScript document.write statements), you might bypass the filter that adds the hidden field to the form. In this case, the form submission will always fail. (This happens because CsrfMiddleware uses a regular expression to add the csrfmiddlewaretoken field to your HTML before the page is sent to the client, and the regular expression sometimes cannot handle wacky HTML.) If you suspect this might be happening, just view the source in your Web browser to see whether csrfmiddlewaretoken was inserted into your <form>.

For more CSRF information and examples, visit http://en.wikipedia.org/wiki/Csrf/.

Form Tools

This module contains a set of high-level tools for working with Django forms (see Chapter 7). Currently, this module contains only one tool, django.contrib.formtools.preview, but there are plans to fill out the module with additional utilities.

django.contrib.formtools.preview

This is an abstraction of a common workflow: display an HTML form, force a preview (of some object created by the form), and then do something with the submission.

Given a Form that you define (see Chapter 7), this takes care of the following:

- Displays the form as HTML on a Web page

- Validates the form data once it's submitted via POST:

  - If it's valid, displays a preview page

  - If it's not valid, redisplays the form with error messages

- At the preview page, if the preview confirmation button is clicked, calls a hook that you define (a done() method)

The framework enforces the required preview by passing a shared-secret hash to the preview page. If somebody tweaks the form parameters on the preview page, the form submission will fail the hash comparison test.

Using FormPreview

Subclass FormPreview and define a done() method:

```
class FormPreview(FormPreview):

    def done(self, request, cleaned_data):
        # ...
```

This method takes an HttpRequest object and a dictionary of the form data after it has been validated and cleaned. It should return an HttpResponseRedirect.

Then, just instantiate your FormPreview subclass by passing it a Form class, and pass that to your URLconf, like so:

```
(r'^post/$', MyFormPreview(MyForm)),
```

The FormPreview class has a few other hooks. You can override any of the methods in Table 14-1 to change the behavior of the tool.

Table 14-1. *Methods on FormPreview That You Can Subclass*

Method	Description
parse_params(self, *args, **kwargs)	Given captured args and kwargs from the URLconf, saves something in self.state and/or raises Http404 if necessary.
security_hash(self, request, form)	Calculates the security hash for the given Form instance. This creates a list of the form field names/values in a deterministic order, pickles the result with the SECRET_KEY setting, and takes an MD5 hash of that. Subclasses may want to take into account request-specific information such as the IP address.
failed_hash(self, request)	Returns an HttpResponse when the security hash check fails.

The framework also uses two templates: 'formtools/preview.html' and 'formtools/form.html'. You can override these by setting preview_template and form_template attributes on your FormPreview subclass:

```
class MyFormPreview(FormPreview):

    preview_template = "myapp/my_form_preview.html"
    form_template = "myapp/my_form_template.html"

    def done(self, request, cleaned_data):
        # ...
```

Look in django/contrib/formtools/templates for the default templates.

Humanizing Data

This application holds a set of Django template filters useful for adding a "human touch" to data. To activate these filters, add 'django.contrib.humanize' to your INSTALLED_APPS setting. Once you've done that, use {% load humanize %} in a template, and you'll have access to the filters described in the following sections.

apnumber

For numbers 1 through 9, this filter returns the number spelled out. Otherwise, it returns the numeral. This follows Associated Press style.

Here are some examples:

- 1 becomes "one".

- 2 becomes "two".

- 10 becomes "10".

You can pass in either an integer or a string representation of an integer.

intcomma

This filter converts an integer to a string containing commas every three digits.

Here are some examples:

- 4500 becomes "4,500".

- 45000 becomes "45,000".

- 450000 becomes "450,000".

- 4500000 becomes "4,500,000".

You can pass in either an integer or a string representation of an integer.

intword

This filter converts a large integer to a friendly text representation. It works best for numbers over 1 million.

Here are some examples:

- 1000000 becomes "1.0 million".

- 1200000 becomes "1.2 million".

- 1200000000 becomes "1.2 billion".

Values up to 1 quadrillion (1,000,000,000,000,000) are supported. You can pass in either an integer or a string representation of an integer.

ordinal

This filter converts an integer to its ordinal as a string.

Here are some examples:

- 1 becomes "1st".

- 2 becomes "2nd".

- 3 becomes "3rd".

You can pass in either an integer or a string representation of an integer.

Markup Filters

The following collection of template filters implements common markup languages:

- `textile`: Implements Textile (`http://en.wikipedia.org/wiki/Textile_%28markup_language%29`)

- `markdown`: Implements Markdown (`http://en.wikipedia.org/wiki/Markdown`)

- `restructuredtext`: Implements ReStructured Text (`http://en.wikipedia.org/wiki/ReStructuredText`)

In each case, the filter expects formatted markup as a string and returns a string representing the marked-up text. For example, the `textile` filter converts text that is marked up in Textile format to HTML:

```
{% load markup %}
{{ object.content|textile }}
```

To activate these filters, add `'django.contrib.markup'` to your `INSTALLED_APPS` setting. Once you've done that, use `{% load markup %}` in a template, and you'll have access to these filters. For more documentation, read the source code in `django/contrib/markup/templatetags/markup.py`.

What's Next?

Many of these contributed frameworks (CSRF, the auth system, etc.) do their magic by providing a piece of *middleware*. Middleware is essentially code that runs before and/or after every single request and can modify each request and response at will. Next, we'll discuss Django's built-in middleware and explain how you can write your own.

Middleware

On occasion, you'll need to run a piece of code on each and every request that Django handles. This code might need to modify the request before the view handles it, it might need to log information about the request for debugging purposes, and so forth.

You can do this with Django's *middleware* framework, which is a set of hooks into Django's request/response processing. It's a light, low-level "plug-in" system capable of globally altering both Django's input and output.

Each middleware component is responsible for doing some specific function. If you're reading this book linearly (sorry, postmodernists), you've seen middleware a number of times already:

- All of the session and user tools that we looked at in Chapter 12 are made possible by a few small pieces of middleware (more specifically, the middleware makes request.session and request.user available to you in views).

- The sitewide cache discussed in Chapter 13 is actually just a piece of middleware that bypasses the call to your view function if the response for that view has already been cached.

- The flatpages, redirects, and csrf contributed applications from Chapter 14 all do their magic through middleware components.

This chapter dives deeper into exactly what middleware is and how it works, and explains how you can write your own middleware.

What's Middleware?

A middleware component is simply a Python class that conforms to a certain API. Before diving into the formal aspects of what that API is, let's look at a very simple example.

High-traffic sites often need to deploy Django behind a load-balancing proxy (see Chapter 20). This can cause a few small complications, one of which is that every request's remote IP (request.META["REMOTE_IP"]) will be that of the load balancer, not the actual IP making the request. Load balancers deal with this by setting a special header, X-Forwarded-For, to the actual requesting IP address.

So here's a small bit of middleware that lets sites running behind a proxy still see the correct IP address in request.META["REMOTE_ADDR"]:

```
class SetRemoteAddrFromForwardedFor(object):
    def process_request(self, request):
        try:
            real_ip = request.META['HTTP_X_FORWARDED_FOR']
        except KeyError:
            pass
        else:
            # HTTP_X_FORWARDED_FOR can be a comma-separated list of IPs.
            # Take just the first one.
            real_ip = real_ip.split(",")[0]
            request.META['REMOTE_ADDR'] = real_ip
```

If this is installed (see the next section), every request's X-Forwarded-For value will be automatically inserted into request.META['REMOTE_ADDR']. This means your Django applications don't need to be concerned with whether they're behind a load-balancing proxy; they can simply access request.META['REMOTE_ADDR'], and that will work whether or not a proxy is being used.

In fact, this is a common enough need that this piece of middleware is a built-in part of Django. It lives in django.middleware.http, and you can read a bit more about it in the next section.

Middleware Installation

If you've read this book straight through, you've already seen a number of examples of middleware installation; many of the examples in previous chapters have required certain middleware. For completeness, here's how to install middleware.

To activate a middleware component, add it to the MIDDLEWARE_CLASSES tuple in your settings module. In MIDDLEWARE_CLASSES, each middleware component is represented by a string: the full Python path to the middleware's class name. For example, here's the default MIDDLEWARE_CLASSES created by django-admin.py startproject:

```
MIDDLEWARE_CLASSES = (
    'django.middleware.common.CommonMiddleware',
    'django.contrib.sessions.middleware.SessionMiddleware',
    'django.contrib.auth.middleware.AuthenticationMiddleware',
    'django.middleware.doc.XViewMiddleware'
)
```

A Django installation doesn't require any middleware—MIDDLEWARE_CLASSES can be empty, if you'd like—but we recommend that you activate CommonMiddleware, which we explain shortly.

The order is significant. On the request and view phases, Django applies middleware in the order given in MIDDLEWARE_CLASSES, and on the response and exception phases, Django applies middleware in reverse order. That is, Django treats MIDDLEWARE_CLASSES as a sort of "wrapper" around the view function: on the request it walks down the list to the view, and on the response it walks back up. See the section "How Django Processes a Request: Complete Details" in Chapter 3 for a review of request and response handling.

Middleware Methods

Now that you know what middleware is and how to install it, let's take a look at all the available methods that middleware classes can define.

Initializer: __init__(self)

Use __init__() to perform systemwide setup for a given middleware class.

For performance reasons, each activated middleware class is instantiated only *once* per server process. This means that __init__() is called only once—at server startup—not for individual requests.

A common reason to implement an __init__() method is to check whether the middleware is indeed needed. If __init__() raises django.core.exceptions.MiddlewareNotUsed, then Django will remove the middleware from the middleware stack. You might use this feature to check for some piece of software that the middleware class requires, or check whether the server is running debug mode, or any other such environment situation.

If a middleware class defines an __init__() method, the method should take no arguments beyond the standard self.

Request Preprocessor: process_request(self, request)

This method gets called as soon as the request has been received—before Django has parsed the URL to determine which view to run. It gets passed the HttpRequest object, which you may modify at will.

process_request() should return either None or an HttpResponse object.

- If it returns None, Django will continue processing this request, executing any other middleware and then the appropriate view.

- If it returns an HttpResponse object, Django won't bother calling *any* other middleware (of any type) or the appropriate view. Django will immediately return that HttpResponse.

View Preprocessor: process_view(self, request, view, args, kwargs)

This method gets called after the request preprocessor is called and Django has determined which view to execute, but before that view has actually been executed.

The arguments passed to this view are shown in Table 15-1.

Table 15-1. *Arguments Passed to process_view()*

Argument	Explanation
request	The HttpRequest object.
view	The Python function that Django will call to handle this request. This is the actual function object itself, not the name of the function as a string.
args	The list of positional arguments that will be passed to the view, not including the request argument (which is always the first argument to a view).
kwargs	The dictionary of keyword arguments that will be passed to the view.

Just like `process_request()`, `process_view()` should return either `None` or an `HttpResponse` object.

- If it returns `None`, Django will continue processing this request, executing any other middleware and then the appropriate view.

- If it returns an `HttpResponse` object, Django won't bother calling *any* other middleware (of any type) or the appropriate view. Django will immediately return that `HttpResponse`.

Response Postprocessor: process_response(self, request, response)

This method gets called after the view function is called and the response is generated. Here, the processor can modify the content of a response; one obvious use case is content compression, such as gzipping of the request's HTML.

The parameters should be pretty self-explanatory: `request` is the request object, and `response` is the response object returned from the view. Unlike the request and view preprocessors, which may return `None`, `process_response()` *must* return an `HttpResponse` object. That response could be the original one passed into the function (possibly modified) or a brand-new one.

Exception Postprocessor: process_exception(self, request, exception)

This method gets called only if something goes wrong and a view raises an uncaught exception. You can use this hook to send error notifications, dump postmortem information to a log, or even try to recover from the error automatically.

The parameters to this function are the same `request` object we've been dealing with all along and `exception`, which is the actual `Exception` object raised by the view function.

`process_exception()` should return either `None` or an `HttpResponse` object.

- If it returns `None`, Django will continue processing this request with the framework's built-in exception handling.

- If it returns an `HttpResponse` object, Django will use that response instead of the framework's built-in exception handling.

■**Note** Django ships with a number of middleware classes (discussed in the following section) that make good examples. Reading the code for them should give you a good feel for the power of middleware. You can also find a number of community-contributed examples on Django's wiki: `http://code.djangoproject.com/wiki/ContributedMiddleware`.

Built-in Middleware

Django comes with some built-in middleware to deal with common problems, which we discuss in the sections that follow.

Authentication Support Middleware

Middleware class: `django.contrib.auth.middleware.AuthenticationMiddleware`

This middleware enables authentication support. It adds the `request.user` attribute, representing the currently logged-in user, to every incoming `HttpRequest` object. See Chapter 12 for complete details.

"Common" Middleware

Middleware class: `django.middleware.common.CommonMiddleware`

This middleware adds a few conveniences for perfectionists:

- *Forbids access to user agents in the* `DISALLOWED_USER_AGENTS` *setting*: If provided, this setting should be a list of compiled regular expression objects that are matched against the user-agent header for each incoming request. Here's an example snippet from a settings file:

```
import re

DISALLOWED_USER_AGENTS = (
        re.compile(r'^OmniExplorer_Bot'),
        re.compile(r'^Googlebot')
)
```

Note the `import re`, because `DISALLOWED_USER_AGENTS` requires its values to be compiled regexes (i.e., the output of `re.compile()`). The settings file is regular Python, so it's perfectly OK to include arbitrary code like `import` statements.

- *Performs URL rewriting based on the* `APPEND_SLASH` *and* `PREPEND_WWW` *settings*: If `APPEND_SLASH` is `True`, URLs that lack a trailing slash will be redirected to the same URL with a trailing slash, unless the last component in the path contains a period. So `foo.com/bar` is redirected to `foo.com/bar/`, but `foo.com/bar/file.txt` is passed through unchanged.

  If `PREPEND_WWW` is `True`, URLs that lack a leading `www.` will be redirected to the same URL with a leading `www.`.

  Both of these options are meant to normalize URLs. The philosophy is that each URL should exist in one—and only one—place. Technically the URL `example.com/bar` is distinct from `example.com/bar/`, which in turn is distinct from `www.example.com/bar/`. A search-engine indexer would treat these as separate URLs, which is detrimental to your site's search-engine rankings, so it's a best practice to normalize URLs.

- *Handles ETags based on the* `USE_ETAGS` *setting*: *ETags* are an HTTP-level optimization for caching pages conditionally. If `USE_ETAGS` is set to `True`, Django will calculate an ETag for each request by MD5-hashing the page content, and it will take care of sending `Not Modified` responses, if appropriate.

■**Note** There is also a conditional GET middleware, covered shortly, which handles ETags and does a bit more.

Compression Middleware

Middleware class: `django.middleware.gzip.GZipMiddleware`

This middleware automatically compresses content for browsers that understand gzip compression (all modern browsers). This can greatly reduce the amount of bandwidth a Web server consumes. The tradeoff is that it takes a bit of processing time to compress pages.

We usually prefer speed over bandwidth, but if you prefer the reverse, just enable this middleware.

Conditional GET Middleware

Middleware class: `django.middleware.http.ConditionalGetMiddleware`

This middleware provides support for conditional GET operations. If the response has an ETag or Last-Modified header, and the request has If-None-Match or If-Modified-Since, the response is replaced by an 304 ("Not modified") response.

It also removes the content from any response to a HEAD request and sets the Date and Content-Length response headers for all requests.

Reverse Proxy Support (X-Forwarded-For Middleware)

Middleware class: `django.middleware.http.SetRemoteAddrFromForwardedFor`

This is the example we examined in the "What's Middleware?" section earlier. It sets `request.META['REMOTE_ADDR']` based on `request.META['HTTP_X_FORWARDED_FOR']`, if the latter is set. This is useful if you're sitting behind a reverse proxy that causes each request's REMOTE_ADDR to be set to `127.0.0.1`.

■**Caution** This middleware does *not* validate HTTP_X_FORWARDED_FOR. If you're not behind a reverse proxy that sets HTTP_X_FORWARDED_FOR automatically, do not use this middleware. Anybody can spoof the value of HTTP_X_FORWARDED_FOR, and because this sets REMOTE_ADDR based on HTTP_X_FORWARDED_FOR, that means anybody can fake his IP address.

Only use this middleware when you can absolutely trust the value of HTTP_X_FORWARDED_FOR.

Session Support Middleware

Middleware class: `django.contrib.sessions.middleware.SessionMiddleware`

This middleware enables session support. See Chapter 12 for details.

Sitewide Cache Middleware

Middleware class: `django.middleware.cache.CacheMiddleware`

This middleware caches each Django-powered page. This was discussed in detail in Chapter 13.

Transaction Middleware

Middleware class: `django.middleware.transaction.TransactionMiddleware`

This middleware binds a database `COMMIT` or `ROLLBACK` to the request/response phase. If a view function runs successfully, a `COMMIT` is issued. If the view raises an exception, a `ROLLBACK` is issued.

The order of this middleware in the stack is important. Middleware modules running outside of it run with commit-on-save—the default Django behavior. Middleware modules running inside it (coming later in the stack) will be under the same transaction control as the view functions.

See Appendix C for more about information about database transactions.

"X-View" Middleware

Middleware class: `django.middleware.doc.XViewMiddleware`

This middleware sends custom `X-View` HTTP headers to HEAD requests that come from IP addresses defined in the `INTERNAL_IPS` setting. This is used by Django's automatic documentation system.

What's Next?

Web developers and database-schema designers don't always have the luxury of starting from scratch. In the next chapter, we'll cover how to integrate with legacy systems, such as database schemas you've inherited from the 1980s.

■ ■ ■

Integrating with Legacy Databases and Applications

Django is best suited for so-called green-field development—that is, starting projects from scratch, as if you were constructing a building on a fresh field of green grass. But despite the fact that Django favors from-scratch projects, it's possible to integrate the framework into legacy databases and applications. This chapter explains a few integration strategies.

Integrating with a Legacy Database

Django's database layer generates SQL schemas from Python code—but with a legacy database, you already have the SQL schemas. In such a case, you'll need to create models for your existing database tables. For this purpose, Django comes with a tool that can generate model code by reading your database table layouts. This tool is called `inspectdb`, and you can call it by executing the command `manage.py inspectdb`.

Using inspectdb

The `inspectdb` utility introspects the database pointed to by your settings file, determines a Django model representation for each of your tables, and prints the Python model code to standard output.

Here's a walk-through of a typical legacy database integration process from scratch. The only assumptions are that Django is installed and that you have a legacy database.

1. Create a Django project by running `django-admin.py startproject mysite` (where `mysite` is your project's name). We'll use `mysite` as the project name in this example.

2. Edit the settings file in that project, `mysite/settings.py`, to tell Django what your database connection parameters are and what the name of the database is. Specifically, provide the `DATABASE_NAME`, `DATABASE_ENGINE`, `DATABASE_USER`, `DATABASE_PASSWORD`, `DATABASE_HOST`, and `DATABASE_PORT` settings. (Note that some of these settings are optional. Refer to Chapter 5 for more information.)

3. Create a Django application within your project by running `python mysite/manage.py startapp myapp` (where `myapp` is your application's name). We'll use `myapp` as the application name here.

4. Run the command `python mysite/manage.py inspectdb`. This will examine the tables in the `DATABASE_NAME` database and print the generated model class for each table. Take a look at the output to get an idea of what `inspectdb` can do.

5. Save the output to the `models.py` file within your application by using standard shell output redirection:

```
python mysite/manage.py inspectdb > mysite/myapp/models.py
```

6. Edit the `mysite/myapp/models.py` file to clean up the generated models and make any necessary customizations. We'll give some hints for this in the next section.

Cleaning Up Generated Models

As you might expect, the database introspection isn't perfect, and you'll need to do some light cleanup of the resulting model code. Here are a few pointers for dealing with the generated models:

- Each database table is converted to a model class (i.e., there is a one-to-one mapping between database tables and model classes). This means that you'll need to refactor the models for any many-to-many join tables into `ManyToManyField` objects.

- Each generated model has an attribute for every field, including `id` primary key fields. However, recall that Django automatically adds an `id` primary key field if a model doesn't have a primary key. Thus, you'll want to remove any lines that look like this:

```
id = models.IntegerField(primary_key=True)
```

Not only are these lines redundant, but also they can cause problems if your application will be adding *new* records to these tables. The `inspectdb` command cannot detect whether a field is autoincremented, so it's up to you to change this to `AutoField`, if necessary.

- Each field's type (e.g., `CharField`, `DateField`) is determined by looking at the database column type (e.g., `VARCHAR`, `DATE`). If `inspectdb` cannot map a column's type to a model field type, it will use `TextField` and will insert the Python comment `'This field type is a guess.'` next to the field in the generated model. Keep an eye out for that, and change the field type accordingly if needed.

  If a field in your database has no ideal Django equivalent, you can safely leave it off. The Django model layer is not required to include every field in your table(s).

- If a database column name is a Python reserved word (such as `pass`, `class`, or `for`), `inspectdb` will append `'_field'` to the attribute name and set the `db_column` attribute to the real field name (e.g., `pass`, `class`, or `for`).

  For example, if a table has an `INT` column called `for`, the generated model will have a field like this:

```
for_field = models.IntegerField(db_column='for')
```

  `inspectdb` will insert the Python comment `'Field renamed because it was a Python reserved word.'` next to the field.

- If your database contains tables that refer to other tables (as most databases do), you might need to rearrange the order of the generated models so that models that refer to other models are ordered properly. For example, if model Book has a ForeignKey to model Author, model Author should be defined before model Book.

- inspectdb detects primary keys for PostgreSQL, MySQL, and SQLite. That is, it inserts primary_key=True where appropriate. For other databases, you'll need to insert primary_key=True for at least one field in each model, because Django models are required to have a primary_key=True field.

- Foreign-key detection only works with PostgreSQL and with certain types of MySQL tables. In other cases, foreign-key fields will be generated as IntegerFields, assuming the foreign-key column was an INT column.

Integrating with an Authentication System

It's possible to integrate Django with an existing authentication system—another source of usernames and passwords or authentication methods.

For example, your company may already have an LDAP server that stores a username and password for every employee. It would be a hassle for both the network administrator and the users themselves if users had separate accounts in LDAP and the Django-based applications.

To handle situations like this, the Django authentication system lets you plug in other authentication sources. You can override Django's default database-based scheme, or you can use the default system in tandem with other systems.

Specifying Authentication Back-Ends

Behind the scenes, Django maintains a list of "authentication back-ends" that it checks for authentication. When somebody calls django.contrib.auth.authenticate() (as described in Chapter 12), Django tries authenticating across all of its authentication back-ends. If the first authentication method fails, Django tries the second one, and so on, until all back-ends have been attempted.

The list of authentication back-ends to use is specified in the AUTHENTICATION_BACKENDS setting. This should be a tuple of Python path names that point to Python classes that know how to authenticate. These classes can be anywhere on your Python path.

By default, AUTHENTICATION_BACKENDS is set to the following:

```
('django.contrib.auth.backends.ModelBackend',)
```

That's the basic authentication scheme that checks the Django users database.

The order of AUTHENTICATION_BACKENDS matters, so if the same username and password are valid in multiple back-ends, Django will stop processing at the first positive match.

Writing an Authentication Back-End

An authentication back-end is a class that implements two methods: get_user(id) and authenticate(**credentials).

The get_user method takes an id—which could be a username, database ID, or whatever—and returns a User object.

The `authenticate` method takes credentials as keyword arguments. Most of the time it looks like this:

```
class MyBackend(object):
    def authenticate(self, username=None, password=None):
        # Check the username/password and return a User.
```

But it could also authenticate a token, like so:

```
class MyBackend(object):
    def authenticate(self, token=None):
        # Check the token and return a User.
```

Either way, `authenticate` should check the credentials it gets, and it should return a `User` object that matches those credentials, if the credentials are valid. If they're not valid, it should return `None`.

The Django admin system is tightly coupled to Django's own database-backed `User` object described in Chapter 12. The best way to deal with this is to create a Django `User` object for each user that exists for your back-end (e.g., in your LDAP directory, your external SQL database, etc.). Either you can write a script to do this in advance or your `authenticate` method can do it the first time a user logs in.

Here's an example back-end that authenticates against a username and password variable defined in your `settings.py` file and creates a Django `User` object the first time a user authenticates:

```
from django.conf import settings
from django.contrib.auth.models import User, check_password

class SettingsBackend(object):
    """
    Authenticate against the settings ADMIN_LOGIN and ADMIN_PASSWORD.

    Use the login name, and a hash of the password. For example:

    ADMIN_LOGIN = 'admin'
    ADMIN_PASSWORD = 'sha1$4e987$afbcf42e21bd417fb71db8c66b321e9fc33051de'
    """

    def authenticate(self, username=None, password=None):
        login_valid = (settings.ADMIN_LOGIN == username)
        pwd_valid = check_password(password, settings.ADMIN_PASSWORD)
        if login_valid and pwd_valid:
            try:
                user = User.objects.get(username=username)
            except User.DoesNotExist:
                # Create a new user. Note that we can set password
                # to anything, because it won't be checked; the password
                # from settings.py will.
                user = User(username=username, password='get from settings.py')
                user.is_staff = True
```

```
            user.is_superuser = True
            user.save()
        return user
    return None

def get_user(self, user_id):
    try:
        return User.objects.get(pk=user_id)
    except User.DoesNotExist:
        return None
```

Integrating with Legacy Web Applications

It's possible to run a Django application on the same Web server as an application powered by another technology. The most straightforward way of doing this is to use Apache's configuration file, httpd.conf, to delegate different URL patterns to different technologies. (Note that Chapter 20 covers Django deployment on Apache/mod_python, so it might be worth reading that chapter before attempting this integration.)

The key is that Django will be activated for a particular URL pattern only if your httpd.conf file says so. The default deployment explained in Chapter 20 assumes you want Django to power every page on a particular domain:

```
<Location "/">
    SetHandler python-program
    PythonHandler django.core.handlers.modpython
    SetEnv DJANGO_SETTINGS_MODULE mysite.settings
    PythonDebug On
</Location>
```

Here, the <Location "/"> line means "handle every URL, starting at the root," with Django.

It's perfectly fine to limit this <Location> directive to a certain directory tree. For example, say you have a legacy PHP application that powers most pages on a domain and you want to install a Django admin site at /admin/ without disrupting the PHP code. To do this, just set the <Location> directive to /admin/:

```
<Location "/admin/">
    SetHandler python-program
    PythonHandler django.core.handlers.modpython
    SetEnv DJANGO_SETTINGS_MODULE mysite.settings
    PythonDebug On
</Location>
```

With this in place, only the URLs that start with /admin/ will activate Django. Any other page will use whatever infrastructure already existed.

Note that attaching Django to a qualified URL (such as `/admin/` in this section's example) does not affect the Django URL parsing. Django works with the absolute URL (e.g., `/admin/people/person/add/`), not a "stripped" version of the URL (e.g., `/people/person/add/`). This means that your root URLconf should include the leading `/admin/`.

What's Next?

Speaking of the Django admin site and bending the framework to fit legacy needs, another common task is to customize the Django admin site. The next chapter focuses on such customization.

CHAPTER 17

■ ■ ■

Extending Django's Admin Interface

Chapter 6 introduced Django's admin interface, and now it's time to circle back and take a closer look.

As we've said a few times before, Django's admin interface is one of the framework's "killer features," and most Django developers find it time-saving and useful. Because the admin interface is so popular, it's common for Django developers to want to customize or extend it.

The last few sections of Chapter 6 offer some simple ways to customize certain parts of the admin interface. Before proceeding with this chapter, consider reviewing that material; it covers how to customize the admin interface's change lists and edit forms, as well as an easy way to "rebrand" the admin interface to match your site.

Chapter 6 also discusses when and why you'd want to use the admin interface, and since that material makes a good jumping-off point for the rest of this chapter, we'll reproduce it here:

> *Obviously, the admin interface is extremely useful for editing data (fancy that). If you have any sort of data entry task, the admin interface simply can't be beat. We suspect that the vast majority of readers of this book will have a whole host of data entry tasks.*
>
> *Django's admin interface especially shines when nontechnical users need to be able to enter data; that's the purpose behind the feature, after all. At the newspaper where Django was first developed, development of a typical online feature—a special report on water quality in the municipal supply, say—goes something like this:*
>
> - *The reporter responsible for the story meets with one of the developers and goes over the available data.*
>
> - *The developer designs a model around this data and then opens up the admin interface to the reporter.*
>
> - *While the reporter enters data into Django, the programmer can focus on developing the publicly accessible interface (the fun part!).*
>
> *In other words, the raison d'être of Django's admin interface is facilitating the simultaneous work of content producers and programmers.*

However, beyond the obvious data entry tasks, we find the admin interface useful in a few other cases:

- *Inspecting data models: The first thing we do when we've defined a new model is to call it up in the admin interface and enter some dummy data. This is usually when we find any data modeling mistakes; having a graphical interface to a model quickly reveals problems.*

- *Managing acquired data: There's little actual data entry associated with a site like* http://chicagocrime.org, *since most of the data comes from an automated source. However, when problems with the automatically acquired data crop up, it's useful to be able to go in and edit that data easily.*

Django's admin interface handles these common cases with little or no customization. As with most design tradeoffs, though, handling these common cases so well means that Django's admin interface doesn't handle some other modes of editing as well.

We'll talk about the cases Django's admin interface *isn't* designed to cover a bit later on, but first, let's briefly digress to a discussion on philosophy.

The Zen of Admin

At its core, Django's admin interface is designed for a single activity:

Trusted users editing structured content.

Yes, it's extremely simple—but that simplicity is based on a whole host of assumptions. The entire philosophy of Django's admin interface follows directly from these assumptions, so let's dig into the subtext of this phrase in the sections that follow.

"Trusted users . . ."

The admin interface is designed to be used by people whom you, the developer, *trust*. This doesn't just mean "people who have been authenticated"; it means that Django assumes that your content editors can be trusted to do the right thing.

This in turn means that there's no approval process for editing content—if you trust your users, nobody needs to approve of their edits. Another implication is that the permission system, while powerful, has no support for limiting access on a per-object basis as of this writing. If you trust someone to edit his or her own stories, you trust that user not to edit anyone else's stories without permission.

". . . editing . . ."

The primary purpose of Django's admin interface is to let people edit data. This seems obvious at first, but again it has some subtle and powerful repercussions.

For instance, although the admin interface is quite useful for reviewing data (as just described), it's not designed with that purpose in mind. For example, note the lack of a "can view" permission (see Chapter 12). Django assumes that if people are allowed to view content in the admin interface, they're also allowed to edit it.

Another more important thing to note is the lack of anything even remotely approaching "workflow." If a given task requires a series of steps, there's no support for enforcing that those steps be done in any particular order. Django's admin interface focuses on *editing*, not on activities surrounding editing. This avoidance of workflow also stems from the principle of trust: the admin interface's philosophy is that workflow is a personnel issue, not something to be implemented in code.

Finally, note the lack of aggregation in the admin interface. That is, there's no support for displaying totals, averages, and so forth. Again, the admin interface is for editing—it's expected that you'll write custom views for all the rest.

"... structured content"

As with the rest of Django, the admin interface wants you to work with structured data. Thus, it only supports editing data stored in Django models; for anything else, such as data stored on a filesystem, you'll need custom views.

Full Stop

It should be clear by now that Django's admin interface does *not* try to be all things to all people; instead, we choose to focus tightly on one thing and do that thing extremely well.

When it comes to extending Django's admin interface, much of that same philosophy holds (note that "extensibility" shows up nowhere in our goals). Because custom Django views can do *anything*, and because they can easily be visually integrated into the admin interface (as described in the next section), the built-in opportunities for customizing the admin interface are somewhat limited by design.

You should keep in mind that the admin interface is "just an app," albeit a very complicated one. It doesn't do anything that any Django developer with sufficient time couldn't reproduce. It's entirely possible that in the future someone will develop a different admin interface that is based on a different set of assumptions and thus will behave differently.

Finally, we should point out that, as of this writing, Django developers are working on a new version of the admin interface that allows for much more flexibility in customization. By the time you read this, those new features may have made their way into the bona fide Django distribution. To find out, ask somebody in the Django community whether the "newforms-admin" branch has been integrated.

Customizing Admin Templates

Out of the box, Django provides a number of tools for customizing the built-in admin templates, which we'll go over shortly, but for tasks beyond that (e.g., anything requiring custom workflow or granular permissions), you'll need to read the section titled "Creating Custom Admin Views" later in this chapter.

For now, though, let's look at some quick ways of customizing the appearance (and, to some extent, behavior) of the admin interface. Chapter 6 covers a few of the most common tasks: "rebranding" the Django admin interface (for those pointy-haired bosses who hate blue) and providing a custom admin form.

Past that point, the goal usually involves changing some of the templates for a particular item. Each of the admin views—the change lists, edit forms, delete confirmation pages, and history views—has an associated template that can be overridden in a number of ways.

First, you can override the template globally. The admin view looks for templates using the standard template-loading mechanism, so if you create templates in one of your template directories, Django will load those instead of the default admin templates bundled with Django. These global templates are outlined in Table 17-1.

Table 17-1. *Global Admin Templates*

View	Base Template Name
Change list	`admin/change_list.html`
Add/edit form	`admin/change_form.html`
Delete confirmation	`admin/delete_confirmation.html`
Object history	`admin/object_history.html`

Most of the time, however, you'll want to change the template for just a single object or application (not globally). Thus, each admin view looks for model- and application-specific templates first. Those views look for templates in this order:

- `admin/<app_label>/<object_name>/<template>.html`

- `admin/<app_label>/<template>.html`

- `admin/<template>.html`

For example, the add/edit form view for a `Book` model in the `books` application looks for templates in this order:

- `admin/books/book/change_form.html`

- `admin/books/change_form.html`

- `admin/change_form.html`

Custom Model Templates

Most of the time, you'll want to use the first template to create a model-specific template. This is usually best done by extending the base template and adding information to one of the blocks defined in that template.

For example, say we want to add a little bit of help text to the top of that book page. Maybe something like the form shown in Figure 17-1.

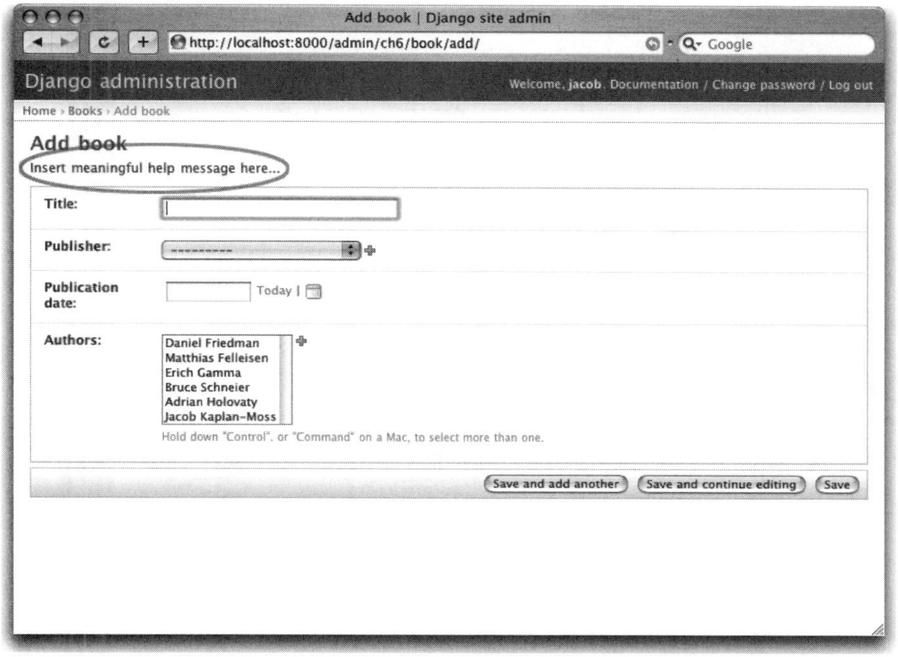

Figure 17-1. *A customized admin edit form*

This is pretty easy to do: simply create a template called `admin/books/book/change_form.html` and insert this code:

```
{% extends "admin/change_form.html" %}

{% block form_top %}
  <p>Insert meaningful help message here...</p>
{% endblock %}
```

All these templates define a number of blocks you can override. As with most programs, the best documentation is the code, so we encourage you to look through the admin templates (they're in `django/contrib/admin/templates/`) for the most up-to-date information.

Custom JavaScript

A common use for these custom model templates involves adding custom JavaScript to admin pages—perhaps to implement some special widget or client-side behavior.

Luckily, that couldn't be easier. Each admin template defines a `{% block extrahead %}`, which you can use to put extra content into the `<head>` element. For example, if you want to include jQuery (`http://jquery.com/`) in your admin history, it's as simple as this:

```
{% extends "admin/object_history.html" %}

{% block extrahead %}
    <script src="http://media.example.com/javascript/jquery.js"
    type="text/javascript">
    </script>
    <script type="text/javascript">

        // code to actually use jQuery here...

    </script>
{% endblock %}
```

■Note We're not sure why you'd need jQuery on the object history page, but, of course, this example applies to any of the admin templates.

You can use this technique to include any sort of extra JavaScript widgets you might need.

Creating Custom Admin Views

At this point, anyone looking to add custom *behavior* to Django's admin interface is probably starting to get a bit frustrated. "All you've talked about is how to change the admin interface *visually*," we hear them cry. "But how do I change the way the admin interface *works*?"

The first thing to understand is that *it's not magic*. That is, nothing the admin interface does is "special" in any way—the admin interface is just a set of views (they live in django.contrib. admin.views) that manipulate data just like any other view.

Sure, there's quite a bit of code in there; it has to deal with all the various options, field types, and settings that influence model behavior. Still, when you realize that the admin interface is just a set of views, adding custom admin views becomes easier to understand.

By way of example, let's add a "publisher report" view to our book application from Chapter 6. We'll build an admin view that shows the list of books broken down by publisher—a pretty typical example of a custom admin "report" view you might need to build.

First, let's wire up a view in our URLconf. We need to insert this line:

```
(r'^admin/books/report/$', 'mysite.books.admin_views.report'),
```

before the line including the admin views. A bare-bones URLconf might look like this:

```
from django.conf.urls.defaults import *

urlpatterns = patterns('',
    (r'^admin/books/report/$', 'mysite.books.admin_views.report'),
    (r'^admin/', include('django.contrib.admin.urls')),
)
```

Why put the custom view *before* the admin inclusion? Recall that Django processes URL patterns in order. The admin inclusion matches nearly anything that falls under the inclusion point, so if we reverse the order of those lines, Django will find a built-in admin view for that pattern, which won't work. In this particular case, it will try to load a change list for a Report model in the books application, which doesn't exist.

Now let's write our view. For the sake of simplicity, we'll just load all books into the context and let the template handle the grouping with the {% regroup %} tag. Create a file, bookstore/admin_views.py, with this code:

```
from mysite.books.models import Book
from django.template import RequestContext
from django.shortcuts import render_to_response
from django.contrib.admin.views.decorators import staff_member_required

@staff_member_required
def report(request):
    return render_to_response(
        "admin/books/report.html",
        {'book_list' : Book.objects.all()},
        RequestContext(request, {}),
    )
```

Because we left the grouping up to the template, this view is pretty simple. However, there are some subtle bits here worth making explicit:

- We use the staff_member_required decorator from django.contrib.admin.views. decorators. This is similar to the login_required decorator discussed in Chapter 12, but this decorator also checks that the given user is marked as a "staff" member, and thus is allowed access to the admin interface.

  This decorator protects all the built-in admin views and makes the authentication logic for your view match the rest of the admin interface.

- We render a template located under admin/. While this isn't strictly required, it's considered good practice to keep all your admin templates grouped in an admin directory. We've also put the template in a directory named books after our application—also a best practice.

- We use RequestContext as the third parameter (context_instance) to render_to_response. This ensures that information about the current user is available to the template.

  See Chapter 10 for more about RequestContext.

Finally, we'll make a template for this view. We'll extend the built-in admin templates to make this view visually appear to be part of the admin interface:

```
{% extends "admin/base_site.html" %}

{% block title %}List of books by publisher{% endblock %}
```

```
{% block content %}
<div id="content-main">
  <h1>List of books by publisher:</h1>
  {% regroup book_list|dictsort:"publisher.name" by publisher as
  books_by_publisher %}
  {% for publisher in books_by_publisher %}
    <h3>{{ publisher.grouper }}</h3>
    <ul>
      {% for book in publisher.list|dictsort:"title" %}
        <li>{{ book }}</li>
      {% endfor %}
    </ul>
  {% endfor %}
</div>
{% endblock %}
```

By extending admin/base_site.html, we get the look and feel of the Django admin "for free." Figure 17-2 shows what the end result looks like.

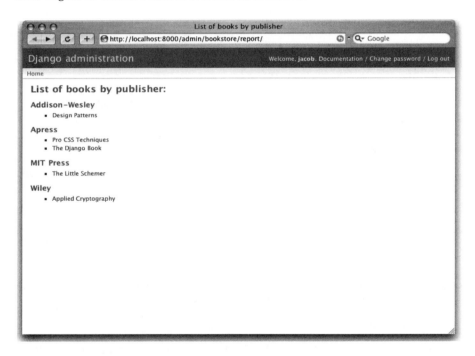

Figure 17-2. *A custom "books by publisher" admin view*

You can use this technique to add anything you can dream of to the admin interface. Remember that these so-called custom admin views are really just normal Django views; you can use all the techniques you learn in the rest of this book to provide as complex an admin interface as you need.

We'll close out this chapter with some ideas for custom admin views.

Overriding Built-in Views

At times the default admin views just don't cut it. You can easily swap in your own custom view for any stage of the admin interface; just let your URL "shadow" the built-in admin one. That is, if your view comes before the default admin view in the URLconf, your view will be called instead of the default one.

For example, we could replace the built-in "create" view for a book with a form that lets the user simply enter an ISBN. We could then look up the book's information from http://isbn.nu/ and create the object automatically.

The code for such a view is left as an exercise for the reader, but the important part is this URLconf snippet:

```
(r'^admin/books/book/add/$', 'mysite.books.admin_views.add_by_isbn'),
```

If this bit comes before the admin URLs in your URLconf, the add_by_isbn view will completely replace the standard admin view.

We could follow a similar tack to replace a delete confirmation page, the edit page, or any other part of the admin interface.

What's Next?

If you're a native English speaker—and we expect that many readers of this English-language book are—you might not have noticed one of the coolest features of the admin interface: it's available in almost 40 different languages! This is made possible by Django's internationalization framework (and the hard work of Django's volunteer translators). The next chapter explains how to use this framework to provide localized Django sites.

Avanti!

CHAPTER 18

■ ■ ■

Internationalization

Django was originally developed smack in the middle of the United States (literally; Lawrence, Kansas, is fewer than 40 miles from the geographic center of the continental United States). Like most open source projects, though, Django's community grew to include people from all over the globe. As Django's community became increasingly diverse, *internationalization* and *localization* became increasingly important. Since many developers have at best a fuzzy understanding of these terms, we'll define them briefly.

Internationalization refers to the process of designing programs for the potential use of any locale. This includes marking text (like UI elements and error messages) for future translation, abstracting the display of dates and times so that different local standards may be observed, providing support for differing time zones, and generally making sure that the code contains no assumptions about the location of its users. You'll often see "internationalization" abbreviated I18N (the number 18 refers to the number of letters omitted between the initial "I" and the terminal "N").

Localization refers to the process of actually translating an internationalized program for use in a particular locale. You'll sometimes see "localization" abbreviated as L10N.

Django itself is fully internationalized; all strings are marked for translation, and settings control the display of locale-dependent values like dates and times. Django also ships with over 40 different localization files. If you're not a native English speaker, there's a good chance that Django is already translated into your primary language.

The same internationalization framework used for these localizations is available for you to use in your own code and templates. In a nutshell, you'll need to add a minimal number of hooks to your Python code and templates. These hooks are called *translation strings*. They tell Django, "This text should be translated into the end user's language, if a translation for this text is available in that language."

Django takes care of using these hooks to translate Web applications, on the fly, according to users' language preferences. Essentially, Django does two things:

- It lets developers and template authors specify which parts of their applications should be translatable.

- It uses that information to translate Web applications for particular users according to their language preferences.

■**Note** Django's translation machinery uses GNU gettext (http://www.gnu.org/software/gettext/) via the standard gettext module that comes with Python.

IF YOU DON'T NEED INTERNATIONALIZATION

Django's internationalization hooks are enabled by default, which incurs a small bit of overhead. If you don't use internationalization, you should set USE_I18N = False in your settings file. If USE_I18N is set to False, then Django will make some optimizations so as not to load the internationalization machinery.

You'll probably also want to remove 'django.core.context_processors.i18n' from your TEMPLATE_CONTEXT_PROCESSORS setting.

Specifying Translation Strings in Python Code

Translation strings specify "This text should be translated." These strings can appear in your Python code and templates. It's your responsibility to mark translatable strings; the system can only translate strings it knows about.

Standard Translation Functions

Specify a translation string by using the function _(). (Yes, the name of the function is the underscore character.) This function is available globally (i.e., as a built-in language); you don't have to import it.

In this example, the text "Welcome to my site." is marked as a translation string:

```
def my_view(request):
    output = _("Welcome to my site.")
    return HttpResponse(output)
```

The function django.utils.translation.gettext() is identical to _(). This example is identical to the previous one:

```
from django.utils.translation import gettext
def my_view(request):
    output = gettext("Welcome to my site.")
    return HttpResponse(output)
```

Most developers prefer to use _(), as it's shorter.

Translation works on computed values. This example is identical to the previous two:

```
def my_view(request):
    words = ['Welcome', 'to', 'my', 'site.']
    output = _(' '.join(words))
    return HttpResponse(output)
```

Translation works on variables. Again, here's an identical example:

```
def my_view(request):
    sentence = 'Welcome to my site.'
    output = _(sentence)
    return HttpResponse(output)
```

(The caveat with using variables or computed values, as in the previous two examples, is that Django's translation string–detecting utility, make-messages.py, won't be able to find these strings. More on make-messages later.)

The strings you pass to _() or gettext() can take placeholders, specified with Python's standard named-string interpolation syntax, for example:

```
def my_view(request, n):
    output = _('%(name)s is my name.') % {'name': n}
    return HttpResponse(output)
```

This technique lets language-specific translations reorder the placeholder text. For example, an English translation may be "Adrian is my name.", while a Spanish translation may be "Me llamo Adrian.", with the placeholder (the name) placed after the translated text instead of before it.

For this reason, you should use named-string interpolation (e.g., %(name)s) instead of positional interpolation (e.g., %s or %d). If you use positional interpolation, translations won't be able to reorder placeholder text.

Marking Strings As No-op

Use the function django.utils.translation.gettext_noop() to mark a string as a translation string without actually translating it at that moment. Strings thus marked aren't translated until the last possible moment.

Use this approach if you have constant strings that should be stored in the original language—such as strings in a database—but should be translated at the last possible point in time, such as when the string is presented to the user.

Lazy Translation

Use the function django.utils.translation.gettext_lazy() to translate strings lazily—when the value is accessed rather than when the gettext_lazy() function is called.

For example, to mark a field's help_text attribute as translatable, do the following:

```
from django.utils.translation import gettext_lazy

class MyThing(models.Model):
    name = models.CharField(help_text=gettext_lazy('This is the help text'))
```

In this example, gettext_lazy() stores a lazy reference to the string, not the actual translation. The translation itself will be done when the string is used in a string context, such as template rendering on the Django admin site.

If you don't like the verbose name gettext_lazy, you can just alias it as _ (underscore), like so:

```
from django.utils.translation import gettext_lazy as _

class MyThing(models.Model):
    name = models.CharField(help_text=_('This is the help text'))
```

Always use lazy translations in Django models (otherwise they won't be translated correctly on a per-user basis). And it's a good idea to add translations for the field names and table names, too. This means writing explicit verbose_name and verbose_name_plural options in the Meta class:

```
from django.utils.translation import gettext_lazy as _

class MyThing(models.Model):
    name = models.CharField(_('name'), help_text=_('This is the help text'))
    class Meta:
        verbose_name = _('my thing')
        verbose_name_plural = _('mythings')
```

Pluralization

Use the function django.utils.translation.ngettext() to specify messages that have different singular and plural forms, for example:

```
from django.utils.translation import ngettext
def hello_world(request, count):
    page = ngettext(
        'there is %(count)d object',
        'there are %(count)d objects', count
    ) % {'count': count}
    return HttpResponse(page)
```

ngettext takes three arguments: the singular translation string, the plural translation string, and the number of objects (which is passed to the translation languages as the count variable).

Specifying Translation Strings in Template Code

Using translations in Django templates involves two template tags and a slightly different syntax than in Python code. To give your template access to these tags, put {% load i18n %} toward the top of your template.

The {% trans %} template tag marks a string for translations:

```
<title>{% trans "This is the title." %}</title>
```

If you only want to mark a value for translation, but translate it later, use the noop option:

```
<title>{% trans "value" noop %}</title>
```

It's not possible to use template variables in {% trans %}—only constant strings, in single or double quotes, are allowed. If your translations require variables (placeholders), use {% blocktrans %}, for example:

```
{% blocktrans %}This will have {{ value }} inside.{% endblocktrans %}
```

To translate a template expression—say, using template filters—you need to bind the expression to a local variable for use within the translation block:

```
{% blocktrans with value|filter as myvar %}
  This will have {{ myvar }} inside.
{% endblocktrans %}
```

If you need to bind more than one expression inside a blocktrans tag, separate the pieces with and:

```
{% blocktrans with book|title as book_t and author|title as author_t %}
  This is {{ book_t }} by {{ author_t }}
{% endblocktrans %}
```

To pluralize, specify both the singular and plural forms with the {% plural %} tag, which appears within {% blocktrans %} and {% endblocktrans %}:

```
{% blocktrans count list|length as counter %}
  There is only one {{ name }} object.
{% plural %}
  There are {{ counter }} {{ name }} objects.
{% endblocktrans %}
```

Internally, all block and inline translations use the appropriate gettext/ngettext call.

When you use RequestContext (see Chapter 10), your templates have access to three translation-specific variables:

- {{ LANGUAGES }} is a list of tuples in which the first element is the language code and the second is the language name (in that language).

- {{ LANGUAGE_CODE }} is the current user's preferred language, as a string (e.g., en-us). (See the "How Django Discovers Language Preference" section for more information.)

- {{ LANGUAGE_BIDI }} is the current language's writing system. If True, it's a right-to-left language (e.g., Hebrew, Arabic). If False, it's a left-to-right language (e.g., English, French, German).

You can also load these values using template tags:

```
{% load i18n %}
{% get_current_language as LANGUAGE_CODE %}
{% get_available_languages as LANGUAGES %}
{% get_current_language_bidi as LANGUAGE_BIDI %}
```

Translation hooks are also available within any template block tag that accepts constant strings. In those cases, just use _() syntax to specify a translation string, for example:

```
{% some_special_tag _("Page not found") value|yesno:_("yes,no") %}
```

In this case, both the tag and the filter will see the already translated string (i.e., the string is translated *before* being passed to the tag handler functions), so they don't need to be aware of translations.

Creating Language Files

Once you've tagged your strings for later translation, you need to write (or obtain) the language translations themselves. In this section we explain how that works.

Creating Message Files

The first step is to create a *message file* for a new language. A message file is a plain-text file representing a single language that contains all available translation strings and how they should be represented in the given language. Message files have a .po file extension.

Django comes with a tool, bin/make-messages.py, that automates the creation and maintenance of these files.

To create or update a message file, run this command:

```
bin/make-messages.py -l de
```

where de is the language code for the message file you want to create. The language code, in this case, is in locale format. For example, it's pt_BR for Brazilian Portuguese and de_AT for Austrian German. Take a look at the language codes in the django/conf/locale directory to see which languages are currently supported.

The script should be run from one of three places:

- The root django directory (not a Subversion checkout, but the one that is linked to via $PYTHONPATH or is located somewhere on that path)

- The root directory of your Django project

- The root directory of your Django application

The script runs over the entire tree it is run on and pulls out all strings marked for translation. It creates (or updates) a message file in the directory conf/locale. In the de example, the file will be conf/locale/de/LC_MESSAGES/django.po.

If the script is run over your project source tree or your application source tree, it will do the same, but the location of the locale directory is locale/LANG/LC_MESSAGES (note the missing conf prefix). The first time you run it on your tree you'll need to create the locale directory.

■**Note** If you don't have the gettext utilities installed, make-messages.py will create empty files. If that's the case, either install the gettext utilities or just copy the English message file (conf/locale/en/ LC_MESSAGES/django.po) and use it as a starting point; it's just an empty translation file.

The format of .po files is straightforward. Each .po file contains a small bit of metadata, such as the translation maintainer's contact information, but the bulk of the file is a list of *messages*—simple mappings between translation strings and the actual translated text for the particular language.

For example, if your Django application contains a translation string for the text "Welcome to my site.", like so:

```
_("Welcome to my site.")
```

then make-messages.py will have created a .po file containing the following snippet, a message:

```
#: path/to/python/module.py:23
msgid "Welcome to my site."
msgstr ""
```

A quick explanation is in order:

- msgid is the translation string, which appears in the source. Don't change it.

- msgstr is where you put the language-specific translation. It starts out empty, so it's your responsibility to change it. Make sure you keep the quotes around your translation.

- As a convenience, each message includes the file name and line number from which the translation string was gleaned.

Long messages are a special case. The first string directly after msgstr (or msgid) is an empty string. Then the content itself will be written over the next few lines as one string per line. Those strings are directly concatenated. Don't forget trailing spaces within the strings; otherwise, they'll be tacked together without whitespace!

For example, here's a multiline translation (taken from the Spanish localization that ships with Django):

```
msgid ""
"There's been an error. It's been reported to the site administrators via e-"
"mail and should be fixed shortly. Thanks for your patience."
msgstr ""
"Ha ocurrido un error. Se ha informado a los administradores del sitio "
"mediante correo electrónico y debería arreglarse en breve. Gracias por su "
"paciencia."
```

Note the trailing spaces.

MIND YOUR CHARSET

When creating a .po file with your favorite text editor, first edit the charset line (search for "CHARSET") and set it to the charset you'll be using to edit the content. Generally, UTF-8 should work for most languages, but gettext should handle any charset you throw at it.

To reexamine all source code and templates for new translation strings and update all message files for *all* languages, run this:

```
make-messages.py -a
```

Compiling Message Files

After you create your message file, and each time you make changes to it, you'll need to compile it into a more efficient form, for use by gettext. Do this with the bin/compile-messages.py utility.

This tool runs over all available .po files and creates .mo files, which are binary files optimized for use by gettext. In the same directory from which you ran make-messages.py, run compile-messages.py like this:

```
bin/compile-messages.py
```

That's it. Your translations are ready for use.

How Django Discovers Language Preference

Once you've prepared your translations—or, if you just want to use the translations that are included with Django—you'll just need to activate translation for your application. Behind the scenes, Django has a very flexible model of deciding which language should be used: installation-wide, for a particular user, or both.

To set an installation-wide language preference, set LANGUAGE_CODE in your settings file. Django uses this language as the default translation—the final attempt if no other translator finds a translation.

If all you want to do is run Django with your native language, and a language file is available for your language, simply set LANGUAGE_CODE.

If you want to let each individual user specify the language he or she prefers, use LocaleMiddleware. LocaleMiddleware enables language selection based on data from the request. It customizes content for each user.

To use LocaleMiddleware, add 'django.middleware.locale.LocaleMiddleware' to your MIDDLEWARE_CLASSES setting. Because middleware order matters, you should follow these guidelines:

- Make sure it's among the first middleware classes installed.

- It should come after SessionMiddleware, because LocaleMiddleware makes use of session data.

- If you use CacheMiddleware, put LocaleMiddleware after it (otherwise users could get cached content from the wrong locale).

For example, your MIDDLEWARE_CLASSES might look like this:

```
MIDDLEWARE_CLASSES = (
    'django.middleware.common.CommonMiddleware',
    'django.contrib.sessions.middleware.SessionMiddleware',
    'django.middleware.locale.LocaleMiddleware'
)
```

LocaleMiddleware tries to determine the user's language preference by following this algorithm:

- First, it looks for a django_language key in the current user's session.

- Failing that, it looks for a cookie called django_language.

- Failing that, it looks at the Accept-Language HTTP header. This header is sent by your browser and tells the server which language(s) you prefer, in order of priority. Django tries each language in the header until it finds one with available translations.

- Failing that, it uses the global LANGUAGE_CODE setting.

In each of these places, the language preference is expected to be in the standard language format, as a string. For example, Brazilian Portuguese is pt-br. If a base language is available but the sublanguage specified is not, Django uses the base language. For example, if a user specifies de-at (Austrian German), but Django has only de available, Django uses de.

Only languages listed in the LANGUAGES setting can be selected. If you want to restrict the language selection to a subset of provided languages (because your application doesn't provide all those languages), set your LANGUAGES setting to a list of languages, for example:

```
LANGUAGES = (
    ('de', _('German')),
    ('en', _('English')),
)
```

This example restricts languages that are available for automatic selection to German and English (and any sublanguage, like de-ch or en-us).

If you define a custom LANGUAGES, it's OK to mark the languages as translation strings—but use a "dummy" gettext() function, not the one in django.utils.translation. You should *never* import django.utils.translation from within your settings file, because that module itself depends on the settings, and that would cause a circular import.

The solution is to use a "dummy" gettext() function. Here's a sample settings file:

```
_ = lambda s: s

LANGUAGES = (
    ('de', _('German')),
    ('en', _('English')),
)
```

With this arrangement, make-messages.py will still find and mark these strings for translation, but the translation won't happen at runtime, so you'll have to remember to wrap the languages in the *real* gettext() in any code that uses LANGUAGES at runtime.

The LocaleMiddleware can only select languages for which there is a Django-provided base translation. If you want to provide translations for your application that aren't already in the set of translations in Django's source tree, you'll want to provide at least basic translations for that language. For example, Django uses technical message IDs to translate date formats and time formats—so you will need at least those translations for the system to work correctly.

A good starting point is to copy the English .po file and to translate at least the technical messages, and maybe the validator messages, too.

Technical message IDs are easily recognized; they're all uppercase. You don't translate the message ID as with other messages; rather, you provide the correct local variant on the provided English value. For example, with `DATETIME_FORMAT` (or `DATE_FORMAT` or `TIME_FORMAT`), this would be the format string that you want to use in your language. The format is identical to the format strings used by the `now` template tag.

Once `LocaleMiddleware` determines the user's preference, it makes this preference available as `request.LANGUAGE_CODE` for each request object. Feel free to read this value in your view code. Here's a simple example:

```
def hello_world(request, count):
    if request.LANGUAGE_CODE == 'de-at':
        return HttpResponse("You prefer to read Austrian German.")
    else:
        return HttpResponse("You prefer to read another language.")
```

Note that with static (i.e., without middleware) translation, the language is in `settings.LANGUAGE_CODE`, while with dynamic (middleware) translation, it's in `request.LANGUAGE_CODE`.

The set_language Redirect View

As a convenience, Django comes with a view, `django.views.i18n.set_language`, that sets a user's language preference and redirects back to the previous page. Activate this view by adding the following line to your URLconf:

```
(r'^i18n/', include('django.conf.urls.i18n')),
```

(Note that this example makes the view available at `/i18n/setlang/`.)

The view expects to be called via the `GET` method, with a `language` parameter set in the query string. If session support is enabled, the view saves the language choice in the user's session. Otherwise, it saves the language choice in a `django_language` cookie.

After setting the language choice, Django redirects the user, following this algorithm:

- Django looks for a `next` parameter in the query string.

- If that doesn't exist or is empty, Django tries the URL in the `Referer` header.

- If that's empty—say, if a user's browser suppresses that header—then the user will be redirected to / (the site root) as a fallback.

Here's example HTML template code:

```
<form action="/i18n/setlang/" method="get">
<input name="next" type="hidden" value="/next/page/" />
<select name="language">
{% for lang in LANGUAGES %}
<option value="{{ lang.0 }}">{{ lang.1 }}</option>
{% endfor %}
</select>
<input type="submit" value="Go" />
</form>
```

Using Translations in Your Own Projects

Django looks for translations by following this algorithm:

- First, it looks for a `locale` directory in the application directory of the view that's being called. If it finds a translation for the selected language, the translation will be installed.

- Next, it looks for a `locale` directory in the project directory. If it finds a translation, the translation will be installed.

- Finally, it checks the base translation in `django/conf/locale`.

This way, you can write applications that include their own translations, and you can override base translations in your project path. Or, you can just build a big project out of several applications and put all translations into one big project message file. The choice is yours.

■**Note** If you're using manually configured settings, the `locale` directory in the project directory will not be examined, since Django loses the ability to work out the location of the project directory. (Django normally uses the location of the settings file to determine this, and a settings file doesn't exist if you're manually configuring your settings.)

All message file repositories are structured the same way:

- `$APPPATH/locale/<language>/LC_MESSAGES/django.(po|mo)`

- `$PROJECTPATH/locale/<language>/LC_MESSAGES/django.(po|mo)`

- All paths listed in `LOCALE_PATHS` in your settings file are searched in that order for `<language>/LC_MESSAGES/django.(po|mo)`

- `$PYTHONPATH/django/conf/locale/<language>/LC_MESSAGES/django.(po|mo)`

To create message files, you use the same `make-messages.py` tool as with the Django message files. You only need to be in the right place—in the directory where either the `conf/locale` (in case of the source tree) or the `locale/` (in case of application messages or project messages) directory is located. And you use the same `compile-messages.py` to produce the binary `django.mo` files that are used by `gettext`.

Application message files are a bit complicated to discover—they need the `LocaleMiddleware`. If you don't use the middleware, only the Django message files and project message files will be processed.

Finally, you should give some thought to the structure of your translation files. If your applications need to be delivered to other users and will be used in other projects, you might want to use application-specific translations. But using application-specific translations and project translations could produce weird problems with `make-messages`. `make-messages` will traverse all directories below the current path and so might put message IDs into the project message file that are already in application message files.

The easiest way out is to store applications that are not part of the project (and so carry their own translations) outside the project tree. That way, make-messages on the project level will only translate strings that are connected to your explicit project and not strings that are distributed independently.

Translations and JavaScript

Adding translations to JavaScript poses some problems:

- JavaScript code doesn't have access to a gettext implementation.

- JavaScript code doesn't have access to .po or .mo files; they need to be delivered by the server.

- The translation catalogs for JavaScript should be kept as small as possible.

Django provides an integrated solution for these problems: it passes the translations into JavaScript, so you can call gettext and friends from within JavaScript.

The javascript_catalog View

The main solution to these problems is the javascript_catalog view, which generates a JavaScript code library with functions that mimic the gettext interface, plus an array of translation strings. Those translation strings are taken from the application, project, or Django core, according to what you specify in either the info_dict or the URL.

You hook it up like this:

```
js_info_dict = {
    'packages': ('your.app.package',),
}

urlpatterns = patterns('',
    (r'^jsi18n/$', 'django.views.i18n.javascript_catalog', js_info_dict),
)
```

Each string in packages should be in Python dotted-package syntax (the same format as the strings in INSTALLED_APPS) and should refer to a package that contains a locale directory. If you specify multiple packages, all those catalogs are merged into one catalog. This is useful if you're depending upon JavaScript that uses strings from different applications.

You can make the view dynamic by putting the packages into the URL pattern:

```
urlpatterns = patterns('',
    (r'^jsi18n/(?P<packages>\S+?)/$', 'django.views.i18n.javascript_catalog'),
)
```

With this, you specify the packages as a list of package names delimited by plus signs (+) in the URL. This is especially useful if your pages use code from different applications, and this changes often and you don't want to pull in one big catalog file. As a security measure, these values can only be either django.conf or any package from the INSTALLED_APPS setting.

Using the JavaScript Translation Catalog

To use the catalog, just pull in the dynamically generated script like this:

```
<script type="text/javascript" src="/path/to/jsi18n/"></script>
```

This is how the admin site fetches the translation catalog from the server. When the catalog is loaded, your JavaScript code can use the standard gettext interface to access it:

```
document.write(gettext('this is to be translated'));
```

There even is an ngettext interface and a string interpolation function:

```
d = {
    count: 10
};
s = interpolate(ngettext('this is %(count)s object', 'this are %(count)s objects',
    d.count), d);
```

The interpolate function supports both positional interpolation and named interpolation. So the preceding code could have been written as follows:

```
s = interpolate(ngettext('this is %s object', 'this are %s objects', 11), [11]);
```

The interpolation syntax is borrowed from Python. You shouldn't go over the top with string interpolation, though—this is still JavaScript, so the code will have to do repeated regular expression substitutions. This isn't as fast as string interpolation in Python, so keep it to those cases where you really need it (e.g., in conjunction with ngettext to produce proper pluralization).

Creating JavaScript Translation Catalogs

You create and update the translation catalogs the same way as the other Django translation catalogs: with the `make-messages.py` tool. The only difference is you need to provide a -d djangojs parameter, like this:

```
make-messages.py -d djangojs -l de
```

This creates or updates the translation catalog for JavaScript for German. After updating translation catalogs, just run compile-messages.py the same way as you do with normal Django translation catalogs.

Notes for Users Familiar with gettext

If you know gettext, you might note these special things in the way Django does translation:

- The string domain is django or djangojs. The string domain is used to differentiate between different programs that store their data in a common message-file library (usually /usr/share/locale/). The django domain is used for Python and template translation strings, and is loaded into the global translation catalogs. The djangojs domain is only used for JavaScript translation catalogs to make sure that those are as small as possible.

- Django only uses gettext and gettext_noop. That's because Django always uses DEFAULT_CHARSET strings internally. There isn't much benefit to using ugettext, because you'll always need to produce UTF-8 anyway.

- Django doesn't use xgettext alone. It uses Python wrappers around xgettext and msgfmt. That's mostly for convenience.

What's Next?

This chapter mostly concludes our coverage of Django's features. You should now know enough to start producing your own Django sites.

However, writing the code is only the first step in deploying a successful Web site. The next two chapters cover the things you'll need to know if you want your site to survive in the real world. Chapter 19 discusses how you can secure your site and your users from malicious attackers, and Chapter 20 details how to deploy a Django application onto one or many servers.

CHAPTER 19

■■■

Security

The Internet can be a scary place.

These days, high-profile security gaffes seem to crop up on a daily basis. We've seen viruses spread with amazing speed, swarms of compromised computers wielded as weapons, a never-ending arms race against spammers, and many, many reports of identify theft from hacked Web sites.

As Web developers, we have a duty to do what we can to combat these forces of darkness. Every Web developer needs to treat security as a fundamental aspect of Web programming. Unfortunately, it turns out that implementing security is *hard*—attackers need to find only a single vulnerability, but defenders have to protect every single one.

Django attempts to mitigate this difficulty. It's designed to automatically protect you from many of the common security mistakes that new (and even experienced) Web developers make. Still, it's important to understand what these problems are, how Django protects you, and—most important—the steps you can take to make your code even more secure.

First, though, an important disclaimer: We do not intend to present a definitive guide to every known Web security exploit, and so we won't try to explain each vulnerability in a comprehensive manner. Instead, we'll give a short synopsis of security problems as they apply to Django.

The Theme of Web Security

If you learn only one thing from this chapter, let it be this:

Never—under any circumstances—trust data from the browser.

You *never* know who's on the other side of that HTTP connection. It might be one of your users, but it just as easily could be a nefarious cracker looking for an opening.

Any data of any nature that comes from the browser needs to be treated with a healthy dose of paranoia. This includes data that's both "in band" (i.e., submitted from Web forms) and "out of band" (i.e., HTTP headers, cookies, and other request information). It's trivial to spoof the request metadata that browsers usually add automatically.

Every one of the vulnerabilities discussed in this chapter stems directly from trusting data that comes over the wire and then failing to sanitize that data before using it. You should make it a general practice to continuously ask, "Where does this data come from?"

SQL Injection

SQL injection is a common exploit in which an attacker alters Web page parameters (such as GET/POST data or URLs) to insert arbitrary SQL snippets that a naive Web application executes in its database directly. It's probably the most dangerous—and, unfortunately, one of the most common—vulnerabilities out there.

This vulnerability most commonly crops up when constructing SQL "by hand" from user input. For example, imagine writing a function to gather a list of contact information from a contact search page. To prevent spammers from reading every single email in our system, we'll force the user to type in someone's username before providing her email address:

```
def user_contacts(request):
    user = request.GET['username']
    sql = "SELECT * FROM user_contacts WHERE username = '%s';" % username
    # execute the SQL here...
```

■**Note** In this example, and all similar "don't do this" examples that follow, we've deliberately left out most of the code needed to make the functions actually work. We don't want this code to work if someone accidentally takes it out of context.

Though at first this doesn't look dangerous, it really is. First, our attempt at protecting our entire email list will fail with a cleverly constructed query. Think about what happens if an attacker types "' OR 'a'='a" into the query box. In that case, the query that the string interpolation will construct will be

```
SELECT * FROM user_contacts WHERE username = '' OR 'a' = 'a';
```

Because we allowed unsecured SQL into the string, the attacker's added OR clause ensures that every single row is returned.

However, that's the *least* scary attack. Imagine what will happen if the attacker submits "'; DELETE FROM user_contacts WHERE 'a' = 'a'". We'll end up with this complete query:

```
SELECT * FROM user_contacts WHERE username = '';
DELETE FROM user_contacts WHERE 'a' = 'a';
```

Yikes! Where'd our contact list go?

The Solution

Although this problem is insidious and sometimes hard to spot, the solution is simple: *never* trust user-submitted data, and *always* escape it when passing it into SQL.

The Django database API does this for you. It automatically escapes all special SQL parameters, according to the quoting conventions of the database server you're using (e.g., PostgreSQL or MySQL).

For example, in this API call:

```
foo.objects.filter(bar__exact="' OR 1=1")
```

Django will escape the input accordingly, resulting in a statement like this:

```
SELECT * FROM foos WHERE bar = '\' OR 1=1'
```

Completely harmless.

This applies to the entire Django database API, with a couple of exceptions:

- The where argument to the extra() method (see Appendix C). That parameter accepts raw SQL by design.

- Queries done "by hand" using the lower-level database API.

In each of these cases, it's easy to keep yourself protected. In each case, avoid string interpolation in favor of passing in *bind parameters*. That is, the example we started this section with should be written as follows:

```
from django.db import connection

def user_contacts(request):
    user = request.GET['username']
    sql = "SELECT * FROM user_contacts WHERE username = %s;"
    cursor = connection.cursor()
    cursor.execute(sql, [user])
    # ... do something with the results
```

The low-level execute method takes a SQL string with %s placeholders and automatically escapes and inserts parameters from the list passed as the second argument. You should *always* construct custom SQL this way.

Unfortunately, you can't use bind parameters everywhere in SQL; they're not allowed as identifiers (i.e., table or column names). Thus, if you need to, say, dynamically construct a list of tables from a POST variable, you'll need to escape that name in your code. Django provides a function, django.db.backend.quote_name, which will escape the identifier according to the current database's quoting scheme.

Cross-Site Scripting

Cross-site scripting (XSS) is found in Web applications that fail to escape user-submitted content properly before rendering it into HTML. This allows an attacker to insert arbitrary HTML into your Web page, usually in the form of <script> tags.

Attackers often use XSS attacks to steal cookie and session information, or to trick users into giving private information to the wrong person (aka *phishing*). This type of attack can take a number of different forms and has almost infinite permutations, so we'll just look at a typical example. Consider this extremely simple "Hello, World" view:

```
def say_hello(request):
    name = request.GET.get('name', 'world')
    return render_to_response("hello.html", {"name" : name})
```

This view simply reads a name from a `GET` parameter and passes that name to the `hello.html` template. We might write a template for this view as follows:

```
<h1>Hello, {{ name }}!</h1>
```

So if we accessed `http://example.com/hello/name=Jacob`, the rendered page would contain this:

```
<h1>Hello, Jacob!</h1>
```

But wait—what happens if we access `http://example.com/hello/name=<i>Jacob</i>`? Then we get this:

```
<h1>Hello, <i>Jacob</i>!</h1>
```

Of course, an attacker wouldn't use something as benign as `<i>` tags; he could include a whole set of HTML that hijacked your page with arbitrary content. This type of attack has been used to trick users into entering data into what looks like their bank's Web site, but in fact is an XSS-hijacked form that submits their bank account information to an attacker.

The problem gets worse if you store this data in the database and later display it on your site. For example, MySpace was once found to be vulnerable to an XSS attack of this nature. A user inserted JavaScript into his profile that automatically added him as your friend when you visited his profile page. Within a few days, he had millions of friends.

Now, this may sound relatively benign, but keep in mind that this attacker managed to get *his* code—not MySpace's—running on *your* computer. This violates the assumed trust that all the code on MySpace is actually written by MySpace.

MySpace was extremely lucky that this malicious code didn't automatically delete viewers' accounts, change their passwords, flood the site with spam, or any of the other nightmare scenarios this vulnerability unleashes.

The Solution

The solution is simple: *always* escape *any* content that might have come from a user. If we simply rewrite our template as follows:

```
<h1>Hello, {{ name|escape }}!</h1>
```

then we're no longer vulnerable. You should *always* use the escape tag (or something equivalent) when displaying user-submitted content on your site.

WHY DOESN'T DJANGO JUST DO THIS FOR YOU?

Modifying Django to automatically escape all variables displayed in templates is a frequent topic of discussion on the Django developer mailing list.

So far, Django's templates have avoided this behavior because it subtly changes what should be relatively straightforward behavior (displaying variables). It's a tricky issue and a difficult tradeoff to evaluate. Adding hidden implicit behavior is against Django's core ideals (and Python's, for that matter), but security is equally important.

All this is to say, then, that there's a fair chance Django will grow some form of auto-escaping (or nearly auto-escaping) behavior in the future. It's a good idea to check the official Django documentation for the latest in Django features; it will always be more up to date than this book, especially the print edition.

Even if Django does add this feature, however, you should *still* be in the habit of asking yourself, at all times, "Where does this data come from?" No automatic solution will ever protect your site from XSS attacks 100% of the time.

Cross-Site Request Forgery

Cross-site request forgery (CSRF) happens when a malicious Web site tricks users into unknowingly loading a URL from a site at which they're already authenticated—hence taking advantage of their authenticated status.

Django has built-in tools to protect from this kind of attack. Both the attack itself and those tools are covered in great detail in Chapter 14.

Session Forging/Hijacking

This isn't a specific attack, but rather a general class of attacks on a user's session data. It can take a number of different forms:

- A *man-in-the-middle* attack, where an attacker snoops on session data as it travels over the wire (or wireless) network.

- *Session forging*, where an attacker uses a stolen session ID (perhaps obtained through a man-in-the-middle attack) to pretend to be another user.

  An example of these first two would be an attacker in a coffee shop using the shop's wireless network to capture a session cookie. She could then use that cookie to impersonate the original user.

- A *cookie-forging* attack, where an attacker overrides the supposedly read-only data stored in a cookie. Chapter 12 explains in detail how cookies work, and one of the salient points is that it's trivial for browsers and malicious users to change cookies without your knowledge.

  There's a long history of Web sites that have stored a cookie like IsLoggedIn=1 or even LoggedInAsUser=jacob. It's dead simple to exploit these types of cookies.

  On a more subtle level, though, it's never a good idea to trust anything stored in cookies; you never know who's been poking at them.

- *Session fixation*, where an attacker tricks a user into setting or resetting the user's session ID.

  For example, PHP allows session identifiers to be passed in the URL (e.g., `http://example.com/?PHPSESSID=fa90197ca25f6ab40bb1374c510d7a32`). An attacker who tricks a user into clicking a link with a hard-coded session ID will cause the user to pick up that session.

  Session fixation has been used in phishing attacks to trick users into entering personal information into an account the attacker owns. He can later log into that account and retrieve the data.

- *Session poisoning*, where an attacker injects potentially dangerous data into a user's session—usually through a Web form that the user submits to set session data.

  A canonical example is a site that stores a simple user preference (like a page's background color) in a cookie. An attacker could trick a user into clicking a link to submit a "color" that actually contains an XSS attack; if that color isn't escaped, the user could again inject malicious code into the user's environment.

The Solution

There are a number of general principles that can protect you from these attacks:

- *Never allow session information to be contained in the URL.* Django's session framework (see Chapter 12) simply doesn't allow sessions to be contained in the URL.

- *Don't store data in cookies directly.* Instead, store a session ID that maps to session data stored on the back-end. If you use Django's built-in session framework (i.e., `request.session`), this is handled automatically for you. The only cookie that the session framework uses is a single session ID; all the session data is stored in the database.

- *Remember to escape session data if you display it in the template.* See the earlier XSS section, and remember that the information there applies to any user-created content as well as any data sent from the browser. You should treat session information as being user created.

- *Prevent attackers from spoofing session IDs whenever possible.* Although it's nearly impossible to detect someone who's hijacked a session ID, Django does have built-in protection against a brute-force session attack. Session IDs are stored as hashes (instead of sequential numbers), which prevents a brute-force attack, and a user will always get a new session ID if she tries a nonexistent one, which prevents session fixation.

Notice that none of those principles and tools prevents man-in-the-middle attacks. These types of attacks are nearly impossible to detect. If your site allows logged-in users to see any sort of sensitive data, you should *always* serve that site over HTTPS. Additionally, if you have an SSL-enabled site, you should set the `SESSION_COOKIE_SECURE` setting to `True`; this will make Django send session cookies only over HTTPS.

Email Header Injection

SQL injection's less well-known sibling, *email header injection*, hijacks Web forms that send email. An attacker can use this technique to send spam via your mail server. Any form that constructs email headers from Web form data is vulnerable to this kind of attack.

Let's look at the canonical contact form found on many sites. Usually this sends a message to a hard-coded email address and, hence, doesn't appear vulnerable to spam abuse at first glance.

However, most of these forms also allow the user to type in his own subject for the email (along with a "from" address, body, and sometimes a few other fields). This subject field is used to construct the "subject" header of the email message.

If that header is unescaped when building the email message, an attacker could submit something like `"hello\ncc:spamvictim@example.com"` (where "\n" is a newline character). That would make the constructed email headers turn into

```
To: hardcoded@example.com
Subject: hello
cc: spamvictim@example.com
```

Like SQL injection, if we trust the subject line given by the user, we'll allow him to construct a malicious set of headers, and he can use our contact form to send spam.

The Solution

We can prevent this attack in the same way we prevent SQL injection: always escape or validate user-submitted content.

Django's built-in mail functions (in `django.core.mail`) simply do not allow newlines in any fields used to construct headers (the "from" and "to" addresses, plus the subject). If you try to use `django.core.mail.send_mail` with a subject that contains newlines, Django will raise a `BadHeaderError` exception.

If you do not use Django's built-in mail functions to send email, you'll need to make sure that newlines in headers either cause an error or are stripped. You may want to examine the `SafeMIMEText` class in `django.core.mail` to see how Django does this.

Directory Traversal

Directory traversal is another injection-style attack, wherein a malicious user tricks filesystem code into reading and/or writing files that the Web server shouldn't have access to.

An example might be a view that reads files from the disk without carefully sanitizing the file name:

```
def dump_file(request):
    filename = request.GET["filename"]
    filename = os.path.join(BASE_PATH, filename)
    content = open(filename).read()

    # ...
```

Though it looks like that view restricts file access to files beneath BASE_PATH (by using os.path.join), if the attacker passes in a filename containing .. (that's two periods, a shorthand for "the parent directory"), she can access files "above" BASE_PATH. It's only a matter of time before she can discover the correct number of dots to successfully access, say, ../../../../../etc/passwd.

Anything that reads files without proper escaping is vulnerable to this problem. Views that *write* files are just as vulnerable, but the consequences are doubly dire.

Another permutation of this problem lies in code that dynamically loads modules based on the URL or other request information. A well-publicized example came from the world of Ruby on Rails. Prior to mid-2006, Rails used URLs like http://example.com/person/poke/1 directly to load modules and call methods. The result was that a carefully constructed URL could automatically load arbitrary code, including a database reset script!

The Solution

If your code ever needs to read or write files based on user input, you need to sanitize the requested path very carefully to ensure that an attacker isn't able to escape from the base directory you're restricting access to. Needless to say, you should *never* write code that can read from any area of the disk!

A good example of how to do this escaping lies in Django's built-in static content-serving view (in django.views.static). Here's the relevant code:

```
import os
import posixpath

# ...

path = posixpath.normpath(urllib.unquote(path))
newpath = ''
for part in path.split('/'):
    if not part:
        # strip empty path components
        continue

    drive, part = os.path.splitdrive(part)
    head, part = os.path.split(part)
    if part in (os.curdir, os.pardir):
        # strip '.' and '..' in path
        continue

    newpath = os.path.join(newpath, part).replace('\\', '/')
```

Django doesn't read files (unless you use the static.serve function, but that's protected with the code just shown), so this vulnerability doesn't affect the core code much.

In addition, the use of the URLconf abstraction means that Django will *never* load code you've not explicitly told it to load. There's no way to create a URL that causes Django to load something not mentioned in a URLconf.

Exposed Error Messages

During development, being able to see tracebacks and errors live in your browser is extremely useful. Django has "pretty" and informative debug messages specifically to make debugging easier. However, if these errors get displayed once the site goes live, they can reveal aspects of your code or configuration that could aid an attacker.

Furthermore, errors and tracebacks aren't at all useful to end users. Django's philosophy is that site visitors should never see application-related error messages. If your code raises an unhandled exception, a site visitor should not see the full traceback—or *any* hint of code snippets or Python (programmer-oriented) error messages. Instead, the visitor should see a friendly "This page is unavailable" message.

Naturally, of course, developers need to see tracebacks to debug problems in their code. So the framework should hide all error messages from the public, but it should display them to the trusted site developers.

The Solution

Django has a simple flag that controls the display of these error messages. If the DEBUG setting is set to True, error messages will be displayed in the browser. If not, Django will render return an HTTP 500 ("Internal server error") message and render an error template that you provide. This error template is called 500.html and should live in the root of one of your template directories.

Because developers still need to see errors generated on a live site, any errors handled this way will send an email with the full traceback to any addresses given in the ADMINS setting.

Users deploying under Apache and mod_python should also make sure they have PythonDebug Off in their Apache conf files; this will suppress any errors that occur before Django has had a chance to load.

A Final Word on Security

We hope all this talk of security problems isn't too intimidating. It's true that the Web can be a wild and wooly world, but with a little bit of foresight, you can have a secure Web site.

Keep in mind that Web security is a constantly changing field; if you're reading the dead-tree version of this book, be sure to check more up-to-date security resources for any new vulnerabilities that have been discovered. In fact, it's always a good idea to spend some time each week or month researching and keeping current on the state of Web application security. It's a small investment to make, but the protection you'll get for your site and your users is priceless.

What's Next?

In the next chapter, we'll finally cover the subtleties of deploying Django: how to launch a production site and how to set it up for scalability.

CHAPTER 20

■■■■

Deploying Django

Throughout this book, we've mentioned a number of goals that drive the development of Django. Ease of use, friendliness to new programmers, abstraction of repetitive tasks—these all drive Django's developers.

However, since Django's inception, there's always been another important goal: Django should be easy to deploy, and it should make serving large amounts of traffic possible with limited resources.

The motivations for this goal are apparent when you look at Django's background: a small, family-owned newspaper in Kansas can hardly afford top-of-the-line server hardware, so Django's original developers were concerned with squeezing the best possible performance out of limited resources. Indeed, for years Django's developers acted as their own system administrators—there simply wasn't enough hardware to need dedicated sysadmins—even as their sites handled tens of millions of hits a day.

As Django became an open source project, this focus on performance and ease of deployment became important for a different reason: hobbyist developers have the same requirements. Individuals who want to use Django are pleased to learn they can host a small- to medium-traffic site for as little as $10 a month.

But being able to scale down is only half the battle. Django also needs to be capable of scaling up to meet the needs of large companies and corporations. Here, Django adopts a philosophy common among LAMP-like Web stacks often called *shared nothing*.

WHAT'S LAMP?

The acronym LAMP was originally coined to describe a popular set of open source software used to drive many Web sites:

- Linux (operating system)

- Apache (Web server)

- MySQL (database)

- PHP (programming language)

Over time, though, the acronym has come to refer more to the philosophy of these types of open source software stacks than to any one particular stack. So while Django uses Python and is database-agnostic, the philosophies proven by the LAMP stack permeate Django's deployment mentality.

There have been a few (mostly humorous) attempts at coining a similar acronym to describe Django's technology stack. The authors of this book are fond of LAPD (Linux, Apache, PostgreSQL, and Django) or PAID (PostgreSQL, Apache, Internet, and Django). Use Django and get PAID!

Shared Nothing

At its core, the philosophy of shared nothing is really just the application of loose coupling to the entire software stack. This architecture arose in direct response to what was at the time the prevailing architecture: a monolithic Web application server that encapsulates the language, database, and Web server—even parts of the operating system—into a single process (e.g., Java).

When it comes time to scale, this can be a major problem. It's nearly impossible to split the work of a monolithic process across many different physical machines, so monolithic applications require enormously powerful servers. These servers, of course, cost tens or even hundreds of thousands of dollars, putting large-scale Web sites out of the reach of cash-hungry individuals and small companies.

What the LAMP community noticed, however, was that if you broke each piece of the Web stack up into individual components, you could easily start with an inexpensive server and simply add more inexpensive servers as you grew. If your $3,000 database server couldn't handle the load, you'd simply buy a second (or third, or fourth) until it could. If you needed more storage capacity, you'd add an NFS server.

For this to work, though, Web applications had to stop assuming that the same server would handle each request—or even each part of a single request. In a large-scale LAMP (and Django) deployment, as many as half a dozen servers might be involved in handling a single page! The repercussions of this are numerous, but they boil down to these points:

- *State cannot be saved locally.* In other words, any data that must be available between multiple requests must be stored in some sort of persistent storage like the database or a centralized cache.

- *Software cannot assume that resources are local.* For example, the Web platform cannot assume that the database runs on the same server; it must be capable of connecting to a remote database server.

- *Each piece of the stack must be easily moved or replicated.* If Apache for some reason doesn't work for a given deployment, you should be able to swap it out for another server with a minimum of fuss. Or, on a hardware level, if a Web server fails, you should be able to replace it with another physical box with minimum downtime. Remember, this whole philosophy is based around deployment on cheap, commodity hardware. Failure of individual machines is to be expected.

As you've probably come to expect, Django handles this more or less transparently—no part of Django violates these principles—but knowing the philosophy helps when it comes time to scale up.

BUT DOES IT WORK?

This philosophy might sound good on paper (or on your screen), but does it actually work?

Well, instead of answering that question directly, let's look at a by-no-means-complete list of a few companies that have based their business on this architecture. You might recognize some of these names:

- Amazon

- Blogger

- Craigslist

- Facebook

- Google

- LiveJournal

- Slashdot

- Wikipedia

- Yahoo

- YouTube

To paraphrase the famous line from the movie *When Harry Met Sally . . .*: "We'll have what they're having!"

A Note on Personal Preferences

Before we get into the details, a quick aside.

Open source is famous for its so-called religious wars; much (digital) ink has been spilled arguing over text editors (emacs vs. vi), operating systems (Linux vs. Windows vs. Mac OS), database engines (MySQL vs. PostgreSQL), and—of course—programming languages.

We try to stay away from these battles. There just isn't enough time.

However, there are a number of choices when it comes to deploying Django, and we're constantly asked for our preferences. Since stating these preferences comes dangerously close to firing a salvo in one of the aforementioned battles, we've mostly refrained. However, for the sake of completeness and full disclosure, we'll state them here. We prefer the following:

- Linux (Ubuntu, specifically) as our operating system

- Apache and mod_python for the Web server

- PostgreSQL as a database server

Of course, we can point to many Django users who have made other choices with great success.

Using Django with Apache and mod_python

Apache with mod_python currently is the most robust setup for using Django on a production server.

mod_python (http://www.djangoproject.com/r/mod_python/) is an Apache plug-in that embeds Python within Apache and loads Python code into memory when the server starts. Code stays in memory throughout the life of an Apache process, which leads to significant performance gains over other server arrangements.

Django requires Apache 2.x and mod_python 3.x, and we prefer Apache's prefork MPM, as opposed to the worker MPM.

■**Note** Configuring Apache is *well* beyond the scope of this book, so we'll simply mention details as needed. Luckily, a number of great resources are available if you need to learn more about Apache. A few of the ones we like are as follows:

- The free online Apache documentation, available via http://www.djangoproject.com/r/ apache/docs/

- *Pro Apache, Third Edition* (Apress, 2004) by Peter Wainwright, available via http://www.djangoproject. com/r/books/pro-apache/

- *Apache: The Definitive Guide, Third Edition* (O'Reilly, 2002) by Ben Laurie and Peter Laurie, available via http://www.djangoproject.com/r/books/apache-pra/

Basic Configuration

To configure Django with mod_python, first make sure you have Apache installed with the mod_python module activated. This usually means having a `LoadModule` directive in your Apache configuration file. It will look something like this:

```
LoadModule python_module /usr/lib/apache2/modules/mod_python.so
```

Then, edit your Apache configuration file and add the following:

```
<Location "/">
    SetHandler python-program
    PythonHandler django.core.handlers.modpython
    SetEnv DJANGO_SETTINGS_MODULE mysite.settings
    PythonDebug On
</Location>
```

Make sure to replace `mysite.settings` with the appropriate `DJANGO_SETTINGS_MODULE` for your site. This tells Apache, "Use mod_python for any URL at or under '/', using the Django mod_python handler." It passes the value of `DJANGO_SETTINGS_MODULE` so mod_python knows which settings to use.

Note that we're using the `<Location>` directive, not the `<Directory>` directive. The latter is used for pointing at places on your filesystem, whereas `<Location>` points at places in the URL structure of a Web site. `<Directory>` would be meaningless here.

Apache likely runs as a different user than your normal login and may have a different path and `PYTHONPATH`. You may need to tell mod_python how to find your project and Django itself:

```
PythonPath "['/path/to/project', '/path/to/django'] + sys.path"
```

You can also add directives such as `PythonAutoReload Off` for performance. See the mod_python documentation for a full list of options.

Note that you should set `PythonDebug Off` on a production server. If you leave `PythonDebug On`, your users will see ugly (and revealing) Python tracebacks if something goes wrong within mod_python.

Restart Apache, and any request to your site (or virtual host if you've put this directive inside a `<VirtualHost>` block) will be served by Django.

■**Note** If you deploy Django at a subdirectory—that is, somewhere deeper than "/"—Django *won't* trim the URL prefix off of your URLpatterns. So if your Apache config looks like this:

```
<Location "/mysite/">
    SetHandler python-program
    PythonHandler django.core.handlers.modpython
    SetEnv DJANGO_SETTINGS_MODULE mysite.settings
    PythonDebug On
</Location>
```

then *all* your URL patterns will need to start with "/mysite/". For this reason we usually recommend deploying Django at the root of your domain or virtual host.

Running Multiple Django Installations on the Same Apache Instance

It's entirely possible to run multiple Django installations on the same Apache instance. You might want to do this if you're an independent Web developer with multiple clients but only a single server.

To accomplish this, just use `VirtualHost` like so:

```
NameVirtualHost *

<VirtualHost *>
    ServerName www.example.com
    # ...
    SetEnv DJANGO_SETTINGS_MODULE mysite.settings
</VirtualHost>

<VirtualHost *>
    ServerName www2.example.com
    # ...
    SetEnv DJANGO_SETTINGS_MODULE mysite.other_settings
</VirtualHost>
```

If you need to put two Django installations within the same `VirtualHost`, you'll need to take a special precaution to ensure mod_python's code cache doesn't mess things up. Use the `PythonInterpreter` directive to give different `<Location>` directives separate interpreters:

```
<VirtualHost *>
    ServerName www.example.com
    # ...
    <Location "/something">
        SetEnv DJANGO_SETTINGS_MODULE mysite.settings
        PythonInterpreter mysite
    </Location>

    <Location "/otherthing">
        SetEnv DJANGO_SETTINGS_MODULE mysite.other_settings
        PythonInterpreter mysite_other
    </Location>
</VirtualHost>
```

The values of `PythonInterpreter` don't really matter, as long as they're different between the two `Location` blocks.

Running a Development Server with mod_python

Because mod_python caches loaded Python code, when deploying Django sites on mod_python you'll need to restart Apache each time you make changes to your code. This can be a hassle, so here's a quick trick to avoid it: just add `MaxRequestsPerChild 1` to your config file to force Apache to reload everything for each request. But don't do that on a production server, or we'll revoke your Django privileges.

If you're the type of programmer who debugs using scattered `print` statements (we are), note that `print` statements have no effect in mod_python; they don't appear in the Apache log, as you might expect. If you have the need to print debugging information in a mod_python setup, you'll probably want to use Python's standard logging package. More information is available at `http://docs.python.org/lib/module-logging.html`. Alternatively, you can add the debugging information to the template of your page.

Serving Django and Media Files from the Same Apache Instance

Django should not be used to serve media files itself; leave that job to whichever Web server you choose. We recommend using a separate Web server (i.e., one that's not also running Django) for serving media. For more information, see the "Scaling" section.

If, however, you have no option but to serve media files on the same Apache `VirtualHost` as Django, here's how you can turn off mod_python for a particular part of the site:

```
<Location "/media/">
    SetHandler None
</Location>
```

Change `Location` to the root URL of your media files.

You can also use `<LocationMatch>` to match a regular expression. For example, this sets up Django at the site root but explicitly disables Django for the media subdirectory and any URL that ends with `.jpg`, `.gif`, or `.png`:

```
<Location "/">
    SetHandler python-program
    PythonHandler django.core.handlers.modpython
    SetEnv DJANGO_SETTINGS_MODULE mysite.settings
</Location>

<Location "/media/">
    SetHandler None
</Location>

<LocationMatch "\.(jpg|gif|png)$">
    SetHandler None
</LocationMatch>
```

In all of these cases, you'll need to set the `DocumentRoot` directive so Apache knows where to find your static files.

Error Handling

When you use Apache/mod_python, errors will be caught by Django—in other words, they won't propagate to the Apache level and won't appear in the Apache `error_log`.

The exception to this is if something is really messed up in your Django setup. In that case, you'll see an "Internal Server Error" page in your browser and the full Python traceback in your Apache `error_log` file. The `error_log` traceback is spread over multiple lines. (Yes, this is ugly and rather hard to read, but it's how mod_python does things.)

Handling a Segmentation Fault

Sometimes, Apache segfaults when you install Django. When this happens, it's almost always one of two causes mostly unrelated to Django itself:

- It may be that your Python code is importing the pyexpat module (used for XML parsing), which may conflict with the version embedded in Apache. For full information, see "Expat Causing Apache Crash" at http://www.djangoproject.com/r/articles/expat-apache-crash/.

- It may be because you're running mod_python and mod_php in the same Apache instance, with MySQL as your database back-end. In some cases, this causes a known mod_python issue due to version conflicts in PHP and the Python MySQL back-end. There's full information in a mod_python FAQ entry, accessible via http://www.djangoproject.com/r/articles/php-modpython-faq/.

If you continue to have problems setting up mod_python, a good thing to do is get a barebones mod_python site working, without the Django framework. This is an easy way to isolate mod_python-specific problems. The article "Getting mod_python Working" details this procedure: http://www.djangoproject.com/r/articles/getting-modpython-working/.

The next step should be to edit your test code and add an import of any Django-specific code you're using—your views, your models, your URLconf, your RSS configuration, and so forth. Put these imports in your test handler function and access your test URL in a browser. If this causes a crash, you've confirmed it's the importing of Django code that causes the problem. Gradually reduce the set of imports until it stops crashing, so as to find the specific module that causes the problem. Drop down further into modules and look into their imports as necessary. For more help, system tools like ldconfig on Linux, otool on Mac OS, and ListDLLs (from SysInternals) on Windows can help you identify shared dependencies and possible version conflicts.

Using Django with FastCGI

Although Django under Apache and mod_python is the most robust deployment setup, many people use shared hosting, on which FastCGI is the only available deployment option.

Additionally, in some situations, FastCGI allows better security and possibly better performance than mod_python. For small sites, FastCGI can also be more lightweight than Apache.

FastCGI Overview

FastCGI is an efficient way of letting an external application serve pages to a Web server. The Web server delegates the incoming Web requests (via a socket) to FastCGI, which executes the code and passes the response back to the Web server, which, in turn, passes it back to the client's Web browser.

Like mod_python, FastCGI allows code to stay in memory, allowing requests to be served with no startup time. Unlike mod_python, a FastCGI process doesn't run inside the Web server process, but in a separate, persistent process.

WHY RUN CODE IN A SEPARATE PROCESS?

The traditional mod_* arrangements in Apache embed various scripting languages (most notably PHP, Python/mod_python, and Perl/mod_perl) inside the process space of your Web server. Although this lowers startup time (because code doesn't have to be read off disk for every request), it comes at the cost of memory use.

Each Apache process gets a copy of the Apache engine, complete with all the features of Apache that Django simply doesn't take advantage of. FastCGI processes, on the other hand, only have the memory overhead of Python and Django.

Due to the nature of FastCGI, it's also possible to have processes that run under a different user account than the Web server process. That's a nice security benefit on shared systems, because it means you can secure your code from other users.

Before you can start using FastCGI with Django, you'll need to install flup, a Python library for dealing with FastCGI. Some users have reported stalled pages with older flup versions, so you may want to use the latest SVN version. Get flup at http://www.djangoproject.com/r/flup/.

Running Your FastCGI Server

FastCGI operates on a client/server model, and in most cases you'll be starting the FastCGI server process on your own. Your Web server (be it Apache, lighttpd, or otherwise) contacts your Django-FastCGI process only when the server needs a dynamic page to be loaded. Because the daemon is already running with the code in memory, it's able to serve the response very quickly.

■**Note** If you're on a shared hosting system, you'll probably be forced to use Web server-managed FastCGI processes. If you're in this situation, you should read the section titled "Running Django on a Shared-Hosting Provider with Apache."

A Web server can connect to a FastCGI server in one of two ways: it can use either a Unix domain socket (a *named pipe* on Win32 systems) or a TCP socket. What you choose is a manner of preference; a TCP socket is usually easier due to permissions issues.

To start your server, first change into the directory of your project (wherever your manage.py is), and then run manage.py with the runfcgi command:

```
./manage.py runfcgi [options]
```

If you specify help as the only option after runfcgi, a list of all the available options will display.

You'll need to specify either a socket or both host and port. Then, when you set up your Web server, you'll just need to point it at the socket or host/port you specified when starting the FastCGI server.

A few examples should help explain this:

- Running a threaded server on a TCP port:

  ```
  ./manage.py runfcgi method=threaded host=127.0.0.1 port=3033
  ```

- Running a preforked server on a Unix domain socket:

  ```
  ./manage.py runfcgi method=prefork ➥
  socket=/home/user/mysite.sock pidfile=django.pid
  ```

- Running without daemonizing (backgrounding) the process (good for debugging):

  ```
  ./manage.py runfcgi daemonize=false socket=/tmp/mysite.sock
  ```

Stopping the FastCGI Daemon

If you have the process running in the foreground, it's easy enough to stop it: simply press Ctrl+C to stop and quit the FastCGI server. However, when you're dealing with background processes, you'll need to resort to the Unix `kill` command.

If you specify the `pidfile` option to your `manage.py runfcgi`, you can kill the running FastCGI daemon like this:

```
kill `cat $PIDFILE`
```

where $PIDFILE is the `pidfile` you specified.

To easily restart your FastCGI daemon on Unix, you can use this small shell script:

```
#!/bin/bash

# Replace these three settings.
PROJDIR="/home/user/myproject"
PIDFILE="$PROJDIR/mysite.pid"
SOCKET="$PROJDIR/mysite.sock"

cd $PROJDIR
if [ -f $PIDFILE ]; then
    kill `cat -- $PIDFILE`
    rm -f -- $PIDFILE
fi

exec /usr/bin/env - \
  PYTHONPATH="../python:.." \
  ./manage.py runfcgi socket=$SOCKET pidfile=$PIDFILE
```

Using Django with Apache and FastCGI

To use Django with Apache and FastCGI, you'll need Apache installed and configured, with mod_fastcgi installed and enabled. Consult the Apache and mod_fastcgi documentation for instructions: http://www.djangoproject.com/r/mod_fastcgi/.

Once you've completed the setup, point Apache at your Django FastCGI instance by editing the httpd.conf (Apache configuration) file. You'll need to do two things:

- Use the FastCGIExternalServer directive to specify the location of your FastCGI server.

- Use mod_rewrite to point URLs at FastCGI as appropriate.

Specifying the Location of the FastCGI Server

The FastCGIExternalServer directive tells Apache how to find your FastCGI server. As the FastCGIExternalServer docs (http://www.djangoproject.com/r/mod_fastcgi/FastCGIExternalServer/) explain, you can specify either a socket or a host. Here are examples of both:

```
# Connect to FastCGI via a socket/named pipe:
FastCGIExternalServer /home/user/public_html/mysite.fcgi ➡
-socket /home/user/mysite.sock

# Connect to FastCGI via a TCP host/port:
FastCGIExternalServer /home/user/public_html/mysite.fcgi -host 127.0.0.1:3033
```

In either case, the the directory /home/user/public_html/ should exist, though the file /home/user/public_html/mysite.fcgi doesn't actually have to exist. It's just a URL used by the Web server internally—a hook for signifying which requests at a URL should be handled by FastCGI. (More on this in the next section.)

Using mod_rewrite to Point URLs at FastCGI

The second step is telling Apache to use FastCGI for URLs that match a certain pattern. To do this, use the mod_rewrite module and rewrite URLs to mysite.fcgi (or whatever you specified in the FastCGIExternalServer directive, as explained in the previous section).

In this example, we tell Apache to use FastCGI to handle any request that doesn't represent a file on the filesystem and doesn't start with /media/. This is probably the most common case, if you're using Django's admin site:

```
<VirtualHost 12.34.56.78>
  ServerName example.com
  DocumentRoot /home/user/public_html
  Alias /media /home/user/python/django/contrib/admin/media
  RewriteEngine On
  RewriteRule ^/(media.*)$ /$1 [QSA,L]
  RewriteCond %{REQUEST_FILENAME} !-f
  RewriteRule ^/(.*)$ /mysite.fcgi/$1 [QSA,L]
</VirtualHost>
```

FastCGI and lighttpd

lighttpd (http://www.djangoproject.com/r/lighttpd/) is a lightweight Web server commonly used for serving static files. It supports FastCGI natively and thus is also an ideal choice for serving both static and dynamic pages, if your site doesn't have any Apache-specific needs.

Make sure mod_fastcgi is in your modules list, somewhere after mod_rewrite and mod_access, but not after mod_accesslog. You'll probably want mod_alias as well, for serving admin media.

Add the following to your lighttpd config file:

```
server.document-root = "/home/user/public_html"
fastcgi.server = (
    "/mysite.fcgi" => (
        "main" => (
            # Use host / port instead of socket for TCP fastcgi
            # "host" => "127.0.0.1",
            # "port" => 3033,
            "socket" => "/home/user/mysite.sock",
            "check-local" => "disable",
        )
    ),
)
alias.url = (
    "/media/" => "/home/user/django/contrib/admin/media/",
)

url.rewrite-once = (
    "^(/media.*)$" => "$1",
    "^/favicon\.ico$" => "/media/favicon.ico",
    "^(/.*)$" => "/mysite.fcgi$1",
)
```

Running Multiple Django Sites on One lighttpd Instance

lighttpd lets you use "conditional configuration" to allow configuration to be customized per host. To specify multiple FastCGI sites, just add a conditional block around your FastCGI config for each site:

```
# If the hostname is 'www.example1.com'...
$HTTP["host"] == "www.example1.com" {
    server.document-root = "/foo/site1"
    fastcgi.server = (
        ...
    )
    ...
}

# If the hostname is 'www.example2.com'...
$HTTP["host"] == "www.example2.com" {
    server.document-root = "/foo/site2"
    fastcgi.server = (
        ...
    )
    ...
}
```

You can also run multiple Django installations on the same site simply by specifying multiple entries in the `fastcgi.server` directive. Add one FastCGI host for each.

Running Django on a Shared-Hosting Provider with Apache

Many shared-hosting providers don't allow you to run your own server daemons or edit the `httpd.conf` file. In these cases, it's still possible to run Django using Web server-spawned processes.

■**Note** If you're using Web server-spawned processes, as explained in this section, there's no need for you to start the FastCGI server on your own. Apache will spawn a number of processes, scaling as it needs to.

In your Web root directory, add this to a file named `.htaccess`:

```
AddHandler fastcgi-script .fcgi
RewriteEngine On
RewriteCond %{REQUEST_FILENAME} !-f
RewriteRule ^(.*)$ mysite.fcgi/$1 [QSA,L]
```

Then create a small script that tells Apache how to spawn your FastCGI program. Create a file, `mysite.fcgi`, and place it in your Web directory, and be sure to make it executable:

```
#!/usr/bin/python
import sys, os

# Add a custom Python path.
sys.path.insert(0, "/home/user/python")

# Switch to the directory of your project. (Optional.)
# os.chdir("/home/user/myproject")

# Set the DJANGO_SETTINGS_MODULE environment variable.
os.environ['DJANGO_SETTINGS_MODULE'] = "myproject.settings"

from django.core.servers.fastcgi import runfastcgi
runfastcgi(method="threaded", daemonize="false")
```

Restarting the Spawned Server

If you change any Python code on your site, you'll need to tell FastCGI the code has changed. But there's no need to restart Apache in this case. Rather, just reupload `mysite.fcgi`—or edit the file—so that the timestamp on the file changes. When Apache sees the file has been updated, it will restart your Django application for you.

If you have access to a command shell on a Unix system, you can accomplish this easily by using the `touch` command:

```
touch mysite.fcg
```

Scaling

Now that you know how to get Django running on a single server, let's look at how you can scale out a Django installation. This section walks through how a site might scale from a single server to a large-scale cluster that could serve millions of hits an hour.

It's important to note, however, that nearly every large site is large in different ways, so scaling is anything but a one-size-fits-all operation. The following coverage should suffice to show the general principle, and whenever possible we'll try to point out where different choices could be made.

First off, we'll make a pretty big assumption and exclusively talk about scaling under Apache and mod_python. Though we know of a number of successful medium- to large-scale FastCGI deployments, we're much more familiar with Apache.

Running on a Single Server

Most sites start out running on a single server, with an architecture that looks something like Figure 20-1.

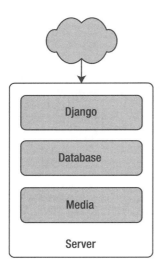

Figure 20-1. *A single-server Django setup*

This works just fine for small- to medium-sized sites, and it's relatively cheap—you can put together a single-server site designed for Django for well under $3,000.

However, as traffic increases you'll quickly run into resource contention between the different pieces of software. Database servers and Web servers love to have the entire server to themselves, so when run on the same server they often end up "fighting" over the same resources (RAM, CPU) that they'd prefer to monopolize.

This is solved easily by moving the database server to a second machine, as explained in the following section.

Separating Out the Database Server

As far as Django is concerned, the process of separating out the database server is extremely easy: you'll simply need to change the DATABASE_HOST setting to the IP or DNS name of your database server. It's probably a good idea to use the IP if at all possible, as relying on DNS for the connection between your Web server and database server isn't recommended.

With a separate database server, our architecture now looks like Figure 20-2.

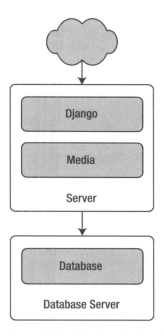

Figure 20-2. *Moving the database onto a dedicated server*

Here we're starting to move into what's usually called *n-tier* architecture. Don't be scared by the buzzword—it just refers to the fact that different "tiers" of the Web stack get separated out onto different physical machines.

At this point, if you anticipate ever needing to grow beyond a single database server, it's probably a good idea to start thinking about connection pooling and/or database replication. Unfortunately, there's not nearly enough space to do those topics justice in this book, so you'll need to consult your database's documentation and/or community for more information.

Running a Separate Media Server

We still have a big problem left over from the single-server setup: the serving of media from the same box that handles dynamic content.

Those two activities perform best under different circumstances, and by smashing them together on the same box you end up with neither performing particularly well. So the next step is to separate out the media—that is, anything *not* generated by a Django view—onto a dedicated server (see Figure 20-3).

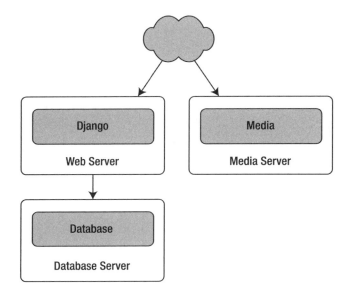

Figure 20-3. *Separating out the media server*

Ideally, this media server should run a stripped-down Web server optimized for static media delivery. lighttpd and tux (http://www.djangoproject.com/r/tux/) are both excellent choices here, but a heavily stripped-down Apache could work, too.

For sites heavy in static content (photos, videos, etc.), moving to a separate media server is doubly important and should likely be the *first* step in scaling up. This step can be slightly tricky, however. Django's admin needs to be able to write uploaded media to the media server (the MEDIA_ROOT setting controls where this media is written). If media lives on another server, however, you'll need to arrange a way for that write to happen across the network.

The easiest way to do this is to use NFS to mount the media server's media directories onto the Web server(s). If you mount them in the same location pointed to by MEDIA_ROOT, media uploading will work as expected.

Implementing Load Balancing and Redundancy

At this point, we've broken things down as much as possible. This three-server setup should handle a very large amount of traffic—we served around 10 million hits a day from an architecture of this sort—so if you grow further, you'll need to start adding redundancy.

This is a good thing, actually. One glance at Figure 20-3 shows you that if even a single one of your three servers fails, you'll bring down your entire site. So as you add redundant servers, not only do you increase capacity, but you also increase reliability.

For the sake of this example, let's assume that the Web server hits capacity first. It's easy to get multiple copies of a Django site running on different hardware—just copy all the code onto multiple machines, and start Apache on both of them.

However, you'll need another piece of software to distribute traffic over your multiple servers: a load balancer. You can buy expensive and proprietary hardware load balancers, but there are a few high-quality open source software load balancers out there.

Apache's mod_proxy is one option, but we've found Perlbal (`http://www.djangoproject.com/r/perlbal/`) to be simply fantastic. It's a load balancer and reverse proxy written by the same folks who wrote Memcached (see Chapter 13).

■**Note** If you're using FastCGI, you can accomplish this same distribution/load-balancing step by separating your front-end Web servers and back-end FastCGI processes onto different machines. The front-end server essentially becomes the load balancer, and the back-end FastCGI processes replace the Apache/mod_python/Django servers.

With the Web servers now clustered, our evolving architecture starts to look more complex, as shown in Figure 20-4.

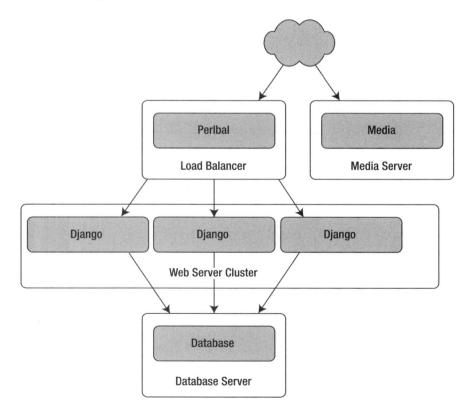

Figure 20-4. *A load-balanced, redundant server setup*

Notice that in the diagram the Web servers are referred to as a "cluster" to indicate that the number of servers is basically variable. Once you have a load balancer out front, you can easily add and remove back-end Web servers without a second of downtime.

Going Big

At this point, the next few steps are pretty much derivatives of the last one:

- As you need more database performance, you'll need to add replicated database servers. MySQL includes built-in replication; PostgreSQL users should look into Slony (http://www.djangoproject.com/r/slony/) and pgpool (http://www.djangoproject.com/r/pgpool/) for replication and connection pooling, respectively.

- If the single load balancer isn't enough, you can add more load balancer machines out front and distribute among them using round-robin DNS.

- If a single media server doesn't suffice, you can add more media servers and distribute the load with your load-balancing cluster.

- If you need more cache storage, you can add dedicated cache servers.

- At any stage, if a cluster isn't performing well, you can add more servers to the cluster.

After a few of these iterations, a large-scale architecture might look like Figure 20-5.

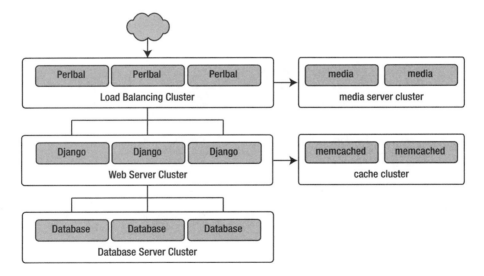

Figure 20-5. *An example large-scale Django setup*

Though we've shown only two or three servers at each level, there's no fundamental limit to how many you can add.

Once you get up to this level, you've got quite a few options. Appendix A has some information from a few developers responsible for some large-scale Django installations. If you're planning a high-traffic Django site, it's worth a read.

Performance Tuning

If you have huge amount of money, you can just keep throwing hardware at scaling problems. For the rest of us, though, performance tuning is a must.

■**Note** Incidentally, if anyone with monstrous gobs of cash is actually reading this book, please consider a substantial donation to the Django project. We accept uncut diamonds and gold ingots, too.

Unfortunately, performance tuning is much more of an art than a science, and it is even more difficult to write about than scaling. If you're serious about deploying a large-scale Django application, you should spend a great deal of time learning how to tune each piece of your stack.

The following sections, though, present a few Django-specific tuning tips we've discovered over the years.

There's No Such Thing As Too Much RAM

As of this writing, the really expensive RAM costs only about $200 per gigabyte—pennies compared to the time spent tuning elsewhere. Buy as much RAM as you can possibly afford, and then buy a little bit more.

Faster processors won't improve performance all that much; most Web servers spend up to 90% of their time waiting on disk I/O. As soon as you start swapping, performance will just die. Faster disks might help slightly, but they're much more expensive than RAM, such that it doesn't really matter.

If you have multiple servers, the first place to put your RAM is in the database server. If you can afford it, get enough RAM to get fit your entire database into memory. This shouldn't be too hard. LJWorld.com's database—including over half a million newspaper articles dating back to 1989—is under 2GB.

Next, max out the RAM on your Web server. The ideal situation is one where neither server swaps—ever. If you get to that point, you should be able to withstand most normal traffic.

Turn Off Keep-Alive

`Keep-Alive` is a feature of HTTP that allows multiple HTTP requests to be served over a single TCP connection, avoiding the TCP setup/teardown overhead.

This looks good at first glance, but it can kill the performance of a Django site. If you're properly serving media from a separate server, each user browsing your site will only request a page from your Django server every ten seconds or so. This leaves HTTP servers waiting around for the next keep-alive request, and an idle HTTP server just consumes RAM that an active one should be using.

Use Memcached

Although Django supports a number of different cache back-ends, none of them even come *close* to being as fast as Memcached. If you have a high-traffic site, don't even bother with the other back-ends—go straight to Memcached.

Use Memcached Often

Of course, selecting Memcached does you no good if you don't actually use it. Chapter 13 is your best friend here: learn how to use Django's cache framework, and use it everywhere possible. Aggressive, preemptive caching is usually the only thing that will keep a site up under major traffic.

Join the Conversation

Each piece of the Django stack—from Linux to Apache to PostgreSQL or MySQL—has an awesome community behind it. If you really want to get that last 1% out of your servers, join the open source communities behind your software and ask for help. Most free-software community members will be happy to help.

And also be sure to join the Django community. Your humble authors are only two members of an incredibly active, growing group of Django developers. Our community has a huge amount of collective experience to offer.

What's Next?

You've reached the end of our regularly scheduled program. The following appendixes all contain reference material that you might need as you work on your Django projects.

We wish you the best of luck in running your Django site, whether it's a little toy for you and a few friends, or the next Google.

PART 3

■ ■ ■

Appendixes

■■■

Case Studies

To help answer questions about how Django works in the "real world," we spoke with (well, emailed) a handful of people who have complete, deployed Django sites under their belts. Most of this appendix is in their words, which have been lightly edited for clarity.

Cast of Characters

Let's meet our cast and their projects.

- *Ned Batchelder* is the lead engineer at Tabblo.com. Tabblo started life as a storytelling tool built around photo sharing, but it was recently bought by Hewlett-Packard for more wide-reaching purposes:

  HP saw real value in our style of web development, and in the way we bridged the virtual and physical worlds. They acquired us so that we could bring that technology to other sites on the Web. Tabblo.com is still a great storytelling site, but now we are also working to componentize and rehost the most interesting pieces of our technology.

- *Johannes Beigel* is a lead developer at Brainbot Technologies AG. Brainbot's major public-facing Django site is http://pediapress.com/, where you can order printed versions of Wikipedia articles. Johannes's team is currently working on an enterprise-class knowledge-management program known as Brainfiler. Johannes tells us that Brainfiler

  . . . is a software solution to manage, search for, categorize, and share information from distributed information sources. It's built for enterprise usage for both the intranet and the Internet and is highly scalable and customizable. The development of the core concepts and components started in 2001. Just recently we have redesigned/reimplemented the application server and Web front-end, which is [now] based on Django.

- *David Cramer* is the lead developer at Curse, Inc. He develops Curse.com, a gaming site devoted to massively multiplayer online games like World of Warcraft, Ultima Online, and others. Curse.com is one of the largest deployed Django sites on the Internet:

  We do roughly 60–90 million page views in an average month, and we have peaked at over 130 million page views [in a month] *using Django. We are a very dynamic and user-centric Web site for online gamers, specifically massively multiplayer games, and are one of the largest Web sites globally for World of Warcraft. Our Web site was established in early 2005, and since late 2006 we have been expanding our reach into games beyond World of Warcraft.*

- *Christian Hammond* is a senior engineer at VMware (a leading developer of virtualization software). He's also the lead developer of Review Board (http://www.review-board.org/), a Web-based code review system. Review Board began life as an internal VMware project, but is now open source:

  In late 2006, David Trowbridge and I were discussing the process we used at VMware for handling code reviews. Before people committed code to the source repository, they were supposed to send out a diff of the change to a mailing list and get it reviewed. It was all handled over email, and as such, it became hard to keep track of reviews requiring your attention. We began to discuss potential solutions for this problem.

  Rather than writing down my ideas, I put them into code. Before long, Review Board was born. Review Board helps developers, contributors, and reviewers to keep track of the code that's out for review and to better communicate with each other. Rather than vaguely referencing some part of the code in an email, the reviewer is able to comment directly on the code. The code, along with the comments, will then appear in the review, giving the developer enough context to work with to quickly make the necessary changes.

  Review Board grew quickly at VMware. Much faster than expected, actually. Within a few short weeks, we had ten teams using Review Board. However, this project is not internal to VMware. It was decided day one that this should be open source and be made available for any company or project to use.

  We made an open source announcement and put a site together, which is available at http://www.review-board.org/. *The response to our public announcement was as impressive as our internal VMware announcement. Before long, our demo server reached over 600 users, and people began to contribute back to the project.*

  Review Board isn't the only code review tool on the market, but it is the first we have seen that is open source and has the extensive feature set we've worked to build into it. We hope this will in time benefit many open source and commercial projects.

Why Django?

We asked each developer why he decided to use Django, what other options were considered, and how the decision to use Django was ultimately made.

Ned Batchelder

Before I joined Tabblo, Antonio Rodriguez (Tabblo's founder/CTO) did an evaluation of Rails and Django, and found that both provided a great quick-out-of-the-blocks rapid development environment. In comparing the two, he found that Django had a greater technical depth that would make it easier to build a robust, scalable site. Also, Django's Python foundation meant that we'd have all the richness of the Python ecosystem to support our work. This has definitely been proven out as we've built Tabblo.

Johannes Beigel

As we have been coding in Python for many years now, and quickly started using the Twisted framework, Nevow was the most "natural" solution for our Web application stuff. But we soon realized that—despite the perfect Twisted integration—many things were getting a little cumbersome and got in the way of our agile development process.

After some Internet research it quickly became clear that Django was the most promising Web development framework for our requirements.

The trigger that led us to Django was its template syntax, but we soon appreciated all the other features that are included, and so Django was pretty much a fast-selling item.

After doing a few years of parallel development and deployment (Nevow is still in use for some projects on customer sites), we came to the conclusion that Django is a lot less cumbersome, results in code that is much better to maintain, and is more fun to work with.

David Cramer

I heard about Django in the summer of 2006, about the time we were getting ready to do an overhaul of Curse, and we did some research on it. We were all very impressed at what it could do, and where it could save time for us. We talked it over, decided on Django, and began writing the third revision to the Web site almost immediately.

Christian Hammond

I had toyed around with Django on a couple of small projects and had been very impressed with it. It's based on Python, which I had become a big fan of, and it made it easy not only to develop Web sites and Web apps, but also to keep them organized and maintainable. This was always tricky in PHP and Perl. Based on past experiences, going with Django was a no-brainer.

Getting Started

Since Django's a relatively new tool, there aren't that many experienced Django developers out there. We asked our "panel" how they got their team up to speed on Django and for any tips they wanted to share with new Django developers.

Johannes Beigel

After coding mostly in C++ and Perl, we switched to Python and continued using C++ for the computationally intensive code.

    [We learned Django by] working through the tutorial, browsing the documentation to get an idea of what's possible (it's easy to miss many features by just doing the tutorial), and trying to understand the basic concepts behind middleware, request objects, database models, template tags, custom filters, forms, authorization, localization . . . Then *[we could]* take a deeper look at those topics when *[we]* actually needed them.

David Cramer

The Web site documentation is great. Stick with it.

Christian Hammond

David and I both had prior experience with Django, though it was limited. We had learned a lot through our development of Review Board. I would advise new users to read through the well-written Django documentation and *[the book you're reading now]*, both of which have been invaluable to us.

■**Note** We didn't have to bribe Christian to get that quote—promise!

Porting Existing Code

Although Review Board and Tabblo were ground-up development, the other sites were ported from existing code. We were interested in hearing how that process went.

Johannes Beigel

We started to "port" the site from Nevow, but we soon realized that we'd like to change so many conceptual things (both in the UI part and in the application server part) that we started from scratch and used the former code merely as a reference.

David Cramer

The previous site was written in PHP. Going from PHP to Python was great programmatically. The only downfall is you have to be a lot more careful with memory management *[since Django processes stay around a lot longer than PHP processes (which are single cycle)]*.

How Did It Go?

Now for the million-dollar question: How did Django treat you? We were especially interested in hearing where Django fell down—it's important to know where your tools are weak *before* you run into roadblocks.

Ned Batchelder

Django has really enabled us to experiment with our Web site's functionality. Both as a startup heat-seeking customers and businesses, and now as a part of HP working with a number of partners, we've had to be very nimble when it comes to adapting the software to new demands. The separation of functionality into models, views, and controllers has given us modularity so we can appropriately choose where to extend and modify. The underlying Python environment gives us the opportunity to make use of existing libraries to solve problems without reinventing the wheel. PIL, PDFlib, ZSI, JSmin, and BeautifulSoup are just a handful of the libraries we've pulled in to do some heavy lifting for us.

The most difficult part of our Django use has been the relationship of memory objects to database objects, in a few ways. First, Django's ORM does not ensure that two references to the same database record are the same Python object, so you can get into situations where two parts of the code are both trying to modify the same record, and one of the copies is stale. Second, the Django development model encourages you to base your data objects on database objects. We've found over time more and more uses for data objects that are not tied to the database, and we've had to migrate away from assuming that data is stored in the database.

For a large, long-lived code base, it definitely makes sense to spend time up front anticipating the ways your data will be stored and accessed, and building some infrastructure to support those ways.

We've also added our own database migration facility so that developers don't have to apply SQL patches to keep their database schemas current. Developers who change the schema write a Python function to update the database, and these are applied automatically when the server is started.

Johannes Beigel

We consider Django as a very successful platform that perfectly fits in the Pythonic way of thinking. Almost everything just worked as intended.

One thing that needed a bit of work in our current project was tweaking the global `settings.py` file and directory structure/configuration (for apps, templates, locale data, etc.), because we implemented a highly modular and configurable system, where all Django views are actually methods of some class instances. But with the omnipotence of dynamic Python code, that was still possible.

David Cramer

We managed to push out large database applications in a weekend. This would have taken one to two weeks to do on the previous Web site, in PHP. Django has shined exactly where we wanted it to.

Now, while Django is a great platform, it can't go without saying that it's not built specific to everyone's needs. Upon the initial launch of the Django Web site, we had our highest traffic month of the year, and we weren't able to keep up. Over the next few months we tweaked bits and pieces, mostly hardware and the software serving Django requests. *[This included modification of our]* hardware configuration, optimization of Django, *[and tuning]* the software we were using to serve the requests (which, at the time, was lighttpd and FastCGI).

In May of 2007, Blizzard (the creators of World of Warcraft) released another quite large patch, as they had done in December when we first launched Django. The first thing going through our heads was, "Hey, we nearly held up in December, this is nowhere near as big, we should be fine." We lasted about 12 hours before the servers started to feel the heat. The question was raised again: was Django really the best solution for what we want to accomplish?

Thanks to a lot of great support from the community, and a late night, we managed to implement several "hot-fixes" to the Web site during those few days. The changes (which hopefully have been rolled back into Django by the time this book is released) managed to completely reassure everyone that while not everyone needs to be able to do 300 Web requests per second, the people who do, can, with Django.

Christian Hammond

Django allowed us to build Review Board fairly quickly by forcing us to stay organized through its URL, view, and template separations, and by providing useful built-in components, such as the authentication app, built-in caching, and the database abstraction. Most of this has worked really well for us.

Being a dynamic *[Web application]*, we've had to write a lot of JavaScript code. This is an area that Django hasn't really helped us with so far. Django's templates, template tags, filters, and forms support are great, but aren't easily usable from JavaScript code. There are times when we would want to use a particular template or filter but had no way of using it from JavaScript. I would personally like to see some creative solutions for this incorporated into Django.

Team Structure

Often successful projects are made so by their teams, not their choice of technology. We asked our panel how their teams work, and what tools and techniques they use to stay on track.

Ned Batchelder

We're a pretty standard Web startup environment: Trac/SVN, five developers. We have a staging server, a production server, an ad hoc deploy script, and so on.

Johannes Beigel

We use Trac as our bug tracker and wiki and have recently switched from using Subversion+SVK to Mercurial (a Python-written distributed version-control system that handles branching/merging like a charm).

I think we have a very agile development process, but we do not follow a "rigid" methodology like Extreme Programming (*[though]* we borrow many ideas from it). We are more like Pragmatic Programmers.

We have an automated build system (customized but based on SCons) and unit tests for almost everything.

David Cramer

Our team consists of four Web developers, all working in the same office space, so it's quite easy to communicate. We rely on common tools such as SVN and Trac.

Christian Hammond

Review Board currently has two main developers (myself and David Trowbridge) and a couple of contributors. We're hosted on Google Code and make use of their Subversion repository, issue tracker, and wiki. We actually use Review Board to review our changes before they go in. We test on our local computers, both by hand and through unit tests. Our users at VMware who use Review Board every day provide a lot of useful feedback and bug reports, which we try to incorporate into the program.

Deployment

The Django developers take ease of deployment and scaling very seriously, so we're always interested in hearing about real-world trials and tribulations.

Ned Batchelder

We've used caching both at the query and response layers to speed response time. We have a classic configuration: a multiplexer, many app servers, one database server. This has worked well for us, because we can use caching at the app server to avoid database access and then add app servers as needed to handle the volume.

Johannes Beigel

Linux servers, preferably Debian, with many gigs of RAM. Lighttpd as the Web server, Pound as the HTTPS front-end and load balancer if needed, and Memcached for caching. SQLite for small databases, Postgres if data grows larger, and highly specialized custom database stuff for our search and knowledge management components.

David Cramer

Our structure is still up for debate . . . *[but this is what's current]:* When a user requests the site they are sent to a cluster of Squid servers using lighttpd. There, servers then check if the user is logged in. If not, they're served a cached page. A logged-in user is forwarded to a cluster of Web servers running apache2 plus mod_python (each with a large amount of memory), which then each rely on a distributed Memcached system and a beastly MySQL database server. Static content is hosted on a cluster of lighttpd servers. Media, such as large files and videos, are hosted (currently) on a server using a minimal Django install using lighttpd plus FastCGI. As of right now we're moving toward pushing all media to a service similar to Amazon's S3.

Christian Hammond

There are two main production servers right now. One is at VMware and consists of an Ubuntu virtual machine running on VMware ESX. We use MySQL for the database, Memcached for our caching back-end, and currently Apache for the Web server. We have several powerful servers that we can scale across when we need to. We may find ourselves moving MySQL or Memcached to another virtual machine as our user base increases.

The second production server is the one for Review Board itself. The setup is nearly identical to the one at VMware, except the virtual machine is being hosted on VMware Server.

Model Definition Reference

Chapter 5 explains the basics of defining models, and we use them throughout the rest of the book. There is, however, a *huge* range of model options available not covered elsewhere. This appendix explains each possible model definition option.

Note that although these APIs are considered very stable, the Django developers consistently add new shortcuts and conveniences to the model definition. It's a good idea to always check the latest documentation online at http://www.djangoproject.com/documentation/0.96/model-api/.

Fields

The most important part of a model—and the only required part of a model—is the list of database fields it defines.

Field Name Restrictions

Django places only two restrictions on model field names:

- A field name cannot be a Python reserved word, because that would result in a Python syntax error, for example:

```
class Example(models.Model):
    pass = models.IntegerField() # 'pass' is a reserved word!
```

- A field name cannot contain more than one underscore in a row, due to the way Django's query lookup syntax works, for example:

```
class Example(models.Model):
    foo__bar = models.IntegerField() # 'foo__bar' has two underscores!
```

These limitations can be worked around, though, because your field name doesn't necessarily have to match your database column name. See the upcoming "db_column" section.

SQL reserved words, such as join, where, and select, *are* allowed as model field names, because Django escapes all database table names and column names in every underlying SQL query. It uses the quoting syntax of your particular database engine.

Each field in your model should be an instance of the appropriate Field class. Django uses the field class types to determine a few things:

- The database column type (e.g., INTEGER, VARCHAR)

- The widget to use in Django's admin interface, if you care to use it (e.g., <input type="text">, <select>)

- The minimal validation requirements, which are used in Django's admin interface

A complete list of field classes follows, sorted alphabetically. Note that relationship fields (ForeignKey, etc.) are handled in the next section.

AutoField

An IntegerField that automatically increments according to available IDs. You usually won't need to use this directly; a primary key field will automatically be added to your model if you don't specify otherwise.

BooleanField

A true/false field.

CharField

A string field, for small- to large-sized strings. For large amounts of text, use TextField.

CharField has an extra required argument, maxlength, which is the maximum length (in characters) of the field. This maximum length is enforced at the database level and in Django's validation.

CommaSeparatedIntegerField

A field of integers separated by commas. As in CharField, the maxlength argument is required.

DateField

A date field. DateField has a few extra optional arguments, as shown in Table B-1.

Table B-1. *Extra DateField Options*

Argument	Description
auto_now	Automatically sets the field to now every time the object is saved. It's useful for "last-modified" timestamps. Note that the current date is *always* used; it's not just a default value that you can override.
auto_now_add	Automatically sets the field to now when the object is first created. It's useful for creation of timestamps. Note that the current date is *always* used; it's not just a default value that you can override.

DateTimeField

A date and time field. It takes the same extra options as DateField.

EmailField

A CharField that checks that the value is a valid email address. This doesn't accept maxlength; its maxlength is automatically set to 75.

FileField

A file-upload field. It has one *required* argument, as shown in Table B-2.

Table B-2. *Extra FileField Option*

Argument	Description
upload_to	A local filesystem path that will be appended to your MEDIA_ROOT setting to determine the output of the get_<fieldname>_url() helper function

This path may contain strftime formatting (see http://docs.python.org/lib/module-time.html), which will be replaced by the date/time of the file upload (so that uploaded files don't fill up the given directory).

Using a FileField or an ImageField in a model takes a few steps:

1. In your settings file, you'll need to define MEDIA_ROOT as the full path to a directory where you'd like Django to store uploaded files. (For performance, these files are not stored in the database.) Define MEDIA_URL as the base public URL of that directory. Make sure that this directory is writable by the Web server's user account.

2. Add the FileField or ImageField to your model, making sure to define the upload_to option to tell Django to which subdirectory of MEDIA_ROOT it should upload files.

3. All that will be stored in your database is a path to the file (relative to MEDIA_ROOT). You'll most likely want to use the convenience get_<fieldname>_url function provided by Django. For example, if your ImageField is called mug_shot, you can get the absolute URL to your image in a template with {{ object.get_mug_shot_url }}.

For example, say your MEDIA_ROOT is set to '/home/media', and upload_to is set to 'photos/%Y/%m/%d'. The '%Y/%m/%d' part of upload_to is strftime formatting; '%Y' is the four-digit year, '%m' is the two-digit month, and '%d' is the two-digit day. If you upload a file on January 15, 2007, it will be saved in the directory /home/media/photos/2007/01/15.

If you want to retrieve the upload file's on-disk file name, or a URL that refers to that file, or the file's size, you can use the get_FIELD_filename(), get_FIELD_url(), and get_FIELD_size() methods. See Appendix C for a complete explanation of these methods.

Whenever you deal with uploaded files, you should pay close attention to where you're uploading them and what type of files they are, to avoid security holes. *Validate all uploaded files* so that you're sure the files are what you think they are.

For example, if you blindly let somebody upload files, without validation, to a directory that's within your Web server's document root, then somebody could upload a CGI or PHP script and execute that script by visiting its URL on your site. Don't let that happen!

FilePathField

A field whose choices are limited to the file names in a certain directory on the filesystem. It has three special arguments, as shown in Table B-3.

Table B-3. *Extra FilePathField Options*

Argument	Description
path	*Required*; the absolute filesystem path to a directory from which this FilePathField should get its choices (e.g., "/home/images").
match	Optional; a regular expression, as a string, that FilePathField will use to filter file names. Note that the regex will be applied to the base file name, not the full path (e.g., "foo.*\.txt^", which will match a file called foo23.txt, but not bar.txt or foo23.gif).
recursive	Optional; either True or False. The default is False. It specifies whether all sub-directories of path should be included.

Of course, these arguments can be used together.

The one potential gotcha is that match applies to the base file name, not the full path. So, the following example:

```
FilePathField(path="/home/images", match="foo.*", recursive=True)
```

will match /home/images/foo.gif but not /home/images/foo/bar.gif because the match applies to the base file name (foo.gif and bar.gif).

FloatField

A floating-point number, represented in Python by a float instance. It has two required arguments shown in Table B-4.

Table B-4. *Extra FloatField Options*

Argument	Description
max_digits	The maximum number of digits allowed in the number
decimal_places	The number of decimal places to store with the number

For example, to store numbers up to 999 with a resolution of two decimal places, you'd use the following:

```
models.DecimalField(..., max_digits=5, decimal_places=2)
```

And to store numbers up to approximately 1 billion with a resolution of ten decimal places, you would use this:

```
models.DecimalField(..., max_digits=19, decimal_places=10)
```

ImageField

Like `FileField`, but validates that the uploaded object is a valid image. It has two extra optional arguments, `height_field` and `width_field`, which, if set, will be autopopulated with the height and width of the image each time a model instance is saved.

In addition to the special `get_FIELD_*` methods that are available for `FileField`, an `ImageField` also has `get_FIELD_height()` and `get_FIELD_width()` methods. These are documented in Appendix C.

`ImageField` requires the Python Imaging Library (http://www.pythonware.com/products/pil/).

IntegerField

An integer.

IPAddressField

An IP address, in string format (e.g., `"24.124.1.30"`).

NullBooleanField

Like a `BooleanField`, but allows `None`/`NULL` as one of the options. Use this instead of a `BooleanField` with `null=True`.

PhoneNumberField

A `CharField` that checks that the value is a valid U.S.-style phone number (in the format XXX-XXX-XXXX).

If you need to represent a phone number from another country, check the `django.contrib.localflavor` package to see if field definitions for your country are included.

PositiveIntegerField

Like an `IntegerField`, but must be positive.

PositiveSmallIntegerField

Like a `PositiveIntegerField`, but only allows values under a certain point. The maximum value allowed by these fields is database dependent, but since databases have a 2-byte small integer field, the maximum positive small integer is usually 65,535.

SlugField

"Slug" is a newspaper term. A *slug* is a short label for something, containing only letters, numbers, underscores, or hyphens. They're generally used in URLs.

Like a `CharField`, you can specify `maxlength`. If `maxlength` is not specified, Django will use a default length of 50.

A `SlugField` implies `db_index=True` since slugs are primarily used for database lookups.

SlugField accepts an extra option, prepopulate_from, which is a list of fields from which to autopopulate the slug, via JavaScript, in the object's admin form:

```
models.SlugField(prepopulate_fpom=("pre_name", "name"))
```

prepopulate_from doesn't accept DateTimeField names as arguments.

SmallIntegerField

Like an IntegerField, but only allows values in a certain database-dependent range (usually –32,768 to +32,767).

TextField

An unlimited-length text field.

TimeField

A time of day. It accepts the same autopopulation options as DateField and DateTimeField.

URLField

A field for a URL. If the verify_exists option is True (the default), the URL given will be checked for existence (i.e., the URL actually loads and doesn't give a 404 response).

Like other character fields, URLField takes the maxlength argument. If you don't specify maxlength, a default of 200 is used.

USStateField

A two-letter U.S. state abbreviation.

If you need to represent other countries or states, look first in the django.contrib.localflavor package to see if Django already includes fields for your locale.

XMLField

A TextField that checks that the value is valid XML that matches a given schema. It takes one required argument, schema_path, which is the filesystem path to a RELAX NG (http://www.relaxng.org/) schema against which to validate the field.

Requires jing (http://thaiopensource.com/relaxng/jing.html) to validate the XML.

Universal Field Options

The following arguments are available to all field types. All are optional.

null

If True, Django will store empty values as NULL in the database. The default is False.

Note that empty string values will always get stored as empty strings, not as NULL. Only use null=True for nonstring fields such as integers, Booleans, and dates. For both types of fields, you will also need to set blank=True if you wish to permit empty values in forms, as the null parameter only affects database storage (see the following section, titled "blank").

Avoid using null on string-based fields such as CharField and TextField unless you have an excellent reason. If a string-based field has null=True, that means it has two possible values for "no data": NULL and the empty string. In most cases, it's redundant to have two possible values for "no data"; Django's convention is to use the empty string, not NULL.

blank

If True, the field is allowed to be blank. The default is False.

Note that this is different from null. null is purely database related, whereas blank is validation related. If a field has blank=True, validation on Django's admin site will allow entry of an empty value. If a field has blank=False, the field will be required.

choices

An iterable (e.g., a list, tuple, or other iterable Python object) of two-tuples to use as choices for this field.

If this is given, Django's admin interface will use a select box instead of the standard text field and will limit choices to the choices given.

A choices list looks like this:

```
YEAR_IN_SCHOOL_CHOICES = (
    ('FR', 'Freshman'),
    ('SO', 'Sophomore'),
    ('JR', 'Junior'),
    ('SR', 'Senior'),
    ('GR', 'Graduate'),
)
```

The first element in each tuple is the actual value to be stored. The second element is the human-readable name for the option.

The choices list can be defined either as part of your model class, as follows:

```
class Foo(models.Model):
    GENDER_CHOICES = (
        ('M', 'Male'),
        ('F', 'Female'),
    )
    gender = models.CharField(maxlength=1, choices=GENDER_CHOICES)
```

or outside your model class altogether:

```
GENDER_CHOICES = (
    ('M', 'Male'),
    ('F', 'Female'),
)
class Foo(models.Model):
    gender = models.CharField(maxlength=1, choices=GENDER_CHOICES)
```

For each model field that has `choices` set, Django will add a method to retrieve the human-readable name for the field's current value. See Appendix C for more details.

db_column

The name of the database column to use for this field. If this isn't given, Django will use the field's name. This is useful when you're defining a model around a database that already exists.

If your database column name is an SQL reserved word, or if it contains characters that aren't allowed in Python variable names (notably the hyphen), that's OK. Django quotes column and table names behind the scenes.

db_index

If `True`, Django will create a database index on this column when creating the table (i.e., when running `manage.py syncdb`).

default

The default value for the field.

editable

If `False`, the field will not be editable in the admin interface or via form processing. The default is `True`.

help_text

Extra "help" text to be displayed under the field on the object's admin form. It's useful for documentation even if your object doesn't have an admin form.

primary_key

If `True`, this field is the primary key for the model.

If you don't specify `primary_key=True` for any fields in your model, Django will automatically add this field:

```
id = models.AutoField('ID', primary_key=True)
```

Thus, you don't need to set `primary_key=True` on any of your fields unless you want to override the default primary-key behavior.

`primary_key=True` implies `blank=False`, `null=False`, and `unique=True`. Only one primary key is allowed on an object.

radio_admin

By default, Django's admin uses a select-box interface (`<select>`) for fields that are `ForeignKey` or have `choices` set. If `radio_admin` is set to `True`, Django will use a radio-button interface instead.

Don't use this for a field unless it's a `ForeignKey` or has `choices` set.

unique

If True, the value for this field must be unique throughout the table.

unique_for_date

Set to the name of a DateField or DateTimeField to require that this field be unique for the value of the date field, for example:

```
class Story(models.Model):
    pub_date = models.DateTimeField()
    slug = models.SlugField(unique_for_date="pub_date")
    ...
```

In the preceding code, Django won't allow the creation of two stories with the same slug published on the same date. This differs from using a unique_together constraint in that only the date of the pub_date field is taken into account; the time doesn't matter.

unique_for_month

Like unique_for_date, but requires the field to be unique with respect to the month of the given field.

unique_for_year

Like unique_for_date and unique_for_month, but for an entire year.

verbose_name

Each field type, except for ForeignKey, ManyToManyField, and OneToOneField, takes an optional first positional argument—a verbose name. If the verbose name isn't given, Django will automatically create it using the field's attribute name, converting underscores to spaces.

In this example, the verbose name is "Person's first name":

```
first_name = models.CharField("Person's first name", maxlength=30)
```

In this example, the verbose name is "first name":

```
first_name = models.CharField(maxlength=30)
```

ForeignKey, ManyToManyField, and OneToOneField require the first argument to be a model class, so use the verbose_name keyword argument:

```
poll = models.ForeignKey(Poll, verbose_name="the related poll")
sites = models.ManyToManyField(Site, verbose_name="list of sites")
place = models.OneToOneField(Place, verbose_name="related place")
```

The convention is not to capitalize the first letter of the verbose_name. Django will automatically capitalize the first letter where it needs to.

Relationships

Clearly, the power of relational databases lies in relating tables to each other. Django offers ways to define the three most common types of database relationships: many-to-one, many-to-many, and one-to-one.

However, the semantics of one-to-one relationships are being revisited as this book goes to print, so they're not covered in this section. Check the online documentation for the latest information.

Many-to-One Relationships

To define a many-to-one relationship, use ForeignKey. You use it just like any other Field type, by including it as a class attribute of your model.

ForeignKey requires a positional argument: the class to which the model is related.

For example, if a Car model has a Manufacturer—that is, a Manufacturer makes multiple cars but each Car has only one Manufacturer—use the following definitions:

```
class Manufacturer(models.Model):
    ...

class Car(models.Model):
    manufacturer = models.ForeignKey(Manufacturer)
    ...
```

To create a *recursive* relationship—an object that has a many-to-one relationship with itself—use models.ForeignKey('self'):

```
class Employee(models.Model):
    manager = models.ForeignKey('self')
```

If you need to create a relationship on a model that has not yet been defined, you can use the name of the model, rather than the model object itself:

```
class Car(models.Model):
    manufacturer = models.ForeignKey('Manufacturer')
    ...

class Manufacturer(models.Model):
    ...
```

Note, however, that you can only use strings to refer to models in the same models.py file—you cannot use a string to reference a model in a different application, or to reference a model that has been imported from elsewhere.

Behind the scenes, Django appends "_id" to the field name to create its database column name. In the preceding example, the database table for the Car model will have a manufacturer_id column. (You can change this explicitly by specifying db_column; see the earlier "db_column" section.) However, your code should never have to deal with the database column name, unless you write custom SQL. You'll always deal with the field names of your model object.

It's suggested, but not required, that the name of a ForeignKey field (manufacturer in the example) be the name of the model, in lowercase letters. You can, of course, call the field whatever you want, for example:

```
class Car(models.Model):
    company_that_makes_it = models.ForeignKey(Manufacturer)
    # ...
```

ForeignKey fields take a number of extra arguments for defining how the relationship should work (see Table B-5). All are optional.

Table B-5. *ForeignKey Options*

Argument	Description
edit_inline	If not False, this related object is edited "inline" on the related object's page. This means that the object will not have its own admin interface. Use either models.TABULAR or models.STACKED, which, respectively, designate whether the inline-editable objects are displayed as a table or as a "stack" of fieldsets.
limit_choices_to	A dictionary of lookup arguments and values (see Appendix C) that limit the available admin choices for this object. Use this with functions from the Python datetime module to limit choices of objects by date. For example, the following: limit_choices_to = {'pub_date__lte': datetime.now} only allows the choice of related objects with a pub_date before the current date/time to be chosen. Instead of a dictionary, this can be a Q object (see Appendix C) for more complex queries. This is not compatible with edit_inline.
max_num_in_admin	For inline-edited objects, this is the maximum number of related objects to display in the admin interface. Thus, if a pizza could have only up to ten toppings, max_num_in_admin=10 would ensure that a user never enters more than ten toppings. Note that this doesn't ensure more than ten related toppings ever get created. It simply controls the admin interface; it doesn't enforce things at the Python API level or database level.
min_num_in_admin	The minimum number of related objects displayed in the admin interface. Normally, at the creation stage, num_in_admin inline objects are shown, and at the edit stage, num_extra_on_change blank objects are shown in addition to all preexisting related objects. However, no fewer than min_num_in_admin related objects will ever be displayed.
num_extra_on_change	The number of extra blank related-object fields to show at the change stage.
num_in_admin	The default number of inline objects to display on the object page at the add stage.
raw_id_admin	Only display a field for the integer to be entered instead of a drop-down menu. This is useful when related to an object type that will have too many rows to make a select box practical. This is not used with edit_inline.
related_name	The name to use for the relation from the related object back to this one. See Appendix C for more information.
to_field	The field on the related object that the relation is to. By default, Django uses the primary key of the related object.

Many-to-Many Relationships

To define a many-to-many relationship, use ManyToManyField. Like ForeignKey, ManyToManyField requires a positional argument: the class to which the model is related.

For example, if a Pizza has multiple Topping objects—that is, a Topping can be on multiple pizzas and each Pizza has multiple toppings—here's how you'd represent that:

```
class Topping(models.Model):
    ...

class Pizza(models.Model):
    toppings = models.ManyToManyField(Topping)
    ...
```

As with ForeignKey, a relationship to self can be defined by using the string 'self' instead of the model name, and you can refer to as-yet undefined models by using a string containing the model name. However, you can only use strings to refer to models in the same models.py file—you cannot use a string to reference a model in a different application, or to reference a model that has been imported from elsewhere.

It's suggested, but not required, that the name of a ManyToManyField (toppings in the example) be a plural term describing the set of related model objects.

Behind the scenes, Django creates an intermediary join table to represent the many-to-many relationship.

It doesn't matter which model gets the ManyToManyField, but you need it in only one of the models—not in both.

If you're using the admin interface, ManyToManyField instances should go in the object that's going to be edited in the admin interface. In the preceding example, toppings is in Pizza (rather than Topping having a pizzas ManyToManyField) because it's more natural to think about a Pizza having toppings than a topping being on multiple pizzas. The way it's set up in the example, the Pizza admin form would let users select the toppings.

ManyToManyField objects take a number of extra arguments for defining how the relationship should work (see Table B-6). All are optional.

Table B-6. *ManyToManyField Options*

Argument	Description
related_name	The name to use for the relation from the related object back to this one. See Appendix C for more information.
filter_interface	Use a nifty, unobtrusive JavaScript "filter" interface instead of the usability-challenged <select multiple> in the admin form for this object. The value should be models.HORIZONTAL or models.VERTICAL (i.e., should the interface be stacked horizontally or vertically).
limit_choices_to	See the description under ForeignKey.

Argument	Description
symmetrical	Only used in the definition of ManyToManyField on self. Consider the following model: class Person(models.Model): friends = models.ManyToManyField("self") When Django processes this model, it identifies that it has a ManyToManyField on itself, and as a result, it doesn't add a person_set attribute to the Person class. Instead, the ManyToManyField is assumed to be symmetrical—that is, if I am your friend, then you are my friend. If you do not want symmetry in ManyToMany relationships with self, set symmetrical to False. This will force Django to add the descriptor for the reverse relationship, allowing ManyToMany relationships to be nonsymmetrical.
db_table	The name of the table to create for storing the many-to-many data. If this is not provided, Django will assume a default name based upon the names of the two tables being joined.

Model Metadata Options

Model-specific metadata lives in a class Meta defined in the body of your model class:

```
class Book(models.Model):
    title = models.CharField(maxlength=100)

    class Meta:
        # model metadata options go here
        ...
```

Model metadata is "anything that's not a field," such as ordering options and so forth.

The sections that follow present a list of all possible Meta options. No options are required. Adding class Meta to a model is completely optional.

db_table

The name of the database table to use for the model.

To save you time, Django automatically derives the name of the database table from the name of your model class and the application that contains it. A model's database table name is constructed by joining the model's "app label"—the name you used in manage.py startapp—to the model's class name, with an underscore between them.

For example, if you have an application called bookstore (as created by manage.py startapp bookstore), a model defined as class Book will have a database table named bookstore_book.

To override the database table name, use the db_table parameter in class Meta.

```
class Book(models.Model):
...
```

If this isn't given, Django will use app_label + '_' + model_class_name. See the section "Table Names" for more information.

If your database table name is an SQL reserved word, or if it contains characters that aren't allowed in Python variable names (notably the hyphen), that's OK. Django quotes column and table names behind the scenes.

db_tablespace

The name of the database tablespace to use for the model. If the back-end doesn't support tablespaces, this option is ignored.

get_latest_by

The name of a DateField or DateTimeField in the model. This specifies the default field to use in your model Manager's latest() method.

Here's an example:

```
class CustomerOrder(models.Model):
    order_date = models.DateTimeField()
    ...

    class Meta:
        get_latest_by = "order_date"
```

See Appendix C for more information on the latest() method.

order_with_respect_to

Marks this object as "orderable" with respect to the given field. This is almost always used with related objects to allow them to be ordered with respect to a parent object. For example, if an Answer relates to a Question object, and a question has more than one answer, and the order of answers matters, you'd do this:

```
class Answer(models.Model):
    question = models.ForeignKey(Question)
    # ...

    class Meta:
        order_with_respect_to = 'question'
```

ordering

The default ordering for the object, for use when obtaining lists of objects:

```
class Book(models.Model):
    title = models.CharField(maxlength=100)

    class Meta:
        ordering = ['title']
```

This is a tuple or list of strings. Each string is a field name with an optional - prefix, which indicates descending order. Fields without a leading - will be ordered ascending. Use the string "?" to order randomly.

For example, to order by a title field in ascending order (i.e., A–Z), use this:

```
ordering = ['title']
```

To order by `title` in descending order (i.e., Z–A), use this:

```
ordering = ['-title']
```

To order by `title` in descending order, and then by `title` in ascending order, use this:

```
ordering = ['-title', 'author']
```

Note that, regardless of how many fields are in `ordering`, the admin site uses only the first field.

permissions

Extra permissions to enter into the permissions table when creating this object. Add, delete, and change permissions are automatically created for each object that has `admin` set. This example specifies an extra permission, `can_deliver_pizzas`:

```
class Employee(models.Model):
    ...

    class Meta:
        permissions = (
            ("can_deliver_pizzas", "Can deliver pizzas"),
        )
```

This is a list or tuple of two-tuples in the format (`permission_code`, `human_readable_permission_name`).

See Chapter 12 for more on permissions.

unique_together

Sets of field names that, taken together, must be unique:

```
class Employee(models.Model):
    department = models.ForeignKey(Department)
    extension = models.CharField(maxlength=10)
    ...

    class Meta:
        unique_together = [("department", "extension")]
```

This is a list of lists of fields that must be unique when considered together. It's used in the Django admin interface and is enforced at the database level (i.e., the appropriate `UNIQUE` statements are included in the `CREATE TABLE` statement).

verbose_name

A human-readable name for the object, singular:

```
class CustomerOrder(models.Model):
    order_date = models.DateTimeField()
    ...

    class Meta:
        verbose_name = "order"
```

If this isn't given, Django will use an adapted version of the class name, in which CamelCase becomes camel case.

verbose_name_plural

The plural name for the object:

```
class Sphynx(models.Model):
    ...

    class Meta:
        verbose_name_plural = "sphynges"
```

If this isn't given, Django will add an "s" to the verbose_name.

Managers

A Manager is the interface through which database query operations are provided to Django models. At least one Manager exists for every model in a Django application.

The way Manager classes work is documented in Appendix C. This section specifically touches on model options that customize Manager behavior.

Manager Names

By default, Django adds a Manager with the name objects to every Django model class. However, if you want to use objects as a field name, or if you want to use a name other than objects for the Manager, you can rename it on a per-model basis. To rename the Manager for a given class, define a class attribute of type models.Manager() on that model:

```
from django.db import models

class Person(models.Model):
    ...

    people = models.Manager()
```

Using this example model, Person.objects will generate an AttributeError exception (since Person doesn't have an objects attribute), but Person.people.all() will provide a list of all Person objects.

Custom Managers

You can use a custom Manager in a particular model by extending the base Manager class and instantiating your custom Manager in your model.

There are two reasons you might want to customize a Manager: to add extra Manager methods and/or to modify the initial QuerySet the Manager returns.

Adding Extra Manager Methods

Adding extra Manager methods is the preferred way to add "table-level" functionality to your models. (For "row-level" functionality—that is, functions that act on a single instance of a model object—use model methods, not custom Manager methods.)

A custom Manager method can return anything you want. It doesn't have to return a QuerySet. For example, this custom Manager offers a method with_counts(), which returns a list of all OpinionPoll objects, each with an extra num_responses attribute that is the result of an aggregate query:

```python
from django.db import connection

class PollManager(models.Manager):

    def with_counts(self):
        cursor = connection.cursor()
        cursor.execute("""
            SELECT p.id, p.question, p.poll_date, COUNT(*)
            FROM polls_opinionpoll p, polls_response r
            WHERE p.id = r.poll_id
            GROUP BY 1, 2, 3
            ORDER BY 3 DESC""")
        result_list = []
        for row in cursor.fetchall():
            p = self.model(id=row[0], question=row[1], poll_date=row[2])
            p.num_responses = row[3]
            result_list.append(p)
        return result_list

class OpinionPoll(models.Model):
    question = models.CharField(maxlength=200)
    poll_date = models.DateField()
    objects = PollManager()

class Response(models.Model):
    poll = models.ForeignKey(Poll)
    person_name = models.CharField(maxlength=50)
    response = models.TextField()
```

With this example, you'd use OpinionPoll.objects.with_counts() to return that list of OpinionPoll objects with num_responses attributes.

Another thing to note about this example is that Manager methods can access self.model to get the model class to which they're attached.

Modifying Initial Manager QuerySets

A Manager's base QuerySet returns all objects in the system. For example, using this model:

```
class Book(models.Model):
    title = models.CharField(maxlength=100)
    author = models.CharField(maxlength=50)
```

the statement Book.objects.all() will return all books in the database.

You can override the base QuerySet by overriding the Manager.get_query_set() method. get_query_set() should return a QuerySet with the properties you require.

For example, the following model has *two* managers—one that returns all objects and one that returns only the books by Roald Dahl:

```
# First, define the Manager subclass.
class DahlBookManager(models.Manager):
    def get_query_set(self):
        qs =  super(DahlBookManager, self).get_query_set()
        return qs.filter(author='Roald Dahl')

# Then hook it into the Book model explicitly.
class Book(models.Model):
    title = models.CharField(maxlength=100)
    author = models.CharField(maxlength=50)

    objects = models.Manager() # The default manager.
    dahl_objects = DahlBookManager() # The Dahl-specific manager.
```

With this sample model, Book.objects.all() will return all books in the database, but Book.dahl_objects.all() will return only the ones written by Roald Dahl.

Of course, because get_query_set() returns a QuerySet object, you can use filter(), exclude(), and all the other QuerySet methods on it. So these statements are all legal:

```
Book.dahl_objects.all()
Book.dahl_objects.filter(title='Matilda')
Book.dahl_objects.count()
```

This example also points out another interesting technique: using multiple managers on the same model. You can attach as many Manager() instances to a model as you'd like. This is an easy way to define common "filters" for your models. Here's an example:

```
class MaleManager(models.Manager):
    def get_query_set(self):
        return super(MaleManager, self).get_query_set().filter(sex='M')

class FemaleManager(models.Manager):
    def get_query_set(self):
        return super(FemaleManager, self).get_query_set().filter(sex='F')
```

```
class Person(models.Model):
    first_name = models.CharField(maxlength=50)
    last_name = models.CharField(maxlength=50)
    sex = models.CharField(maxlength=1, choices=(('M', 'Male'), ('F', 'Female')))
    people = models.Manager()
    men = MaleManager()
    women = FemaleManager()
```

This example allows you to request Person.men.all(), Person.women.all(), and Person.people.all(), yielding predictable results.

If you use custom Manager objects, take note that the first Manager Django encounters (in order by which they're defined in the model) has a special status. Django interprets the first Manager defined in a class as the "default" Manager. Certain operations—such as Django's admin site—use the default Manager to obtain lists of objects, so it's generally a good idea for the first Manager to be relatively unfiltered. In the last example, the people Manager is defined first—so it's the default Manager.

Model Methods

Define custom methods on a model to add custom "row-level" functionality to your objects. Whereas Manager methods are intended to do "tablewide" things, model methods should act on a particular model instance.

This is a valuable technique for keeping business logic in one place: the model. For example, this model has a few custom methods:

```
class Person(models.Model):
    first_name = models.CharField(maxlength=50)
    last_name = models.CharField(maxlength=50)
    birth_date = models.DateField()
    address = models.CharField(maxlength=100)
    city = models.CharField(maxlength=50)
    state = models.USStateField() # Yes, this is America-centric...

    def baby_boomer_status(self):
        """Returns the person's baby-boomer status."""
        import datetime
        if datetime.date(1945, 8, 1) <= self.birth_date \
                                    <= datetime.date(1964, 12, 31):
            return "Baby boomer"
        if self.birth_date < datetime.date(1945, 8, 1):
            return "Pre-boomer"
        return "Post-boomer"

    def is_midwestern(self):
        """Returns True if this person is from the Midwest."""
        return self.state in ('IL', 'WI', 'MI', 'IN', 'OH', 'IA', 'MO')
```

```
@property
def full_name(self):
    """Returns the person's full name."""
    return '%s %s' % (self.first_name, self.last_name)
```

The last method in this example is a *property*—an attribute implemented by custom getter/setter user code. Properties are a nifty trick added to Python 2.2; you can read more about them at http://www.python.org/download/releases/2.2/descrintro/#property.

There are also a handful of model methods that have "special" meaning to Python or Django. These methods are described in the sections that follow.

__str__

__str__() is a Python "magic method" that defines what should be returned if you call str() on the object. Django uses str(obj) in a number of places, most notably as the value displayed to render an object in the Django admin site and as the value inserted into a template when it displays an object. Thus, you should always return a nice, human-readable string for the object's __str__. Although this isn't required, it's strongly encouraged.

Here's an example:

```
class Person(models.Model):
    first_name = models.CharField(maxlength=50)
    last_name = models.CharField(maxlength=50)

    def __str__(self):
        return '%s %s' % (self.first_name, self.last_name)
```

get_absolute_url

Define a get_absolute_url() method to tell Django how to calculate the URL for an object, for example:

```
def get_absolute_url(self):
    return "/people/%i/" % self.id
```

Django uses this in its admin interface. If an object defines get_absolute_url(), the object-editing page will have a "View on site" link that will take you directly to the object's public view, according to get_absolute_url().

Also, a couple of other bits of Django, such as the syndication-feed framework, use get_absolute_url() as a convenience to reward people who've defined the method.

It's good practice to use get_absolute_url() in templates, instead of hard-coding your objects' URLs. For example, this template code is bad:

```
<a href="/people/{{ object.id }}/">{{ object.name }}</a>
```

But this template code is good:

```
<a href="{{ object.get_absolute_url }}">{{ object.name }}</a>
```

The problem with the way we just wrote get_absolute_url() is that it slightly violates the DRY principle: the URL for this object is defined both in the URLconf file and in the model.

You can further decouple your models from the URLconf using the permalink decorator. This decorator is passed the view function, a list of positional parameters, and (optionally) a dictionary of named parameters. Django then works out the correct full URL path using the URLconf, substituting the parameters you have given into the URL. For example, if your URLconf contained a line such as the following:

```
(r'^people/(\d+)/$', 'people.views.details'),
```

your model could have a get_absolute_url method that looked like this:

```
@models.permalink
def get_absolute_url(self):
    return ('people.views.details', [str(self.id)])
```

Similarly, if you had a URLconf entry that looked like this:

```
(r'/archive/(?P<year>\d{4})/(?P<month>\d{1,2})/(?P<day>\d{1,2})/$', archive_view)
```

you could reference this using permalink() as follows:

```
@models.permalink
def get_absolute_url(self):
    return ('archive_view', (), {
        'year': self.created.year,
        'month': self.created.month,
        'day': self.created.day})
```

Notice that we specify an empty sequence for the second argument in this case, because we want to pass only keyword arguments, not named arguments.

In this way, you're tying the model's absolute URL to the view that is used to display it, without repeating the URL information anywhere. You can still use the get_absolute_url() method in templates, as before.

Executing Custom SQL

Feel free to write custom SQL statements in custom model methods and module-level methods. The object django.db.connection represents the current database connection. To use it, call connection.cursor() to get a cursor object. Then, call cursor.execute(sql, [params]) to execute the SQL, and cursor.fetchone() or cursor.fetchall() to return the resulting rows:

```
def my_custom_sql(self):
    from django.db import connection
    cursor = connection.cursor()
    cursor.execute("SELECT foo FROM bar WHERE baz = %s", [self.baz])
    row = cursor.fetchone()
    return row
```

connection and cursor mostly implement the standard Python DB-API (http://www.python.org/peps/pep-0249.html). If you're not familiar with the Python DB-API, note that the SQL statement in cursor.execute() uses placeholders, "%s", rather than adding parameters directly within the SQL. If you use this technique, the underlying database library will automatically add quotes and escaping to your parameter(s) as necessary. (Also note that Django expects the "%s" placeholder, *not* the "?" placeholder, which is used by the SQLite Python bindings. This is for the sake of consistency and sanity.)

A final note: If all you want to do is use a custom WHERE clause, you can just use the where, tables, and params arguments to the standard lookup API. See Appendix C.

Overriding Default Model Methods

As explained in Appendix C, each model gets a few methods automatically—most notably, save() and delete(). You can override these methods to alter behavior.

A classic use-case for overriding the built-in methods is if you want something to happen whenever you save an object, for example:

```
class Blog(models.Model):
    name = models.CharField(maxlength=100)
    tagline = models.TextField()

    def save(self):
        do_something()
        super(Blog, self).save() # Call the "real" save() method.
        do_something_else()
```

You can also prevent saving:

```
class Blog(models.Model):
    name = models.CharField(maxlength=100)
    tagline = models.TextField()

    def save(self):
        if self.name == "Yoko Ono's blog":
            return # Yoko shall never have her own blog!
        else:
            super(Blog, self).save() # Call the "real" save() method
```

Admin Options

The Admin class tells Django how to display the model in the admin site.

The following sections present a list of all possible Admin options. None of these options is required. To use an admin interface without specifying any options, use pass, like so:

```
class Admin:
    pass
```

Adding class Admin to a model is completely optional.

date_hierarchy

Set date_hierarchy to the name of a DateField or DateTimeField in your model, and the change list page will include a date-based navigation using that field.

Here's an example:

```
class CustomerOrder(models.Model):
    order_date = models.DateTimeField()
    ...

    class Admin:
        date_hierarchy = "order_date"
```

fields

Set `fields` to control the layout of admin interface "add" and "change" pages.

`fields` is a pretty complex nested data structure best demonstrated with an example. The following is taken from the `FlatPage` model that's part of `django.contrib.flatpages`:

```
class FlatPage(models.Model):
    ...

    class Admin:
        fields = (
            (None, {
                'fields': ('url', 'title', 'content', 'sites')
            }),
            ('Advanced options', {
                'classes': 'collapse',
                'fields' : ('enable_comments',
                            'registration_required', 'template_name')
            }),
        )
```

Formally, `fields` is a list of two-tuples, in which each two-tuple represents a `<fieldset>` on the admin form page. (A `<fieldset>` is a "section" of the form.)

The two-tuples are in the format (`name`, `field_options`), where `name` is a string representing the title of the fieldset and `field_options` is a dictionary of information about the fieldset, including a list of fields to be displayed in it.

If `fields` isn't given, Django will default to displaying each field that isn't an `AutoField` and has `editable=True`, in a single fieldset, in the same order as the fields are defined in the model.

The `field_options` dictionary can have the keys described in the sections that follow.

fields

A tuple of field names to display in this fieldset. This key is required.

To display multiple fields on the same line, wrap those fields in their own tuple. In this example, the `first_name` and `last_name` fields will display on the same line:

```
'fields': (('first_name', 'last_name'), 'address', 'city', 'state'),
```

classes

A string containing extra CSS classes to apply to the fieldset.

Apply multiple classes by separating them with spaces:

```
'classes': 'wide extrapretty',
```

Two useful classes defined by the default admin site stylesheet are collapse and wide. Fieldsets with the collapse style will be initially collapsed in the admin site and replaced with a small "click to expand" link. Fieldsets with the wide style will be given extra horizontal space.

description

A string of optional extra text to be displayed at the top of each fieldset, under the heading of the fieldset. It's used verbatim, so you can use any HTML and you must escape any special HTML characters (such as ampersands) yourself.

js

A list of strings representing URLs of JavaScript files to link into the admin screen via <script src=""> tags. This can be used to tweak a given type of admin page in JavaScript or to provide "quick links" to fill in default values for certain fields.

If you use relative URLs—that is, URLs that don't start with http:// or /—then the admin site will automatically prefix these links with settings.ADMIN_MEDIA_PREFIX.

list_display

Set list_display to control which fields are displayed on the change list page of the admin.

If you don't set list_display, the admin site will display a single column that displays the __str__() representation of each object.

Here are a few special cases to note about list_display:

- If the field is a ForeignKey, Django will display the __str__() of the related object.

- ManyToManyField fields aren't supported, because that would entail executing a separate SQL statement for each row in the table. If you want to do this nonetheless, give your model a custom method, and add that method's name to list_display. (More information on custom methods in list_display shortly.)

- If the field is a BooleanField or NullBooleanField, Django will display a pretty "on" or "off" icon instead of True or False.

- If the string given is a method of the model, Django will call it and display the output. This method should have a short_description function attribute, for use as the header for the field.

Here's a full example model:

```
class Person(models.Model):
    name = models.CharField(maxlength=50)
    birthday = models.DateField()
```

```
class Admin:
    list_display = ('name', 'decade_born_in')

def decade_born_in(self):
    return self.birthday.strftime('%Y')[:3] + "0's"
decade_born_in.short_description = 'Birth decade'
```

• If the string given is a method of the model, Django will HTML-escape the output by default. If you'd rather not escape the output of the method, give the method an allow_tags attribute whose value is True.

Here's a full example model:

```
class Person(models.Model):
    first_name = models.CharField(maxlength=50)
    last_name = models.CharField(maxlength=50)
    color_code = models.CharField(maxlength=6)

    class Admin:
        list_display = ('first_name', 'last_name', 'colored_name')

    def colored_name(self):
        return '<span style="color: #%s;">%s %s</span>' % \
            (self.color_code, self.first_name, self.last_name)
    colored_name.allow_tags = True
```

• If the string given is a method of the model that returns True or False, Django will display a pretty "on" or "off" icon if you give the method a boolean attribute whose value is True.

Here's a full example model:

```
class Person(models.Model):
    first_name = models.CharField(maxlength=50)
    birthday = models.DateField()

    class Admin:
        list_display = ('name', 'born_in_fifties')

    def born_in_fifties(self):
        return self.birthday.strftime('%Y')[:3] == 5
    born_in_fifties.boolean = True
```

• The __str__() method is just as valid in list_display as any other model method, so it's perfectly OK to do this:

```
list_display = ('__str__', 'some_other_field')
```

- Usually, elements of list_display that aren't actual database fields can't be used in sorting (because Django does all the sorting at the database level).

  However, if an element of list_display represents a certain database field, you can indicate this fact by setting the admin_order_field attribute of the item, for example:

```
class Person(models.Model):
    first_name = models.CharField(maxlength=50)
    color_code = models.CharField(maxlength=6)

    class Admin:
        list_display = ('first_name', 'colored_first_name')

    def colored_first_name(self):
        return '<span style="color: #%s;">%s</span>' % \
            (self.color_code, self.first_name)
    colored_first_name.allow_tags = True
    colored_first_name.admin_order_field = 'first_name'
```

  The preceding code will tell Django to order by the first_name field when trying to sort by colored_first_name in the admin site.

list_display_links

Set list_display_links to control which fields in list_display should be linked to the "change" page for an object.

By default, the change list page will link the first column—the first field specified in list_display—to the change page for each item. But list_display_links lets you change which columns are linked. Set list_display_links to a list or tuple of field names (in the same format as list_display) to link.

list_display_links can specify one or many field names. As long as the field names appear in list_display, Django doesn't care how many (or how few) fields are linked. The only requirement is that if you want to use list_display_links, you must define list_display.

In this example, the first_name and last_name fields will be linked on the change list page:

```
class Person(models.Model):
    ...

    class Admin:
        list_display = ('first_name', 'last_name', 'birthday')
        list_display_links = ('first_name', 'last_name')
```

Finally, note that in order to use list_display_links, you must define list_display, too.

list_filter

Set list_filter to activate filters in the right sidebar of the change list page of the admin interface. This should be a list of field names, and each specified field should be either a BooleanField, DateField, DateTimeField, or ForeignKey.

This example, taken from the `django.contrib.auth.models.User` model, shows how both `list_display` and `list_filter` work:

```
class User(models.Model):
    ...

    class Admin:
        list_display = ('username', 'email', 'first_name', 'last_name', 'is_staff')
        list_filter = ('is_staff', 'is_superuser')
```

list_per_page

Set `list_per_page` to control how many items appear on each paginated admin change list page. By default, this is set to 100.

list_select_related

Set `list_select_related` to tell Django to use `select_related()` in retrieving the list of objects on the admin change list page. This can save you a bunch of database queries if you're using related objects in the admin change list display.

The value should be either `True` or `False`. The default is `False` unless one of the `list_display` fields is a `ForeignKey`.

For more on `select_related()`, see Appendix C.

ordering

Set `ordering` to specify how objects on the admin change list page should be ordered. This should be a list or tuple in the same format as a model's `ordering` parameter.

If this isn't provided, the Django admin interface will use the model's default ordering.

save_as

Set `save_as` to `True` to enable a "save as" feature on admin change forms.

Normally, objects have three save options: "Save," "Save and continue editing," and "Save and add another." If `save_as` is `True`, "Save and add another" will be replaced by a "Save as" button.

"Save as" means the object will be saved as a new object (with a new ID), rather than the old object.

By default, `save_as` is set to `False`.

save_on_top

Set `save_on_top` to add save buttons across the top of your admin change forms.

Normally, the save buttons appear only at the bottom of the forms. If you set `save_on_top`, the buttons will appear at both the top and the bottom.

By default, `save_on_top` is set to `False`.

search_fields

Set search_fields to enable a search box on the admin change list page. This should be set to a list of field names that will be searched whenever somebody submits a search query in that text box.

These fields should be some kind of text field, such as CharField or TextField. You can also perform a related lookup on a ForeignKey with the lookup API "follow" notation:

```
class Employee(models.Model):
    department = models.ForeignKey(Department)
    ...

    class Admin:
        search_fields = ['department__name']
```

When somebody does a search in the admin search box, Django splits the search query into words and returns all objects that contain each of the words, case insensitive, where each word must be in at least one of search_fields. For example, if search_fields is set to ['first_name', 'last_name'] and a user searches for john lennon, Django will do the equivalent of this SQL WHERE clause:

```
WHERE (first_name ILIKE '%john%' OR last_name ILIKE '%john%')
AND (first_name ILIKE '%lennon%' OR last_name ILIKE '%lennon%')
```

For faster and/or more restrictive searches, prefix the field name with an operator, as shown in Table B-7.

Table B-7. *Operators Allowed in search_fields*

Operator	Meaning

^	Matches the beginning of the field. For example, if search_fields is set to ['^first_name', '^last_name'], and a user searches for john lennon, Django will do the equivalent of this SQL WHERE clause:
	`WHERE (first_name ILIKE 'john%' OR last_name ILIKE 'john%')`
	`AND (first_name ILIKE 'lennon%' OR last_name ILIKE 'lennon%')`
	This query is more efficient than the normal '%john%' query, because the database only needs to check the beginning of a column's data, rather than seeking through the entire column's data. Plus, if the column has an index on it, some databases may be able to use the index for this query, even though it's a LIKE query.

=	Matches exactly, case insensitive. For example, if search_fields is set to ['=first_name', '=last_name'] and a user searches for john lennon, Django will do the equivalent of this SQL WHERE clause:
	`WHERE (first_name ILIKE 'john' OR last_name ILIKE 'john')`
	`AND (first_name ILIKE 'lennon' OR last_name ILIKE 'lennon')`
	Note that the query input is split by spaces, so, following this example, it's currently not possible to search for all records in which first_name is exactly 'john winston' (containing a space).

@	Performs a full-text match. This is like the default search method, but it uses an index. Currently this is available only for MySQL.

APPENDIX C

■■■

Database API Reference

Django's database API is the other half of the model API discussed in Appendix B. Once you've defined a model, you'll use this API any time you need to access the database. You've seen examples of this API in use throughout the book; this appendix explains all the various options in detail.

Like the model APIs discussed in Appendix B, though, these APIs are considered very stable, the Django developers consistently add new shortcuts and conveniences. It's a good idea to always check the latest documentation online, available at http://www.djangoproject.com/documentation/0.96/db-api/.

Throughout this reference, we'll refer to the following models, which might form a simple Weblog application:

```python
from django.db import models

class Blog(models.Model):
    name = models.CharField(max_length=100)
    tagline = models.TextField()

    def __str__(self):
        return self.name

class Author(models.Model):
    name = models.CharField(max_length=50)
    email = models.EmailField()

    def __str__(self):
        return self.name

class Entry(models.Model):
    blog = models.ForeignKey(Blog)
    headline = models.CharField(max_length=255)
    body_text = models.TextField()
    pub_date = models.DateTimeField()
    authors = models.ManyToManyField(Author)

    def __str__(self):
        return self.headline
```

Creating Objects

To create an object, instantiate it using keyword arguments to the model class and then call save() to save it to the database:

```
>>> from mysite.blog.models import Blog
>>> b = Blog(name='Beatles Blog', tagline='All the latest Beatles news.')
>>> b.save()
```

This performs an INSERT SQL statement behind the scenes. Django doesn't hit the database until you explicitly call save().

The save() method has no return value.

To create an object and save it all in one, step see the create manager method discussed shortly.

What Happens When You Save?

When you save an object, Django performs the following steps:

1. *Emits a* pre_save *signal*: This provides a notification that an object is about to be saved. You can register a listener that will be invoked whenever this signal is emitted. These signals are still in development and weren't documented when this book went to press; check the online documentation for the latest information.

2. *Preprocesses the data*: Each field on the object is asked to perform any automated data modification that the field may need to perform. Most fields do *no* preprocessing—the field data is kept as is. Preprocessing is only used on fields that have special behavior, like file fields.

3. *Prepares the data for the database*: Each field is asked to provide its current value in a data type that can be written to the database. Most fields require no data preparation. Simple data types, such as integers and strings, are "ready to write" as a Python object. However, more complex data types often require some modification. For example, DateFields use a Python datetime object to store data. Databases don't store datetime objects, so the field value must be converted into an ISO-compliant date string for insertion into the database.

4. *Inserts the data into the database*: The preprocessed, prepared data is then composed into an SQL statement for insertion into the database.

5. *Emits a* post_save *signal*: As with the pre_save signal, this is used to provide notification that an object has been successfully saved. Again, these signals are not yet documented.

Autoincrementing Primary Keys

For convenience, each model is given an autoincrementing primary key field named id unless you explicitly specify primary_key=True on a field (see the section titled "AutoField" in Appendix B).

If your model has an AutoField, that autoincremented value will be calculated and saved as an attribute on your object the first time you call save():

```
>>> b2 = Blog(name='Cheddar Talk', tagline='Thoughts on cheese.')
>>> b2.id      # Returns None, because b doesn't have an ID yet.
None

>>> b2.save()
>>> b2.id      # Returns the ID of your new object.
14
```

There's no way to tell what the value of an ID will be before you call save(), because that value is calculated by your database, not by Django.

If a model has an AutoField but you want to define a new object's ID explicitly when saving, just define it explicitly before saving, rather than relying on the autoassignment of the ID:

```
>>> b3 = Blog(id=3, name='Cheddar Talk', tagline='Thoughts on cheese.')
>>> b3.id
3
>>> b3.save()
>>> b3.id
3
```

If you assign auto-primary-key values manually, make sure not to use an already existing primary key value! If you create a new object with an explicit primary key value that already exists in the database, Django will assume you're changing the existing record rather than creating a new one.

Given the preceding 'Cheddar Talk' blog example, this example would override the previous record in the database:

```
>>> b4 = Blog(id=3, name='Not Cheddar', tagline='Anything but cheese.')
>>> b4.save()  # Overrides the previous blog with ID=3!
```

Explicitly specifying auto-primary-key values is mostly useful for bulk-saving objects, when you're confident you won't have primary key collision.

Saving Changes to Objects

To save changes to an object that's already in the database, use save().

Given a Blog instance b5 that has already been saved to the database, this example changes its name and updates its record in the database:

```
>>> b5.name = 'New name'
>>> b5.save()
```

This performs an UPDATE SQL statement behind the scenes. Again, Django doesn't hit the database until you explicitly call save().

HOW DJANGO KNOWS WHEN TO UPDATE AND WHEN TO INSERT

You may have noticed that Django database objects use the same `save()` method for creating and changing objects. Django abstracts the need to use `INSERT` or `UPDATE` SQL statements. Specifically, when you call `save()`, Django follows this algorithm:

- If the object's primary key attribute is set to a value that evaluates to `True` (i.e., a value other than `None` or the empty string), Django executes a `SELECT` query to determine whether a record with the given primary key already exists.

- If the record with the given primary key does already exist, Django executes an `UPDATE` query.

- If the object's primary key attribute is *not* set, or if it's set but a record doesn't exist, Django executes an `INSERT`.

Because of this, you should be careful not to specify a primary key value explicitly when saving new objects if you cannot guarantee the primary key value is unused.

Updating `ForeignKey` fields works exactly the same way; simply assign an object of the right type to the field in question:

```
>>> joe = Author.objects.create(name="Joe")
>>> entry.author = joe
>>> entry.save()
```

Django will complain if you try to assign an object of the wrong type.

Retrieving Objects

Throughout the book you've seen objects retrieved using code like the following:

```
>>> blogs = Blog.objects.filter(author__name__contains="Joe")
```

There are quite a few "moving parts" behind the scenes here: when you retrieve objects from the database, you're actually constructing a `QuerySet` using the model's `Manager`. This `QuerySet` knows how to execute SQL and return the requested objects.

Appendix B looked at both of these objects from a model-definition point of view; now we'll look at how they operate.

A `QuerySet` represents a collection of objects from your database. It can have zero, one, or many *filters*—criteria that narrow down the collection based on given parameters. In SQL terms, a `QuerySet` equates to a `SELECT` statement, and a filter is a limiting clause such as `WHERE` or `LIMIT`.

You get a `QuerySet` by using your model's `Manager`. Each model has at least one `Manager`, and it's called `objects` by default. Access it directly via the model class, like so:

```
>>> Blog.objects
<django.db.models.manager.Manager object at 0x137d00d>
```

Managers are accessible only via model classes, rather than from model instances, to enforce a separation between "table-level" operations and "record-level" operations:

```
>>> b = Blog(name='Foo', tagline='Bar')
>>> b.objects
Traceback (most recent call last):
  File "<stdin>", line 1, in <module>
AttributeError: Manager isn't accessible via Blog instances.
```

The Manager is the main source of QuerySets for a model. It acts as a "root" QuerySet that describes all objects in the model's database table. For example, Blog.objects is the initial QuerySet that contains all Blog objects in the database.

Caching and QuerySets

Each QuerySet contains a cache, to minimize database access. It's important to understand how it works in order to write the most efficient code.

In a newly created QuerySet, the cache is empty. The first time a QuerySet is evaluated—and, hence, a database query happens—Django saves the query results in the QuerySet's cache and returns the results that have been explicitly requested (e.g., the next element, if the QuerySet is being iterated over). Subsequent evaluations of the QuerySet reuse the cached results.

Keep this caching behavior in mind, because it may bite you if you don't use your QuerySets correctly. For example, the following will create two QuerySets, evaluate them, and throw them away:

```
print [e.headline for e in Entry.objects.all()]
print [e.pub_date for e in Entry.objects.all()]
```

That means the same database query will be executed twice, effectively doubling your database load. Also, there's a possibility the two lists may not include the same database records, because an Entry may have been added or deleted in the split second between the two requests.

To avoid this problem, simply save the QuerySet and reuse it:

```
queryset = Poll.objects.all()
print [p.headline for p in queryset] # Evaluate the query set.
print [p.pub_date for p in queryset] # Reuse the cache from the evaluation.
```

Filtering Objects

The simplest way to retrieve objects from a table is to get all of them. To do this, use the all() method on a Manager:

```
>>> Entry.objects.all()
```

The all() method returns a QuerySet of all the objects in the database. Usually, though, you'll need to select only a subset of the complete set of objects. To create such a subset, you refine the initial QuerySet, adding filter conditions. You'll usually do this using the filter() and/or exclude() methods:

```
>>> y2006 = Entry.objects.filter(pub_date__year=2006)
>>> not2006 = Entry.objects.exclude(pub_date__year=2006)
```

filter() and exclude() both take *field lookup* arguments, which are discussed in detail shortly.

Chaining Filters

The result of refining a QuerySet is itself a QuerySet, so it's possible to chain refinements together, for example:

```
>>> qs = Entry.objects.filter(headline__startswith='What')
>>> qs = qs..exclude(pub_date__gte=datetime.datetime.now())
>>> qs = qs.filter(pub_date__gte=datetime.datetime(2005, 1, 1))
```

This takes the initial QuerySet of all entries in the database, adds a filter, then an exclusion, and then another filter. The final result is a QuerySet containing all entries with a headline that starts with "What" that were published between January 1, 2005, and the current day.

It's important to point out here that QuerySets are lazy—the act of creating a QuerySet doesn't involve any database activity. In fact, the three preceding lines don't make *any* database calls; you can chain filters together all day long and Django won't actually run the query until the QuerySet is *evaluated*.

You can evaluate a QuerySet in any following ways:

- *Iterating*: A QuerySet is iterable, and it executes its database query the first time you iterate over it. For example, the following QuerySet isn't evaluated until it's iterated over in the for loop:

  ```
  qs = Entry.objects.filter(pub_date__year=2006)
  qs = qs.filter(headline__icontains="bill")
  for e in qs:
      print e.headline
  ```

  This prints all headlines from 2006 that contain "bill" but causes only one database hit.

- *Printing it*: A QuerySet is evaluated when you call repr() on it. This is for convenience in the Python interactive interpreter, so you can immediately see your results when using the API interactively.

- *Slicing*: As explained in the upcoming "Limiting QuerySets" section, a QuerySet can be sliced using Python's array-slicing syntax. Usually slicing a QuerySet returns another (unevaluated) QuerySet, but Django will execute the database query if you use the "step" parameter of slice syntax.

- *Converting to a list*: You can force evaluation of a QuerySet by calling list() on it, for example:

  ```
  >>> entry_list = list(Entry.objects.all())
  ```

  Be warned, though, that this could have a large memory overhead, because Django will load each element of the list into memory. In contrast, iterating over a QuerySet will take advantage of your database to load data and instantiate objects only as you need them.

FILTERED QUERYSETS ARE UNIQUE

Each time you refine a QuerySet, you get a brand-new QuerySet that is in no way bound to the previous QuerySet. Each refinement creates a separate and distinct QuerySet that can be stored, used, and reused:

```
q1 = Entry.objects.filter(headline__startswith="What")
q2 = q1.exclude(pub_date__gte=datetime.now())
q3 = q1.filter(pub_date__gte=datetime.now())
```

These three QuerySets are separate. The first is a base QuerySet containing all entries that contain a headline starting with "What". The second is a subset of the first, with an additional criterion that excludes records whose pub_date is greater than now. The third is a subset of the first, with an additional criterion that selects only the records whose pub_date is greater than now. The initial QuerySet (q1) is unaffected by the refinement process.

Limiting QuerySets

Use Python's array-slicing syntax to limit your QuerySet to a certain number of results. This is the equivalent of SQL's LIMIT and OFFSET clauses.

For example, this returns the first five entries (LIMIT 5):

```
>>> Entry.objects.all()[:5]
```

This returns the sixth through tenth entries (OFFSET 5 LIMIT 5):

```
>>> Entry.objects.all()[5:10]
```

Generally, slicing a QuerySet returns a new QuerySet—it doesn't evaluate the query. An exception is if you use the "step" parameter of Python slice syntax. For example, this would actually execute the query in order to return a list of every *second* object of the first ten:

```
>>> Entry.objects.all()[:10:2]
```

To retrieve a *single* object rather than a list (e.g., SELECT foo FROM bar LIMIT 1), use a simple index instead of a slice. For example, this returns the first Entry in the database, after ordering entries alphabetically by headline:

```
>>> Entry.objects.order_by('headline')[0]
```

The preceding is roughly equivalent to the following:

```
>>> Entry.objects.order_by('headline')[0:1].get()
```

Note, however, that the first of these will raise IndexError while the second will raise DoesNotExist if no objects match the given criteria.

Query Methods That Return New QuerySets

Django provides a range of QuerySet refinement methods that modify either the types of results returned by the QuerySet or the way its SQL query is executed. These methods are described in the sections that follow. Some of the methods take field lookup arguments, which are discussed in detail a bit later on.

filter(**lookup)

Returns a new QuerySet containing objects that match the given lookup parameters.

exclude(**kwargs)

Returns a new QuerySet containing objects that do *not* match the given lookup parameters.

order_by(*fields)

By default, results returned by a QuerySet are ordered by the ordering tuple given by the ordering option in the model's metadata (see Appendix B). You can override this for a particular query using the order_by() method:

```
>> Entry.objects.filter(pub_date__year=2005).order_by('-pub_date', 'headline')
```

This result will be ordered by pub_date descending, and then by headline ascending. The negative sign in front of "-pub_date" indicates *descending* order. Ascending order is assumed if the - is absent. To order randomly, use "?", like so:

```
>>> Entry.objects.order_by('?')
```

distinct()

Returns a new QuerySet that uses SELECT DISTINCT in its SQL query. This eliminates duplicate rows from the query results.

By default, a QuerySet will not eliminate duplicate rows. In practice, this is rarely a problem, because simple queries such as Blog.objects.all() don't introduce the possibility of duplicate result rows.

However, if your query spans multiple tables, it's possible to get duplicate results when a QuerySet is evaluated. That's when you'd use distinct().

values(*fields)

Returns a special QuerySet that evaluates to a list of dictionaries instead of model-instance objects. Each of those dictionaries represents an object, with the keys corresponding to the attribute names of model objects:

```
# This list contains a Blog object.
>>> Blog.objects.filter(name__startswith='Beatles')
[Beatles Blog]

# This list contains a dictionary.
>>> Blog.objects.filter(name__startswith='Beatles').values()
[{'id': 1, 'name': 'Beatles Blog', 'tagline': 'All the latest Beatles news.'}]
```

values() takes optional positional arguments, *fields, which specify field names to which the SELECT should be limited. If you specify the fields, each dictionary will contain only the field keys/values for the fields you specify. If you don't specify the fields, each dictionary will contain a key and value for every field in the database table:

```
>>> Blog.objects.values()
[{'id': 1, 'name': 'Beatles Blog', 'tagline': 'All the latest Beatles news.'}],
>>> Blog.objects.values('id', 'name')
[{'id': 1, 'name': 'Beatles Blog'}]
```

This method is useful when you know you're only going to need values from a small number of the available fields and you won't need the functionality of a model instance object. It's more efficient to select only the fields you need to use.

dates(field, kind, order)

Returns a special QuerySet that evaluates to a list of datetime.datetime objects representing all available dates of a particular kind within the contents of the QuerySet.

The field argument must be the name of a DateField or DateTimeField of your model. The kind argument must be "year", "month", or "day". Each datetime.datetime object in the result list is "truncated" to the given type:

- "year" returns a list of all distinct year values for the field.

- "month" returns a list of all distinct year/month values for the field.

- "day" returns a list of all distinct year/month/day values for the field.

order, which defaults to 'ASC', should be either 'ASC' or 'DESC'. This specifies how to order the results.

Here are a few examples:

```
>>> Entry.objects.dates('pub_date', 'year')
[datetime.datetime(2005, 1, 1)]

>>> Entry.objects.dates('pub_date', 'month')
[datetime.datetime(2005, 2, 1), datetime.datetime(2005, 3, 1)]

>>> Entry.objects.dates('pub_date', 'day')
[datetime.datetime(2005, 2, 20), datetime.datetime(2005, 3, 20)]

>>> Entry.objects.dates('pub_date', 'day', order='DESC')
[datetime.datetime(2005, 3, 20), datetime.datetime(2005, 2, 20)]

>>> Entry.objects.filter(headline__contains='Lennon').dates('pub_date', 'day')
[datetime.datetime(2005, 3, 20)]
```

select_related()

Returns a QuerySet that will automatically "follow" foreign key relationships, selecting that additional related-object data when it executes its query. This is a performance booster that results in (sometimes much) larger queries but means later use of foreign key relationships won't require database queries.

The following examples illustrate the difference between plain lookups and select_related() lookups. Here's standard lookup:

```
# Hits the database.
>>> e = Entry.objects.get(id=5)

# Hits the database again to get the related Blog object.
>>> b = e.blog
```

and here's select_related lookup:

```
# Hits the database.
>>> e = Entry.objects.select_related().get(id=5)

# Doesn't hit the database, because e.blog has been prepopulated
# in the previous query.
>>> b = e.blog
```

select_related() follows foreign keys as far as possible. If you have the following models:

```
class City(models.Model):
    # ...

class Person(models.Model):
    # ...
    hometown = models.ForeignKey(City)

class Book(models.Model):
    # ...
    author = models.ForeignKey(Person)
```

then a call to Book.objects.select_related().get(id=4) will cache the related Person *and* the related City:

```
>>> b = Book.objects.select_related().get(id=4)
>>> p = b.author          # Doesn't hit the database.
>>> c = p.hometown        # Doesn't hit the database.

>>> b = Book.objects.get(id=4) # No select_related() in this example.
>>> p = b.author          # Hits the database.
>>> c = p.hometown        # Hits the database.
```

Note that select_related() does not follow foreign keys that have null=True.

Usually, using select_related() can vastly improve performance because your application can avoid many database calls. However, in situations with deeply nested sets of relationships, select_related() can sometimes end up following "too many" relations and can generate queries so large that they end up being slow.

extra()

Sometimes, the Django query syntax by itself can't easily express a complex WHERE clause. For these edge cases, Django provides the extra() QuerySet modifier, a hook for injecting specific clauses into the SQL generated by a QuerySet.

By definition, these extra lookups may not be portable to different database engines (because you're explicitly writing SQL code) and violate the DRY principle, so you should avoid them if possible.

Specify one or more of params, select, where, or tables. None of the arguments is required, but you should use at least one of them.

The select argument lets you put extra fields in the SELECT clause. It should be a dictionary mapping attribute names to SQL clauses to use to calculate that attribute:

```
>>> Entry.objects.extra(select={'is_recent': "pub_date > '2006-01-01'"})
```

As a result, each Entry object will have an extra attribute, is_recent, a Boolean representing whether the entry's pub_date is greater than January 1, 2006.

The next example is more advanced—it does a subquery to give each resulting Blog object an entry_count attribute, an integer count of associated Entry objects:

```
>>> subq = 'SELECT COUNT(*) FROM blog_entry WHERE blog_entry.blog_id = blog_blog.id'
>>> Blog.objects.extra(select={'entry_count': subq})
```

(In this particular case, we're exploiting the fact that the query will already contain the blog_blog table in its FROM clause.)

You can define explicit SQL WHERE clauses—perhaps to perform nonexplicit joins—by using where. You can manually add tables to the SQL FROM clause by using tables.

where and tables both take a list of strings. All where parameters are ANDed to any other search criteria:

```
>>> Entry.objects.extra(where=['id IN (3, 4, 5, 20)'])
```

The select and where parameters described previously may use standard Python database string placeholders, '%s', to indicate parameters the database engine should automatically quote. The params argument is a list of any extra parameters to be substituted:

```
>>> Entry.objects.extra(where=['headline=%s'], params=['Lennon'])
```

Always use params instead of embedding values directly into select or where because params will ensure values are quoted correctly according to your particular database.

Here's an example of the wrong way:

```
Entry.objects.extra(where=["headline='%s'" % name])
```

Here's an example of the correct way:

```
Entry.objects.extra(where=['headline=%s'], params=[name])
```

QuerySet Methods That Do Not Return QuerySets

The following QuerySet methods evaluate the QuerySet and return something *other than* a QuerySet—a single object, value, and so forth.

get(**lookup)

Returns the object matching the given lookup parameters, which should be in the format described in the "Field Lookups" section. This raises AssertionError if more than one object was found.

get() raises a DoesNotExist exception if an object wasn't found for the given parameters. The DoesNotExist exception is an attribute of the model class, for example:

```
>>> Entry.objects.get(id='foo') # raises Entry.DoesNotExist
```

The DoesNotExist exception inherits from django.core.exceptions.ObjectDoesNotExist, so you can target multiple DoesNotExist exceptions:

```
>>> from django.core.exceptions import ObjectDoesNotExist
>>> try:
...     e = Entry.objects.get(id=3)
...     b = Blog.objects.get(id=1)
... except ObjectDoesNotExist:
...     print "Either the entry or blog doesn't exist."
```

create(**kwargs)

This is a convenience method for creating an object and saving it all in one step. It lets you compress two common steps:

```
>>> p = Person(first_name="Bruce", last_name="Springsteen")
>>> p.save()
```

into a single line:

```
>>> p = Person.objects.create(first_name="Bruce", last_name="Springsteen")
```

get_or_create(**kwargs)

This is a convenience method for looking up an object and creating one if it doesn't exist. It returns a tuple of (object, created), where object is the retrieved or created object and created is a Boolean specifying whether a new object was created.

This method is meant as a shortcut to boilerplate code and is mostly useful for data-import scripts, for example:

```
try:
    obj = Person.objects.get(first_name='John', last_name='Lennon')
except Person.DoesNotExist:
    obj = Person(first_name='John', last_name='Lennon', birthday=date(1940, 10, 9))
    obj.save()
```

This pattern gets quite unwieldy as the number of fields in a model increases. The previous example can be rewritten using get_or_create() like so:

```
obj, created = Person.objects.get_or_create(
    first_name = 'John',
    last_name  = 'Lennon',
    defaults   = {'birthday': date(1940, 10, 9)}
)
```

Any keyword arguments passed to get_or_create()—*except* an optional one called defaults—will be used in a get() call. If an object is found, get_or_create() returns a tuple of that object and False. If an object is *not* found, get_or_create() will instantiate and save a new object, returning a tuple of the new object and True. The new object will be created according to this algorithm:

```
defaults = kwargs.pop('defaults', {})
params = dict([(k, v) for k, v in kwargs.items() if '__' not in k])
params.update(defaults)
obj = self.model(**params)
obj.save()
```

In English, that means start with any non-'defaults' keyword argument that doesn't contain a double underscore (which would indicate a nonexact lookup). Then add the contents of defaults, overriding any keys if necessary, and use the result as the keyword arguments to the model class.

If you have a field named defaults and want to use it as an exact lookup in get_or_create(), just use 'defaults__exact' like so:

```
Foo.objects.get_or_create(
    defaults__exact = 'bar',
    defaults={'defaults': 'baz'}
)
```

As mentioned earlier, get_or_create() is mostly useful in scripts that need to parse data and create new records if existing ones aren't available. But if you need to use get_or_create() in a view, please make sure to use it only in POST requests unless you have a good reason not to. GET requests shouldn't have any effect on data; use POST whenever a request to a page has a side effect on your data.

count()

Returns an integer representing the number of objects in the database matching the QuerySet. count() never raises exceptions. Here's an example:

```
# Returns the total number of entries in the database.
>>> Entry.objects.count()
4

# Returns the number of entries whose headline contains 'Lennon'
>>> Entry.objects.filter(headline__contains='Lennon').count()
1
```

count() performs a SELECT COUNT(*) behind the scenes, so you should always use count() rather than loading all of the records into Python objects and calling len() on the result.

Depending on which database you're using (e.g., PostgreSQL or MySQL), count() may return a long integer instead of a normal Python integer. This is an underlying implementation quirk that shouldn't pose any real-world problems.

in_bulk(id_list)

Takes a list of primary key values and returns a dictionary mapping each primary key value to an instance of the object with the given ID, for example:

```
>>> Blog.objects.in_bulk([1])
{1: Beatles Blog}
>>> Blog.objects.in_bulk([1, 2])
{1: Beatles Blog, 2: Cheddar Talk}
>>> Blog.objects.in_bulk([])
{}
```

IDs of objects that don't exist are silently dropped from the result dictionary. If you pass in_bulk() an empty list, you'll get an empty dictionary.

latest(field_name=None)

Returns the latest object in the table, by date, using the field_name provided as the date field. This example returns the latest Entry in the table, according to the pub_date field:

```
>>> Entry.objects.latest('pub_date')
```

If your model's Meta specifies get_latest_by, you can leave off the field_name argument to latest(). Django will use the field specified in get_latest_by by default.

Like get(), latest() raises DoesNotExist if an object doesn't exist with the given parameters.

Field Lookups

Field lookups are how you specify the meat of an SQL WHERE clause. They're specified as keyword arguments to the QuerySet methods filter(), exclude(), and get().

Basic lookup keyword arguments take the form field__lookuptype=value (note the double underscore). For example, the following:

```
>>> Entry.objects.filter(pub_date__lte='2006-01-01')
```

translates (roughly) into this SQL:

```
SELECT * FROM blog_entry WHERE pub_date <= '2006-01-01';
```

If you pass an invalid keyword argument, a lookup function will raise TypeError.
The supported lookup types follow.

exact

Performs an exact match:

```
>>> Entry.objects.get(headline__exact="Man bites dog")
```

This matches any object with the exact headline "Man bites dog".

If you don't provide a lookup type—that is, if your keyword argument doesn't contain a double underscore—the lookup type is assumed to be exact. For example, the following two statements are equivalent:

```
>>> Blog.objects.get(id__exact=14) # Explicit form
>>> Blog.objects.get(id=14) # __exact is implied
```

This is for convenience, because exact lookups are the common case.

iexact

Performs a case-insensitive exact match:

```
>>> Blog.objects.get(name__iexact='beatles blog')
```

This will match `'Beatles Blog'`, `'beatles blog'`, `'BeAtLes BLoG'`, and so forth.

contains

Performs a case-sensitive containment test:

```
Entry.objects.get(headline__contains='Lennon')
```

This will match the headline `'Today Lennon honored'` but not `'today lennon honored'`. SQLite doesn't support case-sensitive `LIKE` statements; when using SQLite, contains acts like icontains.

ESCAPING PERCENT SIGNS AND UNDERSCORES IN LIKE STATEMENTS

The field lookups that equate to `LIKE` SQL statements (iexact, contains, icontains, startswith, istartswith, endswith, and iendswith) will automatically escape the two special characters used in `LIKE` statements: the percent sign and the underscore. (In a `LIKE` statement, the percent sign signifies a multiple-character wildcard and the underscore signifies a single-character wildcard.)

This means things should work intuitively, so the abstraction doesn't leak. For example, to retrieve all the entries that contain a percent sign, just use the percent sign as any other character:

```
Entry.objects.filter(headline__contains='%')
```

Django takes care of the quoting for you. The resulting SQL will look something like this:

```
SELECT ... WHERE headline LIKE '%\%%';
```

The same goes for underscores. Both percentage signs and underscores are handled for you transparently.

icontains

Performs a case-insensitive containment test:

```
>>> Entry.objects.get(headline__icontains='Lennon')
```

Unlike contains, icontains *will* match `'today lennon honored'`.

gt, gte, lt, and lte

These represent greater than, greater than or equal to, less than, and less than or equal to:

```
>>> Entry.objects.filter(id__gt=4)
>>> Entry.objects.filter(id__lt=15)
>>> Entry.objects.filter(id__gte=0)
```

These queries return any object with an ID greater than 4, an ID less than 15, and an ID greater than or equal to 1, respectively.

You'll usually use these on numeric fields. Be careful with character fields since character order isn't always what you'd expect (i.e., the string "4" sorts *after* the string "10").

in

Filters where a value is on a given list:

```
Entry.objects.filter(id__in=[1, 3, 4])
```

This returns all objects with the ID 1, 3, or 4.

startswith

Performs a case-sensitive starts-with:

```
>>> Entry.objects.filter(headline__startswith='Will')
```

This will return the headlines "Will he run?" and "Willbur named judge", but not "Who is Will?" or "will found in crypt".

istartswith

Performs a case-insensitive starts-with:

```
>>> Entry.objects.filter(headline__istartswith='will')
```

This will return the headlines "Will he run?", "Willbur named judge", and "will found in crypt", but not "Who is Will?"

endswith and iendswith

Perform case-sensitive and case-insensitive ends-with:

```
>>> Entry.objects.filter(headline__endswith='cats')
>>> Entry.objects.filter(headline__iendswith='cats')
```

range

Performs an inclusive range check:

```
>>> start_date = datetime.date(2005, 1, 1)
>>> end_date = datetime.date(2005, 3, 31)
>>> Entry.objects.filter(pub_date__range=(start_date, end_date))
```

You can use `range` anywhere you can use BETWEEN in SQL—for dates, numbers, and even characters.

year, month, and day

For date/datetime fields, perform exact year, month, or day matches:

```
# Year lookup
>>>Entry.objects.filter(pub_date__year=2005)

# Month lookup—takes integers
>>> Entry.objects.filter(pub_date__month=12)

# Day lookup
>>> Entry.objects.filter(pub_date__day=3)

# Combination: return all entries on Christmas of any year
>>> Entry.objects.filter(pub_date__month=12, pub_date_day=25)
```

isnull

Takes either True or False, which correspond to SQL queries of IS NULL and IS NOT NULL, respectively:

```
>>> Entry.objects.filter(pub_date__isnull=True)
__isnull=True vs. __exact=None
```

There is an important difference between __isnull=True and __exact=None. __exact=None will *always* return an empty result set, because SQL requires that no value is equal to NULL. __isnull determines if the field is currently holding the value of NULL without performing a comparison.

search

A Boolean full-text search that takes advantage of full-text indexing. This is like `contains` but is significantly faster due to full-text indexing.

Note this is available only in MySQL and requires direct manipulation of the database to add the full-text index.

The pk Lookup Shortcut

For convenience, Django provides a `pk` lookup type, which stands for "primary_key".

In the example Blog model, the primary key is the id field, so these three statements are equivalent:

```
>>> Blog.objects.get(id__exact=14) # Explicit form
>>> Blog.objects.get(id=14) # __exact is implied
>>> Blog.objects.get(pk=14) # pk implies id__exact
```

The use of pk isn't limited to __exact queries—any query term can be combined with pk to perform a query on the primary key of a model:

```
# Get blogs entries  with id 1, 4, and 7
>>> Blog.objects.filter(pk__in=[1,4,7])

# Get all blog entries with id > 14
>>> Blog.objects.filter(pk__gt=14)
```

pk lookups also work across joins. For example, these three statements are equivalent:

```
>>> Entry.objects.filter(blog__id__exact=3) # Explicit form
>>> Entry.objects.filter(blog__id=3) # __exact is implied
>>> Entry.objects.filter(blog__pk=3) # __pk implies __id__exact
```

Complex Lookups with Q Objects

Keyword argument queries—in filter() and so on—are ANDed together. If you need to execute more complex queries (e.g., queries with OR statements), you can use Q objects.

A Q object (django.db.models.Q) is an object used to encapsulate a collection of keyword arguments. These keyword arguments are specified as in the "Field Lookups" section.

For example, this Q object encapsulates a single LIKE query:

```
Q(question__startswith='What')
```

Q objects can be combined using the & and | operators. When an operator is used on two Q objects, it yields a new Q object. For example, this statement yields a single Q object that represents the OR of two "question__startswith" queries:

```
Q(question__startswith='Who') | Q(question__startswith='What')
```

This is equivalent to the following SQL WHERE clause:

```
WHERE question LIKE 'Who%' OR question LIKE 'What%'
```

You can compose statements of arbitrary complexity by combining Q objects with the & and | operators. You can also use parenthetical grouping.

Each lookup function that takes keyword arguments (e.g., filter(), exclude(), get()) can also be passed one or more Q objects as positional (not-named) arguments. If you provide multiple Q object arguments to a lookup function, the arguments will be ANDed together, for example:

```
Poll.objects.get(
    Q(question__startswith='Who'),
    Q(pub_date=date(2005, 5, 2)) | Q(pub_date=date(2005, 5, 6))
)
```

roughly translates into the following SQL:

```
SELECT * from polls WHERE question LIKE 'Who%'
    AND (pub_date = '2005-05-02' OR pub_date = '2005-05-06')
```

Lookup functions can mix the use of Q objects and keyword arguments. All arguments provided to a lookup function (be they keyword arguments or Q objects) are ANDed together. However, if a Q object is provided, it must precede the definition of any keyword arguments. For example, the following:

```
Poll.objects.get(
    Q(pub_date=date(2005, 5, 2)) | Q(pub_date=date(2005, 5, 6)),
    question__startswith='Who')
```

would be a valid query, equivalent to the previous example, but this:

```
# INVALID QUERY
Poll.objects.get(
    question__startswith='Who',
    Q(pub_date=date(2005, 5, 2)) | Q(pub_date=date(2005, 5, 6)))
```

would not be valid.

You can find some examples online at http://www.djangoproject.com/documentation/0.96/models/or_lookups/.

Related Objects

When you define a relationship in a model (i.e., a ForeignKey, OneToOneField, or ManyToManyField), instances of that model will have a convenient API to access the related object(s). For example, an Entry object e can get its associated Blog object by accessing the blog attribute e.blog.

Django also creates API accessors for the "other" side of the relationship—the link from the related model to the model that defines the relationship. For example, a Blog object b has access to a list of all related Entry objects via the entry_set attribute: b.entry_set.all().

All examples in this section use the sample Blog, Author, and Entry models defined earlier.

Lookups That Span Relationships

Django offers a powerful and intuitive way to "follow" relationships in lookups, taking care of the SQL JOINs for you automatically behind the scenes. To span a relationship, just use the field name of related fields across models, separated by double underscores, until you get to the field you want.

This example retrieves all Entry objects with a Blog whose name is 'Beatles Blog':

```
>>> Entry.objects.filter(blog__name__exact='Beatles Blog')
```

This spanning can be as deep as you'd like.

It works backward, too. To refer to a "reverse" relationship, just use the lowercase name of the model.

This example retrieves all Blog objects that have at least one Entry whose headline contains 'Lennon':

```
>>> Blog.objects.filter(entry__headline__contains='Lennon')
```

Foreign Key Relationships

If a model has a ForeignKey, instances of that model will have access to the related (foreign) object via a simple attribute of the model, for example:

```
e = Entry.objects.get(id=2)
e.blog # Returns the related Blog object.
```

You can get and set via a foreign key attribute. As you may expect, changes to the foreign key aren't saved to the database until you call save(), for example:

```
e = Entry.objects.get(id=2)
e.blog = some_blog
e.save()
```

If a ForeignKey field has null=True set (i.e., it allows NULL values), you can assign None to it:

```
e = Entry.objects.get(id=2)
e.blog = None
e.save() # "UPDATE blog_entry SET blog_id = NULL ...;"
```

Forward access to one-to-many relationships is cached the first time the related object is accessed. Subsequent accesses to the foreign key on the same object instance are cached, for example:

```
e = Entry.objects.get(id=2)
print e.blog  # Hits the database to retrieve the associated Blog.
print e.blog  # Doesn't hit the database; uses cached version.
```

Note that the select_related() QuerySet method recursively prepopulates the cache of all one-to-many relationships ahead of time:

```
e = Entry.objects.select_related().get(id=2)
print e.blog  # Doesn't hit the database; uses cached version.
print e.blog  # Doesn't hit the database; uses cached version.
```

select_related() is documented in the "Query Methods That Return New QuerySets" section.

"Reverse" Foreign Key Relationships

Foreign key relationships are automatically symmetrical—a reverse relationship is inferred from the presence of a ForeignKey pointing to another model.

If a model has a ForeignKey, instances of the foreign key model will have access to a Manager that returns all instances of the first model. By default, this Manager is named FOO_set, where FOO is the source model name, lowercased. This Manager returns QuerySets, which can be filtered and manipulated as described in the "Retrieving Objects" section.

Here's an example:

```
b = Blog.objects.get(id=1)
b.entry_set.all() # Returns all Entry objects related to Blog.
```

```
# b.entry_set is a Manager that returns QuerySets.
b.entry_set.filter(headline__contains='Lennon')
b.entry_set.count()
```

You can override the FOO_set name by setting the related_name parameter in the ForeignKey() definition. For example, if the Entry model was altered to blog = ForeignKey(Blog, related_name='entries'), the preceding example code would look like this:

```
b = Blog.objects.get(id=1)
b.entries.all() # Returns all Entry objects related to Blog.

# b.entries is a Manager that returns QuerySets.
b.entries.filter(headline__contains='Lennon')
b.entries.count()
```

You cannot access a reverse ForeignKey Manager from the class; it must be accessed from an instance:

```
Blog.entry_set # Raises AttributeError: "Manager must be accessed via instance".
```

In addition to the QuerySet methods defined in the "Retrieving Objects" section, the ForeignKey Manager has these additional methods:

- add(obj1, obj2, ...): Adds the specified model objects to the related object set, for example:

```
b = Blog.objects.get(id=1)
e = Entry.objects.get(id=234)
b.entry_set.add(e) # Associates Entry e with Blog b.
```

- create(**kwargs): Creates a new object, saves it, and puts it in the related object set. It returns the newly created object:

```
b = Blog.objects.get(id=1)
e = b.entry_set.create(headline='Hello', body_text='Hi', pub_date=datetime.date(2005, 1, 1))
# No need to call e.save() at this point—it's already been saved.
```

This is equivalent to (but much simpler than) the following:

```
b = Blog.objects.get(id=1)
e = Entry(blog=b, headline='Hello', body_text='Hi', pub_date=datetime.date(2005, 1, 1))
e.save()
```

Note that there's no need to specify the keyword argument of the model that defines the relationship. In the preceding example, we don't pass the parameter blog to create(). Django figures out that the new Entry object's blog field should be set to b.

- remove(obj1, obj2, ...): Removes the specified model objects from the related object set:

```
b = Blog.objects.get(id=1)
e = Entry.objects.get(id=234)
b.entry_set.remove(e) # Disassociates Entry e from Blog b.
```

In order to prevent database inconsistency, this method only exists on ForeignKey objects where null=True. If the related field can't be set to None (NULL), then an object can't be removed from a relation without being added to another. In the preceding example, removing e from b.entry_set() is equivalent to doing e.blog = None, and because the blog ForeignKey doesn't have null=True, this is invalid.

- clear(): Removes all objects from the related object set:

```
b = Blog.objects.get(id=1)
b.entry_set.clear()
```

■**Note** This doesn't delete the related objects—it just disassociates them.

Just like remove(), clear() is only available on ForeignKeys where null=True.

To assign the members of a related set in one fell swoop, just assign to it from any iterable object, for example:

```
b = Blog.objects.get(id=1)
b.entry_set = [e1, e2]
```

If the clear() method is available, any pre-existing objects will be removed from the entry_set before all objects in the iterable (in this case, a list) are added to the set. If the clear() method is *not* available, all objects in the iterable will be added without removing any existing elements.

Each "reverse" operation described in this section has an immediate effect on the database. Every addition, creation, and deletion is immediately and automatically saved to the database.

Many-to-Many Relationships

Both ends of a many-to-many relationship get automatic API access to the other end. The API works just as a "reverse" one-to-many relationship (described in the previous section).

The only difference is in the attribute naming: the model that defines the ManyToManyField uses the attribute name of that field itself, whereas the "reverse" model uses the lowercased model name of the original model, plus '_set' (just like reverse one-to-many relationships).

An example makes this concept easier to understand:

```
e = Entry.objects.get(id=3)
e.authors.all() # Returns all Author objects for this Entry.
e.authors.count()
e.authors.filter(name__contains='John')

a = Author.objects.get(id=5)
a.entry_set.all() # Returns all Entry objects for this Author.
```

Like ForeignKey, ManyToManyField can specify related_name. In the preceding example, if the ManyToManyField in Entry had specified related_name='entries', then each Author instance would have an entries attribute instead of entry_set.

HOW ARE THE BACKWARD RELATIONSHIPS POSSIBLE?

Other object-relational mappers require you to define relationships on both sides. The Django developers believe this is a violation of the DRY (Don't Repeat Yourself) principle, so Django requires you to define the relationship on only one end. But how is this possible, given that a model class doesn't know which other model classes are related to it until those other model classes are loaded?

The answer lies in the INSTALLED_APPS setting. The first time any model is loaded, Django iterates over every model in INSTALLED_APPS and creates the backward relationships in memory as needed. Essentially, one of the functions of INSTALLED_APPS is to tell Django the entire model domain.

Queries over Related Objects

Queries involving related objects follow the same rules as queries involving normal value fields. When specifying the value for a query to match, you may use either an object instance itself or the primary key value for the object.

For example, if you have a Blog object b with id=5, the following three queries would be identical:

```
Entry.objects.filter(blog=b) # Query using object instance
Entry.objects.filter(blog=b.id) # Query using id from instance
Entry.objects.filter(blog=5) # Query using id directly
```

Deleting Objects

The delete method, conveniently, is named delete(). This method immediately deletes the object and has no return value:

```
e.delete()
```

You can also delete objects in bulk. Every QuerySet has a delete() method, which deletes all members of that QuerySet. For example, this deletes all Entry objects with a pub_date year of 2005:

```
Entry.objects.filter(pub_date__year=2005).delete()
```

When Django deletes an object, it emulates the behavior of the SQL constraint ON DELETE CASCADE—in other words, any objects that had foreign keys pointing at the object to be deleted will be deleted along with it, for example:

```
b = Blog.objects.get(pk=1)
# This will delete the Blog and all of its Entry objects.
b.delete()
```

Note that delete() is the only QuerySet method that is not exposed on a Manager itself. This is a safety mechanism to prevent you from accidentally requesting Entry.objects.delete() and deleting *all* the entries. If you *do* want to delete all the objects, then you have to explicitly request a complete query set:

```
Entry.objects.all().delete()
```

Extra Instance Methods

In addition to save() and delete(), a model object might get any or all of the following methods.

get_FOO_display()

For every field that has choices set, the object will have a get_FOO_display() method, where FOO is the name of the field. This method returns the "human-readable" value of the field. For example, in the following model:

```
GENDER_CHOICES = (
    ('M', 'Male'),
    ('F', 'Female'),
)
class Person(models.Model):
    name = models.CharField(max_length=20)
    gender = models.CharField(max_length=1, choices=GENDER_CHOICES)
```

each Person instance will have a get_gender_display() method:

```
>>> p = Person(name='John', gender='M')
>>> p.save()
>>> p.gender
'M'
>>> p.get_gender_display()
'Male'
```

get_next_by_FOO(**kwargs) and get_previous_by_FOO(**kwargs)

For every DateField and DateTimeField that does not have null=True, the object will have get_next_by_FOO() and get_previous_by_FOO() methods, where FOO is the name of the field. This returns the next and previous object with respect to the date field, raising the appropriate DoesNotExist exception when appropriate.

Both methods accept optional keyword arguments, which should be in the format described in the "Field Lookups" section.

Note that in the case of identical date values, these methods will use the ID as a fallback check. This guarantees that no records are skipped or duplicated. For a full example, see the lookup API samples at http://www.djangoproject.com/documentation/0.96/models/lookup/.

get_FOO_filename()

For every `FileField`, the object will have a `get_FOO_filename()` method, where `FOO` is the name of the field. This returns the full filesystem path to the file, according to your `MEDIA_ROOT` setting.

Note that `ImageField` is technically a subclass of `FileField`, so every model with an `ImageField` will also get this method.

get_FOO_url()

For every `FileField`, the object will have a `get_FOO_url()` method, where `FOO` is the name of the field. This returns the full URL to the file, according to your `MEDIA_URL` setting. If the value is blank, this method returns an empty string.

get_FOO_size()

For every `FileField`, the object will have a `get_FOO_size()` method, where `FOO` is the name of the field. This returns the size of the file, in bytes. (Behind the scenes, it uses `os.path.getsize`.)

save_FOO_file(filename, raw_contents)

For every `FileField`, the object will have a `save_FOO_file()` method, where `FOO` is the name of the field. This saves the given file to the filesystem, using the given file name. If a file with the given file name already exists, Django adds an underscore to the end of the file name (but before the extension) until the file name is available.

get_FOO_height() and get_FOO_width()

For every `ImageField`, the object will have `get_FOO_height()` and `get_FOO_width()` methods, where `FOO` is the name of the field. This returns the height (or width) of the image, as an integer, in pixels.

Shortcuts

As you develop views, you will discover a number of common idioms in the way you use the database API. Django encodes some of these idioms as shortcuts that can be used to simplify the process of writing views. These functions are in the `django.shortcuts` module.

get_object_or_404()

One common idiom to use `get()` and raise `Http404` if the object doesn't exist. This idiom is captured by `get_object_or_404()`. This function takes a Django model as its first argument and an arbitrary number of keyword arguments, which it passes to the default manager's `get()` function. It raises `Http404` if the object doesn't exist, for example:

```
# Get the Entry with a primary key of 3
e = get_object_or_404(Entry, pk=3)
```

When you provide a model to this shortcut function, the default manager is used to execute the underlying get() query. If you don't want to use the default manager, or if you want to search a list of related objects, you can provide get_object_or_404() with a Manager object instead:

```
# Get the author of blog instance e with a name of 'Fred'
a = get_object_or_404(e.authors, name='Fred')

# Use a custom manager 'recent_entries' in the search for an
# entry with a primary key of 3
e = get_object_or_404(Entry.recent_entries, pk=3)
```

get_list_or_404()

get_list_or_404 behaves the same way as get_object_or_404(), except that it uses filter() instead of get(). It raises Http404 if the list is empty.

Falling Back to Raw SQL

If you find yourself needing to write an SQL query that is too complex for Django's database mapper to handle, you can fall back into raw SQL statement mode.

The preferred way to do this is by giving your model custom methods or custom manager methods that execute queries. Although there's nothing in Django that *requires* database queries to live in the model layer, this approach keeps all your data access logic in one place, which is smart from a code organization standpoint. For instructions, see Appendix B.

Finally, it's important to note that the Django database layer is merely an interface to your database. You can access your database via other tools, programming languages, or database frameworks—there's nothing Django-specific about your database.

APPENDIX D

■ ■ ■

Generic View Reference

Chapter 9 introduces generic views but leaves out some of the gory details. This appendix describes each generic view along with all the options each view can take. Be sure to read Chapter 9 before trying to understand the reference material that follows. You might want to refer back to the Book, Publisher, and Author objects defined in that chapter; the examples that follow use these models.

Common Arguments to Generic Views

Most of these views take a large number of arguments that can change the generic view's behavior. Many of these arguments work the same across a large number of views. Table D-1 describes each of these common arguments; anytime you see one of these arguments in a generic view's argument list, it will work as described in the table.

Table D-1. *Common Arguments to Generic View*

Argument	Description
allow_empty	A Boolean specifying whether to display the page if no objects are available. If this is False and no objects are available, the view will raise a 404 error instead of displaying an empty page. By default, this is False.
context_processors	A list of additional template-context processors (besides the defaults) to apply to the view's template. See Chapter 10 for information on template context processors.
extra_context	A dictionary of values to add to the template context. By default, this is an empty dictionary. If a value in the dictionary is callable, the generic view will call it just before rendering the template.
mimetype	The MIME type to use for the resulting document. It defaults to the value of the DEFAULT_MIME_TYPE setting, which is text/html if you haven't changed it.
queryset	A QuerySet (i.e., something like Author.objects.all()) to read objects from. See Appendix C for more information about QuerySet objects. Most generic views require this argument.
template_loader	The template loader to use when loading the template. By default, it's django.template.loader. See Chapter 10 for information on template loaders.

(Continued)

Table D-1. *(Continued)*

Argument	Description
template_name	The full name of a template to use in rendering the page. This lets you override the default template name derived from the QuerySet.
template_object_name	The name of the template variable to use in the template context. By default, this is 'object'. Views that list more than one object (i.e., object_list views and various objects-for-date views) will append '_list' to the value of this parameter.

"Simple" Generic Views

The module django.views.generic.simple contains simple views that handle a couple of common cases: rendering a template when no view logic is needed and issuing a redirect.

Rendering a Template

View function: django.views.generic.simple.direct_to_template
This view renders a given template, passing it a {{ params }} template variable, which is a dictionary of the parameters captured in the URL.

Example

Given the following URLconf:

```
from django.conf.urls.defaults import *
from django.views.generic.simple import direct_to_template

urlpatterns = patterns('',
    (r'^foo/$',             direct_to_template, {'template': 'foo_index.html'}),
    (r'^foo/(?P<id>\d+)/$', direct_to_template, {'template': 'foo_detail.html'}),
)
```

a request to /foo/ would render the template foo_index.html, and a request to /foo/15/ would render foo_detail.html with a context variable {{ params.id }} that is set to 15.

Required Arguments

- template: The full name of a template to use.

Redirecting to Another URL

View function: django.views.generic.simple.redirect_to
This view redirects to another URL. The given URL may contain dictionary-style string formatting, which will be interpolated against the parameters captured in the URL.

If the given URL is None, Django will return an HTTP 410 ("Gone") message.

Example

This URLconf redirects from `/foo/<id>/` to `/bar/<id>/`:

```
from django.conf.urls.defaults import *
from django.views.generic.simple import redirect_to

urlpatterns = patterns('django.views.generic.simple',
    ('^foo/(?p<id>\d+)/$', redirect_to, {'url': '/bar/%(id)s/'}),
)
```

This example returns a "Gone" response for requests to `/bar/`:

```
from django.views.generic.simple import redirect_to

urlpatterns = patterns('django.views.generic.simple',
    ('^bar/$', redirect_to, {'url': None}),
)
```

Required Arguments

• `url`: The URL to redirect to, as a string. Or `None` to return a 410 ("Gone") HTTP response.

List/Detail Generic Views

The list/detail generic views (in the module `django.views.generic.list_detail`) handle the common case of displaying a list of items at one view and individual "detail" views of those items at another.

Lists of Objects

View function: `django.views.generic.list_detail.object_list`
Use this view to display a page representing a list of objects.

Example

Given the `Author` object from Chapter 5, we can use the `object_list` view to show a simple list of all authors given the following URLconf snippet:

```
from mysite.books.models import Author
from django.conf.urls.defaults import *
from django.views.generic import list_detail

author_list_info = {
    'queryset' :   Author.objects.all(),
    'allow_empty': True,
}
```

```
urlpatterns = patterns('',
    (r'authors/$', list_detail.object_list, author_list_info)
)
```

Required Arguments

- queryset: A QuerySet of objects to list (see Table D-1).

Optional Arguments

- paginate_by: An integer specifying how many objects should be displayed per page. If this is given, the view will paginate objects with paginate_by objects per page. The view will expect either a page query string parameter (via GET) containing a zero-indexed page number, or a page variable specified in the URLconf. See the following "A Note on Pagination" sidebar.

Additionally, this view may take any of these common arguments described in Table D-1:

- allow_empty
- context_processors
- extra_context
- mimetype
- template_loader
- template_name
- template_object_name

Template Name

If template_name isn't specified, this view will use the template <app_label>/<model_name>_list.html by default. Both the application label and the model name are derived from the queryset parameter. The application label is the name of the application that the model is defined in, and the model name is the lowercased version of the name of the model class.

In the previous example using Author.objects.all() as the queryset, the application label would be books and the model name would be author. This means the default template would be books/author_list.html.

Template Context

In addition to extra_context, the template's context will contain the following:

- object_list: The list of objects. This variable's name depends on the template_object_name parameter, which is 'object' by default. If template_object_name is 'foo', this variable's name will be foo_list.

- is_paginated: A Boolean representing whether the results are paginated. Specifically, this is set to False if the number of available objects is less than or equal to paginate_by.

If the results are paginated, the context will contain these extra variables:

- results_per_page: The number of objects per page. (This is the same as the paginate_by parameter.)

- has_next: A Boolean representing whether there's a next page.

- has_previous: A Boolean representing whether there's a previous page.

- page: The current page number, as an integer. This is 1-based.

- next: The next page number, as an integer. If there's no next page, this will still be an integer representing the theoretical next-page number. This is 1-based.

- previous: The previous page number, as an integer. This is 1-based.

- pages: The total number of pages, as an integer.

- hits: The total number of objects across *all* pages, not just this page.

A NOTE ON PAGINATION

If paginate_by is specified, Django will paginate the results. You can specify the page number in the URL in one of two ways:

- Use the page parameter in the URLconf. For example, this is what your URLconf might look like:

  ```
  (r'^objects/page(?P<page>[0-9]+)/$', 'object_list', dict(info_dict))
  ```

- Pass the page number via the page query-string parameter. For example, a URL would look like this:

  ```
  /objects/?page=3
  ```

In both cases, page is 1-based, not 0-based, so the first page would be represented as page 1.

Detail Views

View function: django.views.generic.list_detail.object_detail
This view provides a "detail" view of a single object.

Example

Continuing the previous object_list example, we could add a detail view for a given author by modifying the URLconf:

```
from mysite.books.models import Author
from django.conf.urls.defaults import *
from django.views.generic import list_detail
```

```
author_list_info = {
    'queryset' :    Author.objects.all(),
    'allow_empty': True,
}
author_detail_info = {
    "queryset" : Author.objects.all(),
    "template_object_name" : "author",
}

urlpatterns = patterns('',
    (r'authors/$', list_detail.object_list, author_list_info),
    (r'^authors/(?P<object_id>d+)/$', list_detail.object_detail,
    author_detail_info),
)
```

Required Arguments

- queryset: A QuerySet that will be searched for the object (see Table D-1).

and either

- object_id: The value of the primary-key field for the object.

or

- slug: The slug of the given object. If you pass this field, then the slug_field argument (see the following section) is also required.

Optional Arguments

- slug_field: The name of the field on the object containing the slug. This is required if you're using the slug argument, but it must be absent if you're using the object_id argument.

- template_name_field: The name of a field on the object whose value is the template name to use. This lets you store template names in your data. In other words, if your object has a field 'the_template' that contains a string 'foo.html', and you set template_name_field to 'the_template', then the generic view for this object will use the template 'foo.html'. It's a bit of a brain-bender, but it's useful in some cases.

This view may also take these common arguments (see Table D-1):

- context_processors

- extra_context

- mimetype

- template_loader

- template_name

- template_object_name

Template Name

If `template_name` and `template_name_field` aren't specified, this view will use the template `<app_label>/<model_name>_detail.html` by default.

Template Context

In addition to `extra_context`, the template's context will be as follows:

- `object`: The object. This variable's name depends on the `template_object_name` parameter, which is `'object'` by default. If `template_object_name` is `'foo'`, this variable's name will be `foo`.

Date-Based Generic Views

Date-based generic views are generally used to provide a set of "archive" pages for dated material. Think year/month/day archives for a newspaper, or a typical blog archive.

■**Note** By default, these views ignore objects with dates in the future. This means that if you try to visit an archive page in the future, Django will automatically show a 404 ("Page not found") error, even if there are objects published that day. Thus, you can publish postdated objects that don't appear publicly until their desired publication date.

However, for different types of date-based objects, this isn't appropriate (e.g., a calendar of upcoming events). For these views, setting the `allow_future` option to `True` will make the future objects appear (and allow users to visit "future" archive pages).

Archive Index

View function: `django.views.generic.date_based.archive_index`
This view provides a top-level index page showing the "latest" (i.e., most recent) objects by date.

Example

Say a typical book publisher wants a page of recently published books. Given some `Book` object with a `publication_date` field, we can use the `archive_index` view for this common task:

```
from mysite.books.models import Book
from django.conf.urls.defaults import *
from django.views.generic import date_based

book_info = {
    "queryset"   : Book.objects.all(),
    "date_field" : "publication_date"
}
```

```
urlpatterns = patterns('',
    (r'^books/$', date_based.archive_index, book_info),
)
```

Required Arguments

- `date_field`: The name of the `DateField` or `DateTimeField` in the `QuerySet`'s model that the date-based archive should use to determine the objects on the page.

- `queryset`: A `QuerySet` of objects for which the archive serves.

Optional Arguments

- `allow_future`: A Boolean specifying whether to include "future" objects on this page, as described in the previous note.

- `num_latest`: The number of latest objects to send to the template context. By default, it's 15.

This view may also take these common arguments (see Table D-1):

- `allow_empty`

- `context_processors`

- `extra_context`

- `mimetype`

- `template_loader`

- `template_name`

Template Name

If `template_name` isn't specified, this view will use the template `<app_label>/<model_name>_archive.html` by default.

Template Context

In addition to `extra_context`, the template's context will be as follows:

- `date_list`: A list of `datetime.date` objects representing all years that have objects available according to `queryset`. These are ordered in reverse. For example, if you have blog entries from 2003 through 2006, this list will contain four `datetime.date` objects, one for each of those years.

- `latest`: The `num_latest` objects in the system, in descending order by `date_field`. For example, if `num_latest` is 10, then `latest` will be a list of the latest ten objects in `queryset`.

Year Archives

View function: `django.views.generic.date_based.archive_year`
Use this view for yearly archive pages. These pages have a list of months in which objects exist, and they can optionally display all the objects published in a given year.

Example

Extending the `archive_index` example from earlier, we'll add a way to view all the books published in a given year:

```
from mysite.books.models import Book
from django.conf.urls.defaults import *
from django.views.generic import date_based

book_info = {
    "queryset"   : Book.objects.all(),
    "date_field" : "publication_date"
}

urlpatterns = patterns('',
    (r'^books/$', date_based.archive_index, book_info),
    (r'^books/(?P<year>d{4})/?$', date_based.archive_year, book_info),
)
```

Required Arguments

- `date_field`: As for `archive_index` (see the previous section).

- `queryset`: A `QuerySet` of objects for which the archive serves.

- `year`: The four-digit year for which the archive serves (as in our example, this is usually taken from a URL parameter).

Optional Arguments

- `make_object_list`: A Boolean specifying whether to retrieve the full list of objects for this year and pass those to the template. If `True`, this list of objects will be made available to the template as `object_list`. (The name `object_list` may be different; see the information about `object_list` in the following "Template Context" section.) By default, this is `False`.

- `allow_future`: A Boolean specifying whether to include "future" objects on this page.

This view may also take these common arguments (see Table D-1):

- `allow_empty`

- `context_processors`

- `extra_context`

- mimetype

- template_loader

- template_name

- template_object_name

Template Name

If template_name isn't specified, this view will use the template <app_label>/<model_name>_archive_year.html by default.

Template Context

In addition to extra_context, the template's context will be as follows:

- date_list: A list of datetime.date objects representing all months that have objects available in the given year, according to queryset, in ascending order.

- year: The given year, as a four-character string.

- object_list: If the make_object_list parameter is True, this will be set to a list of objects available for the given year, ordered by the date field. This variable's name depends on the template_object_name parameter, which is 'object' by default. If template_object_name is 'foo', this variable's name will be foo_list.

- If make_object_list is False, object_list will be passed to the template as an empty list.

Month Archives

View function: django.views.generic.date_based.archive_month
This view provides monthly archive pages showing all objects for a given month.

Example

Continuing with our example, adding month views should look familiar:

```
urlpatterns = patterns('',
    (r'^books/$', date_based.archive_index, book_info),
    (r'^books/(?P<year>d{4})/?$', date_based.archive_year, book_info),
    (
        r'^(?P<year>d{4})/(?P<month>[a-z]{3})/$',
        date_based.archive_month,
        book_info
    ),
)
```

Required Arguments

- year: The four-digit year for which the archive serves (a string).

- month: The month for which the archive serves, formatted according to the month_format argument.

- queryset: A QuerySet of objects for which the archive serves.

- date_field: The name of the DateField or DateTimeField in the QuerySet's model that the date-based archive should use to determine the objects on the page.

Optional Arguments

- month_format: A format string that regulates what format the month parameter uses. This should be in the syntax accepted by Python's time.strftime. (See Python's strftime documentation at http://www.python.org/doc/current/lib/module-time.html.) It's set to "%b" by default, which is a three-letter month abbreviation (i.e., "jan", "feb", etc.). To change it to use numbers, use "%m".

- allow_future: A Boolean specifying whether to include "future" objects on this page, as described in the previous note.

This view may also take these common arguments (see Table D-1):

- allow_empty

- context_processors

- extra_context

- mimetype

- template_loader

- template_name

- template_object_name

Template Name

If template_name isn't specified, this view will use the template <app_label>/<model_name>_archive_month.html by default.

Template Context

In addition to extra_context, the template's context will be as follows:

- month: A datetime.date object representing the given month.

- next_month: A datetime.date object representing the first day of the next month. If the next month is in the future, this will be None.

- previous_month: A datetime.date object representing the first day of the previous month. Unlike next_month, this will never be None.

- object_list: A list of objects available for the given month. This variable's name depends on the template_object_name parameter, which is 'object' by default. If template_object_name is 'foo', this variable's name will be foo_list.

Week Archives

View function: django.views.generic.date_based.archive_week
This view shows all objects in a given week.

■**Note** For the sake of consistency with Python's built-in date/time handling, Django assumes that the first day of the week is Sunday.

Example

```
urlpatterns = patterns('',
    # ...
    (
        r'^(?P<year>\d{4})/(?P<week>\d{2})/$',
        date_based.archive_week,
        book_info
    ),
)
```

Required Arguments

- year: The four-digit year for which the archive serves (a string).

- week: The week of the year for which the archive serves (a string).

- queryset: A QuerySet of objects for which the archive serves.

- date_field: The name of the DateField or DateTimeField in the QuerySet's model that the date-based archive should use to determine the objects on the page.

Optional Arguments

- allow_future: A Boolean specifying whether to include "future" objects on this page, as described in the previous note.

This view may also take these common arguments (see Table D-1):

- allow_empty

- context_processors

- extra_context

- mimetype

- template_loader

- template_name

- template_object_name

Template Name

If template_name isn't specified, this view will use the template <app_label>/<model_name>_
archive_week.html by default.

Template Context

In addition to extra_context, the template's context will be as follows:

- week: A datetime.date object representing the first day of the given week.

- object_list: A list of objects available for the given week. This variable's name depends on the template_object_name parameter, which is 'object' by default. If template_object_
  name is 'foo', this variable's name will be foo_list.

Day Archives

View function: django.views.generic.date_based.archive_day
This view generates all objects in a given day.

Example

```
urlpatterns = patterns('',
    # ...
    (
        r'^(?P<year>d{4})/(?P<month>[a-z]{3})/(?P<day>d{2})/$',
        date_based.archive_day,
        book_info
    ),
)
```

Required Arguments

- year: The four-digit year for which the archive serves (a string).

- month: The month for which the archive serves, formatted according to the month_format argument.

- day: The day for which the archive serves, formatted according to the day_format argument.

- queryset: A QuerySet of objects for which the archive serves.

- date_field: The name of the DateField or DateTimeField in the QuerySet's model that the date-based archive should use to determine the objects on the page.

Optional Arguments

- month_format: A format string that regulates what format the month parameter uses. See the detailed explanation in the "Month Archives" section.

- day_format: Like month_format, but for the day parameter. It defaults to "%d" (the day of the month as a decimal number, for example, 01-31).

- allow_future: A Boolean specifying whether to include "future" objects on this page, as described in the previous note.

This view may also take these common arguments (see Table D-1):

- allow_empty
- context_processors
- extra_context
- mimetype
- template_loader
- template_name
- template_object_name

Template Name

If template_name isn't specified, this view will use the template <app_label>/<model_name>_ archive_day.html by default.

Template Context

In addition to extra_context, the template's context will be as follows:

- day: A datetime.date object representing the given day.

- next_day: A datetime.date object representing the next day. If the next day is in the future, this will be None.

- previous_day: A datetime.date object representing the given day. Unlike next_day, this will never be None.

- object_list: A list of objects available for the given day. This variable's name depends on the template_object_name parameter, which is 'object' by default. If template_ object_name is 'foo', this variable's name will be foo_list.

Archive for Today

The django.views.generic.date_based.archive_today view shows all objects for *today*. This is exactly the same as archive_day, except the year/month/day arguments are not used, and today's date is used instead.

Example

```
urlpatterns = patterns('',
    # ...
    (r'^books/today/$', date_based.archive_today, book_info),
)
```

Date-Based Detail Pages

View function: `django.views.generic.date_based.object_detail`
Use this view for a page representing an individual object.

This has a different URL from the `object_detail` view; the `object_detail` view uses URLs like /entries/<slug>/, while this one uses URLs like /entries/2006/aug/27/<slug>/.

■**Note** If you're using date-based detail pages with slugs in the URLs, you probably also want to use the `unique_for_date` option on the slug field to validate that slugs aren't duplicated in a single day. See Appendix B for details on `unique_for_date`.

Example

This one differs (slightly) from all the other examples in that we need to provide either an object ID or a slug so that Django can look up the object in question.

Since the object we're using doesn't have a slug field, we'll use ID-based URLs. It's considered a best practice to use a slug field, but in the interest of simplicity we'll let it go.

```
urlpatterns = patterns('',
    # ...
    (
        r'^(?P<year>d{4})/(?P<month>[a-z]{3})/(?P<day>d{2})/(?P<object_id>[w-]+)/$',
        date_based.object_detail,
        book_info
    ),
)
```

Required Arguments

- `year`: The object's four-digit year (a string).

- `month`: The object's month, formatted according to the `month_format` argument.

- `day`: The object's day, formatted according to the `day_format` argument.

- `queryset`: A `QuerySet` that contains the object.

- `date_field`: The name of the `DateField` or `DateTimeField` in the `QuerySet`'s model that the generic view should use to look up the object according to `year`, `month`, and `day`.

You'll also need either

- `object_id`: The value of the primary-key field for the object.

or

- `slug`: The slug of the given object. If you pass this field, then the `slug_field` argument (described in the following section) is also required.

Optional Arguments

- `allow_future`: A Boolean specifying whether to include "future" objects on this page, as described in the previous note.

- `day_format`: Like `month_format`, but for the day parameter. It defaults to `"%d"` (the day of the month as a decimal number, for example, 01-31).

- `month_format`: A format string that regulates what format the month parameter uses. See the detailed explanation in the "Month Archives" section.

- `slug_field`: The name of the field on the object containing the slug. This is required if you're using the `slug` argument, but it must be absent if you're using the `object_id` argument.

- `template_name_field`: The name of a field on the object whose value is the template name to use. This lets you store template names in the data. In other words, if your object has a field `'the_template'` that contains a string `'foo.html'`, and you set `template_name_field` to `'the_template'`, then the generic view for this object will use the template `'foo.html'`.

This view may also take these common arguments (see Table D-1):

- `context_processors`

- `extra_context`

- `mimetype`

- `template_loader`

- `template_name`

- `template_object_name`

Template Name

If `template_name` and `template_name_field` aren't specified, this view will use the template `<app_label>/<model_name>_detail.html` by default.

Template Context

In addition to `extra_context`, the template's context will be as follows:

- `object`: The object. This variable's name depends on the `template_object_name` parameter, which is `'object'` by default. If `template_object_name` is `'foo'`, this variable's name will be `foo`.

Create/Update/Delete Generic Views

The `django.views.generic.create_update` module contains a set of functions for creating, editing, and deleting objects.

■Note These views may change slightly when Django's revised form architecture (currently under development as `django.newforms`) is finalized.

These views all present forms if accessed with `GET` and perform the requested action (create/update/delete) if accessed via `POST`.

These views all have a very coarse idea of security. Although they take a `login_required` attribute, which if given will restrict access to logged-in users, that's as far as it goes. They won't, for example, check that the user editing an object is the same user who created it, nor will they validate any sort of permissions.

Much of the time, however, those features can be accomplished by writing a small wrapper around the generic view; see "Extending Generic Views" in Chapter 9.

Create Object View

View function: `django.views.generic.create_update.create_object`
This view displays a form for creating an object. When the form is submitted, this view redisplays the form with validation errors (if there are any) or saves the object.

Example

If we wanted to allow users to create new books in the database, we could do something like this:

```
from mysite.books.models import Book
from django.conf.urls.defaults import *
from django.views.generic import date_based

book_info = {'model' : Book}

urlpatterns = patterns('',
    (r'^books/create/$', create_update.create_object, book_info),
)
```

Required Arguments

- `model`: The Django model of the object that the form will create.

■Note Notice that this view takes the *model* to be created, not a `QuerySet` (as all the list/detail/date-based views presented previously do).

Optional Arguments

- `post_save_redirect`: A URL to which the view will redirect after saving the object. By default, it's `object.get_absolute_url()`.

  `post_save_redirect`: May contain dictionary string formatting, which will be interpolated against the object's field attributes. For example, you could use `post_save_redirect="/polls/%(slug)s/"`.

- `login_required`: A Boolean that designates whether a user must be logged in, in order to see the page and save changes. This hooks into the Django authentication system. By default, this is `False`.

  If this is `True`, and a non-logged-in user attempts to visit this page or save the form, Django will redirect the request to `/accounts/login/`.

This view may also take these common arguments (see Table D-1):

- `context_processors`
- `extra_context`
- `template_loader`
- `template_name`

Template Name

If `template_name` isn't specified, this view will use the template `<app_label>/<model_name>_form.html` by default.

Template Context

In addition to `extra_context`, the template's context will be as follows:

- `form`: A `FormWrapper` instance representing the form for editing the object. This lets you refer to form fields easily in the template system—for example, if the model has two fields, `name` and `address`:

```
<form action="" method="post">
  <p><label for="id_name">Name:</label> {{ form.name }}</p>
  <p><label for="id_address">Address:</label> {{ form.address }}</p>
</form>
```

■**Note** `form` is an "old" forms object, which is not covered in this book. See `http://www.djangoproject.com/documentation/0.96/forms/` for details.

Update Object View

View function: django.views.generic.create_update.update_object
This view is almost identical to the create object view. However, this one allows the editing of an existing object instead of the creation of a new one.

Example

Following the previous example, we could provide an edit interface for a single book with this URLconf snippet:

```
from mysite.books.models import Book
from django.conf.urls.defaults import *
from django.views.generic import date_based

book_info = {'model' : Book}

urlpatterns = patterns('',
    (r'^books/create/$', create_update.create_object, book_info),
    (
        r'^books/edit/(?P<object_id>d+)/$',
        create_update.update_object,
        book_info
    ),
)
```

Required Arguments

- model: The Django model to edit. Again, this is the actual *model* itself, not a QuerySet.

and either

- object_id: The value of the primary-key field for the object.

or

- slug: The slug of the given object. If you pass this field, then the slug_field argument (see the next section) is also required.

Optional Arguments

- slug_field: The name of the field on the object containing the slug. This is required if you are using the slug argument, but it must be absent if you're using the object_id argument.

Additionally, this view takes all the same optional arguments as the creation view, plus the template_object_name common argument from Table D-1.

Template Name

This view uses the same default template name (`<app_label>/<model_name>_form.html`) as the creation view.

Template Context

In addition to `extra_context`, the template's context will be as follows:

- `form`: A FormWrapper instance representing the form for editing the object. See the "Create Object View" section for more information about this value.

- `object`: The original object being edited (this variable may be named differently if you've provided the `template_object_name` argument).

Delete Object View

View function: django.views.generic.create_update.delete_object
This view is very similar to the other two create/edit views. This view, however, allows deletion of objects.

If this view is fetched with GET, it will display a confirmation page (i.e., "Do you really want to delete this object?"). If the view is submitted with POST, the object will be deleted without confirmation.

All the arguments are the same as for the update object view, as is the context; the template name for this view is `<app_label>/<model_name>_confirm_delete.html`.

APPENDIX E

■■■■

Settings

Your Django settings file contains all the configuration of your Django installation. This appendix explains how settings work and which settings are available.

■Note As Django grows, it's occasionally necessary to add or (rarely) change settings. You should always check the online settings documentation at http://www.djangoproject.com/documentation/0.96/ settings/ for the latest information.

What's a Settings File?

A *settings file* is just a Python module with module-level variables. Here are a couple of example settings:

```
DEBUG = False
DEFAULT_FROM_EMAIL = 'webmaster@example.com'
TEMPLATE_DIRS = ('/home/templates/mike', '/home/templates/john')
```

Because a settings file is a Python module, the following apply:

- It must be valid Python code; syntax errors aren't allowed.

- It can assign settings dynamically using normal Python syntax, for example:

  ```
  MY_SETTING = [str(i) for i in range(30)]
  ```

- It can import values from other settings files.

Default Settings

A Django settings file doesn't have to define any settings if it doesn't need to. Each setting has a sensible default value. These defaults live in the file `django/conf/global_settings.py`.

Here's the algorithm Django uses in compiling settings:

- Load settings from `global_settings.py`.

- Load settings from the specified settings file, overriding the global settings as necessary.

Note that a settings file should *not* import from `global_settings`, because that's redundant.

Seeing Which Settings You've Changed

There's an easy way to view which of your settings deviate from the default settings. The command `manage.py diffsettings` displays differences between the current settings file and Django's default settings.

`manage.py` is described in more detail in Appendix G.

Using Settings in Python Code

In your Django applications, use settings by importing the object `django.conf.settings`:

```
from django.conf import settings

if settings.DEBUG:
    # Do something
```

Note that `django.conf.settings` isn't a module—it's an object. So importing individual settings is not possible:

```
from django.conf.settings import DEBUG  # This won't work.
```

Also note that your code should *not* import from either `global_settings` or your own settings file. `django.conf.settings` abstracts the concepts of default settings and site-specific settings; it presents a single interface. It also decouples the code that uses settings from the location of your settings.

Altering Settings at Runtime

You shouldn't alter settings in your applications at runtime. For example, don't do this in a view:

```
from django.conf import settings

settings.DEBUG = True    # Don't do this!
```

The only place you should assign to `settings` is in a settings file.

Security

Because a settings file contains sensitive information, such as the database password, you should make every attempt to limit access to it. For example, change its file permissions so that only you and your Web server's user can read it. This is especially important in a shared-hosting environment.

Creating Your Own Settings

There's nothing stopping you from creating your own settings, for your own Django applications. Just follow these conventions:

- Use all uppercase for setting names.

- For settings that are sequences, use tuples instead of lists. Settings should be considered immutable and shouldn't be changed once they're defined. Using tuples mirrors these semantics.

- Don't reinvent an already existing setting.

Designating the Settings: DJANGO_SETTINGS_MODULE

When you use Django, you have to tell it which settings you're using. Do this by using the environment variable DJANGO_SETTINGS_MODULE.

The value of DJANGO_SETTINGS_MODULE should be in Python path syntax (e.g., mysite.settings). Note that the settings module should be on the Python import search path (PYTHONPATH).

Tip A good guide to PYTHONPATH can be found at http://diveintopython.org/getting_to_know_python/everything_is_an_object.html.

The django-admin.py Utility

When using django-admin.py (see Appendix G), you can either set the environment variable once or explicitly pass in the settings module each time you run the utility.

Here's an example using the Unix Bash shell:

```
export DJANGO_SETTINGS_MODULE=mysite.settings
django-admin.py runserver
```

Here's an example using the Windows shell:

```
set DJANGO_SETTINGS_MODULE=mysite.settings
django-admin.py runserver
```

Use the --settings command-line argument to specify the settings manually:

```
django-admin.py runserver --settings=mysite.settings
```

The manage.py utility created by startproject as part of the project skeleton sets DJANGO_SETTINGS_MODULE automatically; see Appendix G for more about manage.py.

On the Server (mod_python)

In your live server environment, you'll need to tell Apache/mod_python which settings file to use. Do that with SetEnv:

```
<Location "/mysite/">
    SetHandler python-program
    PythonHandler django.core.handlers.modpython
    SetEnv DJANGO_SETTINGS_MODULE mysite.settings
</Location>
```

For more information on using Django with mod_python, see Chapter 20.

Using Settings Without Setting DJANGO_SETTINGS_MODULE

In some cases, you might want to bypass the DJANGO_SETTINGS_MODULE environment variable. For example, if you're using the template system by itself, you likely don't want to have to set up an environment variable pointing to a settings module.

In these cases, you can configure Django's settings manually. Do this by calling django.conf.settings.configure(). Here's an example:

```
from django.conf import settings

settings.configure(
    DEBUG = True,
    TEMPLATE_DEBUG = True,
    TEMPLATE_DIRS = [
        '/home/web-apps/myapp',
        '/home/web-apps/base',
    ]
)
```

Pass configure() as many keyword arguments as you'd like, with each keyword argument representing a setting and its value. Each argument name should be all uppercase, with the same name as the settings described earlier. If a particular setting is not passed to configure() and is needed at some later point, Django will use the default setting value.

Configuring Django in this fashion is mostly necessary—and, indeed, recommended—when you're using a piece of the framework inside a larger application. Consequently, when configured via settings.configure(), Django will not make any modifications to the process environment variables. (See the explanation of TIME_ZONE later in this chapter for why this would normally occur.) It's assumed that you're already in full control of your environment in these cases.

Custom Default Settings

If you'd like default values to come from somewhere other than django.conf.global_settings, you can pass in a module or class that provides the default settings as the default_settings argument (or as the first positional argument) in the call to configure().

In this example, default settings are taken from myapp_defaults, and the DEBUG setting is set to True, regardless of its value in myapp_defaults:

```
from django.conf import settings
from myapp import myapp_defaults

settings.configure(default_settings=myapp_defaults, DEBUG=True)
```

The following example, which uses myapp_defaults as a positional argument, is equivalent:

```
settings.configure(myapp_defaults, DEBUG = True)
```

Normally, you will not need to override the defaults in this fashion. The Django defaults are sufficiently tame that you can safely use them. Be aware that if you do pass in a new default module, it entirely *replaces* the Django defaults, so you must specify a value for every possible setting that might be used in the code you are importing. Check in django.conf.settings.global_settings for the full list.

Either configure() or DJANGO_SETTINGS_MODULE Is Required

If you're not setting the DJANGO_SETTINGS_MODULE environment variable, you *must* call configure() at some point before using any code that reads settings.

If you don't set DJANGO_SETTINGS_MODULE and don't call configure(), Django will raise an EnvironmentError exception the first time a setting is accessed.

If you set DJANGO_SETTINGS_MODULE, access settings values somehow, and *then* call configure(), Django will raise an EnvironmentError stating that settings have already been configured.

Also, it's an error to call configure() more than once, or to call configure() after any setting has been accessed.

It boils down to this: use exactly one of either configure() or DJANGO_SETTINGS_MODULE. Not both, and not neither.

Available Settings

The following sections consist of a full list of all available settings, in alphabetical order, and their default values.

ABSOLUTE_URL_OVERRIDES

Default: {} (empty dictionary)

This is a dictionary mapping "app_label.model_name" strings to functions that take a model object and return its URL. This is a way of overriding get_absolute_url() methods on a per-installation basis. Here's an example:

```
ABSOLUTE_URL_OVERRIDES = {
    'blogs.weblog': lambda o: "/blogs/%s/" % o.slug,
    'news.story': lambda o: "/stories/%s/%s/" % (o.pub_year, o.slug),
}
```

Note that the model name used in this setting should be all lowercase, regardless of the case of the actual model class name.

ADMIN_FOR

Default: () (empty list)

This setting is used for admin site settings modules. It should be a tuple of settings modules (in the format 'foo.bar.baz') for which this site is an admin.

The admin site uses this in its automatically introspected documentation of models, views, and template tags.

ADMIN_MEDIA_PREFIX

Default: '/media/'

This setting is the URL prefix for admin media: CSS, JavaScript, and images. Make sure to use a trailing slash.

ADMINS

Default: () (empty tuple)

This is a tuple that lists people who get code error notifications. When DEBUG=False and a view raises an exception, Django will email these people with the full exception information. Each member of the tuple should be a tuple of (full name, email address), for example:

```
(('John', 'john@example.com'), ('Mary', 'mary@example.com'))
```

Note that Django will email *all* of these people whenever an error happens.

ALLOWED_INCLUDE_ROOTS

Default: () (empty tuple)

This is a tuple of strings representing allowed prefixes for the {% ssi %} template tag. This is a security measure, so that template authors can't access files that they shouldn't be accessing.

For example, if ALLOWED_INCLUDE_ROOTS is ('/home/html', '/var/www'), then {% ssi /home/html/foo.txt %} would work, but {% ssi /etc/passwd %} wouldn't.

APPEND_SLASH

Default: True

This setting indicates whether to append trailing slashes to URLs. This is used only if CommonMiddleware is installed (see Chapter 15).

See also PREPEND_WWW.

CACHE_BACKEND

Default: `'simple://'`
This is the cache back-end to use (see Chapter 13).

CACHE_MIDDLEWARE_KEY_PREFIX

Default: `' '` (empty string)
This is the cache key prefix that the cache middleware should use (see Chapter 13).

DATABASE_ENGINE

Default: `' '` (empty string)
This setting indicates which database back-end to use: `'postgresql_psycopg2'`, `'postgresql'`, `'mysql'`, or `'sqlite3'`.

DATABASE_HOST

Default: `' '` (empty string)
This setting indicates which host to use when connecting to the database. An empty string means `localhost`. This is not used with SQLite.

If this value starts with a forward slash (`'/'`) and you're using MySQL, MySQL will connect via a Unix socket to the specified socket:

```
DATABASE_HOST = '/var/run/mysql'
```

If you're using MySQL and this value *doesn't* start with a forward slash, then this value is assumed to be the host.

DATABASE_NAME

Default: `' '` (empty string)
This is the name of the database to use. For SQLite, it's the full path to the database file.

DATABASE_OPTIONS

Default: `{}` (empty dictionary)
This setting is extra parameters to use when connecting to the database. Consult the back-end module's document for available keywords.

DATABASE_PASSWORD

Default: `' '` (empty string)
This setting is the password to use when connecting to the database. It is not used with SQLite.

DATABASE_PORT

Default: `' '` (empty string)
This is the port to use when connecting to the database. An empty string means the default port. It is not used with SQLite.

DATABASE_USER

Default: `' '` (empty string)
This setting is the username to use when connecting to the database. It is not used with SQLite.

DATE_FORMAT

Default: `'N j, Y'` (e.g., Feb. 4, 2003)
This is the default formatting to use for date fields on Django admin change-list pages—and, possibly, by other parts of the system. It accepts the same format as the `now` tag (see Appendix F, Table F-2).

See also `DATETIME_FORMAT`, `TIME_FORMAT`, `YEAR_MONTH_FORMAT`, and `MONTH_DAY_FORMAT`.

DATETIME_FORMAT

Default: `'N j, Y, P'` (e.g., Feb. 4, 2003, 4 p.m.)
This is the default formatting to use for datetime fields on Django admin change-list pages—and, possibly, by other parts of the system. It accepts the same format as the `now` tag (see Appendix F, Table F-2).

See also `DATE_FORMAT`, `DATETIME_FORMAT`, `TIME_FORMAT`, `YEAR_MONTH_FORMAT`, and `MONTH_DAY_FORMAT`.

DEBUG

Default: `False`
This setting is a Boolean that turns debug mode on and off.

If you define custom settings, `django/views/debug.py` has a `HIDDEN_SETTINGS` regular expression that will hide from the `DEBUG` view anything that contains `'SECRET, PASSWORD, or PROFANITIES'`. This allows untrusted users to be able to give backtraces without seeing sensitive (or offensive) settings.

Still, note that there are always going to be sections of your debug output that are inappropriate for public consumption. File paths, configuration options, and the like all give attackers extra information about your server. Never deploy a site with `DEBUG` turned on.

DEFAULT_CHARSET

Default: `'utf-8'`
This is the default charset to use for all `HttpResponse` objects, if a MIME type isn't manually specified. It is used with `DEFAULT_CONTENT_TYPE` to construct the `Content-Type` header. See Appendix H for more about `HttpResponse` objects.

DEFAULT_CONTENT_TYPE

Default: `'text/html'`

This is the default content type to use for all `HttpResponse` objects, if a MIME type isn't manually specified. It is used with `DEFAULT_CHARSET` to construct the `Content-Type` header. See Appendix H for more about `HttpResponse` objects.

DEFAULT_FROM_EMAIL

Default: `'webmaster@localhost'`

This is the default email address to use for various automated correspondence from the site manager(s).

DISALLOWED_USER_AGENTS

Default: `()` (empty tuple)

This is a list of compiled regular expression objects representing user-agent strings that are not allowed to visit any page, systemwide. Use this for bad robots/crawlers. This is used only if `CommonMiddleware` is installed (see Chapter 15).

EMAIL_HOST

Default: `'localhost'`

This is the host to use for sending email. See also `EMAIL_PORT`.

EMAIL_HOST_PASSWORD

Default: `' '` (empty string)

This is the password to use for the SMTP server defined in `EMAIL_HOST`. This setting is used in conjunction with `EMAIL_HOST_USER` when authenticating to the SMTP server. If either of these settings is empty, Django won't attempt authentication.

See also `EMAIL_HOST_USER`.

EMAIL_HOST_USER

Default: `' '` (empty string)

This is the username to use for the SMTP server defined in `EMAIL_HOST`. If it's empty, Django won't attempt authentication.

See also `EMAIL_HOST_PASSWORD`.

EMAIL_PORT

Default: 25

This is the port to use for the SMTP server defined in `EMAIL_HOST`.

EMAIL_SUBJECT_PREFIX

Default: '[Django] '
This is the subject-line prefix for email messages sent with django.core.mail.mail_admins or django.core.mail.mail_managers. You'll probably want to include the trailing space.

FIXTURE_DIRS

Default: () (empty tuple)
This is a list of locations of the fixture data files, in search order. Note that these paths should use Unix-style forward slashes, even on Windows. It is used by Django's testing framework, which is covered online at http://www.djangoproject.com/documentation/0.96/testing/.

IGNORABLE_404_ENDS

Default: ('mail.pl', 'mailform.pl', 'mail.cgi', 'mailform.cgi', 'favicon.ico', '.php')
See also IGNORABLE_404_STARTS and Error reporting via e-mail.

IGNORABLE_404_STARTS

Default: ('/cgi-bin/', '/_vti_bin', '/_vti_inf')
This is a tuple of strings that specify beginnings of URLs that should be ignored by the 404 emailer.
   See also SEND_BROKEN_LINK_EMAILS and IGNORABLE_404_ENDS.

INSTALLED_APPS

Default: () (empty tuple)
This is a tuple of strings designating all applications that are enabled in this Django installation. Each string should be a full Python path to a Python package that contains a Django application. See Chapter 5 for more about applications.

INTERNAL_IPS

Default: () (empty tuple)
A tuple of IP addresses, as strings, that

- See debug comments, when DEBUG is True

- Receive X headers if the XViewMiddleware is installed (see Chapter 15)

JING_PATH

Default: '/usr/bin/jing'
This is the path to the Jing executable. Jing is a RELAX NG validator, and Django uses it to validate each XMLField in your models. See http://www.thaiopensource.com/relaxng/jing.html.

LANGUAGE_CODE

Default: `'en-us'`

This is a string representing the language code for this installation. This should be in standard language format—for example, U.S. English is "en-us". See Chapter 18.

LANGUAGES

Default: A tuple of all available languages. This list is continually growing and any copy included here would inevitably become rapidly out of date. You can see the current list of translated languages by looking in `django/conf/global_settings.py`. The list is a tuple of two-tuples in the format (language code, language name)—for example, (`'ja'`, `'Japanese'`). This specifies which languages are available for language selection. See Chapter 18 for more on language selection.

Generally, the default value should suffice. Only set this setting if you want to restrict language selection to a subset of the Django-provided languages.

If you define a custom `LANGUAGES` setting, it's OK to mark the languages as translation strings, but you should *never* import `django.utils.translation` from within your settings file, because that module in itself depends on the settings, and that would cause a circular import.

The solution is to use a "dummy" `gettext()` function. Here's a sample settings file:

```
gettext = lambda s: s

LANGUAGES = (
    ('de', gettext('German')),
    ('en', gettext('English')),
)
```

With this arrangement, `make-messages.py` will still find and mark these strings for translation, but the translation won't happen at runtime—so you'll have to remember to wrap the languages in the *real* `gettext()` in any code that uses `LANGUAGES` at runtime.

MANAGERS

Default: () (empty tuple)

This tuple is in the same format as `ADMINS` that specifies who should get broken-link notifications when `SEND_BROKEN_LINK_EMAILS=True`.

MEDIA_ROOT

Default: `''` (empty string)

This is an absolute path to the directory that holds media for this installation (e.g., `"/home/media/media.lawrence.com/"`).

See also `MEDIA_URL`.

MEDIA_URL

Default: ' ' (empty string)

This URL handles the media served from MEDIA_ROOT (e.g., "http://media.lawrence.com").
Note that this should have a trailing slash if it has a path component:

- *Correct*: "http://www.example.com/static/"

- *Incorrect*: "http://www.example.com/static"

MIDDLEWARE_CLASSES

Default:

```
("django.contrib.sessions.middleware.SessionMiddleware",
 "django.contrib.auth.middleware.AuthenticationMiddleware",
 "django.middleware.common.CommonMiddleware",
 "django.middleware.doc.XViewMiddleware")
```

This is a tuple of middleware classes to use. See Chapter 15.

MONTH_DAY_FORMAT

Default: 'F j'

This is the default formatting to use for date fields on Django admin change-list pages—and, possibly, by other parts of the system—in cases when only the month and day are displayed. It accepts the same format as the now tag (see Appendix F, Table F-2).

For example, when a Django admin change-list page is being filtered by a date, the header for a given day displays the day and month. Different locales have different formats. For example, U.S. English would have "January 1," whereas Spanish might have "1 Enero."

See also DATE_FORMAT, DATETIME_FORMAT, TIME_FORMAT, and YEAR_MONTH_FORMAT.

PREPEND_WWW

Default: False

This setting indicates whether to prepend the "www." subdomain to URLs that don't have it. This is used only if CommonMiddleware is installed (see Chapter 15).

See also APPEND_SLASH.

PROFANITIES_LIST

This is a tuple of profanities, as strings, that will trigger a validation error when the hasNoProfanities validator is called.

We don't list the default values here, because that might bring the MPAA ratings board down on our heads. To view the default values, see the file django/conf/global_settings.py.

ROOT_URLCONF

Default: Not defined

This is a string representing the full Python import path to your root URLconf (e.g., "mydjangoapps. urls"). See Chapter 3.

SECRET_KEY

Default: (Generated automatically when you start a project)

This is a secret key for this particular Django installation. It is used to provide a seed in secret-key hashing algorithms. Set this to a random string—the longer, the better. `django-admin.py startproject` creates one automatically and most of the time you won't need to change it.

SEND_BROKEN_LINK_EMAILS

Default: `False`

This setting indicates whether to send an email to the `MANAGERS` each time somebody visits a Django-powered page that is 404-ed with a nonempty referer (i.e., a broken link). This is only used if `CommonMiddleware` is installed (see Chapter 15).

See also `IGNORABLE_404_STARTS` and `IGNORABLE_404_ENDS`.

SERIALIZATION_MODULES

Default: Not defined

Serialization is a feature still under heavy development. Refer to the online documentation at `http://www.djangoproject.com/documentation/0.96/serialization/` for more information.

SERVER_EMAIL

Default: `'root@localhost'`

This is the email address that error messages come from, such as those sent to `ADMINS` and `MANAGERS`.

SESSION_COOKIE_AGE

Default: `1209600` (two weeks, in seconds)

This is the age of session cookies, in seconds. See Chapter 12.

SESSION_COOKIE_DOMAIN

Default: `None`

This is the domain to use for session cookies. Set this to a string such as `".lawrence.com"` for cross-domain cookies, or use `None` for a standard domain cookie. See Chapter 12.

SESSION_COOKIE_NAME

Default: `'sessionid'`

This is the name of the cookie to use for sessions; it can be whatever you want. See Chapter 12.

SESSION_COOKIE_SECURE

Default: False
This setting indicates whether to use a secure cookie for the session cookie. If this is set to True, the cookie will be marked as "secure," which means browsers may ensure that the cookie is only sent under an HTTPS connection. See Chapter 12.

SESSION_EXPIRE_AT_BROWSER_CLOSE

Default: False
This setting indicates whether to expire the session when the user closes his browser. See Chapter 12.

SESSION_SAVE_EVERY_REQUEST

Default: False
This setting indicates whether to save the session data on every request. See Chapter 12.

SITE_ID

Default: Not defined
This is the ID, as an integer, of the current site in the django_site database table. It is used so that application data can hook into specific site(s) and a single database can manage content for multiple sites. See Chapter 14.

TEMPLATE_CONTEXT_PROCESSORS

Default:

```
("django.core.context_processors.auth",
"django.core.context_processors.debug",
"django.core.context_processors.i18n")
```

This is a tuple of callables that are used to populate the context in RequestContext. These callables take a request object as their argument and return a dictionary of items to be merged into the context. See Chapter 10.

TEMPLATE_DEBUG

Default: False
This Boolean turns template debug mode on and off. If it is True, the fancy error page will display a detailed report for any TemplateSyntaxError. This report contains the relevant snippet of the template, with the appropriate line highlighted.

　　Note that Django displays fancy error pages only if DEBUG is True, so you'll want to set that to take advantage of this setting.

　　See also DEBUG.

TEMPLATE_DIRS

Default: () (empty tuple)
This is a list of locations of the template source files, in search order. Note that these paths should use Unix-style forward slashes, even on Windows. See Chapters 4 and 10.

TEMPLATE_LOADERS

Default: ('django.template.loaders.filesystem.load_template_source',)
This is a tuple of callables (as strings) that know how to import templates from various sources. See Chapter 10.

TEMPLATE_STRING_IF_INVALID

Default: ' ' (empty string)
This is output, as a string, that the template system should use for invalid (e.g., misspelled) variables. See Chapter 10.

TEST_RUNNER

Default: 'django.test.simple.run_tests'
This is the name of the method to use for starting the test suite. It is used by Django's testing framework, which is covered online at http://www.djangoproject.com/documentation/0.96/testing/.

TEST_DATABASE_NAME

Default: None
This is the name of database to use when running the test suite. If a value of None is specified, the test database will use the name 'test_' + settings.DATABASE_NAME. See the documentation for Django's testing framework, which is covered online at http://www.djangoproject.com/documentation/0.96/testing/.

TIME_FORMAT

Default: 'P' (e.g., 4 p.m.)
This is the default formatting to use for time fields on Django admin change-list pages—and, possibly, by other parts of the system. It accepts the same format as the now tag (see Appendix F, Table F-2).

See also DATE_FORMAT, DATETIME_FORMAT, TIME_FORMAT, YEAR_MONTH_FORMAT, and MONTH_DAY_FORMAT.

TIME_ZONE

Default: 'America/Chicago'
This is a string representing the time zone for this installation. Time zones are in the Unix-standard zic format. One relatively complete list of time zone strings can be found at http://www.postgresql.org/docs/8.1/static/datetime-keywords.html#DATETIME-TIMEZONE-SET-TABLE.

This is the time zone to which Django will convert all dates/times—not necessarily the time zone of the server. For example, one server may serve multiple Django-powered sites, each with a separate time-zone setting.

Normally, Django sets the `os.environ['TZ']` variable to the time zone you specify in the `TIME_ZONE` setting. Thus, all your views and models will automatically operate in the correct time zone. However, if you're using the manually configured settings (described earlier in the section titled "Using Settings Without Setting DJANGO_SETTINGS_MODULE"), Django will *not* touch the TZ environment variable, and it will be up to you to ensure your processes are running in the correct environment.

■**Note** Django cannot reliably use alternate time zones in a Windows environment. If you're running Django on Windows, this variable must be set to match the system time zone.

URL_VALIDATOR_USER_AGENT

Default: `Django/<version> (http://www.djangoproject.com/)`
This is the string to use as the `User-Agent` header when checking to see if URLs exist (see the `verify_exists` option on `URLField`; see Appendix B).

USE_ETAGS

Default: `False`
This Boolean specifies whether to output the ETag header. It saves bandwidth but slows down performance. This is used only if `CommonMiddleware` is installed (see Chapter 15).

USE_I18N

Default: `True`
This Boolean specifies whether Django's internationalization system (see Chapter 18) should be enabled. It provides an easy way to turn off internationalization, for performance. If this is set to `False`, Django will make some optimizations so as not to load the internationalization machinery.

YEAR_MONTH_FORMAT

Default: `'F Y'`
This is the default formatting to use for date fields on Django admin change-list pages—and, possibly, by other parts of the system—in cases when only the year and month are displayed. It accepts the same format as the `now` tag (see Appendix F).

For example, when a Django admin change-list page is being filtered by a date drill-down, the header for a given month displays the month and the year. Different locales have different formats. For example, U.S. English would use "January 2006," whereas another locale might use "2006/January."

See also `DATE_FORMAT`, `DATETIME_FORMAT`, `TIME_FORMAT`, and `MONTH_DAY_FORMAT`.

■■■

Built-in Template Tags and Filters

Chapter 4 lists a number of the most useful built-in template tags and filters. However, Django ships with many more built-in tags and filters. This appendix lists the ones that were included at the time this book was written, but new tags get added fairly regularly.

The best reference to all the available tags and filters is directly in your admin interface. Django's admin interface includes a complete reference of all tags and filters available for a given site. To see it, go to your admin interface and click the Documentation link at the upper right of the page.

The tags and filters sections of the built-in documentation describe all the built-in tags (in fact, the tag and filter references in this appendix come directly from those pages) as well as any custom tag libraries available.

For those without an admin site available, reference for the stock tags and filters follows. Because Django is highly customizable, the reference in your admin site should be considered the final word on the available tags and filters and what they do.

Built-in Tag Reference

block

Defines a block that can be overridden by child templates. See the section on template inheritance in Chapter 4 for more information.

comment

Ignores everything between {% comment %} and {% endcomment %}.

cycle

Cycles among the given strings each time this tag is encountered.

Within a loop, it cycles among the given strings each time through the loop:

```
{% for o in some_list %}
    <tr class="{% cycle row1,row2 %}">
        ...
    </tr>
{% endfor %}
```

Outside of a loop, give the values a unique name the first time you call it, and then use that name each successive time through:

```
<tr class="{% cycle row1,row2,row3 as rowcolors %}">...</tr>
<tr class="{% cycle rowcolors %}">...</tr>
<tr class="{% cycle rowcolors %}">...</tr>
```

You can use any number of values, separated by commas. Make sure not to put spaces between the values—only commas.

debug

Outputs a whole load of debugging information, including the current context and imported modules.

extends

Signals that this template extends a parent template.

This tag can be used in two ways:

- {% extends "base.html" %} (with quotes) uses the literal value "base.html" as the name of the parent template to extend.

- {% extends variable %} uses the value of variable. If the variable evaluates to a string, Django will use that string as the name of the parent template. If the variable evaluates to a Template object, Django will use that object as the parent template.

See Chapter 4 for many usage examples.

filter

Filters the contents of the variable through variable filters.

Filters can also be piped through each other, and they can have arguments—just like in variable syntax.

Here's a sample usage:

```
{% filter escape|lower %}
    This text will be HTML-escaped, and will appear in all lowercase.
{% endfilter %}
```

firstof

Outputs the first variable passed that is not False. Outputs nothing if all the passed variables are False.

Here's a sample usage:

```
{% firstof var1 var2 var3 %}
```

This is equivalent to the following:

```
{% if var1 %}
    {{ var1 }}
{% else %}{% if var2 %}
    {{ var2 }}
{% else %}{% if var3 %}
    {{ var3 }}
{% endif %}{% endif %}{% endif %}
```

for

Loops over each item in an array. This example displays a list of athletes given `athlete_list`:

```
<ul>
{% for athlete in athlete_list %}
    <li>{{ athlete.name }}</li>
{% endfor %}
</ul>
```

You can also loop over a list in reverse by using `{% for obj in list reversed %}`.
The `for` loop sets a number of variables available within the loop (see Table F-1).

Table F-1. *Variables Available Inside {% for %} Loops*

Variable	Description
forloop.counter	The current iteration of the loop (1-indexed).
forloop.counter0	The current iteration of the loop (0-indexed).
forloop.revcounter	The number of iterations from the end of the loop (1-indexed).
forloop.revcounter0	The number of iterations from the end of the loop (0-indexed).
forloop.first	True if this is the first time through the loop.
forloop.last	True if this is the last time through the loop.
forloop.parentloop	For nested loops, this is the loop "above" the current one.

if

The `{% if %}` tag evaluates a variable, and if that variable is "true" (i.e., it exists, is not empty, and is not a false Boolean value), the contents of the block are output:

```
{% if athlete_list %}
    Number of athletes: {{ athlete_list|length }}
{% else %}
    No athletes.
{% endif %}
```

If athlete_list is not empty, the number of athletes will be displayed by the {{ athlete_list|length }} variable.

As you can see, the if tag can take an optional {% else %} clause that will be displayed if the test fails.

if tags may use and, or, or not to test a number of variables or to negate a given variable:

```
{% if athlete_list and coach_list %}
    Both athletes and coaches are available.
{% endif %}

{% if not athlete_list %}
    There are no athletes.
{% endif %}

{% if athlete_list or coach_list %}
    There are some athletes or some coaches.
{% endif %}

{% if not athlete_list or coach_list %}
    There are no athletes or there are some coaches (OK, so
    writing English translations of Boolean logic sounds
    stupid; it's not our fault).
{% endif %}

{% if athlete_list and not coach_list %}
    There are some athletes and absolutely no coaches.
{% endif %}
```

if tags don't allow and and or clauses within the same tag, because the order of logic would be ambiguous. For example, this is invalid:

```
{% if athlete_list and coach_list or cheerleader_list %}
```

If you need to combine and and or to do advanced logic, just use nested if tags, for example:

```
{% if athlete_list %}
    {% if coach_list or cheerleader_list %}
        We have athletes, and either coaches or cheerleaders!
    {% endif %}
{% endif %}
```

Multiple uses of the same logical operator are fine, as long as you use the same operator. For example, this is valid:

```
{% if athlete_list or coach_list or parent_list or teacher_list %}
```

ifchanged

Checks if a value has changed from the last iteration of a loop.

The `ifchanged` block tag is used within a loop. It has two possible uses:

- It checks its own rendered contents against its previous state and displays the content only if it has changed. For example, this displays a list of days, only displaying the month if it changes:

```
<h1>Archive for {{ year }}</h1>

{% for date in days %}
    {% ifchanged %}<h3>{{ date|date:"F" }}</h3>{% endifchanged %}
    <a href="{{ date|date:"M/d"|lower }}/">{{ date|date:"j" }}</a>
{% endfor %}
```

- If given a variable, it checks whether that variable has changed:

```
{% for date in days %}
    {% ifchanged date.date %} {{ date.date }} {% endifchanged %}
    {% ifchanged date.hour date.date %}
        {{ date.hour }}
    {% endifchanged %}
{% endfor %}
```

The preceding shows the date every time it changes, but it only shows the hour if both the hour and the date have changed.

ifequal

Outputs the contents of the block if the two arguments equal each other. Here's an example:

```
{% ifequal user.id comment.user_id %}
    ...
{% endifequal %}
```

As in the {% if %} tag, an {% else %} clause is optional.

The arguments can be hard-coded strings, so the following is valid:

```
{% ifequal user.username "adrian" %}
    ...
{% endifequal %}
```

It is only possible to compare an argument to template variables or strings. You cannot check for equality with Python objects such as `True` or `False`. If you need to test if something is true or false, use the `if` tag instead.

ifnotequal

Just like `ifequal`, except it tests that the two arguments are *not* equal.

include

Loads a template and renders it with the current context. This is a way of "including" other templates within a template.

The template name can be either a variable or a hard-coded (quoted) string, in either single or double quotes.

This example includes the contents of the template "foo/bar.html":

```
{% include "foo/bar.html" %}
```

This example includes the contents of the template whose name is contained in the variable template_name:

```
{% include template_name %}
```

load

Loads a custom template library. See Chapter 10 for information about custom template libraries.

now

Displays the date, formatted according to the given string.

This tag was inspired by, and uses the same format as, PHP's date() function (http://php.net/date). Django's version, however, has some custom extensions.

Table F-2 shows the available format strings.

Table F-2. *Available Date Format Strings*

Format Character	Description	Example Output
a	'a.m.' or 'p.m.'. (Note that this is slightly different from PHP's output, because this includes periods to match Associated Press style.)	'a.m.'
A	'AM' or 'PM'.	'AM'
b	Month, textual, three letters, lowercase.	'jan'
d	Day of the month, two digits with leading zeros.	'01' to '31'
D	Day of the week, textual, three letters.	'Fri'
f	Time, in 12-hour hours and minutes, with minutes left off if they're zero.	'1', '1:30'
F	Month, textual, long.	'January'
g	Hour, 12-hour format without leading zeros.	'1' to '12'
G	Hour, 24-hour format without leading zeros.	'0' to '23'
h	Hour, 12-hour format.	'01' to '12'
H	Hour, 24-hour format.	'00' to '23'
i	Minutes.	'00' to '59'
j	Day of the month without leading zeros.	'1' to '31'

Format Character	Description	Example Output
l	Day of the week, textual, long.	`'Friday'`
L	Boolean for whether it's a leap year.	`True or False`
m	Month, two digits with leading zeros.	`'01' to '12'`
M	Month, textual, three letters.	`'Jan'`
n	Month without leading zeros.	`'1' to '12'`
N	Month abbreviation in Associated Press style.	`'Jan.', 'Feb.', 'March', 'May'`
O	Difference to Greenwich Mean Time in hours.	`'+0200'`
P	Time, in 12-hour hours, minutes, and a.m./p.m., with minutes left off if they're zero and the special-case strings `'midnight'` and `'noon'` if appropriate.	`'1 a.m.', '1:30 p.m.', 'midnight', 'noon', '12:30 p.m.'`
r	RFC 822 formatted date.	`'Thu, 21 Dec 2000 16:01:07 +0200'`
s	Seconds, two digits with leading zeros.	`'00' to '59'`
S	English ordinal suffix for day of the month, two characters.	`'st', 'nd', 'rd' or 'th'`
t	Number of days in the given month.	`28 to 31`
T	Time zone of this machine.	`'EST', 'MDT'`
w	Day of the week, digits without leading zeros.	`'0' (Sunday) to '6' (Saturday)`
W	ISO-8601 week number of year, with weeks starting on Monday.	`1, 23`
y	Year, two digits.	`'99'`
Y	Year, four digits.	`'1999'`
z	Day of the year.	`0 to 365`
Z	Time zone offset in seconds. The offset for time zones west of UTC is always negative, and for those east of UTC it is always positive.	`-43200 to 43200`

Here's an example:

```
It is {% now "jS F Y H:i" %}
```

Note that you can backslash-escape a format string if you want to use the "raw" value. In this example, "f" is backslash-escaped, because otherwise "f" is a format string that displays the time. The "o" doesn't need to be escaped, because it's not a format character:

```
It is the {% now "jS o\f F" %}
```

This would display as "It is the 4th of September".

regroup

Regroups a list of like objects by a common attribute.

This complex tag is best illustrated by use of an example. Say that people is a list of Person objects that have first_name, last_name, and gender attributes, and you'd like to display a list that looks like this:

- Male:
  - George Bush
  - Bill Clinton
- Female:
  - Margaret Thatcher
  - Condoleezza Rice
- Unknown:
  - Pat Smith

The following snippet of template code would accomplish this dubious task:

```
{% regroup people by gender as grouped %}
<ul>
{% for group in grouped %}
    <li>{{ group.grouper }}
    <ul>
        {% for item in group.list %}
        <li>{{ item }}</li>
        {% endfor %}
    </ul>
    </li>
{% endfor %}
</ul>
```

As you can see, {% regroup %} populates a variable with a list of objects with grouper and list attributes. grouper contains the item that was grouped by; list contains the list of objects that share that grouper. In this case, grouper would be Male, Female, and Unknown, and list is the list of people with those genders.

Note that {% regroup %} does not work when the list to be grouped is not sorted by the key you are grouping by! This means that if your list of people was not sorted by gender, you'd need to make sure it is sorted before using it, that is:

```
{% regroup people|dictsort:"gender" by gender as grouped %}
```

spaceless

Removes whitespace between HTML tags. This includes tab characters and newlines. Here's an example:

```
{% spaceless %}
    <p>
        <a href="foo/">Foo</a>
    </p>
{% endspaceless %}
```

This example would return the following HTML:

```
<p><a href="foo/">Foo</a></p>
```

Only space between *tags* is removed—not space between tags and text. In this example, the space around `Hello` won't be stripped:

```
{% spaceless %}
    <strong>
        Hello
    </strong>
{% endspaceless %}
```

ssi

Outputs the contents of a given file into the page.

Like a simple "include" tag, `{% ssi %}` includes the contents of another file—which must be specified using an absolute path—in the current page:

```
{% ssi /home/html/ljworld.com/includes/right_generic.html %}
```

If the optional "parsed" parameter is given, the contents of the included file are evaluated as template code, within the current context:

```
{% ssi /home/html/ljworld.com/includes/right_generic.html parsed %}
```

Note that if you use `{% ssi %}`, you'll need to define `ALLOWED_INCLUDE_ROOTS` in your Django settings, as a security measure.

Most of the time `{% include %}` works better than `{% ssi %}`; `{% ssi %}` exists mostly for backward compatibility.

templatetag

Outputs one of the syntax characters used to compose template tags.

Since the template system has no concept of "escaping," to display one of the bits used in template tags, you must use the `{% templatetag %}` tag.

The argument tells which template bit to output (see Table F-3).

Table F-3. *Valid Arguments to templatetag*

Argument	Output
openblock	{%
closeblock	%}
openvariable	{{
closevariable	}}
openbrace	{
closebrace	}
opencomment	{#
closecomment	#}

url

Returns an absolute URL (i.e., a URL without the domain name) matching a given view function and optional parameters. This is a way to output links without violating the DRY principle by having to hard-code URLs in your templates:

```
{% url path.to.some_view arg1,arg2,name1=value1 %}
```

The first argument is a path to a view function in the format package.package.module.function. Additional arguments are optional and should be comma-separated values that will be used as positional and keyword arguments in the URL. All arguments required by the URLconf should be present.

For example, suppose you have a view, app_name.client, whose URLconf takes a client ID. The URLconf line might look like this:

```
('^client/(\d+)/$', 'app_name.client')
```

If this application's URLconf is included into the project's URLconf under a path such as this:

```
('^clients/', include('project_name.app_name.urls'))
```

then, in a template, you can create a link to this view like this:

```
{% url app_name.client client.id %}
```

The template tag will output the string /clients/client/123/.

widthratio

For creating bar charts and such, this tag calculates the ratio of a given value to a maximum value and then applies that ratio to a constant. Here's an example:

```
<img src="bar.gif" height="10" width="{% widthratio this_value max_value 100 %}" />
```

If this_value is 175 and max_value is 200, the image in the preceding example will be 88 pixels wide (because 175/200 = .875, and .875 * 100 = 87.5, which is rounded up to 88).

Built-in Filter Reference

add

Example:

```
{{ value|add:"5" }}
```

Adds the argument to the value.

addslashes

Example:

```
{{ string|addslashes }}
```

Adds backslashes before single and double quotes. This is useful for passing strings to JavaScript, for example.

capfirst

Example:

```
{{ string|capfirst }}
```

Capitalizes the first character of the string.

center

Example:

```
{{ string|center:"50" }}
```

Centers the string in a field of a given width.

cut

Example:

```
{{ string|cut:"spam" }}
```

Removes all values of the argument from the given string.

date

Example:

`{{ value|date:"F j, Y" }}`

> Formats a date according to the given format (same as the now tag).

default

Example:

`{{ value|default:"(N/A)" }}`

> If the value is unavailable, use the given default.

default_if_none

Example:

`{{ value|default_if_none:"(N/A)" }}`

> If the value is None, use the given default.

dictsort

Example:

`{{ list|dictsort:"foo" }}`

> Takes a list of dictionaries and returns that list sorted by the property given in the argument.

dictsortreversed

Example:

`{{ list|dictsortreversed:"foo" }}`

> Takes a list of dictionaries and returns that list sorted in reverse order by the property given in the argument.

divisibleby

Example:

```
{% if value|divisibleby:"2" %}
    Even!
{% else %}
    Odd!
{% else %}
```

> Returns True if the value is divisible by the argument.

escape

Example:

`{{ string|escape }}`

Escapes a string's HTML. Specifically, it makes these replacements:

- "&" to "&"
- < to "<"
- > to ">"
- '"' (double quote) to '"'
- "'" (single quote) to '''

filesizeformat

Example:

`{{ value|filesizeformat }}`

Formats the value like a "human-readable" file size (i.e., `'13 KB'`, `'4.1 MB'`, `'102 bytes'`, etc.).

first

Example:

`{{ list|first }}`

Returns the first item in a list.

fix_ampersands

Example:

`{{ string|fix_ampersands }}`

Replaces ampersands with & entities.

floatformat

Examples:

`{{ value|floatformat }}`
`{{ value|floatformat:"2" }}`

When used without an argument, rounds a floating-point number to one decimal place—but only if there's a decimal part to be displayed, for example:

- 36.123 gets converted to 36.1.
- 36.15 gets converted to 36.2.
- 36 gets converted to 36.

If used with a numeric integer argument, floatformat rounds a number to that many decimal places:

- 36.1234 with floatformat:3 gets converted to 36.123.

- 36 with floatformat:4 gets converted to 36.0000.

If the argument passed to floatformat is negative, it will round a number to that many decimal places—but only if there's a decimal part to be displayed:

- 36.1234 with floatformat:-3 gets converted to 36.123.

- 36 with floatformat:-4 gets converted to 36.

Using floatformat with no argument is equivalent to using floatformat with an argument of -1.

get_digit

Example:

```
{{ value|get_digit:"1" }}
```

Given a whole number, returns the requested digit of it, where 1 is the rightmost digit, 2 is the second-to-rightmost digit, and so forth. It returns the original value for invalid input (if the input or argument is not an integer, or if the argument is less than 1). Otherwise, output is always an integer.

join

Example:

```
{{ list|join:", " }}
```

Joins a list with a string, like Python's str.join(list).

length

Example:

```
{{ list|length }}
```

Returns the length of the value.

length_is

Example:

```
{% if list|length_is:"3" %}
   ...
{% endif %}
```

Returns a Boolean of whether the value's length is the argument.

linebreaks

Example:

```
{{ string|linebreaks }}
```

Converts newlines into <p> and <br /> tags.

linebreaksbr

Example:

```
{{ string|linebreaksbr }}
```

Converts newlines into <br /> tags.

linenumbers

Example:

```
{{ string|linenumbers }}
```

Displays text with line numbers.

ljust

Example:

```
{{ string|ljust:"50" }}
```

Left-aligns the value in a field of a given width.

lower

Example:

```
{{ string|lower }}
```

Converts a string into all lowercase.

make_list

Example:

```
{% for i in number|make_list %}
    ...
{% endfor %}
```

Returns the value turned into a list. For an integer, it's a list of digits. For a string, it's a list of characters.

phone2numeric

Example:

```
{{ string|phone2numeric }}
```

Converts a phone number (possibly containing letters) to its numerical equivalent. For example, '800-COLLECT' will be converted to '800-2655328'.

The input doesn't have to be a valid phone number. This will happily convert any string.

pluralize

Example:

```
The list has {{ list|length }} item{{ list|pluralize }}.
```

Returns a plural suffix if the value is not 1. By default, this suffix is 's'.

Example:

```
You have {{ num_messages }} message{{ num_messages|pluralize }}.
```

For words that require a suffix other than 's', you can provide an alternate suffix as a parameter to the filter.

Example:

```
You have {{ num_walruses }} walrus{{ num_walrus|pluralize:"es" }}.
```

For words that don't pluralize by simple suffix, you can specify both a singular and plural suffix, separated by a comma.

Example:

```
You have {{ num_cherries }} cherr{{ num_cherries|pluralize:"y,ies" }}.
```

pprint

Example:

```
{{ object|pprint }}
```

A wrapper around Python's built-in pprint.pprint—for debugging, really.

random

Example:

```
{{ list|random }}
```

Returns a random item from the list.

removetags

Example:

```
{{ string|removetags:"br p div" }}
```

Removes a space-separated list of [X]HTML tags from the output.

rjust

Example:

```
{{ string|rjust:"50" }}
```

Right-aligns the value in a field of a given width.

slice

Example:

```
{{ some_list|slice:":2" }}
```

Returns a slice of the list. Uses the same syntax as Python's list slicing. See `http://diveintopython.org/native_data_types/lists.html#odbchelper.list.slice` for an introduction.

slugify

Example:

```
{{ string|slugify }}
```

Converts to lowercase, removes nonword characters (alphanumerics and underscores), and converts spaces to hyphens. It also strips leading and trailing whitespace.

stringformat

Example:

```
{{ number|stringformat:"02i" }}
```

Formats the variable according to the argument, a string formatting specifier. This specifier uses Python string-formatting syntax, with the exception that the leading "%" is dropped. See `http://docs.python.org/lib/typesseq-strings.html` for documentation of Python string formatting.

striptags

Example:

```
{{ string|striptags }}
```

Strips all [X]HTML tags.

time

Example:

```
{{ value|time:"P" }}
```

Formats a time according to the given format (same as the now tag).

timesince

Examples:

```
{{ datetime|timesince }}
{{ datetime|timesince:"other_datetime" }}
```

Formats a date as the time since that date (e.g., "4 days, 6 hours").

Takes an optional argument that is a variable containing the date to use as the comparison point (without the argument, the comparison point is *now*). For example, if blog_date is a date instance representing midnight on 1 June 2006, and comment_date is a date instance for 08:00 on 1 June 2006, then {{ comment_date|timesince:blog_date }} would return "8 hours".

timeuntil

Examples:

```
{{ datetime|timeuntil }}
{{ datetime|timeuntil:"other_datetime" }}
```

Similar to timesince, except that it measures the time from now until the given date or datetime. For example, if today is 1 June 2006 and conference_date is a date instance holding 29 June 2006, then {{ conference_date|timeuntil }} will return "28 days".

It takes an optional argument that is a variable containing the date to use as the comparison point (instead of *now*). If from_date contains 22 June 2006, then {{ conference_date| timeuntil:from_date }} will return "7 days".

title

Example:

```
{{ string|titlecase }}
```

Converts a string into title case.

truncatewords

Example:

```
{{ string|truncatewords:"15" }}
```

Truncates a string after a certain number of words.

truncatewords_html

Example:

```
{{ string|truncatewords_html:"15" }}
```

Similar to truncatewords, except that it is aware of HTML tags. Any tags that are opened in the string and not closed before the truncation point are closed immediately after the truncation.

This is less efficient than truncatewords, so it should be used only when it is being passed HTML text.

unordered_list

Example:

```
<ul>
    {{ list|unordered_list }}
</ul>
```

Recursively takes a self-nested list and returns an HTML unordered list—*without* opening and closing `<ul>` tags.

The list is assumed to be in the proper format. For example, if var contains `['States', [['Kansas', [['Lawrence', []], ['Topeka', []]]], ['Illinois', []]]]`, then `{{ var|unordered_list }}` would return the following:

```
<li>States
<ul>
        <li>Kansas
        <ul>
                <li>Lawrence</li>
                <li>Topeka</li>
        </ul>
        </li>
        <li>Illinois</li>
</ul>
</li>
```

upper

Example:

```
{{ string|upper }}
```

Converts a string into all uppercase.

urlencode

Example:

```
<a href="{{ link|urlencode }}">linkage</a>
```

Escapes a value for use in a URL.

urlize

Example:

```
{{ string|urlize }}
```

Converts URLs in plain text into clickable links.

urlizetrunc

Example:

`{{ string|urlizetrunc:"30" }}`

Converts URLs into clickable links, truncating URLs to the given character limit.

wordcount

Example:

`{{ string|wordcount }}`

Returns the number of words.

wordwrap

Example:

`{{ string|wordwrap:"75" }}`

Wraps words at a specified line length.

yesno

Example:

`{{ boolean|yesno:"Yes,No,Perhaps" }}`

Given a string mapping values for True, False, and (optionally) None, returns one of those strings according to the value (see Table F-4).

Table F-4. *Examples of the yesno Filter*

Value	Argument	Output
True	"yeah,no,maybe"	yeah
False	"yeah,no,maybe"	no
None	"yeah,no,maybe"	maybe
None	"yeah,no"	"no" (converts None to False if no mapping for None is given)

A P P E N D I X   G

■■■

The django-admin Utility

django-admin.py is Django's command-line utility for administrative tasks. This appendix explains its many powers.

You'll usually access django-admin.py through a project's manage.py wrapper. manage.py is automatically created in each Django project and is a thin wrapper around django-admin.py. It takes care of two things for you before delegating to django-admin.py:

- It puts your project's package on sys.path.

- It sets the DJANGO_SETTINGS_MODULE environment variable so that it points to your project's settings.py file.

The django-admin.py script should be on your system path if you installed Django via its setup.py utility. If it's not on your path, you can find it in site-packages/django/bin within your Python installation. Consider symlinking it from some place on your path, such as /usr/local/bin.

Windows users, who do not have symlinking functionality available, can copy django-admin.py to a location on their existing path or edit the PATH settings (under Settings ➤ Control Panel ➤ System ➤ Advanced ➤ Environment) to point to its installed location.

Generally, when working on a single Django project, it's easier to use manage.py. Use django-admin.py with DJANGO_SETTINGS_MODULE or the --settings command-line option, if you need to switch between multiple Django settings files.

The command-line examples throughout this appendix use django-admin.py to be consistent, but any example can use manage.py just as well.

Usage

The basic usage is

```
django-admin.py action [option]
```

or

```
manage.py action [option]
```

action should be one of the actions listed in this document. option, which is optional, should be zero or more of the option listed in this document.

Run django-admin.py --help to display a help message that includes a terse list of all available actions and options.

Most actions take a list of app names. An *app name* is the base name of the package containing your models. For example, if your INSTALLED_APPS contains the string 'mysite.blog', the app name is blog.

Available Actions

The following sections cover the actions available to you.

adminindex [appname appname ...]

Prints the admin-index template snippet for the given application names. Use admin-index template snippets if you want to customize the look and feel of your admin's index page.

createcachetable [tablename]

Creates a cache table named tablename for use with the database cache back-end. See Chapter 13 for more about caching.

dbshell

Runs the command-line client for the database engine specified in your DATABASE_ENGINE setting, with the connection parameters specified in the settings DATABASE_USER, DATABASE_PASSWORD, and so forth.

- For PostgreSQL, this runs the psql command-line client.

- For MySQL, this runs the mysql command-line client.

- For SQLite, this runs the sqlite3 command-line client.

This command assumes the programs are on your PATH so that a simple call to the program name (psql, mysql, or sqlite3) will find the program in the right place. There's no way to specify the location of the program manually.

diffsettings

Displays differences between the current settings file and Django's default settings.

Settings that don't appear in the defaults are followed by "###". For example, the default settings don't define ROOT_URLCONF, so ROOT_URLCONF is followed by "###" in the output of diffsettings.

Note that Django's default settings live in django.conf.global_settings, if you're ever curious to see the full list of defaults.

dumpdata [appname appname ...]

Outputs to standard output all data in the database associated with the named application(s).

By default, the database will be dumped in JSON format. If you want the output to be in another format, use the --format option (e.g., format=xml). You may specify any Django serialization back-end (including any user-specified serialization back-ends named in the SERIALIZATION_MODULES setting). The --indent option can be used to pretty-print the output.

If no application name is provided, all installed applications will be dumped.

The output of dumpdata can be used as input for loaddata.

flush

Returns the database to the state it was in immediately after syncdb was executed. This means that all data will be removed from the database, any postsynchronization handlers will be re-executed, and the initial_data fixture will be reinstalled.

inspectdb

Introspects the database tables in the database pointed to by the DATABASE_NAME setting and outputs a Django model module (a models.py file) to standard output.

Use this if you have a legacy database with which you'd like to use Django. The script will inspect the database and create a model for each table within it.

As you might expect, the created models will have an attribute for every field in the table. Note that inspectdb has a few special cases in its field name output:

- If inspectdb cannot map a column's type to a model field type, it will use TextField and will insert the Python comment 'This field type is a guess.' next to the field in the generated model.

- If the database column name is a Python reserved word (such as 'pass', 'class', or 'for'), inspectdb will append '_field' to the attribute name. For example, if a table has a column 'for', the generated model will have a field 'for_field', with the db_column attribute set to 'for'. inspectdb will insert the Python comment 'Field renamed because it was a Python reserved word.' next to the field.

This feature is meant as a shortcut, not as definitive model generation. After you run it, you'll want to look over the generated models yourself to make customizations. In particular, you'll need to rearrange the models so that models with relationships are ordered properly.

Primary keys are automatically introspected for PostgreSQL, MySQL, and SQLite, in which case Django puts in the primary_key=True where needed.

inspectdb works with PostgreSQL, MySQL, and SQLite. Foreign key detection only works in PostgreSQL and with certain types of MySQL tables.

loaddata [fixture fixture ...]

Searches for and loads the contents of the named fixture into the database.

A *fixture* is a collection of files that contain the serialized contents of the database. Each fixture has a unique name; however, the files that comprise the fixture can be distributed over multiple directories, in multiple applications.

Django will search in three locations for fixtures:

- In the `fixtures` directory of every installed application

- In any directory named in the `FIXTURE_DIRS` setting

- In the literal path named by the fixture

Django will load any and all fixtures it finds in these locations that match the provided fixture names.

If the named fixture has a file extension, only fixtures of that type will be loaded. For example, the following:

```
django-admin.py loaddata mydata.json
```

will only load JSON fixtures called `mydata`. The fixture extension must correspond to the registered name of a serializer (e.g., `json` or `xml`).

If you omit the extension, Django will search all available fixture types for a matching fixture. For example, the following:

```
django-admin.py loaddata mydata
```

will look for any fixture of any fixture type called `mydata`. If a fixture directory contained `mydata.json`, that fixture would be loaded as a JSON fixture. However, if two fixtures with the same name but different fixture types are discovered (e.g., if `mydata.json` and `mydata.xml` were found in the same fixture directory), fixture installation will be aborted, and any data installed in the call to `loaddata` will be removed from the database.

The fixtures that are named can include directory components. These directories will be included in the search path. The following, for example:

```
django-admin.py loaddata foo/bar/mydata.json
```

will search `<appname>/fixtures/foo/bar/mydata.json` for each installed application, `<dirname>/foo/bar/mydata.json` for each directory in `FIXTURE_DIRS`, and the literal path `foo/bar/mydata.json`.

Note that the order in which fixture files are processed is undefined. However, all fixture data is installed as a single transaction, so data in one fixture can reference data in another fixture. If the database back-end supports row-level constraints, these constraints will be checked at the end of the transaction.

The `dumpdata` command can be used to generate input for `loaddata`.

MYSQL AND FIXTURES

Unfortunately, MySQL isn't capable of completely supporting all the features of Django fixtures. If you use MyISAM tables, MySQL doesn't support transactions or constraints, so you won't get a rollback if multiple transaction files are found, or validation of fixture data. If you use InnoDB tables, you won't be able to have any forward references in your data files—MySQL doesn't provide a mechanism to defer checking of row constraints until a transaction is committed.

reset [appname appname ...]

Executes the equivalent of `sqlreset` for the given app names.

runfcgi [option]

Starts a set of FastCGI processes suitable for use with any Web server that supports the FastCGI protocol. See Chapter 20 for more about deploying under FastCGI.

This command requires the Python FastCGI module from `flup http://www.djangoproject.com/r/flup/`.

runserver [optional port number, or ipaddr:port]

Starts a lightweight development Web server on the local machine. By default, the server runs on port 8000 on the IP address 127.0.0.1. You can pass in an IP address and port number explicitly.

If you run this script as a user with normal privileges (recommended), you might not have access to start a port on a low port number. Low port numbers are reserved for the superuser (root).

Do not use this server in a production setting. It has not gone through security audits or performance tests, and there are no plans to change that fact. Django's developers are in the business of making Web frameworks, not Web servers, so improving this server to be able to handle a production environment is outside the scope of Django.

The development server automatically reloads Python code for each request, as needed. You don't need to restart the server for code changes to take effect.

When you start the server, and each time you change Python code while the server is running, the server will validate all of your installed models. (See the upcoming section on the `validate` command.) If the validator finds errors, it will print them to standard output, but it won't stop the server.

You can run as many servers as you want, as long as they're on separate ports. Just execute `django-admin.py runserver` more than once.

Note that the default IP address, 127.0.0.1, is not accessible from other machines on your network. To make your development server viewable to other machines on the network, use its own IP address (e.g., 192.168.2.1) or 0.0.0.0.

For example, to run the server on port 7000 on IP address 127.0.0.1, use this:

```
django-admin.py runserver 7000
```

To run the server on port 7000 on IP address 1.2.3.4, use this:

```
django-admin.py runserver 1.2.3.4:7000
```

Serving Static Files with the Development Server

By default, the development server doesn't serve any static files for your site (such as CSS files, images, things under `MEDIA_ROOT_URL`, etc.). If you want to configure Django to serve static media, read about serving static media at `http://www.djangoproject.com/documentation/0.96/static_files/`.

Turning Off Autoreload

To disable autoreloading of code while the development server is running, use the `--noreload` option, like so:

```
django-admin.py runserver --noreload
```

shell

Starts the Python interactive interpreter.

Django will use IPython (`http://ipython.scipy.org/`) if it's installed. If you have IPython installed and want to force use of the "plain" Python interpreter, use the `--plain` option, like so:

```
django-admin.py shell --plain
```

sql [appname appname ...]

Prints the `CREATE TABLE` SQL statements for the given app names.

sqlall [appname appname ...]

Prints the `CREATE TABLE` and initial-data SQL statements for the given app names.

Refer to the description of `sqlcustom` for an explanation of how to specify initial data.

sqlclear [appname appname ...]

Prints the `DROP TABLE` SQL statements for the given app names.

sqlcustom [appname appname ...]

Prints the custom SQL statements for the given app names. For each model in each specified app, this command looks for the file `<appname>/sql/<modelname>.sql`, where `<appname>` is the given app name and `<modelname>` is the model's name in lowercase. For example, if you have an app news that includes a Story model, `sqlcustom` will attempt to read a file `news/sql/story.sql` and append it to the output of this command.

Each of the SQL files, if given, is expected to contain valid SQL. The SQL files are piped directly into the database after all of the models' table-creation statements have been executed. Use this SQL hook to make any table modifications, or insert any SQL functions into the database.

Note that the order in which the SQL files are processed is undefined.

sqlindexes [appname appname ...]

Prints the `CREATE INDEX` SQL statements for the given app names.

sqlreset [appname appname ...]

Prints the `DROP TABLE` SQL, and then the `CREATE TABLE` SQL, for the given app names.

sqlsequencereset [appname appname ...]

Prints the SQL statements for resetting sequences for the given app names.

You'll need this SQL only if you're using PostgreSQL and have inserted data by hand. When you do that, PostgreSQL's primary key sequences can get out of sync from what's in the database, and the SQL emitted by this command will clear it up.

startapp [appname]

Creates a Django application directory structure for the given app name in the current directory.

startproject [projectname]

Creates a Django project directory structure for the given project name in the current directory.

syncdb

Creates the database tables for all applications in INSTALLED_APPS whose tables have not already been created.

Use this command when you've added new applications to your project and want to install them in the database. This includes any applications shipped with Django that might be in INSTALLED_APPS by default. When you start a new project, run this command to install the default applications.

If you're installing the django.contrib.auth application, syncdb will give you the option of creating a superuser immediately. syncdb will also search for and install any fixture named initial_data. See the documentation for loaddata for details on the specification of fixture data files.

test

Discovers and runs tests for all installed models. Testing was still under development when this book was being written, so to learn more you'll need to read the documentation online at http://www.djangoproject.com/documentation/0.96/testing/.

validate

Validates all installed models (according to the INSTALLED_APPS setting) and prints validation errors to standard output.

Available Option

The sections that follow outline the option that django-admin.py can take.

--settings

Example usage:

```
django-admin.py syncdb --settings=mysite.settings
```

Explicitly specifies the settings module to use. The settings module should be in Python package syntax (e.g., `mysite.settings`). If this isn't provided, `django-admin.py` will use the `DJANGO_SETTINGS_MODULE` environment variable.

Note that this option is unnecessary in `manage.py`, because it takes care of setting `DJANGO_SETTINGS_MODULE` for you.

--pythonpath

Example usage:

```
django-admin.py syncdb --pythonpath='/home/djangoprojects/myproject'
```

Adds the given filesystem path to the Python import search path. If this isn't provided, `django-admin.py` will use the `PYTHONPATH` environment variable.

Note that this option is unnecessary in `manage.py`, because it takes care of setting the Python path for you.

--format

Example usage:

```
django-admin.py dumpdata --format=xml
```

Specifies the output format that will be used. The name provided must be the name of a registered serializer.

--help

Displays a help message that includes a terse list of all available actions and options.

--indent

Example usage:

```
django-admin.py dumpdata --indent=4
```

Specifies the number of spaces that will be used for indentation when pretty-printing output. By default, output will *not* be pretty-printed. Pretty-printing will be enabled only if the indent option is provided.

--noinput

Indicates you will not be prompted for any input. This is useful if the `django-admin` script will be executed as an unattended, automated script.

--noreload

Disables the use of the autoreloader when running the development server.

--version

Displays the current Django version.
    Example output:

```
0.9.1
0.9.1 (SVN)
```

--verbosity

Example usage:

```
django-admin.py syncdb --verbosity=2
```

Determines the amount of notification and debug information that will be printed to the console. 0 is no output, 1 is normal output, and 2 is verbose output.

--adminmedia

Example usage:

```
django-admin.py --adminmedia=/tmp/new-admin-style/
```

Tells Django where to find the various CSS and JavaScript files for the admin interface when running the development server. Normally these files are served out of the Django source tree, but because some designers customize these files for their site, this option allows you to test against custom versions.

■ ■ ■

Request and Response Objects

Django uses request and response objects to pass state through the system.

When a page is requested, Django creates an HttpRequest object that contains metadata about the request. Then Django loads the appropriate view, passing the HttpRequest as the first argument to the view function. Each view is responsible for returning an HttpResponse object.

We've used these objects often throughout the book; this appendix explains the complete APIs for HttpRequest and HttpResponse objects.

HttpRequest

HttpRequest represents a single HTTP request from some user-agent.

Much of the important information about the request is available as attributes on the HttpRequest instance (see Table H-1). All attributes except session should be considered read-only.

Table H-1. *Attributes of HttpRequest Objects*

Attribute	Description
path	A string representing the full path to the requested page, not including the domain—for example, "/music/bands/the_beatles/".

method	A string representing the HTTP method used in the request. This is guaranteed to be uppercase. For example:
	
	`if request.method == 'GET':`
	    `do_something()`
	`elif request.method == 'POST':`
	    `do_something_else()`

GET	A dictionary-like object containing all given HTTP GET parameters. See the upcoming QueryDict documentation.
POST	A dictionary-like object containing all given HTTP POST parameters. See the upcoming QueryDict documentation. It's possible that a request can come in via POST with an empty POST dictionary—if, say, a form is requested via the POST HTTP method but does not include form data. Therefore, you shouldn't use if request.POST to check for use of the POST method; instead, use if request.method == "POST" (see the method entry in this table). Note: POST does *not* include file-upload information. See FILES.

Continued

Table H-1. *Continued*

Attribute	Description
REQUEST	For convenience, a dictionary-like object that searches POST first, and then GET. Inspired by PHP's $_REQUEST. For example, if GET = {"name": "john"} and POST = {"age": '34'}, REQUEST["name"] would be "john", and REQUEST["age"] would be "34". It's strongly suggested that you use GET and POST instead of REQUEST, because the former are more explicit.
COOKIES	A standard Python dictionary containing all cookies. Keys and values are strings. See Chapter 12 for more on using cookies.
FILES	A dictionary-like object containing all uploaded files. Each key in FILES is the name from the <input type="file" name="" />. Each value in FILES is a standard Python dictionary with the following three keys: • filename: The name of the uploaded file, as a Python string • content-type: The content type of the uploaded file. • content: The raw content of the uploaded file. Note that FILES will contain data only if the request method was POST and the <form> that posted to the request had enctype="multipart/form-data". Otherwise, FILES will be a blank dictionary-like object.
META	A standard Python dictionary containing all available HTTP headers. Available headers depend on the client and server, but here are some examples: • CONTENT_LENGTH • CONTENT_TYPE • QUERY_STRING: The raw unparsed query string • REMOTE_ADDR: The IP address of the client • REMOTE_HOST: The hostname of the client • SERVER_NAME: The hostname of the server • SERVER_PORT: The port of the server Any HTTP headers are available in META as keys prefixed with HTTP_, for example: • HTTP_ACCEPT_ENCODING • HTTP_ACCEPT_LANGUAGE • HTTP_HOST: The HTTP Host header sent by the client • HTTP_REFERER: The referring page, if any • HTTP_USER_AGENT: The client's user-agent string • HTTP_X_BENDER: The value of the X-Bender header, if set

user	A django.contrib.auth.models.User object representing the currently logged-in user. If the user isn't currently logged in, user will be set to an instance of django.contrib.auth.models.AnonymousUser. You can tell them apart with is_authenticated(), like so:
	
	`if request.user.is_authenticated():`
	`    # Do something for logged-in users.`
	`else:`
	`    # Do something for anonymous users.`
	
	user is available only if your Django installation has the AuthenticationMiddleware activated.
	For the complete details of authentication and users, see Chapter 12.

session	A readable and writable, dictionary-like object that represents the current session. This is available only if your Django installation has session support activated. See Chapter 12.
raw_post_data	The raw HTTP POST data. This is useful for advanced processing.

Request objects also have a few useful methods, as shown in Table H-2.

Table H-2. *HttpRequest Methods*

Method	Description
__getitem__(key)	Returns the GET/POST value for the given key, checking POST first, and then GET. Raises KeyError if the key doesn't exist. This lets you use dictionary-accessing syntax on an HttpRequest instance. For example, request["foo"] is the same as checking request.POST["foo"] and then request.GET["foo"].
has_key()	Returns True or False, designating whether request.GET or request.POST has the given key.
get_full_path()	Returns the path, plus an appended query string, if applicable. For example, "/music/bands/the_beatles/?print=true".
is_secure()	Returns True if the request is secure; that is, if it was made with HTTPS.

QueryDict Objects

In an HttpRequest object, the GET and POST attributes are instances of django.http.QueryDict. QueryDict is a dictionary-like class customized to deal with multiple values for the same key. This is necessary because some HTML form elements, notably <select multiple="multiple">, pass multiple values for the same key.

QueryDict instances are immutable, unless you create a copy() of them. That means you can't change attributes of request.POST and request.GET directly.

QueryDict implements all standard dictionary methods, because it's a subclass of dictionary. Exceptions are outlined in Table H-3.

Table H-3. *How QueryDicts Differ from Standard Dictionaries*

Method	Differences from Standard dict Implementation
__getitem__	Works just like a dictionary. However, if the key has more than one value, __getitem__() returns the last value.
__setitem__	Sets the given key to [value] (a Python list whose single element is value). Note that this, like other dictionary functions that have side effects, can be called only on a mutable QueryDict (one that was created via copy()).
get()	If the key has more than one value, get() returns the last value just like __getitem__.
| update() | Takes either a QueryDict or standard dictionary. Unlike the standard dictionary's update method, this method *appends* to the current dictionary items rather than replacing them:<br><br>```
>>> q = QueryDict('a=1')
>>> q = q.copy() # to make it mutable
>>> q.update({'a': '2'})
>>> q.getlist('a')
['1', '2']
>>> q['a'] # returns the last
['2']
``` |
| items() | Just like the standard dictionary items() method, except this uses the same last-value logic as __getitem()__:<br><br>```
>>> q = QueryDict('a=1&a=2&a=3')
>>> q.items()
[('a', '3')]
``` |
| values() | Just like the standard dictionary values() method, except this uses the same last-value logic as __getitem()__. |

In addition, `QueryDict` has the methods shown in Table H-4.

Table H-4. *Extra (Nondictionary) QueryDict Methods*

Method	Description
`copy()`	Returns a copy of the object, using `copy.deepcopy()` from the Python standard library. The copy will be mutable—that is, you can change its values.
`getlist(key)`	Returns the data with the requested key, as a Python list. It returns an empty list if the key doesn't exist. It's guaranteed to return a list of some sort.
`setlist(key, list_)`	Sets the given key to `list_` (unlike `__setitem__()`).
`appendlist(key, item)`	Appends an item to the internal list associated with key.
`setlistdefault(key, l)`	Just like `setdefault`, except it takes a list of values instead of a single value.

`lists()`	Like `items()`, except it includes all values, as a list, for each member of the dictionary. For example:
	`>>> q = QueryDict('a=1&a=2&a=3')`
	`>>> q.lists()`
	`[('a', ['1', '2', '3'])]`

`urlencode()`	Returns a string of the data in query-string format (e.g., `"a=2&b=3&b=5"`).

A Complete Example

For example, given this HTML form:

```
<form action="/foo/bar/" method="post">
<input type="text" name="your_name" />
<select multiple="multiple" name="bands">
    <option value="beatles">The Beatles</option>
    <option value="who">The Who</option>
    <option value="zombies">The Zombies</option>
</select>
<input type="submit" />
</form>
```

if the user enters "`John Smith`" in the your_name field and selects both "The Beatles" and "The Zombies" in the multiple select box, here's what Django's request object would have:

```
>>> request.GET
{}
>>> request.POST
{'your_name': ['John Smith'], 'bands': ['beatles', 'zombies']}
>>> request.POST['your_name']
'John Smith'
>>> request.POST['bands']
'zombies'
>>> request.POST.getlist('bands')
['beatles', 'zombies']
```

```
>>> request.POST.get('your_name', 'Adrian')
'John Smith'
>>> request.POST.get('nonexistent_field', 'Nowhere Man')
'Nowhere Man'
```

> ■**Note** The GET, POST, COOKIES, FILES, META, REQUEST, raw_post_data, and user attributes are all lazily loaded. That means Django doesn't spend resources calculating the values of those attributes until your code requests them.

HttpResponse

In contrast to HttpRequest objects, which are created automatically by Django, HttpResponse objects are your responsibility. Each view you write is responsible for instantiating, populating, and returning an HttpResponse.

The HttpResponse class lives at django.http.HttpResponse.

Construction HttpResponses

Typically, you'll construct an HttpResponse to pass the contents of the page, as a string, to the HttpResponse constructor:

```
>>> response = HttpResponse("Here's the text of the Web page.")
>>> response = HttpResponse("Text only, please.", mimetype="text/plain")
```

But if you want to add content incrementally, you can use response as a filelike object:

```
>>> response = HttpResponse()
>>> response.write("<p>Here's the text of the Web page.</p>")
>>> response.write("<p>Here's another paragraph.</p>")
```

You can pass HttpResponse an iterator rather than passing it hard-coded strings. If you use this technique, follow these guidelines:

- The iterator should return strings.

- If an HttpResponse has been initialized with an iterator as its content, you can't use the HttpResponse instance as a filelike object. Doing so will raise Exception.

Finally, note that HttpResponse implements a write() method, which makes is suitable for use anywhere that Python expects a filelike object. See Chapter 11 for some examples of using this technique.

Setting Headers

You can add and delete headers using dictionary syntax:

```
>>> response = HttpResponse()
>>> response['X-DJANGO'] = "It's the best."
```

```
>>> del response['X-PHP']
>>> response['X-DJANGO']
"It's the best."
```

You can also use has_header(header) to check for the existence of a header.

Avoid setting Cookie headers by hand; instead, see Chapter 12 for instructions on how cookies work in Django.

HttpResponse Subclasses

Django includes a number of HttpResponse subclasses that handle different types of HTTP responses (see Table H-5). Like HttpResponse, these subclasses live in django.http.

Table H-5. *HttpResponse Subclasses*

Class	Description
HttpResponseRedirect	The constructor takes a single argument: the path to redirect to. This can be a fully qualified URL (e.g., http://search.yahoo.com/) or an absolute URL with no domain (e.g., '/search/'). Note that this returns an HTTP status code 302.
HttpResponsePermanentRedirect	Like HttpResponseRedirect, but it returns a permanent redirect (HTTP status code 301) instead of a "found" redirect (status code 302).
HttpResponseNotModified	The constructor doesn't take any arguments. Use this to designate that a page hasn't been modified since the user's last request.
HttpResponseBadRequest	Acts just like HttpResponse but uses a 400 status code.
HttpResponseNotFound	Acts just like HttpResponse but uses a 404 status code.
HttpResponseForbidden	Acts just like HttpResponse but uses a 403 status code.
HttpResponseNotAllowed	Like HttpResponse, but uses a 405 status code. It takes a single, required argument: a list of permitted methods (e.g., ['GET', 'POST']).
HttpResponseGone	Acts just like HttpResponse but uses a 410 status code.
HttpResponseServerError	Acts just like HttpResponse but uses a 500 status code.

You can, of course, define your own HttpResponse subclass to support different types of responses not supported out of the box.

Returning Errors

Returning HTTP error codes in Django is easy. We've already mentioned the HttpResponseNotFound, HttpResponseForbidden, HttpResponseServerError, and other subclasses. Just return an instance of one of those subclasses instead of a normal HttpResponse in order to signify an error, for example:

```
def my_view(request):
    # ...
    if foo:
```

```
        return HttpResponseNotFound('<h1>Page not found</h1>')
    else:
        return HttpResponse('<h1>Page was found</h1>')
```

Because a 404 error is by far the most common HTTP error, there's an easier way to handle it.

When you return an error such as HttpResponseNotFound, you're responsible for defining the HTML of the resulting error page:

```
return HttpResponseNotFound('<h1>Page not found</h1>')
```

For convenience, and because it's a good idea to have a consistent 404 error page across your site, Django provides an Http404 exception. If you raise Http404 at any point in a view function, Django will catch it and return the standard error page for your application, along with an HTTP error code 404. Here's an example:

```
from django.http import Http404

def detail(request, poll_id):
    try:
        p = Poll.objects.get(pk=poll_id)
    except Poll.DoesNotExist:
        raise Http404
    return render_to_response('polls/detail.html', {'poll': p})
```

In order to use the Http404 exception to its fullest, you should create a template that is displayed when a 404 error is raised. This template should be called 404.html, and it should be located in the top level of your template tree.

Customizing the 404 (Page Not Found) View

When you raise an Http404 exception, Django loads a special view devoted to handling 404 errors. By default, it's the view django.views.defaults.page_not_found, which loads and renders the template 404.html.

This means you need to define a 404.html template in your root template directory. This template will be used for all 404 errors.

This page_not_found view should suffice for 99% of Web applications, but if you want to override the 404 view, you can specify handler404 in your URLconf, like so:

```
from django.conf.urls.defaults import *

urlpatterns = patterns('',
    ...
)

handler404 = 'mysite.views.my_custom_404_view'
```

Behind the scenes, Django determines the 404 view by looking for handler404. By default, URLconfs contain the following line:

```
from django.conf.urls.defaults import *
```

That takes care of setting `handler404` in the current module. As you can see in `django/conf/urls/defaults.py`, `handler404` is set to `'django.views.defaults.page_not_found'` by default. There are three things to note about 404 views:

- The 404 view is also called if Django doesn't find a match after checking every regular expression in the URLconf.

- If you don't define your own 404 view—and simply use the default, which is recommended—you still have one obligation: to create a `404.html` template in the root of your template directory. The default 404 view will use that template for all 404 errors.

- If `DEBUG` is set to `True` (in your settings module), then your 404 view will never be used, and the traceback will be displayed instead.

Customizing the 500 (Server Error) View

Similarly, Django executes special-case behavior in the case of runtime errors in view code. If a view results in an exception, Django will, by default, call the view `django.views.defaults.server_error`, which loads and renders the template `500.html`.

This means you need to define a `500.html` template in your root template directory. This template will be used for all server errors.

This `server_error` view should suffice for 99% of Web applications, but if you want to override the view, you can specify `handler500` in your URLconf, like so:

```
from django.conf.urls.defaults import *

urlpatterns = patterns('',
    ...
)

handler500 = 'mysite.views.my_custom_error_view'
```

Index

Numbers

404 (page not found) errors, 23, 28, 126
  archive pages and, 365
  customizing, 431
  flatpages and, 218
500 (server) errors, 218, 432
7-Zip, 12

Symbols

\ backslash, addslashes filter for, 405
^ caret character, 20
_ underscore, 347
  __ double underscore, 75
  _() method, 252, 255
{ } braces, 32, 135
{# #} comments, 45
{% %} braces and percent sign, 32
% percent sign, 347
| pipe character, 32, 46
# hash character, 68
$ dollar sign character, 20
& ampersand, 407
/ slash, 20
" " quotes, 46
. dot character, 37
>>> greater-than signs, 33

A

About page, 126, 216
ABSOLUTE_URL_OVERRIDES setting, 383
activating
  middleware, 228
  models, 68
active flag, 79
add filter, 405
add-ons, 209–226
addslashes filter, 46, 405
Admin class, options for, 326–332
admin directory, 247
admin framework, 209
admin index page, customizing, 93
admin interface, 83–94
  activating, 83
  authentication and, 190
  customizing, 91, 241–249
  deleting objects and, 90
  managing groups via, 195
  newer version of, 243

reasons for using, 94
referencing templates/filters, 395
--adminmedia option (django-admin utility),
  423
admin templates
  customizing, 93, 243
  stored in admin directory, 247
admin tool, 184
admin users, 91
admin views, 246, 249
adminindex command, 416
ADMINS setting, 273, 384
ADMIN_FOR setting, 384
ADMIN_MEDIA_PREFIX setting, 384
all() method, 74, 337
ALLOWED_INCLUDE_ROOTS setting, 384
ALTER TABLE statement, 79
ampersand (&), fix_ampersands filter for,
  407
Apache, 216, 278–282
  error_log file and, 281
  httpd.conf file and, 239
apnumber filter, 225
appendlist() method, 428
APPEND_SLASH setting, 231, 384
applications
  application-specific translations and,
    261
  creating, 64
  legacy, integrating with Django, 239
  vs. projects, 64
app_directories template loader, 142
archive for today view, 372
archive index view, 365
AssertionError, 344
Atom feeds, 162–168
  publishing in tandem with RSS feeds,
    168
  syndication framework and, 168
attacks
  brute-force, 191
  cookie-forging, 269
  man-in-the-middle, 178, 269–270
  phishing, 268, 270
  snooping, 178
  vulnerabilities and, 265–273
auth/auth system, 183–196
authenticate() method, 186, 237–238

You Need the Companion eBook

Your purchase of this book entitles you to buy the companion PDF-version eBook for only $10. Take the weightless companion with you anywhere.

We believe this Apress title will prove so indispensable that you'll want to carry it with you everywhere, which is why we are offering the companion eBook (in PDF format) for $10 to customers who purchase this book now. Convenient and fully searchable, the PDF version of any content-rich, page-heavy Apress book makes a valuable addition to your programming library. You can easily find and copy code—or perform examples by quickly toggling between instructions and the application. Even simultaneously tackling a donut, diet soda, and complex code becomes simplified with hands-free eBooks!

Once you purchase your book, getting the $10 companion eBook is simple:

❶ Visit **www.apress.com/promo/tendollars/**.

❷ Complete a basic registration form to receive a randomly generated question about this title.

❸ Answer the question correctly in 60 seconds, and you will receive a promotional code to redeem for the $10.00 eBook.

2560 Ninth Street • Suite 219 • Berkeley, CA 94710

eBookshop

THE EXPERT'S VOICE™